From Grandeville - A Tale
Book 9

Holiday.

A Time For Celebration, Gift Giving, and Being Happy
With What You Have.

George R. Mead

E-Cat Worlds Press

This is a work of fiction. All the characters and events portrayed are creations of the imagination, nothing more, nothing less.
Comments and questions? –> gmead01@gmail.com

Holiday

Copyright 2010 by George R. Mead

All rights reserved. No part of this document may be reproduced, stored in a retrieval system, or transmitted, in any form or by an means, electronic, mechanical, photocopying, or otherwise, with out prior permission of E-Cat Worlds Press. This includes a prohibition on rebinding.

LCCN 2009929088

Mead, George R.
Holiday. A Time for Celebration, Gift Giving, and Being Happy With What You Have./
George R. Mead.
p. cm. – (From Grandeville, a tale; Tale 9)
ISBN-13 978-0-9817446-1-2
1. Fantasy. I. Title. II. Series.

E-Cat Worlds established its publishing program as a reaction to the large commercial publishing houses currently dominating the book industry and the smaller intellectual clones. It is interested in publishing works of fiction and non-fiction that are often deemed insufficiently profitable or commercial or that are not necessarily reflective of literary trends and fads.

E-Cat Worlds, 57744 Foothill Road, La Grande OR 97850
www.ecatworldspress.com
SAN 255-6383

In the middle of nowhere - Creativity.

First Edition:
Printed in the United States of America

From Grandeville.

Tales Told

Portal
Lair
Search
Not Again
And Again.
Magiwitch
Rebirth
Offspring
Holiday

Tales Yet To Be Told

Treasure
Two
Seemna
Choice

With controlled chaos,
> a large dose of confusion,
and seven radically different ideas about how to do the deed,
> the deed was done.

It was finally done.

And over with.
> Really . . . it was.
>> Done!
> Really and truly.
>> Done!

All agreed on that.
> And now. . .
>> And now. . .
> And now . . .

He had stayed away, allowing the process, such as it was, or is, or whatever, to operate. He knew better than to get in their way. In normal times, it was difficult enough.

> But this was a special occasion.
>> A holiday.

So, it was done, this deed.
> And he knew it.

He felt it.
    Deep inside, he felt it.

So, he came downstairs.
    To the living room.
First stopping for awhile in the kitchen.

They had felt him in there.
    In the kitchen.
        Doing something.

And then he walked into the living room.
    From the kitchen.
        Through the dining room.

And he looked at . . . IT!

Chapter One.

So, It Is A Very Merry Time Of Year.

Grandeville. Tinker's Place. Evening.
"Certainly big all right."
Seven happy female faces nodded. All were dressed in pajamas, men's pajamas, their costume of choice for relaxed living. The tops were, more or less, buttoned. Each wore their favorite color.
"It will be beautiful," bubbled Messenger (pale green), dragging strings of lights from one of the several boxes. Waggling the first string of the many to come at him. "Really really." She popped up onto her toes and kissed the side of his face.
"Your turn," grumbled Chantal (powder blue - silk). "We did the hard part." She dropped into one of the couches and stared at it.
Everything in the large living room, almost all of the furniture, had been shoved around until the object of their concern was properly situated and the furniture was properly situated. But what was properly situated had been a long and hotly debated topic. But with much

pushing and pulling and shoving of furniture. and it, from here to there and back again, a correct location had been finally established.

The focus of all the discussion and debate had been placed to take advantage of the high canted ceiling The living room was a large room, easily accommodating it and the numerous pieces of furniture.

Off to one side, near the east wall, flanked by two large windows, sat a large wood burning stove, muttering softly to itself. Two of the smaller couches sat at angles to each other, facing the stove. They were not too close, just close enough that occupants could relax and soak up the radiant heat from the stove when they felt like it.

So, he stood there.
    And admired it, the Christmas tree.
And nodded. "Yep. Big," he said.
    Then he admired them.
All the rest of himself.
    And went to work.

Taking the first string of tree lights from Messenger, he started placing them on the tree. "You guys want some egg-nog? I made a bunch. It is in the frig."

"Yum, yum," said Fair Morn (soft rose with white trim). She headed for the kitchen.

"I will get the mugs." Smoke (jet black - the ends

of her top tied just above the lower ribs) stepped into the dining room.

Princess Chicken (bright yellow) kissed him and handed him another string of lights. "Most noble a'deed, Our Prince." She held yet another string of lights at the ready, bright blue eyes twinkling at him, her face framed by sandy brown hair.

And the egg-nog was passed around.

And the tree lights were strung.

"It will look all right," he mumbled, taking another string. Working his way around the tree. Busily fixing the lights here and there.

They started hanging the ornaments as he wound his way higher and higher, up and around the tree, headed for the top.

And the egg-nog was passed around.

Again.

"Most tasty nog of eggs." Chicken stretched, reached, and pinched him. Just for the fun of it.

R-Bar (bright red) and Ran (soft brown) began to unpack another box of ornaments, whispering quietly to each other as they did, eyes jumping his way, and that way, and back again.

Taking yet another string of lights from Messenger, he dragged the ladder around to a better spot. "Any idea what the witchy pair are up to?" he whispered, indicating R-Bar and Ran.

"Nope." Messenger peered up at him as he stepped higher. "Nope, nope, nope," she whispered, and giggled. She had caught him peering down inside her pajama top. She thought that it was just fine.

And the egg-nog was handed around, again. Refills. For the refills.

"Me'Lord?" Chicken climbed the ladder steps and handed him a full mug. He was sitting on top of the ladder waiting for another string of lights to be handed up.

He took the cup, took a sip. And smiled down at the tree decorators busily at work.

"Damn Cheshire Cat," muttered Chantal, her grey-green eyes staring up at him as she slumped further down into a couch which faced the tree, swiping at the dark brown hair that had flopped over one side of her forehead.

"All your fault." He cleared his throat. "Ahem. It is the fault of you-all collectively, so to speak."

Chantal grumbled up at him, "Grinch! Scrooge! Bah Humbug!"

He handed down his empty mug in exchange for another string of lights. He was approaching the top of the tree. He was almost done. Well, almost, he had one last thing to do.

Stretching, leaning way out, reaching, wobbling, on the verge of tipping over, Tinker managed to place the Angel on top of the tree. It looked suspiciously like a black-clad witch.

Smoke grabbed and anchored the ladder which was threatening to topple him into the tree. He wobbled and sat down, on the top. And glared down at Chantal glaring up at him. "Humbug to you too. Keep that up and I will scratch you off my Christmas list. Ho, ho, ho, ho, ho, ho." And took a sip from the newly filled mug just handed up by Chicken.

Messenger hurried back into the room, carrying a large grocery bag. "We bought just lots and lots of that tinsel, glitter, shiny stuff." She rattled the bag at Chantal. "It will be beautiful, our tree."

"Bugger off," growled Chantal.

Eyes stared at her from all around the tree.

Tinker clattered down the ladder, handed his now empty mug to Chicken, and dropped heavily into the couch next to Chantal. "Ummmmmmm?"

She slumped sideways against him. "Christmas blues, John. Always happens. Gimme a hug, Simba Leader."

He did.

And then they were buried by all the others. All trying to do the same thing.

"OOOOOOF." It was Tinker. On the bottom, as per usual. Somehow they had all wound up on the floor in a tangled heap. On top of him. As per usual.

Someone's silent tears wet his face. "O.K.," he grumbled. "Who's leaking?"

Chantal sniffed loudly. "Let's finish decorating that damn tree."

So they unpiled.

>>> 5 <<<

And somehow.
Eventually.
Finished decorating the tree.
More or less.

They also managed to become heavily festooned with tinsel.

He picked an errant strand of tinsel from the side of her face, slid his arms around her waist and kissed the back of her neck. "Better?" And looked at the tree.

"Yah." Chantal leaned back against his chest.

"How did we get that stuff everywhere?"

Silver threads floated down around them. They had escaped from a clump that Ran had sent floating up to the higher reaches of the tree.

Messenger, now standing on top of the ladder, a ladder held firmly in place by Fair Morn, gaily tossed streamers, mostly at the tree.

"Happy kids," observed Tinker, turning a little, patting Chantal's hip. He thought that it was a very nice hip.

"I am not a child," growled R-Bar, yanking her pajama top half off, snatching away pieces of the final tree decoration that had managed to get inside. She glanced over at him and leered. "As you can plainly see. And as you well know."

"It is beautiful, our tree thingy," gurgled Messenger, dispersing another handful toward the tree. "Shorty."

R-Bar stomped over and shook the ladder and glared up at her. "I am not short. Either. I am four feet, eleven and three-quarters inches tall, as measured in the strange system of this elseplace."

"I am," stated Messenger firmly, wobbling from side to side, "five feet tall, and a little bit more." She stared down at the glowering witch. "So there! Shorty!"

R-Bar snarled and kicked the side of the ladder. She didn't like being called short.

Messenger lurched and toppled from the ladder, and landed happily in Smoke's arms.

"Thanks, mom. We have any more egg-nog?" Messenger smiled at Smoke, and sang, way off key, "It's yummy for your tummy. Do daaaaaaaah!"

Tinker tickled Chantal, just a little, and laughed. "I think that we have kicked off the twelve days of Christmas with a roar. Must be the rum in the egg-nog."

"We will have to cut cards for the unused nights," suggested Chantal. "Seven babes, twelve nights." She twisted around and kissed him. "Lover." And loosened a button on his pajama top. His had red and green stripes this time.

Chicken walked into the room with a large bowl. Full. "We did Us make more, Noble Lord, and Ladies."

"Watch it," snapped R-Bar.

Ran stood close and nudged Tinker's side. "Amtar, it is not nice to call witches ladies."

He shoved one arm around Chantal's shoulders, the another around Ran's. Chantal did the same thing.

To him. But around his waist.

"How'd you stay undecorated?" he asked, choosing to ignore her remark.

"Worked on the far side." Ran slipped her arm around his waist. "This is very strange, your ceremony."

"Not my ceremony," he mumbled.

"Tradition," sang Chantal, swaying from side to side. A little.

"Deck us all with brolly lolly." Messenger, singing happily, joined them, carrying a large tray with three filled mugs. "Boop, boop, boop, boop, boop, boop."

Each took one of the mugs.

Messenger swung away, and flapped Chicken across the backside with the flat of the tray.

"Raucous wench," snarled Chicken, grabbing her. And hugging her.

"Brolly lolly?" asked Tinker.

"Beats me, Cowboy." Chantal emptied her mug, set it on a handy table, and slowly licked her lips clean of the foam. She popped the first and second buttons loose on her top and tickled his side with her free hand.

"Unknown," added Ran.

"Eeeeeeeeeeek!" squeaked Messenger.

Chicken had slipped one hand down Messenger's back and inside her pajama bottoms.

"Two," he said.

Chantal stepped away, just a little and yanked

her top forward, peering inside. "The usual number," she observed.

"Raucous wenches." He laughed. And snapped his head around. Some ornament on the tree had moved.

He stepped over to take a look. "What are you doing in there?"

"Watching the Princess abuse Messenger," explained Dat as she walked out on a limb.

"Am I not beautiful?" The tiny indjinn had wrapped tinsel here and there around herself. Her hand caressed her torso.

"Gorgeous. You gonna stay in there all through the holiday season?"

She shook her head. "Messenger put me up here. A little time ago."

"Jump down," said Chantal, walking over, staring up at Dat. "Have some egg-nog." She held up one hand, stretching out her arm.

Dat leaped, hit Chantal's forearm, bounced, and tumbled inside the mostly open pajama top.

"Nice catch," suggested Tinker. "But very unorthodox." He admired the open top.

Chantal pulled her garment forward. "Watch those claws, damn it!"

Dat scrambled out and up, clenching the material, until she sat on Chantal's shoulder. Then she leaned forward and peered down. "Yum, yum, yum, yum. Almost as beautiful and shapely as me."

Chantal stepped over to the table where the egg-nog bowl sat. "Down."

Dat jumped to the table and walked around the bowl. Just to take a taste, here and there.

Chantal handed him another mug, just filled, and sat on the nearest couch.

Smoke turned off the room lights and turned on the tree lights, bathing the room and its habitants in multi-colors.

Ran walked over to select music.

Tinker joined Chantal on the couch. And admired them both. The tree and her. "Ever tell you what a babe you are?"

"All the time, Cowboy, all the time." She kissed him on the temple.

"Whoosh," he gasped as he took and swallowed a mouthful. "Certainly Princess made."

Chicken dropped against his free side. "Most true, Our Verra Own Bonny Prince." Her grin was getting rather crooked. "We do Ourself bespeak pon this not some few moments past." She slipped her arm under his.

Smoke leaned over the back of the couch, nibbled on his ear, and draped one arm over and across Chicken, tickling her.

"CEASE AND DESIST!" cried Chicken, writhing against Tinker.

"TIME!" he announced as he stood, waving his arms and his empty cup, "It is time to hit the hay, everyone is pretty well wrecked, and the party is getting rowdy."

He headed into the hallway and for his bedroom, leaving his cup to join the others on a table. "Nite all."

They all followed except for Smoke. She remained behind and loaded the wood stove, set the damper carefully, and turned off the tree lights. The stove would burn at a low rate all night long.

Early Morning.

It was the soft pawing at his cheek that did it.

His eyes flew open.

From deep sleep to full wide awake.

More or less.

He rolled his head sideways. Two feline eyes blinked at him. And then soft fur rubbed against his face. He blew at it. And struggled to free his arm. It was pinned in place by a sleeping body. With a quick yank he was almost free. The body mumbled.

And something ran over them, him and the sleeping body. Right over the top. From one side to the other. Followed by another.

He gave another yank, and freed at last, sat up and stared into the early morning light flooding his bedroom with soft. "What is going on in here?"

The door flew open and Messenger hurtled into the room. "Kittens!" And smiled at him. And at them. "There you are."

She began to pick them up and stuff them inside

her pajama top, holding one arm across her waist to keep them from tumbling out.

He blinked and stared at her. "Kittens?"

She nodded. And stuffed the third one inside. "Aren't they nice?" And giggled. "Sorta tickles."

"Baby cats?"

Smoke slipped into the room. "We have mice." She held her arm across her mid-section. Her pajama top was also making strange bumping motions.

Tinker cleared his throat. "How many? Are there?"

Chantal, the warm body next to him, yanked the blanket around and up and over her head, grumbling softly. "Too damn early for this."

"Six, the entire litter." Messenger beamed happily at him. "Two males, four females."

"We are gonna be overrun with cats." He frowned at her and at Smoke. "They are as bad as rabbits."

One of Chantal's arms poked out from under the mound. She made scissor motions with her fingers. "Clip, clip, clip. When they are old enough. No charge. All six of them. Just your friendly neighborhood Veterinarian."

Chicken leaned in through the doorway and smiled at everyone. "Fair Morn, Me'Lord. Do thee know we do be fair overrun with rodents small?"

"I heard," he grumbled, wondering why everyone was up so early this morning, especially after last night.

Chicken frowned. "Buggers do be most brazen and bold."

He scooted back a little and leaned against the wall. "Wouldn't it be just a wee bit easier to have R-Bar zap a little death spell on them?"

R-Bar pushed past Chicken, tying the botton of her top across her mid-section. "Can't do that, Tink. You would have little dead bodies rotting all over the house."

Messenger wrinkled her nose at the thought. "Pee-you. Yuck, yuck, yuck, yuck. OOOPS!"

A kitten had poked up through the gap in her pajama top, squirmed free, leaped, landed on the bed, and quickly pushed beneath the heap of blankets. It began to purr loudly.

"I am not your mother," growled Chantal, sitting up, and carefully removing the kitten from the joint between her neck and her shoulder. She held it out and peered at it. "Pretty healthy looking."

Ran twisted past Chicken and sat at the foot of the bed. "They were going to be a surprise for your religious ceremony. But they escaped from your Messenger's room."

"Huh?" He slumped at little and really wondered what was going on this time.

"Gifting," explained Ran. "Your custom."

He nodded. And yawned.

"Christmas present, John." Chantal buttoned her

pajama top and stood. "Certainly a friendly bunch."

Messenger grinned at her. "And lots and lots of fun." She nodded violently. "Really really."

"Yah," stated Fair Morn, dragging her pajama top on as she pushed Chicken into the room.

He looked at her. "What?"

Chicken nodded. "For irritating rodents t'will be most great a'terror."

"So there," stated Messenger firmly, scratching another kitten behind the ear. It had tried to make its escape.

He glared at them all. "What exactly are you guys going on about? Anyway?" He knew he hadn't said anything to provoke all this.

"Keeping the kittens," mumbled Chantal.

"I didn't say anything," stated Tinker. He looked at Chicken. "Did I?"

She nodded. "Most true, Our Prince."

He looked at R-Bar who was glowering darkly at something. "Then what is your problem, witch little?"

"Witches are not allowed pets," she hissed. "Not real pets." And threw her shoulders back. "And I am not little."

Ran nodded at him. "And we would like one." She glanced sideways at R-Bar. "Amtar, your R-Bar should not show off like that."

He laughed, and pointed at the kittens held by Messenger and Chantal and Smoke. "Take two, they're small." Then he checked each face. "There are only six of them. Who goes without?"

"None," stated Ran.

"We share," explained R-Bar. "Ran and I."

"Oh, you do, do you?"

"Yesssss," she hissed. Ran nodded.

"And where is mine?" he demanded.

Chantal handed the kitten she was holding to Messenger and threw an arm around his shoulders as she sat back down. "Meow, meow, meow." And smiled at him.

"Who's making breakfast?" he mumbled, having decided they might as well get started.

"Tis Me'self and Fair Morn, this morn, Great Grumble Lord." Chicken stood and headed for the door.

"Me too," said Messenger

They scattered. Messenger, assisted by Smoke, took the kittens back to Messenger's room and carefully closed the door, trapping the herd inside.

The last one out of his room slammed the door shut.

"Well, Cowboy?" asked Chantal, sliding one hand inside his pajama top.

"What?"

"You gonna pet me?"

"Sure."

She toppled him over.

They missed the start of breakfast.

"Me'thinks Our Animal Doctor Self do lose her mood sad." Chicken looked around the dining room table at the others.

"Yep." Messenger grabbed a pancake out from under Fair Morn's reaching fork. "Really really."

"I will make more." Fair Morn started to rise as Smoke stepped from the kitchen and thumped a large, heavy plate onto the table, heaped with pancakes. "Too late."

A mob of round-bellied kittens wobbled from the kitchen, headed for the living room and one of the couches.

"They were hungry." Smoke sat and hooked two pancakes onto her plate. "Pass the syrup, please." She shoved the platter toward Fair Morn. Smoke knew that she was always ready to eat more, a very high metabolic rate.

"Deck us all with brolly lolly," sang Messenger quietly to herself, stirring a pancake piece around in the syrup on her plate with her fork. "Boop, boop, boop, boop, boop." She looked up. "How many more days until this Christmas thing of his?"

"So now we have a herd of kittens?"

He and Chantal had eventually joined the others for breakfast.

Chicken nodded and filled his coffee cup. "Most true, Me'Lord. A clutch of cats." She passed the coffee pot in the general direction of Chantal.

He slumped in his chair and sipped.

Chantal mumbled something, eyes marginally open.

They had gone back to sleep and had just come awake for breakfast.

The kittens, having made a run down the hallway from the large living room, skidded through the kitchen and then into the dining room, galloped past his chair, headed back toward the large living room, humping, bumping, and knocking each other over.

Messenger giggled.

Chantal hissed at her.

"Oh, sorry." Messenger ducked her head. She had forgotten again that Chantal liked quiet when she was waking up.

Chicken smiled at Tinker. "Do thee ne'blue Our Doctor Self?"

"Dun know," he mumbled. "Ask her."

"Merry, merry, merry," grumbled Chantal. "And brolly lolly to one and all." Half-open eyes looked around the table, at the once again mostly empty platters. "Who's cooking?"

Messenger popped up from her chair. "Me, me, me, sourdough pancakes. I started them last night." She knew that they were Chantal's favorites. She had let Smoke do the first batches of regular ones.

R-Bar joined her in the kitchen. "I'll help." It was one of the few things that she would cook. She liked to watch the bubbles form and break as the pancakes cooked.

Chantal nodded at Chicken. "I feel fine."

"True?"

She nodded again. "Yep. Nothing like a Simba mauling to chase away the blues." She winked lewdly at Tinker.

Smoke stood and walked around the table to lean over and whisper in his ear, "MindMate, I feel blue." One hand slipped inside his robe and tickled him as she kissed his cheek.

"Go away," he grumbled, hoping that they were not starting up.

She pinched his side. "Spoil sport." And went back to her chair, and started cutting the pancake she had left on her plate into pieces.

"Maul us all in the hall," sang Fair Morn, more or less on key. "Fa la la, la la la la." And beamed at him. And took a couple more pancakes.

Tinker frowned down the table at Chantal. "See what you started?" He knew that it was too late, the conversation was already headed downhill.

"Amtar?" asked Ran.

"What?" He sat straighter and looked at her. He was beginning to wake up.

"I prefer dusky brown." She nodded at him and plucked at her pajama top.

"O.K."

"And I wish to be mauled as well." She nodded

again.

"Take a number," he mumbled, leaning his chin in his hand, elbow on the table.

"Three!" she stated firmly, looking over at Smoke and Fair Morn.

As he signed heavily, Messenger popped in with a platter heaped with pancakes. "FOUR! I am four." She slipped the platter in front of Chantal, then dropped into her seat next to Smoke. She leaned sideways and whispered loudly, "Mom, what happens when you get mauled?"

Smoke shrugged and took another pancake. She had given up trying to stop Messenger and Fair Morn from calling her mom.

Chicken held in her laughter and looked at Tinker, her eyes twinkling. "Our Lord du Maulier, praps thee might to this Our Verra Own Kitten explain?"

He slumped a little more and ate some pancake. "I pass."

Chantal swallowed the piece that she was chewing and smiled at Messenger. "Really good, a treat. Thanks." And winked at her. "It is more fun finding out."

"Oh, boy." Messenger beamed at him and sat straighter. "May I be green?"

He lurched to his feet, leaned forward, shoved his plate to one side, rapped on the tabletop with one knuckle, and announced sternly, "Hello out there in

Rowdyland."

Messenger sank in her chair. "Oh, oh." And leaned closer to Smoke. "What did we do? This time?"

"Not much," replied Smoke, taking another pancake. She liked sourdough pancakes as well.

Fair Morn shoved the syrup in her direction.

He carefully looked from face to face. "Let us take it as an act of faith, shall we, that you guys may be any color that you might wish to be?" He glared at Chantal. "Except for you. Blue is out!" And then he looked at each watching face. "O.K.?"

"Not giving up my p.j.'s," mumbled Chantal. Everyone else nodded.

"Good." Smoke smiled at him. "I like black."

R-Bar sat straighter. "Tink?"

"And I am not changing the color of my p.j.'s either," grumbled Chantal.

"What?" He sat down.

"Maul one, maul all," stated R-Bar. She rapped on the table top with the end of her knife. "Fair is fair."

He slumped. "Merde." And looked unhappy at them all. It was a look that they tended to ignore. They did, this time as well.

Chicken reached over and topped up his cup. And gently kicked the side of his foot. It was a soft kick. She was wearing large, fuzzy slippers.

He glowered at her.

Chantal laughed. "That's what I like, Cowboy. A really jolly Santa Claus."

"Chantal," he warned, looking darkly at her.

"Ho, ho, ho, ho, ho," she replied. "Ho, ho, ho."

"How about, Ms. Santa Clausette, you just slip your concept of maul to them?"

Their seven minds flowed together as she did.

"GOSH." Messenger blushed. And looked all round-eyed at him.

"Ooooops." Chantal grinned at Tinker. "Got a little too graphic."

He sighed. "May we change the topic, please?"

"Indeed, Sweet Prince. Pon which topic shall we begin fair discourse?" Chicken smiled at him.

"Everyone got their shopping done?"

They all nodded.

"And . . . wrapped?"

Heads shook.

"Nay, Our Love. Most gaily wrapped a'gifts be yet to be."

"Right," agreed R-Bar.

Smoke and Fair Morn stood and began to clear the table.

Chantal tugged Messenger from the room. "Let's go get the wrapping materials."

R-Bar looked at them. "We can take what we need to our rooms so no one may see. Is that not correct?" After all, it was his custom not her's.

"Yep."

Ran poked R-Bar in the side. "Most strange ceremonial custom."

Chicken joined them, leaned close, and spoke softly. "This do for him have great emotional feelings." She kissed each on the side of the face. "And tis jolly good fun."

The wrapping materials arrived by the armfuls, were dumped on the dining room table, and shoved here and there as each grabbed what ever they thought was most appropriate.

All hurried to their rooms.

He relaxed in the large living room, staying clear of all that activity, and entertained the kittens.

And then, several hours were spent in the wrapping process as everyone hurried from bedroom to bedroom, swapping materials back and forth, until they were finally satisfied.

It was late in the day.

He was reading.

Messenger bounded into the room and dropped onto the couch next to him, beaming happily.

He bounced a little.

"I like it," she announced.

The jumble of kittens on his other side woke up, yawned, stretched, and went back to sleep.

They had been bounced a little as well.

"What?" He dropped his book onto the floor, place properly marked.

"Your Christmas thingee." She grinned. "Really really."

"Holiday. And it is not mine."

She leaned against him and reached across his lap and tickled one of the kittens with her fingers. "I like it anyway."

Then she said, all soft voice, "MyTinker, why are you blue, also?"

"Huh?"

"I can feel it."

He slipped an arm around her. "Christmas is a special time of the year when families get together. And feel sorta special doing it. Parents. Grandparents. Kids."

"Oh." She leaned back and looked at him, a very serious look. "We are all here. Aren't we family?" And blinked.

He kissed her and hugged her tight. "Certainly are. Best family that I ever had"

The air began to darken and shimmer in the open space in the middle of the room.

Then it was Farth and Sedeem. She was tall. He was taller, and large, very large.

"Hi, Pop." She walked over, leaned, and gave him a kiss. "Certainly a heap of kittens."

Then she kissed Messenger. "Hi, Mom. Merry Christmas. Beautiful tree." And stepped back. "Corner room available?"

"Yep," said Tinker and Messenger.

Messenger smiled at her. "We have just lots and lots of pretty wrapping stuff. It is in the Chamber."

"Let's put our packages in our room and go find

some of this pretty wrapping stuff." Sedeem smiled at Farth, standing so patiently, his arms full of bundles.

He nodded at her, then at Tinker. "Great Lord, we came for your festival. Your dutiful daughter explained and demanded that we come." He bowed as well as he could. And followed his wife to the corner room.

Messenger pinched Tinker. "See?"

"OUCH! What?"

"Our daughter is family. And so is Farth."

"Yep." R-Bar joined them, scouping up the kittens so she could sit by his side. And gave him a jab with one finger.

"Stop that!" He jerked as she did it again.

"I could send a call to my sisters." She grinned wickedly. "I have a large family."

"Never mind." He didn't think that he needed a house full of witches.

"Heh, heh, heh," she cackled.

"Never mind," he restated louder. "Two witches are more than enough."

"Reep and J. C. are planning on coming for the Eve Fest." R-Bar tickled a furry belly. The owner of the belly purred loudly. "J. C. said that he usually spends the Day Christmas with Doc and the others."

"Right. Until he married Reep, Doc and the others were all the family that J. C. had, not counting an Uncle out there somewhere."

Someone entered the room, leaned on the back of

the couch and slipped their arms around him. "Merry Christmas, Pop."

"You too," he grumbled, swiping his hair back into place after she had finished messing it up.

"Hi, Mom."

"Hayou, daughter," said R-Bar. "Come and sit. You may hold some."

Sedeem sat next to R-Bar. "Certainly have fat bellies."

Messenger leaned around Tinker. "They just eat lots and lots. We have mice."

"So we took the entire litter." Smoke sat in a chair and smiled at Sedeem.

"They had them hidden in Messenger's room," he said.

"Mom, why'd you do that?" Sedeem looked at Smoke.

"It was going to be a surprise for him only they escaped and paid him a visit."

"In the middle of the night," he grumbled.

"For Thy Verra Own Merry Yule." Chicken joined them. "T'was fair morn." And smiled at Sedeem. "Thee do pear most well, Fair Princess Our Own."

Sedeem jumped up and hugged and kissed her. "That's me, Mom."

Then she spun and attacked Smoke. And whispered in her ear, "Most wicked a gleam in your eyes, Mom."

Smoke touched the side of Sedeem's face with

the ornate ring she wore on one finger.

Sedeem straightened up. Smoke winked at her.

"The kittens were going to be my Christmas gift?" Tinker watched Chicken as she sat where Sedeem had been and scooped the remaining kittens into her lap.

She nodded at him, and smiled. "Most true, Our Love? As We Ourself do say a'fore."

Messenger bumped him. "You are not supposed to leave your bedroom door open, even slightly. So it was your fault." Not when one of them was in his bed.

"I thought that you guys said that they were your cats?"

Chicken nodded at him again. "Indeed, tis most true."

"My gift, your cats?"

"Thee has it."

He laughed. "Certainly an interesting way to give gifts."

Sedeem laughed with him. "Makes perfectly good sense to me, Dad."

Fair Morn and Ran joined the group, each taking a kitten from R-Bar.

"Hi, Moms."

"Hi, Sedeem." Fair Morn sat next to Messenger, then handed her the kitten, stood, and headed for the kitchen. She had just remembered something that needed doing.

"Amtarene." Ran sat on the couch next to

Chicken.

"New term," said Sedeem. She sat on one of the arms of Smoke's chair, her arm over Smoke's shoulders.

Ran bowed her head. "The daughter of an Amtar."

"Awfully formal," said Tinker.

"Best greeting," explained Ran. She smiled. "Hello, Daughter of Us All."

Sedeem looked at her, carefully looked at her. "You have changed, Mom."

Ran nodded. "I am now, again, Ranfer of the Tanpak. But I prefer the name Ran."

Sedeem leaned forward, sliding her arm from around Smoke's shoulders. "Tell me how." She wanted to know how Ran had regained her magic.

Ran stood. "We may talk in my room."

Sedeem stood. "Let's go."

They headed for the hallway, then toward Ran's bedroom.

Tinker looked at R-Bar, his brow wrinkling. "They aren't going to do something, are they?"

"I do not think so. But Sedeem always wants to know about new things."

Farth walked in and looked around.

"Sit thee down," ordered Chicken, indicating a chair, a sturdy chair. "She do go with Ran for to some conversation private have." She set a kitten in his lap as he did as ordered. He filled the chair. It creaked.

Farth stared at the kitten. "Does it attack?" It was

a strange beast. Small, but strange.

"Do be but mere infant," explained Chicken.

"What manner of beast is it?" He watched it carefully.

"It is a baby cat," explained Smoke. "A small domesticated carnivore household pet of this elseplace. Perfectly safe." She petted the one she held. "Do this, they like it."

Farth did. Very, very carefully. "It makes noise."

Messenger beamed at him. "That means that the kitten likes you to do that."

"Ah." Farth petted the kitten some more. Very gently. "A strange creature."

Fair Morn returned and smiled broadly at everyone, especially at Tinker. She was holding a few cookies. Just a little snack in the making.

He glanced up at her. "Now what?"

"Ho, ho, ho, ho."

"What?"

Her smile grew even broader as she stated loudly, "HO, HO, HO!"

Frowning darkly, he growled at her, "All right, Christmas Mothra, what's going on this time?"

Two arms draped around him from behind the couch as someone leaned over and nuzzled the side of his neck. "A Very Merry Christmas to The Heart of Our Heart, Vander Lord."

"Sa'ar?" he gasped.

"Ho, ho, ho, ho, ho," restated Fair Morn. And bit

one of the cookies.

Messenger twisted around and smiled happily at their new house guest. "Did they all come?"

"Oh no," grumbled Tinker. Not a whole house full of Vander magicians.

Sa'ar nipped him on the ear and straightened up. "Mostly me." And caressed the side of his face. "They were all very disappointed."

"Gonna have to stay that way," he mumbled. "Mostly?"

"Bye, Aunts." She disappeared. To visit her parents, and her brother. And his wife. In town. In Grandeville.

"See," demanded Messenger.

"Most beautiful," said Chicken. Sa'ar had looked even more lovely than the last time they had seen her.

"A real looker," agreed Fair Morn, winking at Tinker. She started on the last of the cookies.

"You have just lots and lots of family," stated Messenger. "Really really."

"And beautiful babes hanging all over you," added Chantal, stepping in from the hall. She had been watching Sa'ar appear and disappear. And in between.

"Ho, ho, ho," he grumbled.

"That's the holiday spirit, Hon . . . ney." Chantal leaned over and bit his ear.

"Hey!" He reached up and rubbed the offended member.

She breathed into his ear. "Looked like fun,

Vander Lord."

"Don't start."

"Lordy, lordy, lordy," giggled Messenger, dropping a kitten into his lap.

"Goes for you too."

"Grump, grump, grump," stated R-Bar.

"Don't need Vander all over the place," he growled.

"Not even the mother of your son?" She stepped into the room, soft flowing pants and billowing blouse of pale violet.

"IMDAR! I didn't mean you." He smiled.

"Our son and his wife demanded that I come here as this time of Ceremony had great meaning for you. This is true?" She watched his face carefully.

"Stay," he said.

"See," whispered Messenger.

"Most true," agreed Chicken. Imdar looked lovely as well.

"Rate that we are going," observed Chantal, "twelve days of Christmas aren't going to be enough, Simba Leader."

Smoke leered at him. "Many many." And licked her upper lip.

"Ummmm, how does that song go?" Chantal frowned at him.

"What song, pray tell?" asked Chicken,

"Ahem." Chantal cleared her throat and started to sing.

"On the first day of Christmas my True Love gave to me, one ornate ring."

Smoke waggled a finger at him, the one wearing the ornate ring, and licked her lips again, eyes sliding half-closed.

"On the second day of Christmas, My True Love gave to me, two Vander babes bouncing in my beddie."

"HOLD IT." Tinker glared at her. "Whoa there, Cowgirl!"

Imdar looked at him. "Is there something wrong?"

"Nope," said Smoke.

"Most sweetly sung a'song," observed Chicken, smiling at Tinker.

"Doooo DAH!" finished Messenger.

R-Bar nodded at Imdar. "He just gets touchy now and then."

"Certainly does," agreed Fair Morn. "Big Stud!" She winked at him.

"Bah humbug!" stated Tinker.

"I knew it," laughed Chantal. "A Christmas Grinch."

Imdar smiled at him. "I brought someone with me."

His eyes flew wide. "What? Not more Vander?"

"Hello, Father."

"Hi, Unc, you big hunk."

Rorx and Szaifeh had appeared, standing next to Imdar.

Szaifeh walked over, bent and kissed him. "UMMMM." And laughed when she stepped back. "Daughter-in-law privilege."

"Since when," snarled R-Bar, not liking any other witch taking freedoms with her mate-for-life. Except for Ran of course.

"Szai," cautioned Rorx. "Hello, Father."

"Yes, husband," she said, as contrite as a witch ever was, which was not much. "Sorry, Aunt." And grinned at Tinker. "You going to have a big New Year's Eve party?"

"You and the mothers all look well," said Rorx.

"You, too. Both of you." Tinker smiled at Szaifeh. "Even prettier. Your father will he surprised."

"Dad's part of the house has an extra room, we are staying there." She nodded at Rorx.

"We will visit back and forth," explained Rorx, touching his mother lightly on the arm.

"Do," said Imdar.

He nodded.

They disappeared.

Rorx and Szaifeh.

To visit her parents, Reep and J. C.

"Bigger and bigger." Messenger smiled at him.

Imdar looked at Tinker as she sat in a vacant chair. "We have taught him almost all that we know. For Vander males. The Vander are healed and well."

"Good news, indeed," replied Chicken. "Thee also do appear much prettier than in times past."

Imdar nodded. It was the way of the Vander.

"Think thee not," prodded Chicken as she smiled sly at him.

He nodded at her, and sighed. "Right." And then frowned at her. "Goes for Sa'ar too, before you decide to ask."

Imdar reached over and laid a gentle hand on Smoke's forearm. "Aada, Moonda, Cazor, and Tobtz wanted to come for his time as well, but Our Heart thought it best that they stayed behind, saying we must have his permission first. They were very, very sad."

Smoke rolled her eyes at him.

"No," he stated.

"Very, very, very, very sad," said Imdar softly, watching his face.

"Ohhhhhhhhhh," gurgled Messenger. She thought that it was terrible that they couldn't come.

"Seven, eight, nine," counted Chantal loudly. "And three more makes eleven. You have only got one day left, Cowboy. Nope. Tobtz makes twelve. BINGO!"

"Knock it off," he growled.

"Better eat lots," she suggested. "Keep your, ahem, strength up, so to speak."

"Aada wept," sighed Imdar.

"Merde," he grumbled.

"Be thee so cruel a'heart, My Lord." Chicken tried to look sad.

He sighed, just to let them know. "Snookered again. Right?" He nodded. "O.K."

Four violet clad figures appeared, dropped to their knees and bowed their heads. One looked up.

"Vander Lord," stated Aada. "We are in your debt."

"Oh no you're not!" He leaned forward and glared at them all. "One more word about debt and you can all go home, understand?"

"To hear is to obey," intoned Aada. She stood, walked over and kissed him. "First Greetings, Lord."

So did Cazor, Moonda, and Tobtz. Then they all sat on the floor. Near him.

Cazor smiled at him. "Our Warlock and his witch-mate told us of this special time of your's as did Our Heart."

"And," continued Moonda, "we who fought alongside you and your's at the Great Battle wished to experience this thing, Vander Lord."

Tobtz nodded.

"O.K., all right. Relax. Welcome to Grandeville."

Four very warm smiles radiated in his direction. Then they asked Smoke about the small animals. She began to explain.

"May I enter?" asked a female voice, trying to sound polite.

"Bingo! Again." Chantal nodded. "Baker's dozen of days. Ho, ho, ho, ho."

"Thee may," replied Chicken.

She appeared and nodded at them. "Uncle. Aunts. Vander."

"Shitar," said Tinker.

"Where's Deem? She sent the call." Shitar looked around the room, the air crackling softly around her. "Who needs killing?"

"Certainly going to be busy twelve days, plus one," observed Chantal. "You had better get lots of rest and take lots of vitamins."

"No one," he replied to Shitar while glowering at Chantal.

"No one," echoed Sedeem walking in from the hall, dragging one hand over Farth's shoulder as she passed by to hug her cousin. "I just thought that you could join us for the holiday. Szai, and Shar, and Shem and his wife will all get together here, off and on. So I thought that our rangle cousin should be here as well."

"We do room have." Chicken nodded at Tinker, a motion that said it is so.

"Sure," he agreed. "The Princess is in charge of who gets which room." He smiled at Chicken.

She stuck out her tongue.

The Vander looked from one to the other and wondered.

Shitar looked down. "What are those strange creatures?"

"Fun beasts," explained Cazor, petting the kitten she held.

"A native creature of this elseplace," added Moonda.

"They belong to the Vander Lord," stated Aada.

"Kittens," said Messenger.

"Young cats," added Smoke.

"We have mice in the house," explained Fair Morn.

"When they get older they will catch and eat those bothersome creatures." R-Bar smiled.

Shitar stared at the kittens and then looked at her Aunt. "True?"

"Most fiercely." Chicken smiled at the young witch. "Thee do be most welcome for holiday a'visiting."

Ran agreed. "Do stay."

"I will." Shitar waved over a chair and sat.

Bounce, bounce, bounce. It was Chantal.

You are going to be in deep kimshee, if you don't knock it off.

Not me that is going to be knocking things off, she snarled.

Everyone is going to behave. Including you.

Smoke rolled her eyes at them. *MindMate, perhaps you should drag Our Doctor Self into your bedroom and maul her vigorously. Again.* She smiled at him.

"Oh my," gasped Messenger. "Does she have the blues again?"

"Who?" asked Sedeem.

Farth looked at Sedeem.

"Slang for sad," she said. He nodded.

"Never mind." Tinker cut into that conversation, hoping to head off whatever they were going before they did.

"Shannon, Deke, and the twins are coming to visit," said Chantal. "Gonna be a full house." She thought that her sister and family ought to come up for at least one day.

"See?" Messenger beamed at him again.

Vander eyes jumped from speaker to speaker. Except Imdar. She was more familiar with Tinker and company and wasn't bothered by this type of seemingly disjointed conversation. She made a slight hand motion telling the others that everything was all right.

Aada reached over and gently touched the side of his leg, having moved closer during all that puzzling conversation. "Vander Lord."

He jerked. "What?" He hadn't noticed her getting closer.

"We do not have to participate in your Special Time. We will leave, if you so wish." Her eyes focused tightly on his. He was the Vander Lord after all.

He shook his head. "Nope. Plenty of room at the inn. Here and there. If need be, one of you can bunk with Chantal. And some of the others." He smiled.

No damn way, Cowboy!

He smiled, wider.

Tobtz looked up and over at Chantal, her eyes slowly sliding over her face and form, appraising, caressing. "What does one do?" It was a silken soft question.

Chantal stared back. "When?"

Cazor banged Tobtz on one shoulder. "Ask her in private."

Chantal frowned at both of them. "About what?"

Moonda looked at her, face carefully composed, showing no expression at all. "Our Soul wishes to know what will happen when you bunk her?"

Tinker quickly stifled his laughter and looked at Chantal, one corner of his mouth violently twitching.

"Sleep," snapped Chantal. "It just means to sleep in someone's room. That's all. Just sleep." And glared at him. *Not funny!*

Tobtz nodded. So did the other Vander.

"The term comes from a type of bed, a certain style, called a bunk bed." Chantal felt that somehow it all needed more explanation.

"Very interesting language." Cazor ran a lazy finger along Aada's ribs.

"Can I help anyone with dinner?" Sedeem looked around the room.

"Yep." Smoke stood. "You may help Chantal and me."

Messenger shoved the kittens she had been holding into Tinker's lap and jumped to her feet. "Me too. I'll just make lots and lots of salad." And hurried after the others.

Chicken stood. "From dusty below will We Ourself fetch ample libations for most festive a'meal." She headed for the kitchen and the wine cellar, the space under the kitchen where they stored wine and other food stuffs.

Fair Morn crooked a finger at the four Vander. "Come with me and I'll show you where you can." She winked at Chantal. "Bunk."

Imdar smiled up at her. "I will stay in the same room as before."

Fair Morn led the four away.

"It will be permissible?" she asked Tinker.

"Sure."

"May I hold one of the Fun Beasts?"

He dumped all three into her lap. "Here."

R-Bar nudged him, "Where did Shitar go?"

He shrugged. "With all the bodies in here, I lost track." And looked down. "I think one of the kittens urped in my lap, I better change." And stood. "Be right back."

R-Bar and Ran selected some music for dinner.

He dumped his trousers in the laundry hamper, hurried through the open space of the chamber and into his bedroom, yanked open a dresser drawer and snatched out another pair of jeans.

"Really muscular legs."

He whipped around. "What are you doing in here?"

Shitar looked up at him. From his bed. It was set flush with the floor. "I am staying here."

"No, you are not."

He yanked on his jeans and pointed at the door.

"Out!"

"Witches may stay wherever they wish," she stated firmly. As firmly as only a witch could be when she was being firm.

He shook his head. "Nope! In my house, in my home, you will stay wherever we choose to put you. Witch or not!"

"Tink!" hissed R-Bar at him from the open doorway.

"Amtar?" Ran stepped past her.

The air crackled around the bed, the blankets puffed and settled flat.

R-Bar glared at him as she and Ran edged further inside.

"She was already in here when I came in. Maybe you ought to sent her home."

Shitar peered in at them from outside the room around the edge of the door jamb. "Uncle, you are not nice."

R-Bar whipped around, snarling. "Young Witch, he is MINE!"

"Ours," amended Ran.

"Share," demanded Shitar.

Ran reached down a small purple clear sphere.

"Gar dip dit dit," growled Shitar, yanking her head back."

"Very coarse," observed Ran. Shitar was very Faan witch.

R-Bar crooked one finger, yanked the resisting

young witch in from the outside open space, her feet sliding across the polished wood.

"OUCH, OUCH, OUCH." Something was pinching her. In embarrassing places.

R-Bar looked at Tinker. "She may stay in the room next to mine, Ran's room. Ran will stay with me."

"Good as any," agreed Tinker. "She staying?" He glanced at Shitar.

Her lower lip pushed out. She looked up at him through her eyebrows and choked on the word. "Please?"

He looked at R-Bar and Ran. "Well?"

So did Shitar. "Aunts?"

Then they all looked at him.

He nodded. "O.K. But you stay out of here. All right?"

"Gib dak!" hissed Shitar.

"I'll take that as a big yes." He slipped his feet into his slippers and started for the door. "How come you witches are all like that?" And shook his head. "Never mind, I don't want to know."

He paused, and looked at Shitar. She really was quite beautiful. He smiled. "Nice offer though. But, I'm booked."

Shitar gasped and touched his chest with one hand. "AUNT! Do something."

He sighed. And mumbled to R-Bar, "You explain. Please? I'm tired."

Dinner was boisterous.
	But no more than was usual.
It wasn't the visitors.
	It was the locals

"Worse than kids," he mumbled to no-one in particular.
	Sedeem beamed down the length of the crowded dining table and held up her glass. "Merry Christmas, Dad, Moms."
	Messenger laughed and smiled at her. "Lots and lots and lots."
	Glasses were emptied and refilled.
	He looked at the rest of himself. *Merry Christmas, gang. Love ya all.*
	Seven pairs of eyes twinkled in various ways at him. Chantal leaned sideways and kissed Sedeem on the side of the face. "Thanks for coming, Daughter. From us all." Then she leaned forward and smiled at Farth. "You too. Thanks."
	Farth looked embarrassed. And fizzled.
	"Shhhhh," said Sedeem. To Farth.
	Then Chantal looked across the table at them. "Thanks for coming. Sa'ar was correct. This is a Special Time and I am happy that you would come to join us." She held up her glass and toasted the Vander. And looked down the table at Tinker. *Ho, ho, ho, ho, ho!*
	He winked back at her.
	"There do be cake more," announced Chicken,

standing. "Who another piece do wish?"

"Me," chorused Fair Morn and Smoke. They were always ready to eat.

Everyone else agreed.

So, the cake was demolished.

And then they sat.

Sipping coffee, enjoying one another's company.

The front door banged open and in a moment they heard it bang shut. All wondered who had come to visit and entered without knocking.

Three people stepped into the dining room from the large living room. The woman in front was wildly banging snow from her clothes in all directions. "Messhuggener weather you have here, John."

Chicken gaped at her. "Tis the loud Mirf."

Mirf looked up from her efforts and smiled. "Came for your Christmas. Always enjoy primitive celebrations."

She slowly looked over the folk gathered around the dining room table. "ZOWIE! Now you've got them in all colors and flavors." She grinned broadly at him. "A short but happy life, I am sure. Never met anyone that would even think of doing something like that. Seven, eight, nine, ten, eleven, twelve, thirteen."

"Mirf," grumbled Tinker loudly, knowing that nothing would deter her.

"Fourteen," gurgled Mirf, indicating Shitar. "If you count sulky face."

Someone bounded from behind Mirf and

wrapped her arms around Tinker. And hugged his chest, patted his cheeks, and ruffled his hair, all at the same time. And then kissed him on the side of the face. "Chirp."

Mirf shrugged. "So they wanted to come. Who can deny their assistants? Especially assistants such as these. You have more chairs, glasses, and wine, in that order." She looked expectant.

Messenger bounced up and hurried into the living room, giggling happily.

"Stop that, Fred." Tinker batted at the various arms and hands.

"Nak," said her husband, Quan. The suk-dragon bobbled her head and walked the long way around the table hugging and kissing everyone that she knew before stopping by her husband's side, folding her second pair of arms over her chest, the third pair held behind, her hands clasped together in the small of her back.

"She is even prettier." Messenger carried in a chair for Mirf. Fred and Quan went into the living room to fetch two more.

Mirf dropped into the proffered chair, emptied her glass, and held it out for a refill. "Mazel tove, Chosen One. Everyone looks healthy."

Fred and Quan joined her, sitting close to Mirf who was sitting close to Tinker. His end of the table and the dining room were getting crowded.

"You really just here for Christmas?" he asked,

starting to worry. He always figured Mirf was up to something whenever she turned up. She usually was.

"Right-o-rooney," replied Mirf. She shrugged one shoulder. "So we decided to take a little vacation, me and my assistants. Monetary Control can afford it. So, here we are. Chin chin. Christmas comes but once a year. Various poets and folk like that there said it."

She held out her empty glass in Chicken's direction and waited for her to fill it.

"We are running out of rooms," he mumbled.

"There is room in the Corporate Building," announced Fair Morn.

Mirf cooed, gurgled, and batted her eyes at Tinker. "Hey there, Big Boy, wanna try a Baker's Dozen or so, I am still single?" And laughed loudly. "As long as you are still collecting." She unbuttoned the top of her blouse.

"Mirf!"

"You're right." She winked at him. "I'd probably be the straw that broke the camel's back, metaphorically speaking." And laughed even louder. "Of course, as someone said, they found the Lady in the straw. Or in your case, Ladies." She grinned at him.

"So, how's the big guy with the wife with the spooky eyeballs? And the klutz?" she asked.

"Everyone is fine," replied Tinker. "They will all be visiting off and on."

"Vunderbar." She slumped, just a little, and popped another button loose. "So what are you doing

>>> 45 <<<

with all these Vander babes?" She waved one seemingly disjoined arm vaguely in the correct direction. "Or is that an indelicate question?"

Imdar reached over and lightly touched Mirf's arm. "Our Heart brought us for his Special Time. She is a native of this elseplace and explained how important it is."

"Sa'ar," explained Tinker. "Shem's twin sister. Ramp's children."

"Ah sooooo," hissed Mirf. "Maybe she'll talk to me, help fill in our records. Monetary Control doesn't have much information on the Vander Guild yet."

"Of course," said Aada, leaning back in her chair and smiling warmly at Mirf.

Mirf swivelled her head back toward Tinker. "That look could over-stimulate a male moth at two of your miles away. How do you stay so calm?"

Imdar leaned close to her. "He allowed us to repay our debt."

"So I won't ask how," stage whispered Mirf. And yawned widely. "Someone show us to our rooms, we have had a long, long day."

Fair Morn stood and headed for the large living room. "This way."

"Merry, Merry, Merry Christmas," bubbled Messenger, smiling at everyone around the table.

R-Bar jabbed Shitar in the side. "He is not going to do anything with Mirf either."

Shitar's lower lip had been pushing even further

out.

"Except visit."

"Yes, Aunt," she replied, getting a very witchy look in her eyes.

"You are not ready to have children," growled R-Bar.

"Yes, Aunt." Shitar sat straighter. "May I visit Szai?"

"Reach out. She will tell you."

Shitar did.

And vanished.

"Visiting Szaifeh," explained R-Bar to the table at large.

Fair Morn returned. "Snowing again. Hard. Let's watch a movie."

Everyone relocated into the large living room.

It was a great movie.

So they watched another one.

And made and ate lots of popcorn.

It was a new experience for Aada, Cazor, Moonda, and Tobtz.

Snow.

Movies.

Popcorn.

At the end of the second flick, Tinker started yawning. It wasn't that the movie was dull, it was just that he was feeling the end of a rather long day.

So they all, one by one by one, headed for their bedrooms.

And he suggested, loudly, before everyone scattered, that there was no need for anyone to be rising early. No one needed to pop up at the crack of dawn.

One eye opened.
Then the other.
It was dark.
It wasn't even close to dawn.

The digital clock glared red numerals at him.
12:10.

She nudged him.
From under his bedcovers.

She nudged him.

He sat up. And reached over, hands sliding across soft skin.

"What are you doing in here? Sa'ar, right?"

"Know anyone else that feels this nice?" She sat up and breathed warmth into his ear.

"Yes. Times seven."

"Not very complimentary, Vander Lord."

He slipped down, flat on his back and stared up at the ceiling, just now beginning to become stripped with moonlight easing into the room through his window. And grumbled at her and the ceiling.

"The Vander debt was repaid, as I recall."

She lay back down and hitched up against him. "True." He was nice and warm. And somehow radiated comfort.

"Then?"

An arm slithered over his chest as she rolled onto her side. "I am The Heart of the Vander as Tobtz is The Soul."

"I know that," he grumbled.

A leg slipped over one of his. "And you are The Vander Lord."

"I know that. Also." His grumble deepened.

"Ummmm," she sighed, settling on top of him. "A Vander gift for Christmas, Lord of Us All." Her fingers clenched his shoulders. "Merry Christmas from One and All."

Red numerals stared at him from the clock.
2:00.

She nibbled on his shoulder. "Nothing like a little rest." And tickled him.

"Stop that."

"Everyone wanted to come and visit."

"How many?"

"We now number twelve. There are those who you know from The Great Battle. And there are new members who only know you through our story history."

She laughed softly. "They all wanted to give you a personal gift, a very personal gift."

"How personal?" He sounded worried. He was.

"Roll this way."

He did.

"You guys think that my anatomy can do things like that?"

She wiggled gently. "The Vander have many spells, lotions, and ointments. It would be an experience that none have ever had."

His lips tickled her's. "They are not coming, right?"

"Uh...huh." She breathed out soft sigh. "Cazor, Moonda, Aada, and Tobtz were allowed because they were there when you aided us in the battle against our great enemy. Imdar is special to you. And we also feel special to you."

4:30

She yanked the blankets back into order and kissed his stomach.

"Not now dear, I have a headache."

She sat up and touched his forehead. "No, you do not."

"Joke."

Moonlight flooded white down the bedroom's

walls and over the floor.

"Did you know that you guys are kinna faint purple, um, here and there?"

She smiled. "It happens. I am The Brooch Wearer and The Vander Heart. But all guild members, as they study and learn and practice, get some small touch of Vander tinge."

She slipped lower, brushing her lips over his. And said ever so softly, "Vander Lord, I found in our archives an ancient tome written long early in our beginnings that described in some detail, in some very graphic detail, the proper thing, things actually, that The Vander Lord and The Vander Heart are supposed to do during special ceremonial occasions.

"Oh?"

"Most true. In those ancient days it was expected."

"Uh huh?" He frowned into the darkness and soft white of her face illuminated by the moonlight.

"It would be an immense breach of proper Vander conduct if we did not."

She whispered in his ear.

His eyes flew wide. "You're kidding?"

"No. You must. We must."

So they did.

Her scream blasted through all their collective minds.

Chantal jerked awake, rolled from her bed, and snatched her revolver from the night stand.

The others jumped from their beds and produced weapons of various kinds.

Smoke reached out to them. *Go back to sleep. Everyone is safe.*

They did.

But they all wondered.

He stared past her at the window. "We are never going to do that again. Ever." And reached down and dragged a blanket up and over them.

She began to shake. "Hold me, hold me."

Dragging up another blanket, he did. "Your cultural ancestors were either hardier than we are or they lied a whole bunch."

"Hold me," she mumbled.

"I am."

"Tighter, tighter."

Someone dropped beside their bed, knelt, and yanked the covers away and hissed at him, "Tink, what did you do to her?"

"You do not want to know. What are you doing in here?"

"She requires help."

Ran slipped into the room and sank to her knees next to R-Bar. And touched Sa'ar, then Tinker, and sucked in her breath.

"What?" asked Tinker and R-Bar.

"Mage burn."

R-Bar leaped away as Ran brought in a deep green crystal clear sphere. "Careful, careful. Ran, protect yourself." Darkness swirled around R-Bar.

Yanking the covers further away, Ran hurtled down the clear sphere, jumped sideways and into R-Bar, tumbling them both into a wall.

The pair in the bed flared green, white, violet, and then not at all.

R-Bar crawled over to inspect the two bodies. "Alive. Well."

Ran stood, nodded, and dragged the blankets back into place. "Something very powerful happened in here."

R-Bar nodded. "We will talk to her in the morning. These Vander mage experiment too much."

Ran nodded.

And wobbled from the room.

Followed by R-Bar. Who wobbled some small bit as well.

Morning.

After a leisurely shower and a wonderful soak in the hot tub, they wandered into the kitchen.

Chicken stood at the range. "Thy breakfast do be most ready, Me'Lord, Sweet Vander Heart. Set thyselfs down do."

They did.

Messenger bustled in, filled their cups, set a

coffee pot on a trivet, and kissed each of them. "Merry, Merry, Merry Christmas," she bubbled as she headed for the living room."

And when the pair were finished, R-Bar and Ran walked in

"Sa'ar, we must talk."

Ran nodded.

The three of them disappeared.

Tinker refilled his cup, picked it up, and headed into the living room to see what the rest of them were up to.

The three magical users stood in R-Bar's room

Ran and R-Bar stepped closer to Sa'ar.

"Tell us what you did to him last night," demanded R-Bar, her face held witch blank.

Sa'ar stepped back, and shook her head.

"It is a Vander secret."

R-Bar and Ran stepped closer.

"You are the daughter magician of my sister magician, Ramp, and are also Faan. As you well know, all the power flows down the Faan female line. Tell us that secret!" R-Bar's eyes were starting to witch glitter.

Sa'ar stepped back, almost touching the wall. "NO! It is a Vander secret from our ancient times. I am Vander and The Heart of the Vander as well as Faan. No!"

Suddenly Sa'ar's head twisted back and forth, mouth open, eyes near shut.

R-Bar released her and snapped at Ran,

"ENOUGH! She is falling inside."

Sa'ar's head fell forward. "Aaaaaahhhhhh. What did you do?"

"It is a Tanpak secret." Ran nodded. "I turned the Vander magic against you. That knowledge has passed down the Tanpak line from before forever. None have ever used it, but all knew it as a weapon against the Vander." She grabbed Sa'ar. "Protect yourself."

The air crackled and fell silent.

Sa'ar moaned deep in her throat, "I cannot."

Ran let go. And watched and waited. "Now, protect yourself."

The air buzzed.

Ran reached. And quickly yanked her hand back as something snapped angrily.

R-Bar leaned close to her niece. "She said that a Vander taken unaware could be consumed in any manner chosen. Do you believe this?"

Sa'ar swallowed loudly. "Yes."

"I will tell you this secret so the Vander may be forever safe from it," stated Ran.

"In exchange," added R-Bar.

"I agree, Aunts. But I must sit down as my knees are buckling." Sa'ar slid down the wall and sat on the floor.

They sat close.

R-Bar tugged Sa'ar's garment back over her shoulders.

Sa'ar leaned forward and began to whisper to

them the secret.

"Hum, hum, hum," gasped R-Bar as Sa'ar finished.

Ran nodded.

They shoved Sa'ar over and fell on top of her. And then Ran whispered into Sa'ar's ear and told her the Tanpak secret.

They were lounging in the great hot tub, Sa'ar, R-Bar, and Ran, when the outer door banged open and closed as Chantal clumped in and began to shed snow and several layers of clothes.

And joined them in the gigantic hot tub. "Bringing fire wood around from the main pile. Pretty cold out there." She stared at Sa'ar.

Sa'ar stared back and winced. "Do not be angry, Aunt. He is The Vander Lord."

"I am not angry. I do not like it. But I do understand. As strange as that is." Her eyes darted from R-Bar to Ran. "We all do."

And cleared her throat. "AHEM. But whatever you are doing, I'd stop it if I was you. You are getting some very dark bags under your eyes."

R-Bar touched Sa'ar on the shoulder. "When will you tell him?"

"What?" asked Chantal, sinking up to her chin in the hot water, eyes closed to mere slits.

Sa'ar sank deeper and looked at her. "The Vander Lord, there is never more than one at a time, is very carefully selected by the Vander Heart."

"Uh huh," mumbled Chantal. "It sounded pretty casual to me."

"Not nice," grumbled R-Bar, frowning at Chantal.

Sa'ar sank deeper, almost up to her lips, and near whispered to Chantal, "The Vander Lord may command us to do anything."

Chantal's eyes popped wide. "WHAT?"

"Any wish, any request, must be given. Anything."

"Holy cow," gasped Chantal, heaving herself upward. "And John is The Vander Lord?"

Sa'ar nodded, raised her face up above the waves sloshing back and forth

"And all you purple babes are his to do anything with, or to, or whatever?" Chantal grinned at the three of them. "Boy, is he ever going to be surprised."

"As The Vander Lord commands so it will be," intoned Sa'ar. "To hear is to obey."

"And he does not know this," said Ran.

"Yet." R-Bar frowned at Sa'ar.

"We were afraid of what he might . . . wish," sighed Sa'ar. "My decision was long coming. The Heart decides."

Chantal started to laugh. And to laugh. And to laugh. "You made a really good choice, a really good choice."

She smiled broadly at Sa'ar. "Now he can relax

around you Vander. He is always worried about what you guys might try to do. And you have been worrying about what he might try to do."

She started laughing again. "Boy, is everyone safe."

Tinker sat up.
Violently.
Suddenly.

Sa'ar had just told him.

He had been lying on one of the couches. Now he stared at them, gathered close by. Sa'ar, Cazor, Moonda, Aada, Imdar, and Tobtz.

"Really?" He stared at them.

Sa'ar nodded. "To hear is to obey," she stated solemnly.

His eyes danced from serious face to serious face to serious face. He beckoned Aada over with a finger. She walked close, eyes watching his face.

"Anything?"

She nodded.

"Take off all your clothes."

She nodded and began to unfasten her upper garment.

"STOP!"

She stopped and waited, her eyes fastened upon his.

"Just checking," he said. "O.K., Vander, just be

your usual selves. And if I need anything, I'll let you know."

He sagged back and slumped in the couch.

They all nodded. And smiled at him.

Sa'ar dropped onto the couch by his side. Imdar took the other. The rest settled on the floor, very close.

He sighed, heavily he sighed. "Guess that I will have to work on my phraseology, see if I can't find a happy medium."

Sa'ar and Imdar kissed the sides of his face.

He nudged Sa'ar. "You feel all right?"

"Tired."

"Go take a nap."

She nodded and stood.

"Ahhhhhhh," he hastily added. "Only if you want to."

"I do." Sa'ar headed for Imdar's bedroom.

He looked at Imdar. "You guys going to jump every time I say something?"

"The Vander Lord commands The Vander Heart. The Vander Heart commands the Vander body."

She smiled and leaned against him. "To hear is to obey."

He sighed. And began to ponder how to speak to them.

Two hands slithered over him from behind the couch. "Me'Lord, wouldst help this, thy Verra Own Queen, in fair messy a'kitchen?"

He jumped up. "Sure." Leaned over and kissed

Imdar. "Relax, do whatever."

And followed Chicken, making his escape.

"Fair randy, thy test, Great Vander Lord."

He winked at her. "Just the first thing that came to mind. Figured that if she protested that they were pulling my leg or were up to something."

She shook her head. "T'were nay Vander jest, that."

He stared at the kitchen. "What happened in here?"

"Naught but mere cooking, Sweet Prince."

He looked at the shambles. And then at her. And spun slowly around. "What kind of cooking does all this? What were you guys doing in here?"

"Nay guys, t'were none but Us."

He turned back and grinned at her. "Just you? Did all this?"

She nodded. "Indeed, We do Us make great Christmas Merry a'dessert." She stepped close to him. "Mighty Warrior?"

"Oh oh."

"Oh, oh, Us not." Her fingers fiddled with the buttons on his shirt.

"The Lady Chen do say Great Emperors of Yore do be measured mighty do they have but a few wives. Thee, Our Lord, do have seven, most willing and obedient, hand maidens."

"Hold it!"

"My Lord?" She looked up through her eyebrows at him. A small smile puckered at the corners of her mouth.

"So far, I only thing that I will agree to in this conversation is seven. Willing and obedient is stretching the truth a whole lot, bright blue eyes."

She kissed him. "And twelve thy concubines."

"Oh no they're not!" He jerked back and glared at her. "No! Nope!"

She stepped close and leaned against him. "Tell Us true, Our King?" Her arms slipped around and gently rubbed up and down his back.

"What?" It was a very cautious question.

"What manner of bed tussle do thee inflict pon fair nubile Vander wench for to cause such mighty a'fatigue?"

"Don't ask me, Princess Curiosity Cat." He sighed and held her. "Go ask her or the witchy pair. Sa'ar looked just fine at breakfast before she went off with them somewhere."

"Indeed?"

"Yep. Didn't you notice?" He stuffed his hands into her back pockets.

"Nay."

"And they certainly aren't talking." He smiled. "Nice butt."

"Passing fair." She nodded. "Leave off Our Verra Own Hindquarters, Sirrah, else kitchen t'will ne'er clean becomen."

He did. "O.K, Slim, where do we start?"
She told him. And they started.

It took quite awhile.
But then.
Finally.
The kitchen was clean.
Again.

The kitchen cleaners made hot cocoa and carried pots and cups into the living room which was now well cluttered with bodies dressed in various styles of costumes.

The Vander had relaxed, as ordered, and were back to behaving normally. Rather like large tabby cats as far as Tinker was concerned.

Most of the rest of himself had finished various chores, inside and outside, and had shifted into pajamas, men's pajama, their native costume. And had convinced several of the Vander to try this form of dress.

Shitar had popped back in, looked askance at Sa'ar and then held a quiet conversation with her. Sa'ar's nap had helped her recover.

R-Bar and Ran walked over and leaned close to Tinker's ears, R-Bar raising up on her toes to do so.

"It is a very private thing," whispered R-Bar.

"And only for Sa'ar to tell you if she does chose to do so," added Ran.

R-Bar nuzzled the side of his neck and murmured, "Of course if the Vander Lord told her to say so."

"Forget it," he growled at them. "I am not about to start prying into their private matters."

His eyes popped wide. "Holy cow!"

Aada and Cazor had just entered the large living room from the hall, wearing pajamas. The pajamas emphasized rather than obscured as their Vander garb tended to do.

They stopped in front of him and bowed.

Aada smiled. "This dress style is very pleasant. May we keep?" She plucked at her top with two fingers.

Tinker looked around. Seven voices answered in his mind. *Yes.*

"Sure," he replied. "Have some cocoa." He indicated the pot and the extra cups.

They did.

And then everyone scattered again.

He went upstairs to his office to work.

Hours later came a soft knock on the door and someone pushed it open.

"LordLove, tis none but Us." Chicken peered around the doorjamb.

He sat, hunched over a paper strewn desktop, working on this or that, marking pages with various colors of ink. His concentration was total.

She stepped inside. "We do Ourself bring coffee

and most tasty of cookies."

"Huh?" He spun around, his swivel chair raspy rust squeal. Somehow oiling it didn't seem to have any effect. "Oh. Princess. Come in. Almost at a break point." He spun around to finish a section.

Chicken found a more or less clear spot, set the tray down, carefully unpiled a chair, and sat.

In a minute or so, he spun around and smiled at her. "Takes care of that." She poured and handed him a cup.

He took it, slouched, sipped, and sighed happily. "Messenger is right, you know."

"Bout?" She munched loudly.

"Merry, Merry, Merry Christmas."

She nodded. "Indeed." And smiled back. "Most full a'house. Most merry a'group."

"Everyone behaving?"

"Of course, Our Prince." She handed him another cookie.

"Witches and magicians getting along?"

She grinned. "As thee do command, so it shall be."

Suddenly their minds were filled with a scene of violent combat.

Snow balls and bodies were flying in all directions.

Fair Morn was watching from the safety of her balcony, three stories above the battle. They were seeing whatever she was watching. It appeared that most of the house had emptied outside.

Smoke, Messenger, and Chantal had lured Cazor, Aada, Tobtz and Moonda outside to play in the snow, The Vander were dressed warmly in borrowed and shared clothing.

One, for folk who didn't know about snow or winter like this, the Vander have certainly adapted fast.

Fair Morn's gaze shifted.

Cazor and Aada had pinned Chantal down while Moonda stuffed snow up under her jacket. Then Smoke and Messenger piled into Aada and dragged her up a high snow bank, over the lip and down into the hole they had dug on the backside. And kicked a snow cornice loose and down on top of her.

They trundled toward the house as Tobtz pelted them from behind with well aimed snowballs.

R-Bar and Ran were attempting to hit Fair Morn who ducked back and into her room.

"Most well behaved," observed Chicken.

He laughed. "They will need hot cocoa."

Doing it, Tink.

R-Bar and Ran had hurried into the house, had rapidly shed their outer wear and were now in the kitchen making cocoa aided by a grumbling Shitar, who being a witch, did not like doing things with food. Nor being assaulted with cold white stuff.

Imdar, The Healer, ordered Sa'ar back to bed and handed her various medicines to drink.

"Our Noble Prince, thy son Rorx and his fair wife

Szaifeh will this very night with us dine. Smoke did promise most fine a'meal."

"Smoke is cooking?"

After warming up, said Smoke.

"I am helping." Fair Morn poked her head through the doorway and crooked a finger at Chicken. "You too."

"Tomorrow we will have to shop for food, MindMate." Smoke handed him a list as he walked into the kitchen, peeking over shoulders at things cooking or being prepared.

"Much neater."

Smoke smiled as she slipped something into an oven. "Our Princess Queen is a very enthusiastic cook."

"Right," he agreed. "Messy."

Fair Morn whirled around, grabbed him and kissed him. And after awhile, released him and pointed up. "Missile toes."

He looked up. "I don't see anything. And it is mistletoe, a plant of some sort."

"Satellite," she explained. "OH! There goes another one." And grabbed him and kissed him even more enthusiastically than the previous time.

"Bug nuts," he mumbled after he was released.

"Buzz, buzz, buzz," buzzed Fair Morn.

Smoke stepped over, held something over his head and tapped him on the shoulder. When he looked at her, she kissed him. And grinned. "Poh Tae Toe. A

>>> 66 <<<

distant relative."

He made his escape through the dining room.

And was grabbed as he entered the large living room.

And kissed.

And held firmly.

"Merry Christmas to you, Uncle Father-in-law."

"Szaifeh." He stared into great dark eyes, twinkling happily.

"Just arrived, Unc." She whispered in his ear, "Rorx told me." And kissed him again.

"What?" he whispered back.

"Mighty Vander Lord," she purred, arms still wrapped tightly around him.

"Merry Christmas, Father." Rorx looked over Szaifeh's shoulder. And tapped her gently.

She released Tinker and stepped back. Then looked at the Vander wearing pajamas. They all had changed into them this time.

"Hum, hum, hum." She grinned wickedly at him.

Tinker shook his head. "Nothing going on. But I think that we may have started a new fashion trend."

Messenger bounced in carrying a tray. "We are having little thingees before dinner."

Shitar joined them, shoved Szaifeh aside, wrapped her arms around Tinker, and kissed him, leaned back, and grinned into his startled expression.

"It is your custom, I believe." She stepped back and grabbed an appetizer from the tray. "I helped

Messenger make these things. I put the pink stuff on."

She chewed, swallowed, licked her lips, leaned forward, and kissed him again. "And Aunt may not complain." Her eyes glanced upward.

So did Tinker's.

"A magic plant of some sort," she purred.

It was mistletoe. Thumb tacked to the ceiling.

He stepped to one side. "Safe."

Chicken patted the couch cushion next to herself. "Sit thy own self here, My Lord."

He did.

She grinned. "We do Ourself attach fair plant pon ceiling thus. And do explain to one and all this most jolly custom a'Christmas."

"How nice."

She nodded. "We do so think so, We do." And winked. "As all do so think t'was most wonderfully fine." And laughed softly.

Murkland Obscuratan. A Place Never Visited.

He opened his eyes.

And turned his head.

And realized two things.

He was lying in a bed.

And she was sitting there, in a chair right next to the bed, sitting still as death.

The hood of her forest green almost black robe was thrown back and draped down her back. A short gold staff was laying in her lap.

He swallowed.

It was one of them.

A Sister of Death.

Then he remembered.

And sat up.

"What happened?"

She smiled, warmly.

He almost fell back, almost.

"This one feels that it was a shock to your beliefs. All were very concerned. This one was concerned." Small wrinkles creased her forehead just between her eye brows. "You are our consort."

Swinging his legs over and down, he sat on the edge of the bed next to her chair.

And cleared his throat. "Hard to believe." He watched her face, very carefully he watched her face.

"This one is rejected?"

Swallowing loudly, he shook his head, and rasped, after clearing his throat once again. "NO! Not at all. Just a surprise, that's all. A very great surprise, a very great, sudden surprise." He cleared his throat again.

"Does your, ah, um, order allow this?" he asked.

"A rare event. But none disagree. We do as we do." A delicate hand lightly touched the side of his face. "Are you well?"

"Yes." He realized that it was true, very much so. He felt really good.

The hand slid away, forefinger pointing. "New

clothes are there. This one thinks that the ever so clever Ransapal should wear something before leaving this room." Her smile dimpled at the corners.

"Oh, my!" He leaped from the bed and hastily dressed.

She flowed to her feet, gold staff held in her right hand. "We have elseplaces to visit."

Grandeville. Tinker's Place. Morning. Again. Another Day.

He was sprawled on one of the couches watching the day creep first bright patches across the floor.

Smoke slipped on silent bare feet into the room, coffee pot in hand, refilled his cup and set the pot on a low table, And sprawled. Next to him. "Best part of the day."

"Uh huh."

Hitching closer, she breathed in his ear. "All sleep soundly."

"Uh huh."

She purred loudly.

"Just like the kittens," he mumbled.

"I suppose."

"They like their stomachs tickled also."

"Also?"

She took his cup, reached around and set it on the floor. And mashed him flat.

"Watch it," he gasped.

And as morning light splashed snow drift blue

white across the living room, they came in.

One by one by one by one. To kiss him, and her.

"Morning greetings," each said.

Tobtz, the last, smiled warm soft and straightened up, fingers slowly drifting away. And tugged Smoke's robe closed.

"Very smooth, near Vander."

"Tobtz," he said. "Behave."

She looked at him, eyebrows furrowed. "I am always well behaved, Vander Lord."

"Ahh, O.K., never mind."

"Very Vander," said Smoke sitting up. "Everyone ready for breakfast."

"Cazor will help," said Tobtz, sitting next to him as Smoke headed for the kitchen. Followed by Cazor.

Moonda and Aada went down the hall headed for the shower.

She turned and slipped one hand inside his robe.

"How was I ill-behaved, Vander Lord?"

He batted at her hand. "My mistake."

"We would not displease you deliberately, Heart of our Heart."

He sighed. "I know." And batted at her hand again.

A small smile pushed at one corner of her mouth. "The Smoke has very smooth skin, almost Vander."

"I heard your comment."

"Would you like to verify my truth?" She leaned a little.

He jerked more upright. "No." And slipped sideways, a little.

"She has many scars."

He looked into violet eyes. "I know."

She saw the pain of remembrance in his eyes. "I could take them away."

"No." He swallowed. "It is how we, I, remember why doing things out there is not such a good idea."

She leaned closer. "The Chosen One of Legend has special duty and obligations."

"Ummmm?" He didn't like the direction this conversation had suddenly taken.

"Lord?"

"Let's talk about something else."

Her lips brushed across his. "We are your's, Lord. To command. To have."

He jerked. "Pretty sneaky."

She smiled softly. "I would ease your pain." And gently touched lips to lips.

Someone loudly cleared their throat. "AHEM!"

Tobtz rose smoothly and bowed to her. "Our Heart?"

Sa'ar made slight gestures with one hand.

Tobtz shook her head.

Smoke leaned into the room. "Almost ready."

"Breakfast?" He looked at Sa'ar.

She nodded and kissed Tobtz morning greetings. And said to him, "It seems that all prefer pajamas."

Tobtz nodded. "A uniquely comfortable type of

covering. Moonda believes that Arktan will be able to easily copy them once we return."

"Arktan," explained Sa'ar, slipping her arms around him as he stood, "is our newest member. Very adept at material things."

"Time to eat," announced Moonda. "The Smoke orders us in."

They all drifted in, in various stages of awake. For breakfast.

"Hi, Pop." Sedeem joined them, Farth in tow. She headed for her seat, dragging fingers over Sa'ar in passing. "Looking good."

"Morning, morning, morning." Messenger bubbled in and dropped into her chair.

Smoke and Cazor set more platters on the table and joined the gathering.

"Fair Morn, Me'Lord." Chicken refilled his cup and kissed his cheek before sitting down.

Shitar slipped past the Vander and sat next to Sedeem.

"Morn, Rangle Puss," said Sedeem, soft and low.

"I haven't done anything," grumbled Shitar softly as she handed her cup to Sedeem who passed it to Farth who filled it and passed the cup back.

"Hum," said Sedeem to her cousin.

"Dir tik," suggested Shitar.

"Pretty grumpy, Tar."

She frowned. "I am bothered, not grumpy!"

Sedeem's eyebrows shot up in surprise. "Who

would dare?"

Shitar shook her head. "Not here. Out there. Something."

Sedeem leaned sideways. "What?"

Shitar hissed softly. "I can not tell see feel know. Yet."

"Tar, a favor?"

"Of course. What?"

"Don't mention this to Dad, please? It would ruin his holiday."

Shitar nodded. "Pass the scorched bread."

Sedeem did. "It is called toast."

"Boy, does she ever look sour." Tinker had leaned toward Chicken and was indicating the quiet conversation at the far end of the long dining table.

"Indeed, My Lord, Sweet Niece do seem a'vexed most be."

"Think that I ought to talk to her?"

No, MindMate, Shitar wishes to be left alone. Smoke looked at him and passed the jelly down the table. *Just have to pounce on someone else.* She nudged Messenger and handed her the ornate ring.

Messenger slipped it on her left thumb and smiled happily at Tinker.

And now it was late afternoon.

Sedeem had convinced her father, right after lunch, to let them use The Den. 'Them' being herself, Shitar, Szaifeh, and Sa'ar.

The four cousins wanted to visit in a comfortable place and catch each other up on all that they had been doing and seeing since they had last been together, traveling, doing wander together.

Now he was in the kitchen making cocoa, helping Messenger and Fair Morn.

Most of the rest had spent a good portion of the day outside in the cold clear blue-sky winter day.

She appeared

In the living room.

A tall woman.

Dressed totally in black.

She looked at the bodies sprawled on the furniture and on the floor. Her jet black hair tumbled over one side of her face, hiding her cheek.

"Hum, hum, hum." She poked the nearest body in the side with her boot, not all that gently.

"Is this the elseplace and housing of the one called Chosen?"

Tobtz looked up. She had been the one poked. And blinked. And glued the sole of that offending boot to the floor. "Who are you, witch?"

Snapping her fingers, she released her boot. And cocked her head to one side. "Not nice, magician."

"STOP!" Ran stepped into the room from the hallway. She had felt the witch magic pulse.

A pale blue crystal clear sphere floated from her open hand and hovered by his frowning person.

Who crooked one finger, beckoning Ran over.

"Step close, witch."

Ran did. And reached over and touched the tiny orange dot that suddenly appeared on this woman's check. And nodded at her. "We are clan linked. I am Ranfer of The Tanpak." The pale blue crystal clear sphere disappeared.

R-Bar hurtled into the room. "RANNA! What are you doing here? Sister?"

Tobtz flowed to her feet and nodded. Her cheek now bore a similar small orange dot. "Clan linked. I am Tobtz, Soul of the Vander."

"As you heard, I am Ranna of the Faan. Most sorry."

"Nothing," replied Tobtz.

"Well?" demanded R-Bar. "Eldest sister."

"Rangle runt," snapped Ranna. "I was requested to do this!"

"By?" R-Bar glared at her.

"Ripple. She and her's travel elsewhere."

R-Bar growled, black shifting around her. "If this is trouble, take it out!"

Ranna bent and frowned at her. "I am The Eldest, young witch!"

"Glab poky," spat R-Bar.

Ranna straightened up. "Wonderfully coarse." She waggled one hand. And they appeared.

A man.

A woman.

Two teenaged children.

The man smiled at R-Bar.

The woman bowed. "Our Husband, The King, did say that we should visit for this your special feast."

TINK, more house guests. R-Bar called to him in private.

He handed the spoon he was using to Messenger and headed for the living room, announcing in a loud voice as he entered, "Full up!" And stopped and stared.

"Highness?"

"Great Lord?"

He laughed and stepped toward them. "How did you guys get here?"

Chicken hurtled past him and wrapped herself around the man. "Brother, what means this?"

Willawa, the Queen, swung an arm around each of her children, who were trying very hard to not stare at everyone and everything.

"Our children have never traveled any way other than by beast."

"Certainly have grown since we last saw them," laughed Tinker. He glanced at the tall witch and wondered who she was.

"The eldest, Ranna," explained R-Bar. "She brought them."

Ranna nodded. "May I stay, runt?" It was proper witch manners to ask the mate-witch.

"Why not?" Tinker smiled at R-Bar. He had decided that one more guest, more or less wasn't going to make all that much difference. He swung his arms at them and the furniture. "Sit, sit. Toucan, you know where everything is, more or less. Back in a flash. I am helping with the cocoa."

R-Bar beckoned to her sister. "You may use Ran's room. She is sleeping with me."

"Husband King?" asked Willawa as they sat on one of the couches. "The Lord Tinker is working in the kitchen? This is a very strange castle. They have dead vegetation in here."

"Sweet My Queen, this Lord does live most differently than thee and I."

Tinker, Messenger, and Fair Morn carried in trays. The Vander took them and began to serve everyone.

Tinker carefully set a marshmallow in each young person's cup. "Try it, you'll like it. Prince. And Princess."

"Most kind, Lord," said the Prince. The Princess smiled at him.

Willawa reached over and touched her King's shoulder and indicated the tree. "It is a most be'baubled thing."

Tinker dragged over a chair. "How long can you stay?"

He felt all the others coming from various parts of the house.

And, after the Prince and the Princess were introduced to everyone, Willawa smiled at him.

"Tinker Lord, you have even more Personal

Guard than when last we did meet."

"Ahhhhh, some. The Vander are just here, ummmmm, visiting, for the holidays."

He smiled and indicated Mirf and her Assistants. "They are all Monetary Control. You already know Mirf. These are her Assistants, Fred and Quan."

Then his smile widened. "This is Rorx, my son. Sedeem, my daughter, is still upstairs. The big guy is Farth, her husband, a Silver Ranger."

Messenger perched on the arm of Tinker's chair and tickled him. And said to Willawa, "We are having a Merry, Merry, Merry Christmas."

Chicken stepped around and smiled at their new guests. "Praps, Noble Queen, Fair Princess, Noble King and Prince, thee would be comfortable more in less courtly attire? Here we do be most casual."

She plucked at her pajamas. "Tis our folk costume herein." And turned and winked at Tinker. "Be this not so, Lord?"

"Sure. You guys fix them up. Ahh, Princess?"

"Great King?" replied the Princess, licking the cocoa from her upper lip.

"Ooops, wrong Princess." He patted Chicken on the hip. "Figure out the room arrangements. O.K.? Umm, I think that The King and The Queen may use the den. After the kids stop visiting in there."

"Be this acceptable?"

"Sure." He tickled Messenger in return. "Well?"

"Gosh." Messenger giggled. And blushed.

Kitten, cautioned Smoke.

Messenger ducked her head.

Chicken and Smoke ushered the Royals from the room.

"Hum, hum, hum," noted Ranna, standing back into the living room. R-Bar had talked her into wearing pajamas as well. Some of Smoke's. They were black.

She tugged at her garments. "Most not-witch. But comfortable." And looked pointedly at R-Bar. "The correct color."

R-Bar was wearing her usually color. Red. She winked at Tinker. "Looks pretty good, huh?"

Don't start, he grumbled. "Yes, fine."

R-Bar took Ranna elsewhere in the house.

The four cousins came in, eyes twinkling, took cups and poured cocoa for themselves. And filled the couch, part of it. It was the largest couch.

"Vander Lord?" Sa'ar looked up at him through her eyebrows.

"Oh, oh. What?"

"The Princess told us of your new guests. I will take my sister mage to my home. There are many extra rooms there. All may sleep there. And come and go as they please. Mother will not mind." She smiled at him. "Neither will Father."

"Ahhhh?"

"Yes?"

"Will they mind?" He indicated the rest of the Vander watching them.

She smiled at him. "As you wish, so shall it be." And bowed her head.

He nodded. "Putting it on my back, huh?"

Tobtz stepped up behind him and ran a light tickle finger along the back of his neck. "We will not mind. But."

He reached around and grabbed that pesky hand. "What?"

"Imdar stays."

"Sure." He released her hand. She set it lightly on his shoulder. And pinched him gently. And then sat in another couch.

The Vander settled around him.

"What is this white ball?" Aada poked at the marshmallow with a finger, bobbing it up and down.

"Mostly sugar," explained Sedeem. "It sorta melts into the cocoa, a sweetening."

Shitar sat up. "Aunt calls." And disappeared, taking her cup with her.

She looked at the three witches, standing, waiting. "You will share your room, Ran's room," stated R-Bar.

Shitar's eyes shifted to the tall woman.

"I am Ranna, the eldest."

Shitar nodded. "I am Ripple Daughter Shitar."

Ranna looked her over. "Hum. I see your mother there." This daughter had the same pouty expression as her sister. She slipped a light spell over Shitar. "I travel muchly elsewhere. We have not yet met."

Shitar nodded. And countered. It was a fast cast to the front.

"Hum," said Ranna, sending the spell out. "A strong daughter." Dark grabbed her from behind. She stabbed backward. And hissed at Shitar. "That was vile."

Shitar nodded. And watched her Aunt very carefully.

"Rangle mother, rangle daughter." Ranna nodded at Shitar. "You will room share?"

"Yes, Aunt."

R-Bar relaxed.

Ranna nodded.

Ran waited.

Shitar nodded.

Then all sat on the floor and talked.

Downstairs the Vander finished their cocoa and vanished.

"Ummmmm?" Tinker looked around.

"Dad?"

"Unc?"

"They were all still wearing pajamas."

Chicken came in leading their new guests. "Tis nay wrong, My Lord." She indicated The Royals.

"The Vander," he explained.

"They went to visit Sa'ar's home," said Sedeem.

Szaifeh grinned. "Big surprise."

The Hardcastle Residence.

In the library.

Ramp looked up from behind her desk and smiled. "Daughter?"

"Tinker's house is full. May they, we, all sleep here?"

Ramp looked from one to the other. "Do Vander always travel in such?"

Sa'ar shook her head. The air shimmered around them. And the Vander were Vander dressed again.

"Hum," said Ramp.

"MOTHER! That is not nice." Sa'ar looked shocked at her mother.

The door popped open. And Shem came in, tripping over some small thing that wasn't there. "Sa'ar."

"Shem."

His eyes jumped to the others and then back to his sister, asking a twin silent question.

"Just visiting," replied Sa'ar. "You remember Cazor, Moonda, Aada, and Tobtz?"

The four Vander smiled warmly at him. Shem blushed.

"Daughter?" asked Ramp.

"Vander private," said Sa'ar. "May we, Mother?"

Ramp smiled. "There are many rooms. Your grandparents will enjoy the company. So will your father and I."

Sa'ar nodded. "We will change into Grandeville,

first." And led the group out into the hall and upstairs.

Shem looked at his mother.

"John Tinker's house is full. They wish to sleep here."

Tajaar hurried into the room. "Vander are here." She fingered the hilt of the long dagger hung on her belt.

"I know." Shem slipped an arm around his wife, holding her, calming her down.

"Visiting," stated Ramp.

Hard walked into the room. "Isn't she a little too old to be having slumber parties?" He sat on the corner of Ramp's desk and bumped a tall vase of flowers. It rocked back and forth.

Ramp touched the vase, then her husband. "They are visiting John Tinker, but sleeping here."

"Oh. Want some lunch?"

"We do." Ramp stood and looked at Shem. "Ask them to join us."

He nodded. And headed upstairs. Tajaar went with him.

"What's Tinker doing?" They walked down the hall toward the kitchen.

"Celebrating your, emm, holiday, Husband."

"Oh. With them?" He looked surprised and puzzled.

"Sa'ar will explain."

Tinker's Place.

Lech, lech, lech, giggled Messenger, standing next to his side, fighting to not burst into laughter.

He turned his head, glared at her, and cleared his throat as he looked back. "Ahem, you do not have to wear them, you know. We can outfit you in some other stuff."

Willawa plucked at her pajamas, a pair of Chantal's. Silk. Blue. "Most comfortable, this tribal garb of thine. Your court is rather, ahh, unconventional, Lord." She would have preferred white, her kingdom's color.

He nodded. "It is that all right." And waved them toward a couch. "You guy's hungry?"

"I will fix it." Messenger headed for the kitchen.

Fair Queen do fair fill Fair Chantal's garb, do she not, Our Prince? Chicken nudged him as she sat on the arm of his chair.

Knock it off. He wasn't ready for another of those conversations having to do with comparing this person's anatomy or that.

Toucan leaned forward, arms on his knees. "Highness, I did tell all bout most magical devices of this thy elseplace." He smiled. "Might I, with thy leave, show these things?"

"Wander as you wish. We have lots of warm gear, if you want to go outside."

Toucan ushered his wife and children toward the kitchen.

Tinker sighed.

"Most heavy a'sigh, Our Love." Chicken leaned against him, one arm snaking around his shoulders.

"You gonna tell me?"

"Bout what, do pray tell?"

"How you guys managed to invite everyone for Christmas?" He tickled some handy ribs.

"Cease!" She squirmed and squeaked. "And this We will most certainly do."

He did.

So she did.

"Almost an overdose," he mumbled.

"Our kitten do feel thy need most greatly. So we do the deed, we do."

"My need?"

"Merry Christmas from us all." She bent around and kissed him and somehow wound up in his lap with her legs sticking out over one arm of the chair.

"Lunch time," announced Smoke. "Dessert later." She leered at him from the doorway to the dining room.

Much Later.

All day long, people had poked and peeked and prodded and gently shook all the gaily decorated packages under the tree.

Now it was later afternoon.

Much later.

"Oh boy, oh boy, oh boy, oh boy," chortled

Messenger. "There are just lots and lots." She nodded violently. "Really really."

Smoke nodded. "Many many."

Tinker slumped in one of the couches. "Made it! To the day before Christmas." He sighed.

Messenger dropped onto the couch and snuggled against his side, "Merry, Merry, Merry."

He tickled her, just a little. "Certainly has been quite a holiday season, all right."

Chantal joined them and poked his other side. "You grumbling, Simba Leader?"

"Nope."

"Don't see how you could be. You are awash in gorgeous babes." She laughed and hastily amended the statement. "Friends, you are awash in friends."

R-Bar sat down, nudged Messenger, who made room, so R-Bar could sit tight against Tinker. "Heh, heh, heh."

A thin gold chain around her neck was strung through a large ornate ring.

"Ummmm," he said, yanking an arm free and slipping it around her. "Certainly a full house."

Most of the living room was covered, furniture and floor. And all the chairs dragged from the dining room. With people.

He gave her a little tickle-poke. "What is wrong with your sister?"

"Eh?"

"Ranna. Look over there."

R-Bar did. Ranna stood in a far corner, wedged in, carefully watching everyone.

"Looks magician bothered to me."

"Huh?"

R-Bar grabbed his hand and jabbed him in the ribs with her elbow. "Remember? Witches and magicians? They may not get too close. Most of the time? Most of them?"

He nodded. "Right. Forgot." And leaned forward and peered around her. "Kitten, you wanna go fix Ranna?"

"Gosh!" Messenger frowned at him. "Maybe Chantal ought to look at her. She is a kind of a Doctor."

Chantal tapped him hard on the shoulder. "Exactly what did you have in mind, Stud Butt?" She took a cup of punch from the tray shoved at her by Fair Morn.

"You developing a taste for witch other than your own? Besides, I only work on animals. The non-human kind. And I do not neuter people of any type."

"Punch." Fair Morn stepped around the couch and shoved the tray at him. "Can't get at your gifts until later."

He sighed heavily. "I thought that Messenger might do to her what she did to the others. So Ranna could associate with the magicians."

"I will go ask her. It will be safer if I do." R-Bar pushed his arm away and stood. And intoned, in deep tones, deep for her, "I'll be back."

She slipped across the room and began to talk with her oldest sister. Reep floated over and joined them.

And after some heated discussion between the three witches, they gathered in Imdar's bedroom. Messenger shut the door behind them.

Ranna glowered at her. "You did this thing to my sisters, urh-witch?"

Messenger nodded. "It doesn't hurt."

"I will be unchanged except for that?" Ranna looked doubtful.

Reep looked at her, pushing her enormous sunglasses up on top of her head.

"DO NOT!" screamed Ranna, pulling down all the protection that she knew, squinting her eyes.

The slight figure drifted higher and kissed her sister. "She gave me control over that as well, eldest sister," sighed the soft shadows.

"Witch true?" Ranna opened her eyes and looked deep into those pools of death, Reep's eyes.

Reep nodded and settled to the floor.

R-Bar looked Ranna. "I told you that it was true. And safe."

"Hum, hum," said Ranna.

"Don't be nasty," snapped R-Bar. She nodded at Messenger.

Messenger stepped close and said, "You have to get rid of all that black stuff. Otherwise I can't see what I am doing."

Ranna gulped. "You can see magic! I thought that Ripple was child telling."

"Nope," stated R-Bar. "Relax."

Reep nodded.

Ranna did.

More or less.

Relax.

As much as a witch ever did.

And Messenger smiled at Ranna, looked inside, and reached. And jerked back. "There is white stuff in there. White magic!"

Three witches stared at her.

"Parquor the White," gurgled Ranna, sagging backward, thumping into the wall.

R-Bar hissed. Something large and dark formed behind her.

Reep held a long silver and green wand, eyes seeming to grow larger and larger.

Messenger whispered to R-Bar, "Who's that?"

"A mage of some unique power," growled R-Bar. She snapped at Ranna, "What did you do?"

"Yes," whispered the shadows. Dark was gathering around Reep, eddying in great folds.

"On Omanlap. He wanted something that I did not wish to give. To him." Ranna shuddered and heaved herself upright. Her eyes flickered, deep down dark fire.

"He will walk tilted forever."

R-Bar stared at her. "He got you?"

"NO! A sharp throw." She looked at Messenger. "You could see white?"

Messenger nodded. "It chokes a bundle."

"I couldn't feel it."

Messenger shrugged one shoulder.

"Can you remove it?"

"Yes."

"Take it out!" snapped Ranna, throwing her shoulders back.

"It might hurt."

"Of no importance." Ranna sucked in a deep breath. "Do it!" she ordered.

Messenger began.

Ranna gasped, gurgled, moaned. And collapsed, toppling over Messenger, knocking her to the floor under heavy dead weight.

R-Bar and Reep leaped over and dragged their sister away, rolling her onto her back.

"Kitten, finish it." R-Bar helped Messenger sit up.

Messenger nodded. And did. "There."

"Now," said R-Bar. "Leave us. We have work to do."

Messenger nodded, stood, and did.

R-Bar and Reep grabbed Ranna as her eyes flickered opened.

Much, Much Later.

And then.

Finally.

Finally.

It was Christmas Eve.
It was . . . The Evening.

Really and truly.
Dinner was over.
Libations were sampled.

And Tinker had surprised everyone. Somehow, and he wasn't telling how, he had wrapped gifts for everyone.

Sa'ar handed him a very small package. And smiled at him, a very small, very sly, very warm smile. "From The Vander, from each and everyone."

"Oh my gosh," gasped Messenger, looking at Tinker as he took the ring from the box. The ring was constructed from three braided strands.

Twisted.
Entwined.
Purple.
Lavender.
Violet.

"Purple mist." She stared at it.

Sa'ar touched his arm and then a finger on his left hand. "It wears itself here, Vander Lord. From beyond beyond, from before before, comes this ring design. Each of us put in. This ring is the Sigil of The Vander Lord."

He looked into sparking violet eyes. And then from Vander face to Vander face. "This thing safe?"

"Of course." Sa'ar smiled.

"Umm." He slowly slipped the ring on the indicated finger. And looked over at Messenger.

It is not doing anything, MyTinker. Not even shedding purple mist now.

He looked back at Sa'ar. "Thanks."

Sa'ar leaned in and kissed him and said, "We leave in the morning." And stepped back.

Then each of the Vander stepped in and said goodbye.

When Imdar stopped, she had been the last, he mumbled, "Good thing that the rest of them stayed at home. I probably wouldn't have survived the whole bunch." And smiled at her. And at the rest.

They had all settled to the floor, near him. Tobtz tickled his foot. "These pajamas are goodgift. Nice color."

Tinker laughed. All their gift pajamas were a light lavender color.

Ranna sat on the couch, next to Messenger, reached over and carefully touched her thigh with one fingertip. "Witch debt, urh-witch. May I gift you?"

Messenger's eyes popped round. "Gosh." She shook her head. "I really do not need anything."

Ranna took Messenger's hand, lifted it and

slipped a white band ornamented with fine blue lines onto her third finger. "Your's. Now."

Messenger stared from the ring to the witch. "Don't you want to keep it, it is very powerful?"

"Not required." Ranna frowned. "I must gift. A gift for a gift."

"Oh." Messenger nodded and smiled. "All right. Thank you."

"Once it was Parquor's. Then it was mine. Now it is your's."

Messenger looked at the ring and ran one fingertip over it, then looked at Ranna. "It did not like him. He was not nice."

Ranna stared at her and jerked away. And banged into Reep. Who hissed, feather soft whisper. Which caused J. C. to laugh. And to tickle her.

Ranna stared from J. C. to Messenger to Reep. "Sister, this elseplace is strange strange."

"Home," sighed the evening.

"Hum," replied Ranna. Reep nodded.

Messenger leaned close and whispered to the obviously agitated witch. "Do you feel all right? Thank you for the ring."

"I will speak with Ripple," growled Ranna. "She did not tell all."

The smallest of twitches occurred at one corner of Reep's mouth.

"Don't laugh at your eldest sister," softly whispered J. C. in her ear, throwing an arm around her shoulders and tugging her close.

    And then, finally, the last gift was opened.
        And then.
    The champagne was poured.
        And the cake served.
    And everyone went to bed.
        Or home.
        And then to bed.

Later. Dark Night.
    "Heh, heh, heh."
    "Huh? Ouch!"
    She rolled back. "Sorry."
    "Kiddo, you could just put that chain and ring somewhere else."
    R-Bar slipped the chain over her head and set it on the floor. "Forgot."
    He yawned. "What were you cackling about?"
    "I was not cackling."
    "What ever it was."
    She tickled him. "I am the last."
    He jerked upright. "Stop that! WHAT?"
    "Gift."
    He crashed back. Flat. And stared up at the ceiling. He couldn't see it. The room was pitch black.
    "Roll this way."
    He did.
    "Welllll?"

He sighed. "Lovely. Gorgeous. Absolutely delectable. Not small, just right."

"What?"

"Isn't that the question? Or questions? Usually?"

R-Bar hissed at him.

He laughed. "You roll over a kitten?"

She growled at him. "I wanted to know whether it was a Merry Christmas Special Day for you?"

So he tickled her. "Yep. Best one that I have ever had. Lot's of gifts."

She hitched closer. "Really?"

"Yep. Even if the last one is kinna short and growls." He kissed her.

"I am not. Either one."

He laughed.

She growled.

And shoved him onto his back.

And pounced.

Somewhat Early In the Evening. A Week Later.

She curled against his side and gave him a sharp jab in the ribs.

"Ooof."

They were sitting on one of the couches.

"You and the moms gonna carouse and usher in the New Year, Dad?"

"Ummmm, maybe. Why?"

"No reason. Just wondered, now that the house is empty."

"Not exactly."

"All the guests are gone. Almost."

He nodded. "Right. We are down to our last witch."

Shitar glared at him. From the other side of Sedeem.

"Don't took at any of our clocks," he mumbled.

"Dad?" Sedeem nudged him again. More gently this time.

He suppressed his grin and indicated Shitar. "Expression like that would stop the Buggers dead in their tracks." He laughed.

"Dar pol tak," growled Shitar.

"Tar," cautioned Sedeem.

R-Bar joined them and sat against his free side. And tickled a rib or two. "What have you been doing to her?" She looked at Shitar.

"Nuttin." He tickled her back. "Think that I should?"

Shitar watched him carefully, leaning forward to peer around Sedeem at him.

"Hum," said R-Bar.

Sedeem laughed.

    Shitar grumbled.

"Where's Farth?"

"Smoke and Fair Morn took him outside to shovel snow," said Sedeem. "They are cleaning off the parking space."

The front door banged open.

They all looked that way.

"Boots!" commanded their father as two small children hurtled inside. They jolted to a halt and yanked off heavy coats, gloves, hats, and snow boots. Their father piled everything next to the wall as they shot for the couch.

"Tinkle," they yelled as they piled into and onto his lap. Crawling across the adjoining laps as they did.

"Pretty excited all right," stated Morgan, setting a large paper sack that clinked on a side table, slipping off his jacket. "Happy New Year."

Shannon closed the door behind him and grabbed the heavy garment from her husband's hands. "Where do we dump everything? Including them?"

"No need," replied Sedeem, tickling the young girl now entirely on her lap.

Chantal walked in and threw her arm around her sister's waist. "The others coming?"

"Nope. Cattlemen's group is throwing a big blowout down at the place."

Morgan laughed. "Thought that it might be quieter up here. The sisters et al are using our barn."

Messenger popped into the room and began to carry away all the shed clothing, smiling happily

Chicken carried in a tray of glasses, removed the bottles from their paper sack, opened one, and poured, handing the glasses around. "Most Happy a New Year."

"We can't stay late." Morgan dropped into an

empty chair.

"Maybe even earlier than that," laughed Shannon, dropping into Morgan's lap. "The weather forecast is for a big storm this evening. If it really starts blowing and snowing we are heading for home."

"Leave the outside lights on." Tinker took a sip. "That way we can see if it does, if it starts."

"HAPPY NEW YEAR!" Szaifeh and Rorx came in from the hallway. She leaned over the back of the couch and kissed Tinker on the cheek. And slipped around to talk with Shitar.

Ran brought more things from the kitchen. Glasses. Munchies.

Szaifeh leaned against her cousin and whispered witch soft in her ear. "Pretty grumpy looking, Tar."

"Thinking about going home."

"Hum, hum."

"Don't be coarse, Szai."

Szaifeh laughed and beckoned to Rorx and whispered to him when he joined them. Whispered so only he and Shitar could hear. "Husband, this witch needs a mate? Is there not some sly Vander thing you might do?"

"Behave!" snapped Rorx.

"Zig tar tar ptar," snarled Shitar at Szaifeh.

"Take her into a bedroom and rip off her clothes," snorted Szaifeh.

Rorx touched his wife's forehead.

Szaifeh blinked and looked at Shitar. "Sorry,

Tar."

"Started drinking brandy with her parents and the rest of them at Doc's. Some while past." Rorx sat down, reached over and gently touched Shitar on the side of the neck. "Hum." And looked at his wife. "I am mage trained, not witch."

Shitar twisted around and threw an arm around each of their necks. "I am all right. What kind of Celebration Ceremony is this New Year thing?"

Later.

She slipped in front of him.

"Amtar. Shannon, her children and her's have gone down to her house."

He was leaning in the open double-doorway arch between the large living room and the dining room, against one wall, feeling pretty good.

Chantal had headed for the kitchen to bring back a few more bags of munchies.

Ran stepped close to him. He hooked an arm around her waist. "Happy New Year."

She leaned closer. "One of your horrible white storm weathers is now swirling around your house."

His hand slipped up her back and ruffled though her black, black hair. "Ran fur." He smiled.

"Shall I lower the lights?"

"Huh?"

"Really gross," grumbled Chantal, rejoining them, ripping open a bag of pretzels.

"What?"

Chantal nudged Ran. "I get him primed and you move in."

"What?" asked Tinker.

Ran took a handful of pretzels. "I came to tell him that your sister and her's had hurried away as we were being enfolded by all that white stuff you have here in this elseplace."

"Happy, happy, happy, happy, happy, happy, happy," bubbled Messenger as she joined them. "Newp Year!"

Tinker squinted at her. "I think that all you guys are drunk."

"Nope." Messenger shook her head from side to side and jabbed him in the ribs with one finger. "Ran is pouching." She nodded. Violently. "Really really."

"Huh?" They certainly sounded drunk to him.

"Kitten, the term," explained Chantal, "is poaching. As in stealing someone else's game."

"He was unguarded," explained Ran to one and all.

"What?" asked Tinker

"You know what happens to poachers?" Chantal frowned at Ran.

"What?" asked Messenger.

"What?" he asked again.

"Get their ass shot off." Chantal cocked one finger, jabbed Ran on the flank with it, and said, "BANG!"

"Gosh," gasped Messenger, all round eyed.

Ran slumped against him, wrapping her arms around his waist. And gurgled, "Amtar, your overly endowed Doctor Lady has grievously wounded your own Ran."

He stared at Chantal over one of Ran's shoulders. "What?"

"Code of The West," announced Chantal, taking another handful of pretzels and glancing down at her shirt front. "I am not overly endowed." She kissed his check. "Much."

Ran tugged his shirt loose from the back. "You will have to carry this your own Ran to her bedroom and inspect the damage, carefully."

Messenger patted Ran on the hip pocket. "You look all right to me."

Chantal shoved one hand between Ran and Tinker. Ran jerked back.

"I think that I will just go into the living room," he mumbled, sliding sideways, making his escape. He thought that it was probably the safest thing to do.

"Pretty well endowed yourself," snarled Chantal at Ran.

Szaifeh grabbed him. "Happy New Year, Unc!" And kissed him. And stepped back. "We are leaving."

Rorx slipped an arm around her waist and nodded. "Happy New Year, Father, Mothers." They disappeared.

Sedeem walked over and kissed his cheek. "Us

too, Dad." And grabbed Farth's hand. "We are going to Au Tba Koy. It is warm and sunny. And Farth heard that there might be a Silver Ranger unit there." She smiled at everyone. "Bye Moms. Happy New Year." They faded away.

Chicken leaned against his back and tugged his shirt completely loose. And slid her arms around his waist. "Most Happy a'New Year, My Lord." And patted his bare stomach.

Smoke nodded.

Fair Morn looked at the clock and announced, "Ten past midnight."

R-Bar stepped away from one of the large windows. "All white out there. Shitar left."

"She did?" He looked over at her.

She nodded. "Yep. Went on a wander. She said that maybe she would bump into her parents." And pointed at Ran while looking at Tinker. "There is nothing wrong with her backside."

He frowned at her. "I didn't say anything."

Messenger peeked around Fair Morn. "Chantal shot her in the butt. For claim jumping."

"Claim jumping?" He batted at Chicken's hands. She was unbuttoning his shirt.

"Right," announced Chantal, grabbing him by the shoulder. "I had claimed this slightly used piece of territory before Ran moved in. I reclaim it, shoddy as it is."

"Wait a minute," he snarled.

Chicken stepped back. "Thee wert most late a'comer."

"So what? I got my claim in first." Chantal looked over at the clock on the wall. "Fifteen past the New Year."

"I am not territory," he grumbled. "To he claimed."

Messenger jumped from behind Fair Morn and pointed at Chantal. "That's the Evil Doer, Sheriff. Goes around shooting people in the rump."

"Which one, Pilgrim?" asked Fair Morn, using her John Wayne voice. "Can you describe her?"

"Oh sure." Messenger nodded violently. "Sorta narrow in the hips, sorta wide in the shoulders. Beautiful grey-green eyes. And round, globular . . ."

"Hold it!" He glowered at her.

"Shirt fillers," finished Messenger.

"Nobody is holding anything, no how," grumbled Chantal.

"And she grabs people," added Ran.

"Unless I ask," mumbled Chantal.

"Drunker than skunks," he observed.

"Well, they are," stated Messenger firmly. "Really really."

"Looks dangerous, Sheriff." Smoke eased up alongside Fair Morn.

"They do?" Messenger stared at Chantal's shirt front.

"Where?" asked Fair Morn.

"Like this." Ran grabbed R-Bar.

"Dir dit!" snapped R-Bar.

"Just demonstrating," explained Ran, releasing her. "See, ahhh, Sheriff? What is that?"

"Officer of the law," explained Chicken, tugging Tinker sideways. "We do put Us, Our Verra Own Self, this territory into most Royal a'custody."

"I resign," sighed Tinker. "It is time for bed."

Messenger hiccuped.

"No, you do not." Chantal waggled her hand in Chicken's direction. Something glittered on one of her fingers.

"Ga'zooks, tis The Ring." Chicken cringed dramatically.

"Heh, heh, heh," said Chantal.

"The grey-green eyed, globular shirt filler strikes again," announced Fair Morn in rolling tones. "The Law can't touch her."

Messenger nodded violently. "The one with the dangerous . . . "

A hand muffled the rest of Messenger's sentence. It was Smoke.

"BED TIME!" he announced loudly, heading for the hallway.

Fair Morn grabbed him by one forearm. "Hold on there, Pardner," she drawled.

"What?" he growled.

Smoke released Messenger and kissed the side of his face. "Take that trouble maker with you before she grabs someone else."

Fair Morn kissed the other side of his face.

Messenger walked around and kissed him. "Or before she shoots someone in the be . . . hind." And hiccuped.

"Happy New Year, Me'Lorp." Chicken slipped past them, headed for her bedroom.

"Let's go, Simba Leader," stated Chantal, grabbing his arm and yanking him into motion. "Your pride of Lady Lions is following your orders. Headed for bed." She winked at him. "Your place or mine?"

Chapter Two.

Well, It Was A Happy New Year.

Grandeville. Tinker's Place.

"Sha boom, sha boom, chug'ah, chug'ah, ree bop, whang dang a doo dah, boob boop de do, rattle dattle, ya ta ta ta, ah haaaaaaaa . . ."

The voice sang its way down the hall, through the living room, into the dining room, and out into the kitchen, slowly fading. Almost, but not entirely, gone.

Tinker lurched a little higher and kissed Chantal on her temple as she grumbled at him. They were slouched deep, watching the Rose Parade, from one of the couches, from under a quilt, tucked up to their chins, backs propped up by pillows.

"What on earth was that?" he mumbled.

"Kitten."

"Sit up a little," he grumbled. "I know that. But what was she singing?"

Chantal sat up, a little more, and grumbled back at him. "Don't be a grump. Sounds like she merged 50's and 60's rock and roll."

"Really different."

"Yep."

"I am not doing anything today," he mumbled. "Except lying right here and watching football games."

"Me too. Who's going to get the coffee?"

"Morning, morning, morning, morning," bubbled Messenger. "I brought it. Any room for me?"

"Guess we could share the couch and sit up, or vice verse," said Tinker.

Chantal swung her legs around and down. "O.K., John, let's do it."

They did.

He rearranged his arms and tugged Messenger close to his other side, holding the cup carefully out in front. "You certainly have been bubbly this holiday season."

"Yep." She kissed his cheek, tugged the blanket higher, slipped her arm around and behind him. "Oooop."

"Watch it," snapped Chantal, hitching sideways.

"I really enjoyed your holiday." Messenger kissed him again.

Chantal pushed her arm behind Tinker. "Lean forward. A little."

He did.

"EEEEEEK." Messenger jerked violently.

"What's going on?" He sighed, looking from side to side. "I thought that we were watching a parade?"

"She poked me," said Messenger.

"Returning the favor," replied Chantal.

"Well, I didn't know that you were pressing your dangerous, ummm, self, umm, selves, against him that way." Messenger lunged.

Chantal jerked sideways and laughed. "Missed, Miss Grabby Green Eyes."

"Time!" He didn't know which one to glare at first. So, he leaned around Messenger and refilled his coffee cup.

Which gave Chantal an opportunity to lunge the other way. Again.

"EEEEEK EEEEEK, EEEEEK," squeaked Messenger.

"Ha, ha," sneered Chantal, straightening up, yanking the quilt up to her chin.

"YAAAAAARGH! Your hands are COLD!"

Chicken had just leaned over the back of the couch and plunged her hands and arms over Chantal's shoulders, past her neck, and beneath the quilt.

"Thee do be most warm," laughed Chicken. "Abuser of our Kitten."

"Merde," mumbled Tinker, sitting back. "Does anyone want to watch this parade? Besides me?"

Chicken kissed Chantal on top of the head and straightened up, releasing her. "Most globular, indeed. How some ever, ne'dangerous, Me'thinks. We would

Ourself watch most fair parade, Me'Lord. Do be there room?"

"Big couch," he grumbled, resettling the blankets and the quilt.

Chantal made room, snuggling against Tinker. "But you keep your cold hands to yourself," she said to Chicken. And nudged him. "Course you can mess around, Cowboy, if you, pardon the pun, feel like it."

He sighed. And mumbled something. And thought, to himself, it just never stops.

Chicken settled next to Chantal. Tucking her legs up, she spread the comforter she had snatched from the other couch. "Most warm, enow." And smiled at Tinker. "Coffee, please?"

He sighed again, and frowned, and gave her his cup. "Here."

"Most kind, Our Prince." She sipped loudly.

He slumped.
    And watched the parade.
Everyone did.
    Slump and watch.

Towards the end of the parade, it happened.
    Breakfast.

"Couch. Poh. Tae. Toe. ZZZZZ," snarled Smoke as she pushed a cart into the living room. And handed each of them a tray, dinnerware, and cups to those still needing cups. And poured the coffee.

"Eggs," said Fair Morn, heaping their plates full. "With cottage cheese and green chili."

"Toast and jelly," added Smoke.

Ran and R-Bar joined them.

Then they all ate breakfast.

"Most slow a'rising this morn," observed Chicken, looking at the witches.

"That was great." Chantal sat up, straighter, now fully awake. And buttoned her pajama top.

Everyone smiled at the cooks.

They smiled back.

"Who poked the hole in the snow drift that covered the back door?" asked Smoke.

"We do Us Ourself but for to peek some outside," said Chicken.

Chantal gasped. "No wonder your hands were so cold."

Chicken winked at her.

Tinker stretched and yawned and snatched up the control from the floor. The TV screen went dead.

"When does the game start?" asked Chantal, snuggling against his side,

"Two-o-clock, more or less. Why?" He shoved at the quilt.

She slid her hand over his thigh. "Plenty of time, Simba Leader." And gave him a gentle squeeze.

He looked at her from the corners of his eyes.

"You guys made a resolution last night to behave."

"Most well behaved be," observed Chicken, holding out her cup.

Fair Morn poured and nodded. "I'd say so."

"Well behaved? For what?" he asked.

"Us," quickly answered Messenger, standing up, shoving blankets to the floor. "Gonna go outside." She hurried from the room. Smoke and Fair Morn went with her.

"Great and Mighty King," intoned Chicken. "To barn will We Our Verra Own Self attend." She followed the others.

"Me also, Amtar," said Ran.

"Cluck, cluck, cluck," said R-Bar, trailing after them.

Chantal kissed him. "Take a nap, John. I will wake you in time for the game." And winked slowly.

"There is always halftime." She stood and watched him stretch out. Then she poked the quilt here and there around him, and headed from the room.

Sometime, not long after, as he slid from deep doze into heavy sleep, he heard someone filling the woodstove.

A Strange Place This Is.

"Wake up!"

His shoulder was being violently shaken by someone.

"Wake up!"

The someone became more insistent.

"WAKE UP!"

His eyes popped open. "Huh?"

An out-of-focus face peered down at him. "Are you awake?"

"No." His eyes closed.

The slap rocked his head sideways.

He moved.

Violently.

He moved.

One fist snapped out and back again. Into her solar plexus. The other arm, the forearm, struck against her neck, under her chin, toppling the body back to thud heavily on the floor.

He was up, on his feet, not too close, waiting, ready, standing. "Who are you?"

The room was grey, floor, walls, ceiling. Dim light.

"Where am I?"

There were bodies laying here and there.

One was half-propped against a far wall. That person was leaking dark stains from many wounds.

The one he had toppled over glared up at him, curled tight, arms around knees, sucking in deep rasping breaths.

"I'll wait." He reached out. And felt all the rest of himself. Near. Asleep. He shook his head But where was here? They certainly weren't at home.

She slowly slowly uncurled, sat up, and cleared

her throat. "I am Faan witch Ranna."

He leaned forward a little and stared at her.

One side of her face was puffy, multi-colored. Her clothes were torn and filthy. Ugly stains were slowly spreading on her dark attire.

He stepped close and squinted at her. "Kinna hard to tell who you are."

She lurched to her feet and snarled at him. "Thank you for the gift of your native costume, pajamas."

She turned away and stomped over to the propped up body against the wall and knelt by her side. "Sister, stay. Help is here, help is here."

"Dim, dim, dim, dim, dim, dim."

Tinker whirled in the direction of that snarling voice.

R-Bar was sitting up, growling, and looking at their surroundings. Something dark was forming alongside her. She leaned sideways and banged a slumped over figure on the shoulder.

"Ran, wake up."

Ran rolled over and stared up at the ceiling. The air shimmered up there, along the ceiling.

"Careful!" hissed R-Bar as she stood and glared around. "Why are we here, in this dar-space?"

Ran sat up then stood. "Not nice"

They slowly turned and faced the tall woman wobbling from side to side near Tinker.

"RANNA." R-Bar hurried to her side.

"It is mine," said Ranna. "And her's." She indicated the other.

R-Bar walked over, bent, and peered into the other's face. "Rekel?"

The head lifted. One eye opened, then the other. She squinted. "Funny clothes, Runt."

R-Bar straightened up and spun to face her oldest sister. "Who did that?"

"Talk later, little sister. She needs healing. Now. Quickly." Ranna stepped closer to Rekel.

R-Bar nodded and beckoned Ran over.

Ran knelt next to Rekel and leaned close, staring into the unfocused eyes. "Near far." She crushed a red-blue clear sphere and sprinkled the dust over Rekel.

Then she stood and said to R-Bar, "We must work fast."

R-Bar jumped up, grabbed her hand and one of Ranna's. "Join, join."

The air bent and crackled around them as R-Bar cast and threw.

Rekel gasped, gurgled, and slumped sideways. On each of the wounded spots the skin healed, the swelling began to go down.

Ranna hugged R-Bar and Ran. "Witch debt, witch debt."

Rekel heaved herself upright with one arm and stared up at the three witches and rasped, "Witch debt Runt, witch debt."

R-Bar kicked her in the ankle. "I am R-Bar, not

runt." And bent over. "How do you heal?"

"I am alive," rasped the answer. "Happy to see you . . . R-Bar, sister."

Tinker helped Messenger up, then Chicken. "I think we are in deep doo-doo, gang." He didn't like the looks of this place.

Chicken stared at the rest. "My Lord, we all do still in pajamas be."

And no one had a weapon.

"Yep." Smoke and Fair Morn joined them.

"Where's your top?" hissed Tinker.

Fair Morn shrugged. "Home. I guess."

"We were all sleeping," said Smoke.

"Napping," added Fair Morn. "In comfort."

He spun around and glared in the general direction of the witches. "One of you guys feel like explaining what is going on? This time? Why we are here? Little things like that?"

R-Bar left Rekel and walked over, nudging her elder sister to come along. "You tell him."

Ran joined them.

"This," Ranna waved one arm. "Is a safe place." She stared at Fair Morn as Fair Morn stared back.

"Her dar-space," explained R-Bar.

"Where's your top?" Ranna asked Fair Morn

"Uh huh?" said Tinker.

"Home," said Fair Morn.

"Hard to explain," said Ran.

"Hum, hum," said Ranna, her eyes wandering

over Fair Morn's torso.

"It is her dar-space," repeated R-Bar.

"Infolded nine ways," said Ranna, looking back at Tinker. "I pulled all of you here. It was all I could do."

She nodded at R-Bar. "Else Rekel would have gone far."

R-Bar nodded at Tinker. "She knows, Tink."

"What?" He looked at Chicken. She shrugged one shoulder.

"About us," added R-Bar.

"Huh?"

Ranna carefully touched his arm. "I needed her skills. So, you all had to come."

"Ahhh," said Tinker. "HA!" And frowned at R-Bar. "Blabber mouth."

"Didn't do anything," grumbled R-Bar.

"Oh, my," said Messenger.

All eyes swung her way.

Messenger ducked her head. "It must have happened when I fixed her. I suppose." She smiled a weak smile at Tinker. And tugged the top of her pajamas closed.

"No," interrupted Ranna. "Not at all." She pointed at Chantal. "I heard that one talking with my sister magician Ramp. During your Great Ceremony."

"Oh," said Tinker, now frowning at Chantal "Word does seem to be getting around."

He nodded and looked back at Ranna. "So, are

we done here?" Then at R-Bar. "Your sister fixed up?"

"Best we can do here," replied R-Bar.

Ran nodded.

"Good. Take us home."

R-Bar shook her head. "Can't. It is her dar-space."

"Oh." He shifted his gaze to Ranna. "Well?"

"We," she said. "Rekel and I." And whispered, "Need your help." It was very bold, and hard, for a witch to ask for help.

"For what?" he snapped.

"Watch your tone of voice," hissed Ranna.

"Sister," growled R-Bar.

Ranna jerked back and sucked in a quick breath. "Nervous, nervous." And shuddered. "Not well."

She stepped forward and threw an arm around R-Bar's shoulders. "Gargoyle quetl." And leaned heavily against her.

R-Bar leaped away, hissing loudly.

Ranna tilted sideways.

"Almost ruined Rekel into far." Ranna started to sag. "I am near done." Dark poured from her to R-Bar. "All . . . ," sighed Ranna, knees giving out.

The dar-space exploded.

Grandeville. Tinker's Place.

They thudded down.

Gouts of white puffed upward and were ripped away, white swirling rush in the freezing wind blast.

Figures struggled to rise, lurching, standing, stumbling toward the dimly seen building not too far away.

"HELP, TINK, HELP! I NEED HELP!"

He staggered over to her and grabbed her roughly. "INSIDE!" he shouted over the roar of the blizzard. "INSIDE. WE'VE GOT TO GET INSIDE QUICKLY."

R-Bar yanked at his arm. "IT'S RANNA! I NEED HELP!"

He nodded, bent, and heaved the limp form into his arms, the storm banging horizontal wet cold onto him, coating his face. "GUIDE ME, I AM HAVING TROUBLE SEEING IN THIS STUFF."

R-Bar tugged him toward the glare of light pouring from the suddenly thrown open front door.

Smoke and Fair Morn hurtled back out and grabbed them, helping them inside.

R-Bar spun around, quickly checking the room. "Where's Rekel?"

She spun and ran outside, "SISTERRRRRRR."

Smoke and Fair Morn raced after her.

Ran and Messenger staggered into the living room from the hall, arms piled high with blankets and quilts.

"Cold, cold, cold," mumbled Messenger, shivering violently.

Chicken knelt in front of the stove, yanked the door wide and heaved in large pieces of wood.

The front door slammed shut behind Fair Morn as she lurched toward and into one of the couches, R-Bar cradled in her arms.

Ran draped blankets over them and ran toward the kitchen. "I will make hot cocoa."

Chicken ran after her, a blanket swung around her shoulders, carrying another under one arm.

"Home? We home?" mumbled Tinker.

Smoke laid her burden on the other couch and shoved blankets around her. She snatched up another blanket and tossed it around her own shoulders. And lifted Ranna from Tinker's arms and set her on the last open couch near the stove.

"Yes, MindMate, we are at home." She wiped the snow from his eye sockets. "Peek-a-boo."

Messenger handed him a towel. "You have snow all over your face. And everywhere else." And wrapped her arms around him. "Cold, MyTinker, cold." And shivered violently.

He shivered with her. "Me too, kitten, me too. " He smiled at her. "Of course you are kinna nice and warm."

The house creaked.

The stove muttered.

It was their usual conversation.

He sighed. "Good thing we were so close to the house and the front door. With that storm we would have been icicles in no time."

He wiped Messenger's hair back from her

forehead. Then pulled her closer. "Dressed as we were."

They sat on the couch with Ranna, near her feet. He dragged a blanket over them.

"One?" Fair Morn looked at him from her place on a couch, only her upper face visible from under the quill piled all around her. "Do you think that I got frost bite?"

"What?"

"No top."

"With your high metabolic rate and body heat, I doubt it."

Her face poked out, all the way out. "Wanna check?"

R-Bar heaved her blanket around. "Me too, Tink. Check one, check all."

"Well," he mumbled. "That sounds normal enough. How is everyone else doing?"

"Most warm, My Lord." Chicken had returned, carrying a tray laden with mugs. She was now wearing one of the thick white robes. Her feet were stuffed into fuzzy slippers. "Ran do bring most warm hot cocoa."

She handed around the mugs, then bent and checked Ranna and Rekel.

Ranna mumbled something. Chicken handed her one of the extra mugs.

Ran carried in a tray with two large steaming pots on it. Smoke took one, Chicken the other.

Cups were quickly filled.

"Amtar," said Ran, sitting next to Tinker and

Messenger, dropping the empty tray on top of Ranna. "Your Ran does not like your white stuff cold weather stuff."

He reached over and tugged the top of her heavy white robe closed. "We weren't dressed for it."

"We could have died." She glared at Ranna.

"Derpta," grumbled Ranna. "R-Bar did it."

"HAD TO, HAD TO!" R-Bar frowned at them over the top of her cup, held in both hands. "Ranna was going in." She sipped noisily. And mumbled. "Had to."

Fair Morn threw another blanket around the small witch and hugged her with one arm.

"Right." Tinker looked around the room. "We are home. We are warm. We are alive." He smiled at Chicken. "And we need to turn down the damper before we melt the stove."

Chicken quickly made adjustments. And grinned over at him. "Most warm, Our Prince, enow."

"Couldn't have been gone too long if the stove was still burning when we returned." He yawned. And jerked upright. "Where's Chantal?"

Hot tub, Cowboy. We are all home, so relax.

He slumped.

They all stared at him.

"I am all right," he mumbled. And stood, and looked at the clock on the wall. "And I am going to bed. We will work on whatever the problem is in the morning. Or tomorrow afternoon. Or whenever."

He headed down the hall, trailing a blanket tail,

grumbling, as he looked once again at the clock. "Missed all the bowl games."

"You are nice and warm."
"Better than a hot water bottle?"
"You betcha." Chantal yanked the blankets around. "Damn witches are always causing trouble."
He kissed the back of her neck.
"Don't mess around," she grumbled. "Just hold me."
"This is my bed, you know," he mumbled, slipping an arm over her waist. "Really grumpy." And slid his palm here and there. "Nice smooth skin."
"All your's," she mumbled back. Then she kicked the blankets around some more. "O.K., let's amend that."
"Huh?"
"Damn witches. Hold me. And, you can mess around."

Morning came sooner than anyone was ready for it to come. The storm still swirled around the house, snow drifting higher and higher.

Smoke slipped on silent feet into Fair Morn's room and looked out the window, three stories above the ground. All she could see was blowing snow.

Visibility was only a few feet. She could hardly see the tree that stood near the house, just at the edge of the rear deck and swimming pool. That storm had blasted past them all night long.

"I am not going out there."

Smoke nodded and turned around.

"Not," repeated Fair Morn, sitting up.

"We can wait until this afternoon. There should be enough wood stacked on the front porch until then."

Smoke sat on the edge of Fair Morn's bed. "What's a gargoyle?"

Fair Morn shrugged. And reached out with her mind. "Oooooop."

Smoke smiled. "He's busy. And the witches are closed up." She handed Fair Morn her pajama top. "Certainly don't look frost bitten to me. Let's go downstairs. You can look it up and read it to me."

Fair Morn closed the large dictionary and leaned close to Smoke, and whispered, "I don't understand at all. How can a Gothic roof ornament be a problem?"

"Let's have breakfast," suggested Smoke.

"Good idea. Lost a lot of energy last night." Fair Morn grinned. "I didn't think anything was frost bitten either."

So they made breakfast. Steak and eggs and hash browns and toast and jelly. A light breakfast. For them.

As they finished their meal, Fair Morn nudged Smoke's elbow. "You still miss her, don't you?"

"Who?"

"Ferrelden."

Smoke nodded. And stood. "We better start

cooking. The rest are stirring."

After breakfast, Chantal went in and looked at Rekel's wounds. "Witches must have feline genes. You heal fast."

"My sister must have gotten strange strange," grumbled Rekel, "to put up with gir nop."

R-Bar stomped into the room and wacked Rekel on top of the head with the flat of one hand. "Am tak tak, sister." And bent and snarled into her face, "In my home you will behave."

She yanked the blanket up to Rekel's neck. "And you will eat what I give you to eat." She straightened up and whirled around, tromping for the kitchen.

Chantal looked down at Rekel. "You are a real beauty, you are."

She turned and walked over to check on the other couch occupant. "So, how are you doing?"

"I am alive. Witch debt." Dark eyes carefully watched her.

Smoke walked in, carrying a tray, accompanied by Fair Morn, and waited until Chantal had lifted Ranna into a better sitting position. Then she set the tray in Ranna's lap. "I cut everything into small pieces."

R-Bar clomped back into the living room, carrying a laden tray. "Set that am tak do tak Rekel up so she can eat."

Fair Morn and Smoke did, carefully. And stepped away.

R-Bar thumped the tray down into her sister's lap. "Are you able to feed yourself? Sister?"

Rekel nodded, shrugging off the blanket. "Yes." And slowly dragged one arm over and began to eat "Witch debt, Sister."

And then they all drifted into the room. And settled here and there. And took away dishes and trays as Ranna and Rekel finished eating.

"Sister?" murmured Rekel, looking around for R-Bar.

"What?" R-Bar leaped from the place by the window where she had been staring out at the storm. She hurried over. "What?"

"If I have permission?"

"To do what?"

"Ask."

"Hum, hum."

Rekel's brow wrinkled. "I am hardly capable of that."

"What?"

"Why have you dragged that dead piece of vegetation into your house and festooned it so garishly?"

Ranna laughed.

Rekel glared at her.

"Custom of this elseplace for this time of the year," explained R-Bar.

"Strange strange," said Rekel.

"Tik tik," snapped R-Bar.

Rekel looked indignant.

Ranna laughed again.

Chicken joined R-Bar and threw a comradely arm around her shoulders. "Be thee ne'agitated so, Our Sweet witch Self. This thy Sister has ne'knowledge pon our ways."

Rekel gasped. And stared from Chicken to R-Bar. "Sweet? She said . . . sweet . . . witch?" Then she blinked and stared at R-Bar. "You are trying to bother me, are you not?"

"Rekel . . . ," hissed R-Bar, dark puffing around her ankles.

"SISTER," barked Ranna. "Calm, calm, calm."

"Me'thinks." said Chicken, hugging R-Bar, "this thy Sister has much learning for to do."

"Right," growled R-Bar, leaning toward Rekel. "And if you start making comments about my clothes, or anything else, I will put you back into a snow bank."

"Pretty grumpy," observed Tinker slipping into the safety of his chair.

R-Bar whipped around, stomped over, shoved one of his arms off the arm rest of the chair and dropped over it and onto his lap. "You betcha. Hold me." And curled against his chest. "Make a better lap."

He did. "Yes, Boss."

R-Bar growled softly. He slid his arms around her.

Ran looked over his shoulder at her. "Muchly bothered."

"Ahhhhhhhhhhhhhh?" said Tinker.
"What?" asked R-Bar.
"This going to go on all the time?"
"Sister," said Rekel very, very softly, "I will try."
R-Bar's head snapped around, eyes flying wide.
"I will," stated Rekel.
"Hum," said Ranna.
"Well," said Tinker, looking around the room. "We have things to do. Shall we?"
They scattered.
Leaving their patients to rest.

Several hours later, he came down from his office, stopped at the correct closet, dressed in the necessary layers, and headed outside to help.

Grumbling loudly, he clumped through the house and out through the living room door. The back door had drifted completely over. Again.

Ranna watched him pass. Rekel slept on.

He followed the bright yellow guide rope tied from post to post across the front deck and out into the swirling whiteness of blizzard howl. This was turning into a monster of a storm.

And arrived at the large wood shed where the diligent crew had hacked their way through a large swallowing drift and into the interior and now waited along with row after row of split and stacked fire wood.

Inside the calm of the shed, he looked at them.

White.

Snow encrusted.

Marginally recognizable lumps under multiple layers of clothes and hats and goggles and gloves.

"Worse and worse out there," he said to the lumps.

One of the lumps turned toward him. "MindMate, we shall have to carry this fire wood, piece by piece to the front deck. We can not get the cart through this much snow without digging a new path."

"Can't we just witch it over? A whole bunch?"

One of the shorter lumps shook her head. "Nope. Too close. We might miss, break a window, or even a wall."

A taller lump nodded. "Most true, Amtar."

"Grab some wood, Cowboy," ordered a larger lump. "Let's get this show on the road."

He did.

They all did.

And then.

Finally.

They clumped inside, back inside the living room.

Behind them, on the front deck, they had stacked rows of fire wood, leaving just a narrow path.

Garments heavy with snow were hung on the wall pegs, boots lined up underneath. And layer after layer peeled away as bodies sought the heat of the wood stove. Chicken and Chantal hurried to the kitchen It was cocoa time.

Ranna hitched herself more upright and watched them. And Tinker as he removed a number of pieces of clothing. "Hum, hum, hum."

"Mine," snapped R-Bar at Ranna.

"Our's," growled Ran at them both.

"Touchy," mumbled Ranna.

Rekel's eyes popped open. She struggled to sit up. "What?" She had felt witch agitation.

Fair Morn leaned over the back of the couch and gently pushed her back down. "Just us."

Tinker sat on the longest couch and stretched bare feet toward the stove. He was down to his last few layers: jeans, thermal underwear. And looked over at Ranna. "Feel like telling us about what ever it was that got you into this state?"

She looked at him.

And nodded.

One brief, sharp nod.

Lism Heavr.

She had first heard of the strange elseplace from an Amp'tar in the Great Small on Lism Heavr. It was a new thing to hear.

Ranna had been admiring certain dark things at a certain dark shop when the owner, an Amp'tar of The Green String, had asked for a favor. And, as these creatures were known to have all manner of arcane secrets not often shared, Ranna had carefully discussed the matter.

And had gone off to dinner to think and ponder over the favor wanted. During her meal, she had spotted her sister Rekel drifting through, called her over, and proceeded to enlist the aid of this prickly and bothering sister in her scheme.

Ranna stopped her tale and looked over at the other couch. Rekel frowned back at her. "It is rare," explained Ranna, "that one meets another on wander."

And so they had returned and helped the Amp'tar of The Green string. Who then told them of a certain orange magic located on Amtittle. And how to find Amtittle, a strange place.

It was difficult. One had to twist out, down, down and around.

Something not usually done.

Something little known.

Amtittle.

"Oom pa'tak," hissed Rekel as they thudded down.

"Amtittle," said Ranna, ignoring the remark.

The two witches turned slowly and scanned their surroundings.

Amtittle was mostly flat to the distant horizons.

In all directions.

Green.

Flat.

Punctuated by truncated pyramids. These were wide-based, four-sided, grey squat things, slightly higher than the top of Ranna's head. Rekel was half a head shorter than her sister, her tallest sister.

"Sister?" asked Rekel, staring at their strange surroundings.

"We are out, down, down and around. I did not know of this layer of elseplaces."

"Hum."

"And neither did you," hissed Ranna.

"What lives in this strange strange?"

Ranna shrugged a shoulder and looked down at her slightly shorter sister. "That Amp'tar did not tell. Look for one with orange pulse." She pointed at the rows of truncated pyramid. "Be careful."

"I," stated Rekel, "am always careful." She cast a search. She was careful.

They waited. Rekel polished a smudge from the tip of one shiny boot.

And little by little, some time later, little by more, Rekel nodded. And pointed. "There. That way."

They walked that way. Into the pyramid field.

"Far?"

"Not far," said Rekel. "Not close."

Far beyond sight there was a stirring.
    Nests unfolded.
        Grey green wings opened.

Nesery stretched and grumbled. Silver wing claws flexed as agitation bubbled through The Clutch.

They glared at each and blinked in the bright light.

Three soft barks brought them into the air as The Fit soared up.

The Clutch swirled around, snapping, tasting unknown smell in the air. Hitching higher and higher.

"There."

Ranna indicated the pyramid just ahead. "I can see a soft orange pulse on top."

Standing next to it, she stretched up onto her toes and peered over the top edge. "Hum, hum, hum."

What?" hissed Rekel.

Ranna reached up and over and waggled her hand over the smooth feeling top. And yanked her arm down. Dangling from her clenched fist, two fine chains, each holding a small orange rock, each chain made of fine orange metal links.

"One for each." Ranna handed Rekel a chain.

Rekel took it and stared at it.

Ranna yanked her hat off and slipped the chain over her head, fluffed out her hair, and dropped the chain and rock inside her blouse.

"Orange," said Rekel. Witch was black, not orange.

"See look," commanded Ranna, setting her hat just so.

Rekel did. There was no sign of the orange.

"Keep or give." Ranna held out her hand.

Rekel snatched off her hat, threw the chain over her head, and banged her hat back into place. And stuffed chain and rock down her shirt. "In dik" She glared at Ranna. "Orange is not witch." And buttoned the collar of her military cut tunic, then tugged everything into the proper order, just so.

Ranna nodded and hurtled the orange bolt.

"OOOK," gasped Rekel, staring at her chest, at the thing piercing her. And collapsed.

Ranna held the other bolt and stared at it. Then sucking in a deep breath, she yanked it hard, inward, exhaling sharply, slumping to the ground. The Amp'tar had said that this was the only way to activate the orange.

Keening rage anger, The Fit ripped higher and higher, seeking direction.

Stealers were here.

Ugly unknown was here.

The Clutch whirled and swirled. And snapped frustration at each other.

The bodies were found and carried away to Krepkar. One was dumped in the center, one draped over Zimat.

The Clutch jostled angrily around Zimat, stepping on the other body, sharp claws cutting, digging, finger claws nipping at the thing Zimat held.

One dark eye popped open. Ranna stared at them upside down. At the things tearing at her.

She reached, took from Rekel, and ripped them out.

"To our dar-space." Ranna looked at Tinker. "And I pulled you. We required help."

He nodded, and stretched out a little more. "How do you feel?"

"Better." She looked around, from face to face, ending with R-Bar. "Safe. Comfort feeling safe."

R-Bar looked from Ranna to Tinker and back. "Show us this orange magic."

"Can not."

"Oh?" R-Bar straightened up, back stiffening, arms on the rests of her chair, fingers tightening. "Oh?"

"Not." Ranna nodded. "I do not have it here. Neither does she."

Ran stood and walked over to stand behind R-Bar, gently laying her hands on the back of the chair.

"Lost to those things?" asked Ran.

"No. I sent it elseplace." Ranna looked over at Rekel. "Even if we went far, the orange would remain Faan."

R-Bar sucked in her breath. "Who?"

A slight tug at the side of Ranna's mouth. "Guess."

Rekel hitched upright, struggled with the quilt,

and finally managed to shove it sideways. She ripped her tunic open and slid her hand across the base of her neck. Then sagged back. "Pak, pak, pak, pak, pak." She glared at Ranna. "Return," she growled.

"Our sister will have to do that," said Ranna.

R-Bar jumped to her feet. "Ripple! You sent it to Ripple."

Ranna nodded. Rekel hissed. And coughed.

Fair Morn stepped over, shoved her back down against the pillows, and tugged the quilt back up to Rekel's neck. "You better calm down. You are not really well."

"Ripple!" restated R-Bar, sitting back.

"Of course," said Ranna. "She is clan head. And the most rangle of us all. Who else?"

"So," interjected Tinker, interjecting, feeling the dark undercurrent to their conversation. "What were those things you stole this orange magic from?"

"Not their's," gurgled Rekel.

Ranna looked at him. "The Amp'tar of The Green String said that it had been there long before before. The gargoyles arrived later." She slid one arm free and lightly touched Tinker's arm.

"Gargoyles are child fright tell tale name. I do not know what they were. Other than duquar creatures."

Ran leaped to her feet And started toward Ranna.

Smoke grabbed her halfway there, and clamped

her hand around the arm reaching back, ready to hurl the glistening yellow crystal dagger.

"S'Hag," snarled Ran at Ranna, lurching at her, trying to yank her arm free.

Chantal jumped from her chair and helped Smoke hold the wildly struggling witch.

Black flowed and billowed around them.

The air crackled.

R-Bar crashed into them. "RAN, STOP!"

Something boomed.

The air cleared.

"Ummmm?" said Tinker.

Chicken watched Smoke, Chantal, and R-Bar lead Ran from the room, headed for their chambers. "Most agitated, indeed."

"Ummmmm?" said Tinker.

"That dagger was witch kill," snarled Ranna, struggling to her feet.

Tinker yanked her back down. "Sit down." And glared back at her. "And don't snarl at me. Either." He really didn't need this, all this agitation.

"Gosh." Messenger stared from Ranna to Rekel. "What did you do?"

"Ummmmm?" repeated Tinker.

"Nothing," said Ranna to Messenger. "What?" she asked Tinker.

"Duquar?"

"Duquar," shrugged Ranna, "is duquar." It was obvious.

"Clear as mud," replied Tinker, wondering why it was so hard to ever get an answer.

"Of course not," snapped Ranna.

"Coffee?" Chicken headed for the kitchen.

Tinker looked at Fair Morn. "I do not like this, not even a little bit."

"One?" Fair Morn frowned and wondered whether she ought to go and get her cannon.

"Bad feeling." He sighed as he slumped. And grumbled loudly, "Damn Faan are doing it again. Dragging us into more bad stuff. Wonder if they will ever learn?"

"Watch your mouth," hissed Ranna, sending a dark look at him.

Loud humming began to come from a far corner.

Ranna twisted around and lifted up to see what it was. Hissing loudly, she stood and took two steps. And sagged.

Fair Morn caught her and helped her back onto the couch. "You are still not fully recovered. Either."

Tinker stood and stared into the dark corner. "Be quiet," he said.

It stood, propped up in a corner, point down. The golden glow coming from the jewel set on the tip of the great black sword's hilt faded. The humming softly stopped.

He spun and dropped back onto the couch. "Even worse, if that thing is getting excited."

Ranna squirmed into the furthest corner of the

couch and carefully watched him, her mouth set in a hard thin line.

"And what is your problem?" Tinker frowned at her. "Now?" This was getting out of hand. And they had hardly done anything. Yet.

Before she could answer, a body dropped from elsewhere and thudded onto the floor trailing green fumes and smoke. The remnants of her black garb burst into flame.

Rekel heaved herself up and toppled from the couch.

Fair Morn grabbed a blanket, flopped it on top of the figure and fell on top of the body, smothering the fire.

Messenger gasped as Tinker jumped over and helped Fair Morn. "It's another one of them," said Fair Morn.

"Roll her over gently," said Tinker. "Let's see who it is, this time."

Fair Morn nodded.
And they did.

Messenger knelt alongside them and gently brushed the matted, tangled dark hair away from the face. "OH. MY. It is Shitar. Again."

R-BAR, GET DOWN HERE. His mental command banged outward.

OUCH! Tink that hurt. Not so loud. I'm coming.

And soon, she joined them. And stood and

stared. "I wonder what she has been doing? This time?"

His head swivelled around. "Whatever it is, or was, your bunch seems to be tangled up in something even worse than usual."

TINK!

"I am not the one that has all the ugly enemies," he grumbled. "I am not the one all beat up and flopping around on the floor, burned and smoking." His arms waved wildly.

"The couches are cluttered with bodies. And more keep arriving. We will have to put her in one of the spare bedrooms." He knelt and heaved the limp form into his arms and lurched to his feet.

"OOOOOOF. I'm beginning to feel like Florence Nightingale." He looked back over his shoulder as he stepped into the hall. "Someone want to put Rekel back on the couch?"

When he returned, Messenger lightly touched his arm. "MyTinker, why do you feel like a bird?"

"Huh?"

"A bird?"

Fair Morn reached over and poked her with one fingertip. "Better take a peck inside, kitten."

Messenger did, reached into his memories. "OH." And looked sheepish.

"Strange, strange," mumbled Rekel, back on the couch, trying to follow this rather unusual conversation.

Ranna watched them equally carefully. "My

sister has chosen tan kanyt emdur."

"Who? Did what?" Messenger looked at Ranna.

"The Runt," said Ranna, giving all the explanation that she was going to give.

Smoke slipped into the room. "Ran sleeps. Deep."

Tinker nodded. "How long until these two are well enough to travel?" He glowered at their "guests."

Smoke looked from witch to witch. "Ranna, two more weeks. Rekel, at least another month."

He jerked his head. "And?"

Smoke blinked.

What?

Unless R-Bar can do something that niece is gone.

Messenger gasped, burst into tears, jumped up, and bolted from the room.

Ramp and Reep? He stared at Smoke.

R-Bar joined their conversation. *They are on the way, Tink.*

The air in the center of the living room shimmered.

And formed.

"Where?" whispered dark soft.

"This way," said Smoke, leading Reep toward the correct bedroom.

Rekel struggled to sit up, a little more upright. And whispered at her eldest sister. "She had nothing hiding her eyes. Our niece will be killed."

"No," snapped Ranna. "The Silent One has

control. Now." She indicated Tinker with her chin. "His urh-witch did it."

"Where is my niece." Ramp shimmered in, stood there.

"IN HERE," called Smoke.

Ramp hurried that way.

"Worse, worse," whispered Rekel, mostly to herself. "Merge contact will kill them all. Horribly." She cringed deeper into the couch.

"No," stated Ranna firmly. "His urh-witch fixed that."

"Sister," wept Rekel. "This is gak talk." She wiped one sleeve across her face. "If I could, I would leave now."

Messenger returned, from the kitchen, carrying a cup of cocoa. "I made just lots and lots." She looked from face to face. "Really really."

"Come here," commanded Ranna, throwing blankets and quilt aside, beckoning at Messenger.

Messenger did.

Slowly Ranna lifted her hand. "Hold my hand."

"DO NOT!" screamed Rekel, knowing that such a direct contact between a witch and another magical type most often ended in a fatal blast of competing magics. Except for mates-for-life. Or when one was engaged in using counter spells. Sometimes.

Messenger twitched, cocoa sloshed from her cup, mostly on the hardwood floor, and grabbed Ranna's hand.

"YAAAAAAA!" bellowed Rekel, trying to call in protection. And failing. She still wasn't healthy enough for that. Then she peered at them through the cracks between the fingers covering her face and eyes. "Not possible."

"Look. Learn," said Ranna. "This urh-witch fixed me also. Now I may touch my sister magician Ramp."

Rekel fell back dragging the blankets up to her chin, eyes staring at the ceiling. "I have been brain damaged, false fixed, magic'd foul." She blinked. "Doom, doomed."

"You are bothersome as bothersome can be," growled Ranna. "Same as ever ever." Her lower tip pushed out. "Look at me."

Rekel turned her head and did.

"Our sister witch R-Bar has changed much much," said Ranna. "You have been wandering long, too long." She laid back, exhaling a long soft breath. "Must sleep . . . sleep." And sagged limply. Asleep.

Messenger released Ranna's hand and tucked the blanket and quilt around her, poking it in with gentle touches here and there.

"Touch me, urh-witch," whispered Rekel.

Messenger whirled and gasped, "Oh, no, you might be injured."

Dark midnight eyes peered round and round at Messenger. "Urh-witch, I would be not so . . . outside."

Messenger looked at Tinker. He nodded And sighed. "Might as well. What harm can it do?" And finished mopping up the cocoa spill.

"Will it cause great pain?" Rekel looked up as Messenger approached and knelt next to her couch,

"Nope." Messenger looked. "OH MY. Really really tangled. How did everything get so messy." And she reached in and straightened out the magical strands. And did something else. And leaned forward and kissed Rekel on the forehead. "There."

Rekel yelped. And gasped. "Nothing happened. Ranna true told." She stared at Messenger, then at Fair Morn, then at Tinker. "Alone. I need alone." And closed her eyes.

He stood, cocoa blotched cloth in hand. "Sure. Come on. Let's go check on Shitar. After I drop this in the kitchen."

They crowded around the door and peered inside.

Reep and R-Bar stood on one side of the bed, Ramp on the other. Chantal was sponging blood, dirt, and other stains from the pale limp body. The tattered remains of Shitar's clothes were tossed in a heap in one corner of the bedroom. Chicken handed Chantal a clean bowl of water and looked over at the crowd by the door. *Bad, My Lord. Fair Niece do abused be in most foul a'manner.*

R-Bar and Reep talked in low tones. Dark began to seep around them. Ramp threw her hood over her head and stuffed her arms into the wide baggy sleeves of her robe. And leaned forward, bending at the waist.

Tinker looked at Chicken.

They do all that they know, Our Prince. She pushed past him and headed down the hall with the bowl of dirty water.

Shitar lurched uptight, claws, fangs, wings appearing. And lunged toward Tinker.

Fair Morn charged, caught her in full flight and smashed her back down into the bed.

Smoke shoved Tinker sideways and pounced, helping Fair Morn clamp flailing arms and legs in place.

"What's going on?" He stared at the creature thrashing and snarling at the restraining arms and hands.

Reep stared at it.

"DON'T," hissed R-Bar. She gestured a vague blue form down. "Not yet."

Ramp shuddered.

Tendrils of smoke, grey smoke, seeped from her robe. Yanking her hands from her sleeves, she reached high above her head into somewhere, and plunged the flaming red wand down, pinning the howling beast through the chest to the bed.

Smoke and Fair Morn rolled, twisting away.

It gurgled and went limp.

And snarled at them. "All of you are ingmep."

And collapsed.

And began to fade away. Leaving only a faint blue ghost with a scarlet shaft poking up from the mattress.

"OH." Messenger wrapped her arms around Tinker. "OH. Oh. Oooohhhhhhh."

He gently turned and twisted her around so she couldn't see the bed and held her gently. "Shhhhhhhh, kitten, shhhh." And then watched what else was happening.

Reep began to toss handfuls of something black at the vague shape. The air crackled around her and R-Bar.

Ramp hastily backed up until she banged into the wall. "Careful, sisters, careful." And started to sag. Fair Morn quickly stepped over and grabbed her.

Suddenly she was there, dark eyes staring at them. A thick tongue slowly moistened parched lips. Then she croaked, "Dir dir ptar dar tak."

Ramp lurched from Fair Morn's arms and snatched the glowing red wand up and out and threw it somewhere. And toppled backwards against Fair Morn who wrapped her arms around Ramp's chest and held the sagging magician upright. Again.

Chantal nudged them aside, scooped Shitar into her arms, and headed for the door. "We need another bed. A clean one. Get out of the way." And headed down the hall. Reep went with her.

R-Bar stepped in front of Tinker and Messenger as Fair Morn headed Ramp toward the living room.

R-Bar tickled Messenger and smiled up at Tinker.

"She all right?" he asked.

R-Bar nodded. "Judging from the coarseness of her last comment, I would say that she is herself. And alive. Mostly."

Chicken joined them. "Most strange, that."

He nodded, eased one arm free, and wrapped it around R-Bar. "Think your clan will ever stop bringing all that kind of stuff down around our ears?"

R-Bar glared at him.

"Let us to living room go," said Chicken.

They did

Tinker settled into his chair, and took a tentative sip from the hot coffee in his mug, furnished by Fair Morn who had brought a pot and cups to the living room. He looked at Ranna, then at Rekel.

Ranna was sitting up. Rekel was propped half up by large collection of pillows poked behind her back.

The two witches eyed him carefully as he looked from one to the other. "I want you guys to do me a favor," he said.

Both nodded.

"Witch debt," stated Ranna.

He nodded back at them. "'I'd really like all of you, everyone, to try and keep your problems and troubles away from me, from us."

R-Bar growled at him, and hissed loudly.

Rekel stared at him.

One corner of Ranna's mouth twitched. She nodded. "Hum."

R-Bar glared at her.

"It had to be done," explained Ranna. "The runt, umm, R-Bar was needed. I do not know why the daughter of Ripple fell here."

"She lives," said R-Bar before either of her sisters could ask. "Almost far. Kar twisted spell bent."

"What?" hissed Ranna.

"How?" whispered Rekel.

Smoke joined them, sat on the arm of his chair, and slipped one arm around his shoulders. "She sleeps deep. It will be sometime before Shitar leaves that bed."

She looked at Ranna. "Was she with you two?"

"No. We most most-travel alone, Rekel and I."

"I have no idea what that niece natdar," grumbled Rekel.

R-Bar shifted her glare to Rekel.

Rekel yanked the quilt up to her chin. And mumbled, "Even in training she did."

Chantal walked in and dropped onto the couch used by Ranna. "Gimme some room." And stared at Tinker. "Bodies all over the damn place."

Chicken handed her a mug.

Fair Morn took the pot and poured. "Watch it, it is hot."

Chantal blew on the black liquid and frowned at him. "So, Simba Leader, what are we going to do about it?"

"What?"

"Damn witch bodies."

He shrugged. "Get 'em healed and shipped out, I suppose."

Messenger dragged her chair over and around. "We have lots and lots of room."

The silent figure slipped into the room. "Going home," whispered the shadows. Reep disappeared.

"Me too," said Ramp as she stood. "I will ask Shem to search his books." She bent and kissed R-Bar on the forehead. "Close, close." And faded away.

"Most weary a'looking," said Chicken.

R-Bar nodded. And yawned. "Used up a lot of energy. Think I will take a nap." She stood and headed down the hallway.

Chantal shoved her legs straight out and slurped loudly. "Grumble, grumble," she mumbled.

He admired her legs. "What?"

"Grumble, grumble, grumble," she grumbled.

He sighed.

Smoke leaned against him.

"Oh my," said Messenger.

"Prithee, Our Sister Self, what portends this thy grumbles?" Chicken joined Chantal on the couch.

"I think that we are in deep doo doo," stated Chantal, staring at Tinker. "Also."

Ranna looked at her and frowned, wondering what that term meant.

"Witch crap," explained Chantal. "And I do not

want to go out there again. Either."

"I'm hungry," announced Fair Morn, standing, and heading for the kitchen. "I'll bring the coffee cake back. Someone else can bring the cocoa."

Tinker looked around the room. "Then we have some more things to do. The storm has finally blown itself out."

Ranna lurched from the living room and joined them at the dining room table for their late dinner.

Everyone had spent the rest of the day shoveling snow from all those areas that needed drifts removed.

She looked down the table at him as he ate his dessert. "In one week I shall start the cast."

He looked at her. "Huh?" mumbled Tinker around a mouthful, and swallowed. "What?"

"Witch ward."

"No, you will not!" R-Bar rapped on the table top with the butt end of a grey smoking wand.

Ranna looked across the table at her. "It is what he wants."

"Dik dir," snapped R-Bar.

Ranna smiled a slight smile at her.

"What?" he asked.

"My old sister," began R-Bar.

"Oldest," corrected Ranna, sitting just a little straighter, throwing her shoulders back, just a little, unfastening the top button on her shirt.

"Wants to cast a spell that would prevent any

witch from approaching here."

"Yes," agreed Ranna. "Including me."

"And our daughter, maybe," snarled R-Bar. "And Reep. And her daughter."

"Bad idea," said Tinker.

"Indeed," stated Chicken. "Most."

"How bout," suggested Tinker, "that you just agree to leave your troubles elsewhere? Instead?"

"Never mind," snapped Chantal, heading off what she knew he was feeling, smiling at Ranna. "We know that you had no choice. Let's go in and watch a movie."

Ranna nodded at her. She had a very witchy look in her eyes.

And then, it was two weeks later.

And as Smoke had said, Ranna was healed.

And up and about, doing this and that, helping anyone who did anything. She was determined to understand this elseplace where her youngest sister witch lived. And what they were, exactly.

Besides, she did not like to just sit around doing nothing. She was a witch, after all. They did not like to be still just for the sake of being still. With one exception, their sister Reep.

Rekel was sitting up and looking healthy, but still weak.

Shitar was still in bed. Just lying there. Sometimes her eyes were open, sometimes they were not.

So everyone checked on her.

"Healing slowly." Smoke peered over his shoulder at her. "Much too slowly."

They turned and headed for the kitchen. And found R-Bar teaching Ranna how to make cocoa. Ran was helping. She had slowly accepted what Ranna and Rekel had done. And Ranna had acknowledged Ran's agitation.

Ranna was carefully stirring. Cooking was not something most of the witch clan enjoyed. "Strange, strange," she mumbled.

"Just stir," demanded R-Bar. "It is almost ready."

A small figure ran lightly across the counter top, the range top, and stretched and peered over the lip of the cocoa pan. Then she looked up at Ranna. "Aren't you done yet?"

"GAB DAK!" Ranna lurched backward, then swung with her wooden spoon, batting the thing back against the wall, splattering everything with brown spots.

"Dim, dim, dim," snarled R-Bar.

"Im patkak mek," growled Ran.

"OUCH," cried the small being as she hit the wall. Then she stood and stalked forward, low hung billowing trousers soft silk flowing. Growling, stepping bare toes in and out of the blue gas flame, she pointed at Ranna but spoke to Tinker. "This a new one of your houris?"

"Nope. But . . . "

The blast knocked Ranna backward, to the floor, doubling her over. "URK."

"DAT! STOP!" Tinker bent over, then knelt next to Ranna. "You hurt?"

"Ra tak FAR par," gasped Ranna.

"That is really nasty," said R-Bar, glaring down at her.

Ran nodded. "Vile ugly."

Dat stepped to the edge of the counter top and glared down at the curled up witch. "Is the cocoa ready?"

Tinker helped Ranna stand. "The little cocoa freak is Dat. Dat, this is Ranna, one of R-Bar's sisters. There is another one in the living room."

"I am his indjinn," stated Dat. "And I do not like being hit with a wooden spoon. I saw the other one on the couch."

Ranna rubbed her stomach and stared at the tiny figure. "An indjinn?"

"Yes." Dat smiled up at her, running her hands up and down her bare torso. "A very beautiful indjinn."

"I think that the . . . cocoa, is ready." Ranna picked up the spoon and gave the cocoa one last stir. And eyed Dat.

Dat stomped over and bit her hand.

"DIT PTAR." Ranna jerked away from the stove

top.

"And I do not like spells being cast over me, either."

Ranna bent forward and peered at her. "Small being, large demands." She poked one crackling finger at the indjinn.

"STOP IT!" Tinker grabbed Ranna's arm. "Both of you. You two want to squabble, go outside."

"Sister," hissed R-Bar. "Behave. Dat is very agitated and he is getting that way." A very agitated mate-for-life was something to worry about. And her sister ought to know that.

Ranna straightened up. "Of no importance." And indicated Dat.

A hand grabbed her shoulder and dragged her around. Chantal leaned close. "WRONG! You are about to become an unwelcome guest. You stand in our debt. Go in the living room, talk with Rekel." Her other hand was balled into a tight fist.

Ranna's eyes shifted sideways at R-Bar.

"Strong debt, Eldest Sister. And you know it."

Ranna nodded, once, and walked away.

"I'm gonna get my gun," mumbled Chantal. "If I don't punch her lights out first."

"Cool it, Cowgirl," said Tinker.

"Is the cocoa ready?" asked Dat.

"Yes," said Ran. "It is ready."

Chicken and Messenger joined them.

Chicken grabbed a tray. "Let us to living room

go."

Messenger banged open a cabinet. "I've got the cookies."

Dat ran up the outstretched arm of Chantal. And sat on her shoulder, one hand clenching Chantal's collar. She looked at Tinker as the rest left. "Great Master, do you want me to do something to that tall unpleasant female person witch nik nik?"

"No!" snapped Tinker. "I want you to behave. Or go back into that ring."

"Gimble, gimble," grumbled Dat.

As they started for the living room, Tinker stopped Chantal.

"What?" she asked.

"And you are not to punch her either."

"Gimble, gimble." Chantal smiled. Dat nodded and kissed Chantal's cheek.

He sighed.

Dat stood up, one hand digging into Chantal's hair. "I will leave, Great Master, if you wish to play with this one."

This generated another, longer sigh. "Umm, Dat? Oh, never mind, wouldn't do any good anyway." He nudged Chantal toward the hallway. "I want to stop in Shitar's room, first."

"Meow, meow," said Chantal. And laughed.

Ranna leaned back in the couch and looked from Ran to R-Bar. "Sorry, sorry. I was bothered much. How did your's get one of those?"

"It was a gift," explained Messenger, dropping a marshmallow into Rekel's cup.

Rekel eyed the white ball with some suspicion.

"We do buy most fine ring at Foregather," added Chicken.

"It was The Eye of Dat," said Ran.

"You let that indjinn roam free?" Ranna stared around the room.

"Yep," said Smoke.

"Sure," said Fair Morn. "Why not?"

"She is well behaved," added R-Bar, emphasizing the words 'well behaved.'

"And in my debt forever," croaked someone as she wobbled from the hallway.

Four witches sucked in their breath.

Chantal quickly looped an arm around Shitar and helped her to one of the large chairs.

"I, ah, just remembered," said Tinker, stepping in. "That Dat fixed up Chantal in the elseplace of the Dark Emp."

"So he asked her if she could do something for Shitar." Chantal dropped into another chair.

"Somebody did not like her very much," said Dat, sitting on Chantal's shoulder. "Very, very, very much."

Ranna jumped up, stepped over, and fell to her knees facing Chantal, and said to Dat, "How may I gift you, Indjinn Dat?"

"I do not need anything," answered Dat. "Thank you."

Ranna looked at R-Bar.

R-Bar looked at Dat. "It is not polite to refuse a gift. From a witch. Perhaps some jewelry? Something to compliment your beauty?"

Dat nodded. "Translucent green gems?"

"A necklace?" suggested Ranna, standing.

"Really really would be pretty," added Messenger.

"All right," agreed Dat.

Ranna nodded. A thin line of green sparkle formed around Dat's neck. A lower pendant of three gems hung past her sternum. "Beautiful," breathed Ranna.

Dat lifted the necklace up to her eyes. "It is a very nice gift." She cleared her throat. "Ahem. Thank you. You are a nice person." She bit off the lowest gem and crunched loudly. "Very nice."

Ranna jerked back, and went back to her spot on the couch. And stared at Shitar, now encircled by a thick comforter, pulled up to her neck.

"I am healing, Aunt," mumbled Shitar. "What is wrong with Aunt Rekel? She looks . . . strange."

So Ranna told her.

      And then Chicken told Shitar all the rest. And then.

      It was Shitar's turn.

Chapter Three.

One Finds Many Things On Wander.

Flora Sopatch. Warm and Pleasant.

Flora Sopatch, the garden elseplace, all shades of green. It was renown as a place to come to for relaxation. Few witches ever came. They were not good at it, relaxing.

But, Hanred had convinced Ripple to give it a try. As a sort of holiday celebration. So they had. Come here. To relax. They had been here for two days. And Ripple was beginning to fidget.

He shrugged. "Oh well. We can always travel tomorrow." And reached across the table and filled her goblet. Again.

"Master Illusionist, are you up to no good?" She was beginning to slur her words. She set her goblet down and undid another button on her blouse.

"Of course." He admired the large amount of pale skin showing in the ever widening gap of her blouse.

She smiled. "Good." And shoved her goblet across the table at him. Empty again. "I feel in the mood for no good."

He filled her's, then his.

Waving over the waiter, Hanred ordered a number of beverages and smiled across the table. "As soon as he returns, let us retire to our rooms, Dark Delight."

"Hum, hum, hum." She blinked at him. "Husband, is the light in here suddenly orange tinged?"

Something crackled, way up there, near the ceiling, and fell onto the table, right in front of her.

Hanred leaped to his feet. And hastily stepped around to stand by her side. "What are those? Necklaces?"

Ripple carefully poked at them with a sparkling golden wand. They buzzed, and spit at her.

"Rekel touched, Ranna sent." She scooped them into a pouch colored a deep black and cinched the top closed. And handed the pouch to him. "Keep these. They will come looking for them." She pushed her chair back and stood.

The waiter rushed up and started to hand Hanred a number of ornate vessels. Hanred dropped the pouch into one jacket side pocket and filled her arms with the jugs. Then he shooed the waiter away. "Shall we?"

Ripple nodded and headed for the staircase, clinking softly.

In front of the door, five flights up, she fumbled with the door lock. He fumbled with her blouse.

Banging the door open, they lurched into the first room.

"Dap dap dir tak!" exploded Ripple.

"Hayou, Mother. Hayou, Father."

"Daughter?" Hanred hastily yanked Ripple's blouse back up and over her shoulder. "What are you doing here?"

The ceiling grumbled at Shitar. And Ripple glared. And walked to one side and set all the jugs on a small table.

"Visiting," said Shitar, watching her mother carefully.

Ripple shoved a jug at her. Then grabbed another, and flopped onto the couch, and beckoned at her daughter to join her. "Speak tell."

"I can talk to you in the morning."

"Now." Ripple looked at Hanred. He handed her a mug, then one to his daughter.

And filled his own, using his own supply. "A surprise. How did you find us?"

"Heh, heh, heh," replied Shitar.

"Gib dip," grumbled Ripple, her lower lip pushing out.

"You were not trying to be not found." Shitar's lower lip pushed out, looking just like her mother. She frowned at her parents.

Hanred nodded. "True." They were both too

agitated for comfort, mother and daughter. Agitated witches were always a hazard.

"Just getting away from the court," said Ripple. "Just prowling a little."

"Hum, hum," said Shitar.

"It was a holiday of a sort," added Hanred.

"That also." Ripple patted her daughter's thigh. "Until you got here."

"Didn't mean to interrupt," mumbled Shitar, looking at her mother from the corners of her eyes. "Also?"

"So? Speak." Dark seeped sideways.

"Mother," growled Shitar. "Don't." Something popped.

Ripple jerked. And nodded. "Tale tell."

Shitar's frown deepened. "I just felt the need to leave them, Aunt R-Bar and all the others." Her lower lip quivered. "All have their's . . . "

"Hum," said Ripple.

"Oh," said Hanred, looking at Ripple.

"Eventime," said Shitar. She disappeared.

"Clap spat," growled Ripple.

He flopped down next to her and slid one arm behind the small of her back and then hooked it around her waist. "That is new." He hadn't heard that particular epitaph before.

"Dark trouble," she hissed, rolling her head sideways.

"Ahhhhh?"

"Husband, Wise Master Illusionist . . ."

He blanched. "What?" he whispered.

"Every once in a great passage of time, not often, few few, it can happen. Dark trouble." She turned and grabbed him, releasing her cup and jug. They floated out of the way. "Weird witch magic."

He stared into those seemingly bottomless black eyes with the glowing red fire deep down. "What . . . are you . . . talking . . . about?"

"Our daughter, the unmated rangle witch. Of them all, she has not found. Of her clan name group."

He nodded. "True. But many of your sisters also have not." He gently tugged her closer.

"Husband, a kan-witch has no control. I heard of one, long ago, before before, two clans over. She had to be hunted down." Her eyes bored into his. "And taken apart."

"What?"

She shook her head. "No more. I can speak of this no more. Take me to bed." She wobbled to her feet. "Bring the bottles."

As they ate breakfast, a voice spoke to them from somewhere. "May I?"

"Enter," said Ripple. "Very polite," she grumbled.

Shitar faded in, waved over a chair, and sat. "Looks edible."

Hanred smiled and pushed over a covered

container. "Most edible." And as his daughter served herself, he carefully searched her face for signs of . . . something. He refilled his cup, then Ripple's, and cleared his throat. "Ahem, I hear that there is A Grand Fest on Ander's Back."

"Hum," said Shitar, loading her plate.

"Hum, hum," said Ripple, looking at him, wondering why he had this sudden interest in a magical gathering with large magical crowds.

Hanred shrugged elegantly. "Bound to be large numbers of males there. All kinds, all classes." He smiled broadly. "Maybe even an Illusionist, or two."

"Hum," said Shitar.

"Ander's Back has a nice climate," offered Ripple. What a clever mate he was.

"And," added Hanred quietly. "We could buy something special for The Prince and The Princess."

Ripple gently touched her daughter's arm. "Find new spells."

Hanred stared at his wife. "Does she need more?"

"Of course." One corner of Ripple's mouth puckered. "I even might find some . . . interesting, there as well."

"Ahhhh," said Hanred. "We are going." He could tell that she had made up her mind.

Shitar looked up, from one to the other. "Travel?" Was her mother actually inviting her to go along.

Ripple's eyes glittered. "Of course. I shall widen your arcana skills."

Hanred clenched his wife's forearm. "Is that safe? To do?" He frowned at them both. "Our daughter already biggdals dark. Is there not a limit?"

"Rangle be rangle," stated Ripple firmly, very witch firmly. She gently patted the hand still gripping her forearm. "Husband, we are Faan. And her clan name group moves in new ways."

Hanred released her arm. "I deter in such matters to you."

Ripple sat straighter. "Our daughter will be clan center. Time by time. Out there." She looked deep into her daughter's eyes, black staring into black. "It will be detrak to pass over. Soon, daughter, soon."

Shitar stared back. "Do The Aunts, all The Aunts, Young and Old, and Cousins, agree?"

Ripple shrugged one shoulder. "Of no import. Center to center is the rule. If you were a sister's daughter, it would still be so."

"Mother? Why not Sedeem? She is power beyond power. Or Szaifeh? She is double-trained."

Ripple sat back and folded her hands over her stomach. "Szaifeh is Vander tied, cross-tied by her mate-for-life. Sedeem is something beyond, not just Faan witch magician. Sa'ar is Vander Heart. Of your name group you are Faan, the only pure rangle Faan."

Shitar nodded agreement. "I am the only one."

"Now," said Ripple. "But there will be a cousin

and sister more."

"MOTHER." Shitar leaped to her feet. And stared at her.

"Your sister is named Santar. Reep has not yet name selected."

"WHEN?"

"Soon. Sit. Daughter." Ripple waited until Shitar did. She tapped a knuckle on the table."You will help teach."

"Yes."

"Shall we go?" asked Hanred.

Ripple nodded.

And took them away.

Leaving a glittering stack of gold coins on the table top.

Ander's Back. Hordes and Hordes.

Ander's Back

The Grand Fest.

Thronged.

Mobbed.

All kinds of folk.

"Lodging," said Ripple.

This way." Hanred led them to a small, out of the way inn. The sign over the entrance read **JAK**.

He talked with a rather short fellow and received the key to a suite of rooms, handed over by the smiling owner of the inn.

Unlocking the door, Hanred ushered them

inside. "Rasjak is an old acquaintance. And always holds rooms open for certain old friends just in case they might come visiting."

"Hum," said Shitar.

"Hum, hum," said Ripple. "And you are one of these, an old friend."

Smiling broadly, he dropped into a large piece of furniture. "Dusky Delight, that I am. And lucky we are, for otherwise there would be nary a lodging place to be found. Not during The Grand Fest."

"Drink," stated Ripple.

Hanred jumped to his feel. "I know just the booth." And taking wife and daughter, each by the arm, he led them outside and deep into the heart of the sea of tents, and booths, to a certain favored tent, nodded at the owner, and was ushered to a private side table. After ordering, they were left alone.

"Another old friend?" Ripple stared at him. This was a side of him she had not yet seen.

"Another," said Hanred. He winked at Shitar. "Before I settled down, I traveled muchly."

Their drinks arrived. Ripple took a sip, winced, and grunted.

"Poison," gasped Shitar. The air crackled wildly around her.

"Noooo," hissed Ripple. "Santar." She grabbed Hanred's arm. "We must return to Bahn Duhr Tohr. A daughter is arriving."

He nodded. "Of course."

Ripple took the black pouch from Hanred and shoved it across the tabletop to Shitar. "Here. Aunts Rekel and Ranna will come to you. Looking for these."

She stood. "Enjoy The Great Fest. Buy something for the young Royals. And visit soon." She would have to do something for Shitar when she did.

Ripple nodded at her daughter. And they were gone.

"Dir dik dit," growled Shitar, gesturing for the waitress. "Another," she demanded. The waitress hurried away. And hurried back, banging down the order. "Food?"

"No!" snapped Shitar. Waving her away, she took a long swallow from her long glass. And noticed the man dressed all in dark green drift through the crowd in her direction.

He sat down. Across the table from her. Without asking. He just sat down. At her table.

"A dark dark. Yet this is a large table, open. Hard to find such at The Grand Fest." He waggled one hand in the air and then ordered from the startled waitress as soon as she rushed up.

"You there," he said, looking across the table. "Another? I pay." Soft orange brown eyes watched her face.

Shitar glared at him. She was not in the mood for company. Even if the company was quite pleasant to look upon.

"WELL?" he demanded. "Do you speak?" He

decided that she had a very nice sulky look.

"Yesssssssss," she hissed.

His eyes flew wide, then he leaned forward, and stared at her very carefully. "Are you one of the Lamia's children?" And leaned back, and waggled one hand loosely. "Of no concern." He looked up at the nervous waitress. "Bring her another of whatever she is having. And I will require a meal. A very large meal."

The waitress fled. Even for a Great Fest, there was something about that pair that did not set well with the waitress.

He looked at Shitar and the growing dark forming behind her. "Never met one of her offspring before. Do not see any scales."

"Cretin," snapped Shitar. "Go away. Flee." She waggled a hand at him.

"Hum duk bid bid, snaky one. I will leave after I eat." He nodded at her. "You just sit there and hiss quietly." He began to loosen the ties on the collar of his heavy traveling cloak. And finally threw it back from wide shoulders and over the chair back.

His tunic was colored a soft green. It matched the jewel on the black ring he wore. He sipped from his cup. "Thought you looked witch, not Lamia." He shrugged. "Never tell by looks, they say."

He nodded at her. "Of course, you are lovely to look at, much much. Even for a reptile daughter." And smiled warmly at her, eyes dancing here and there. "Nice nice." And stared at the gap in her blouse.

"Lovely pale skin."

She wacked the back of his hand with a long bronze wand that sparkled small flashes of fire. "I am Faan witch Shitar, do darp."

"Coarse, of course." He nodded to himself. "That witch clan." And he reached over and tapped the back of her hand with one fingertip. It left a green stain.

Shitar looked at the mark, and then slowly looked up, calling down a deep dark. It settled around them.

"Very nice," he said, picking up something and chewing thoughtfully. She was very attractive. And very witch.

"Name me a name," she growled.

He nodded. "Mantara." And swallowed.

"Clan," she demanded.

"None. I am one of a few." And reached for another tidbit on his plate.

"Few? What?"

"Grenzanr."

Shitar leaped up. And twisted to her rooms.

Sometime Later in The Week.

It had been three days since her Mother and Father had departed.

She was watching a display of ganko.

He grabbed her right forearm. "Gim dik to! I have searched for three days. You leave a very twisted trail, Faan witch Shitar."

Her downstroke enveloped him. She stabbed with a blue wand. It struck his chest. And bent. Jerking wildly, she bit his wrist.

"OUCH!" His tangle twisted around her as he jerked the wounded member back.

All around them folk pushed at each other to make room and to get away. This was not a safe place to be.

He glared at her and wiped healing over the wound. "That will probably leave a scar." She was certainly witch.

She sent something that grabbed him from behind and coated him nine ways before he could react.

"Hum," she said. "What is this that would so tangle one so rangle?" And stepped around Mantara and loosened Ripple.

"Faan witch, I am Zwar witch Surlindar. We are debt tied, clan tied. Your R-Bar did do this thing." She had felt their clan link as she had wandered past this spot and turned to visit.

Shitar nodded. And noted the small orange dot on Surlindar's cheek bone.

"Ahm, ahm," said Surlindar. And nodded. "What shall we do with this male who would agitate one so pale?"

Ripple leaned close and whispered. "He is named Mantara. Of the Grenzanr."

Surlindar sucked in her breath. And turned to peer at him. "One of The Green?"

Mantara watched her carefully. It was all he could do. He blinked.

Surlindar slid a glowing red wand over his cheek, the tip coming to rest just below one eye. "If we unbind you, you oath say no harm to either do?"

Mantara blinked.

Surlindar released his face. "Say, speak."

"No harm," croaked Mantara. "To either."

Surlindar looked at Shitar.

Shitar nodded.

Mantara was released.

He cleared his throat. "Lovely witches, allow me to offer you a drink. Or food."

Shitar nodded, pointed at an open booth. The previous occupants had fled during the action between the two witches and Mantara. "There."

They walked over and sat. Mantara waited until the witches were settled, then he sat next to Shitar. She growled. He sat closer. She gurgled.

He ignored her and nodded to Surlindar. "Zwar and Faan. Interesting cross-tie."

Surlindar looked at him. "And Tanpak."

Mantara jerked. "Them as well? A three link?"

She nodded.

Mantara gasped. "That is mant'ble ramdam."

"Very vulgar," hissed Shitar.

"As vulgar as a certain hissing Faan witch?" Mantara slipped one arm around her back, lightly stroking her ribs. "OOOF."

Ripple's elbow had nearly cracked one of his ribs.

Surlindar reached across the table and filled their mugs. "Ahm ahm," she said.

Shitar frowned at her, turned, grabbed Mantara's head with both hands and twisted it around until he was looking at her.

He blinked.

She stared into his eyes, those lovely orange brown eyes. "Hum, hum, hum."

"Dark beauty?" asked Mantara. She had beautiful eyes, midnight black, bottomless with a faint glow of red fire deep within.

She released him. "Take this googark from my hand." And lifted her hand in front of his face.

He kissed it. "My pleasure, Faan witch Shitar." And held it. The green stain faded away. He looked across the table. "You are beautiful also, Zwar witch Surlindar."

"The Green are solitary spin twist," said Surlindar.

"So it is told," replied Mantara.

"Stand," commanded Shitar.

He did. Releasing her hand.

"Turn around. Slowly."

He did.

Slowly Shitar stood and faced him. "Mother will certainly be surprised."

"Ahm ahm," said Surlindar.

"What?" said Mantara.

"Mine," breathed Shitar, leaning close.

"Let us speak on this," said Mantara.

Surlindar stood, sent the table and the chairs somewhere, and swirled a nop-space in and around them. Twisting a ring from one finger, one ring of many, she held it out to Mantara. "Gift gift."

Shitar grabbed his hand, snatched the ring from Surlindar's hand, and jabbed it on the appropriale finger. "Father will be so surprised."

"Are you sure?" Mantara stared at the ring. The inscription read, in witch twisted script, "Bound to Shitar."

Shitar nodded. "They will be."

He looked up. "Is this ring Zwar?"

Surlindar nodded.

He tugged at it. "It stays."

"Yes," said Surlindar.

"Mine," sighed Shitar, tugging him close. She looked at Surlindar. "Mother was correct." So was father, she added to herself.

Surlindar blinked at her. "The Great Fest calls." She pulled out.

"I would go to Doth Lamex," said Shitar. It was considered a good place to take a mate-for-life first.

"First, Indermal," answered Mantara, kissing her, tasting that wild witch taste of her.

"Hum," said Shitar.

"I have a small, very much alone, place spot there." He plucked a button loose on her blouse. Then another.

Shitar nodded. "Can you?"

"Yes."

He turned them to it.

Grandeville. Tinker's Place.

Shitar stared around the room.

"Not a few days later they fell on us as we stood on a hill top. Hordes of karpakars. I barely twisted out."

She slumped deeper into the thick comforter.

"Karpakar?" asked Tinker.

"It is what Mantara screamed."

"I will go to Indermal," announced Ranna. "Those karpakar must have been the gargoyles. Where are the orange?"

"There." Shitar pointed at one of the shelves in the bookcase. A small sack sat there.

Ranna stood, walked over and grabbed the sack, emptying it into her other hand. Then she stepped back and handed one necklace to Rekel, slipping the other over her own neck. "There. Now I will see to these karpakar."

"HOLD IT!" Tinker leaped up and grabbed her arm. "You are not going anywhere. You have barely recovered from your last encounter with them."

"I was not ready. Then."

R-Bar jumped to her other side. "Right. We will go with you. I think that you are going to need help."

Ranna stared down her nose at her shorter sister.

"I do not require assistance."

"Damn dumb," observed Chantal. "Barely healed and ready to get beat up again."

"Nik nik," snarled Ranna.

"Sister!" snapped Rekel. "Sit. They are correct."

Ranna glared at her.

Rekel glared back, and hissed. "Shitar near went far. As I was."

Tinker released Ranna's arm. "I think we all ought to talk about what these karpakar are capable of doing before we rush off for a visit. A little thought is needed. This time."

He nodded as Shitar insisted that she should go as well. "Right. When you are healthy. That gives us plenty of time to think about it."

Ranna stepped over and sat next to Shitar, gently touching her shoulder. "Your's was a Green?"

"Yes."

"Did he go far?"

"I do not know. I think that he was taken. By those things. I still feel him alive."

"Hum." Ranna turned toward Tinker. "I will look."

She stood.

And turned.

And was gone.

"Merde," mumbled Tinker as he dropped into his chair.

"My Lord? Chicken frowned in his direction.

Smoke tapped Fair Morn on the shoulder. "Let's go. We might as well get everything ready."

Chantal stood. "I'll help."

"HEY." He stared at them.

"Can't have ugly what ever they are snatching our niece's hunny bunch." Chantal went with Smoke and Fair Morn. "Can we?" she asked back over her shoulder.

"Nope," relied R-Bar, dropping into his lap. "Can we?"

"OOOOF!" He nodded. "Sure. I am tired of getting beat up." He frowned at her.

Messenger leaned against the back of his chair and threw her arms around his neck. "Hum buggy doo de doo."

"Yah," said R-Bar.

Shitar stared at them. "Uncle?"

"What?" he growled.

"When I am well, I will take care of those dodark dit dar." Nothing could injure her mate-for-life and survive for long. "By myself."

He nodded at her. "Right. Did just fine the last time."

"Gip dit ptar." Shitar glowered at him. She didn't like being talked to that way. Unless it was by her mate-for-life. Witches did not appreciate people disagreeing with them, especially non-witches.

"Good thing that you are sick," grumbled R-Bar. "Foul mouth niece."

The telephone rang and interrupted them.

He stood, set R-Bar on her feet and answered it. It was J. C.

"Congratulations," said Tinker.

"How'd you know?"

"Witchy grapevine. What's up?"

"Need any help? I could come up, shovel snow, stuff like that there. Use Doc's new snowmobile."

"Nope."

"Reep just left. To visit Ripple. Ahhhh, Tinker?"

"Ummmm?"

"Think that I can get Morgan to get his sneaky corporate attorneys to whip up another birth certificate? I'm gonna need one. Soon."

"I imagine we can get him to do that. What is your daughter's name?"

"Reep said that it was Sha'gar. Supposed to be an ancient name indicating quiet strength."

Tinker laughed. "That would be nice. Quiet, that is."

J. C. laughed with him. "Can't be any more quiet than Reep. Your house full?"

"Getting there."

"Going out there?"

Tinker sighed.

"Want me to come along?"

"Umm, no. We're not going anywhere yet."

"O.K. Give me a call. I do house sitting, right?"

"Right."

Tinker hung up and turned to his audience. The rest had slipped up to listen. "Their daughter's name is Sha'gar."

Witches nodded. It was a good name.

Rekel slowly shoved quilts and blankets aside, stood and stepped over to Shitar, bent and cracked her across the side of the face with the flat of one hand, rocking Shitar's head to one side.

"NIECE! That is not proper language to use when addressing your Uncle. Sick or not." She banged Shitar's head the other way. "Without him, you would have gone far." Then she slowly turned, lurched back to the couch and toppled into it.

"Great bedside manner," mumbled Tinker.

"Hist, Our Prince." Chicken hurried over and tucked Rekel's legs back up and poked the blankets and quilts into order.

"Sorry sorry, Uncle," whispered Shitar.

"How about some cocoa," he asked no one in particular.

"I will make it." Messenger hurried toward the kitchen. Ran was already there.

"That niece is very rangle," she said to Messenger.

"I suppose. Get the milk."

Chapter Four.

Surprise, Surprise.

Grandeville. Tinker's Place.
"My Lord, those things do be most vile." Chicken banged a fist into an open palm.

"Uh huh."

"Need killing, Tink." R-Bar frowned at the floor.

Ran nodded. "Yes, Amtar."

"Uh huh."

"That all that you can say, Cowboy?" Chantal poked another piece of wood into the stove. "Uh huh?"

"Uh huh."

Smoke stared at him, intently. "MindMate?" Checking for illness.

He looked over. "What?"

"Just checking." She stood. "I will get a fresh pot of coffee."

"Me'Lord?" Chicken leaned toward him. "For what reason do thee uh huh pon us so?"

He slumped deeper. "Everyone just assumes that we are going to hard charge straight ahead, out there again, right?" And frowned at her.

She nodded. "Pears so, Our Prince."

"Well?"

"Fair scowling Lord?"

"Are we going?"

She frowned at him. "Our Heart, thee do discombobulate this, Thy Verra Own Queen."

He sighed. "Why do you think that we are going? Or need to be going anywhere? Anyhow?"

Chicken grinned. "Why, for to rescue Sweet Niece husband from most foul beasties."

"He alive?"

She shrugged.

"Why did they snatch him?"

"Most great irritation bout poaching witches, me'thinks." She nodded. It was fairly obvious. To her.

"Right. They stole the orange magic and those things came looking for it. I think these guys can clean up after themselves."

"Coffee?" Smoke had returned with a full pot, and was waiting for Tinker to hold up his cup. She looked at the witches, who were in various stages of astonishment, staring at Tinker. "What did you do to them, MindMate?" She indicated the startled looking group. "This time?"

"Not much," he grumbled. "Just getting tired of cleaning the Aegean Barns. Or whatever it was." He nodded at the witches. "None of them are named Hera either."

Chicken chewed on one corner of her lower lip.

"Most literary a'grump."

His head snapped around to glare at her. "I told you. I am tired of out there. And pain. And agony." He surged to his feet and headed for the hallway, striding quickly, up to The Den. He needed to be alone.

"Oh . . . my . . ." Messenger looked at Smoke as she refilled various of the cups. With those wanting cocoa.

Shitar shoved herself more upright. "Uncle is quite correct. I will see to those beasts." She would kill them all. By herself.

"But not just yet." Smoke gently pushed her back and yanked a blanket up and around her. "You are still a very weak kitten. When you are healthy it will be time enough to talk of hunting." And it would give them more than enough time to calm him down. Once that was done then they could bring up the idea of going out there again.

Fair Morn leaned in from the dining room. "Soup's on. Chicken soup. So it is supposed to be good for whatever ails you." She winked at the Princess. "Tee hee."

Chicken frowned at her as she stood. "Passing poor a'jest, it do a'Us seem."

"Stay there," said Smoke to Shitar and Rekel. "We will bring you your's."

"Soup du poulette, Princess," said Fair Morn, ladling from the large tureen, and setting a filled bowl in front her.

Chicken nodded. And looked around the table.

"I'll do it." Chantal stood, grabbed a tray and set a filled bowl, a spoon, and a heap of crackers on it. "If I am not back in ten minutes, send a rescue party." She headed upstairs for The Den. She and Chicken were the best at getting him to calm down.

Ranna, just returned, looked at R-Bar. "Does he often get violent? And beat you?" She frowned worry at her sister. There was a deep history to this in the witch clans.

"No," replied Fair Morn. "She was just joking."

"He was very bothered." Smoke took a tray into Shitar, followed by Ran carrying one for Rekel.

"Hum," said Ranna.

R-Bar frowned at her.

Ranna shrugged. It was a problem about mates-for-life. Their potential for violence.

Messenger poked a cracker to the bottom of her bowl with her spoon. "They do seem to be causing an awfully large amount of trouble."

"Kitten," grumbled R-Bar.

Chicken looked down the table. "Tis most true. And ne'possible for to be overlooken."

"Dir zir gap gap," grumbled R-Bar.

Ranna stared at her. That was pretty vile, even for a witch.

"Can't deny the obvious," said Fair Morn, refilling her bowl. "Anyone want some more?"

R-Bar nodded. "Let's talk about something else."

She didn't want to hear anymore about witches causing problems.

Chicken looked at Ranna. "Healthy enow?"

"I am." Ranna took more soup. And beckoned over the cracker tray. "When Rekel and our niece are ready, we will see to those beasts. There was no trace of Mantara at Indermal."

She kicked on the door. "Knock, knock, knock. Hello in there. Anything at home?"

The door swung in. "What?"

"Brought you some lunch, Cowboy. You wanna eat?" He looked calmer.

"Sure. Come in."

"Is it safe?" She leaned forward, just a little. "I'm not in the mood for assault or rape."

He took the tray. "You eat?"

"Nope. But I am beatin' feet down the hall toot sweet."

"Thanks."

"You all right, John?" Her hand lightly touched his shoulder.

"Sure. Feel fine." He sighed. "Just needed some space. Away from agitated witches and all their problems."

"We know," she whispered. "Don't keep us out too long. O.K.?" She stepped back and gently closed the door. And headed toward downstairs. "Damn witches." They all needed to have their butts kicked.

"Whoosh," said Chicken, looking at Smoke.

"Tred softly, Princess," cautioned Smoke.

"Indeed." She filled her cup and settled back in her chair.

Chantal walked in and dropped into her chair and growled loudly. "The first one that gives me any lip gets her ass kicked. Pass that damn coffee, please."

Messenger slumped in her chair, eyes going all round. "Oh, my."

Ranna looked at Chantal.

"Not a word," snapped Chantal, hunching over her cup. "Not one damn word."

R-Bar gently touched her sister on the arm and shook her head, one short quick jerk.

Ranna nodded. And took more soup. Ran called the crackers over.

Fair Morn headed for the living room and passed back through, carrying trays and dirty dishes.

And then they talked about travel.

And other things.

And finished the soup.

"YAAAAAAAAAAAAAAAAA!"

It was Rekel, screaming terror. Trying to call down protection.

"SHUT UP, AUNT! SHUT UP!"

It was Shitar yelling through the scream.

They all poured into the living room.

Ran grabbed Ranna, jerking her to a halt.

R-Bar jumped in front of her and shouted at her sister. "DO NOT!"

"Kartz," gasped Messenger.

"What are you doing here?" demanded Chantal.

Smoke knelt next to Rekel, a tightly coiled up ball of witch. "Relax. She is a friend." And carefully touched the witch, gently pushing in calm with her minds.

"A witch bane," hissed Ranna, calling down dark things.

R-Bar reached up and slapped her across the face. "Stop that. And they are called Nagar."

Rekel exhaled loudly and slowly straightened out. "Friend?" Her eyes watched Smoke's face.

Ranna growled at R-Bar. "How can she be a friend?" And carefully didn't look at the dark fiend. Witches didn't have friends.

Footsteps thudded down the hall and burst into the living room. "Now what's going on?" He jolted to a halt. "Kartz?"

She flowed over to him and wrapped him in a close embrace, arms and legs, pressing. "Are those safe?" she breathed in his ear.

Ranna stared from R-Bar to Smoke and Rekel and back again and hissed ever so softly, "What do you mean friend?" And how could her sister let that thing hug her mate like that?

"Long story. Tell you later." R-Bar turned toward Smoke. "Rekel?"

Smoke looked up. "All right. Coming around."

Rekel's eyes wobbled around and stared over at Tinker and that, that . . . person he was holding in his arms. "How?" she gasped.

Smoke leaned close. "Don't worry, she really is our friend." And straightened out the blankets.

"Ando, ando," mumbled Rekel. "This elseplace is ando anzik."

Tinker looked at them past Kartz' head. "Everyone going to behave?" He was keeping her from turning around.

She was using the opportunity to nuzzle the side of his neck. She thought that it was fun.

"Her also, Tink." R-Bar poked Kartz in the side. "He is mine."

Tinker disengaged and stared into dark eyes. "You going to behave also?"

"Yeel," said Kartz. What he wanted, she would do. Nagar debt.

"Good." He spun her around by the shoulders. "The tall one is Ranna. The one under all the blankets is Rekel. They are both R-Bar's sisters. Everyone will behave."

Kartz nodded. And blinked. Something dangerous in their surroundings faded away. She turned and kissed him. And smiled. Warmly. He was comforting.

"Mine," snapped R-Bar, poking Kartz in the side again.

"Ahem," said Tinker. "How did you get here?

Why are you here? Kartz?"

"Dedmund bring, Love Lover."

He looked around the room. "Here?"

She pointed.

"Outside?"

She nodded.

"Ahhhhhhhh, better bring whatever it is inside before it freezes to death."

She nodded.

The air snapped and crackled as Ranna drew down protection.

Rekel gasped. "Help, sister, help." They were all going to die.

"Oh, no." Tinker stared at it.

It just stood there shedding patches of snow onto the floor.

"Greetings, Master Boss." It pointed one glistening talon at Kartz. "Your horror slurb brought me to this terrible elseplace."

"An a'demon," gasped Messenger.

"Oooo," cooed the a'demon, looking at her. "It is the green-eyed lust lure."

"Hey," said Tinker.

Its head snapped around. And leered at Rekel. "How about that one? Looks tenderized already." It licked its lips, large nubby tongue slowly sliding back and forth.

"What are you doing here?" He didn't really need this.

The head swivelled back around. "Nothing, Master Boss." One ear waggled as it glanced around the room at all the others staring at it. "Nice parts. Tasty looking."

"How did you get here? I thought that you guys put a demon block all around this elseplace."

"Oh, we did. Just as you ordered, Master Boss. And hard work it was also." It slithered closer, eyeing Ranna as it passed. "We never could come on our own. That taste did it." It indicated Kartz. "As I said."

"Came and took me here. Ripped Argkild's ear badly. You should have left that horror slurb in the afrite hold." It took a piece of cloth from a rear pocket and began to polish one large lower tusk.

Kartz turned and jabbed it with one fingertip. "Speak true, ugly worb."

"Thank you," said the a'demon. "I am, aren't I?"

It looked at Tinker. "Master Boss, a large gobmob of fright wings pangled through. Ak-tasting, but not too bad. Have to tear the wings off first. You need to boil them for a long time, though." The a'demon burped softly.

"Why," said Tinker firmly, "are . . . you . . . here?"

"Oh, that. Of course." It looked at him with one eye expectantly.

Kartz frowned at the a'demon.

"Phoo bug bug, horror slurb, don't do that. It is impolite in public." It waggled both ears at her.

"Speak, speak," demanded Kartz.

Laying its ears back, the a'demon sidled around her and inched closer to Tinker. "The gobmob had one of your sort, green wrapped. That taste yelled shitar at us. Some sort of a weak spell. Nothing happened. Then this horror slurb came up, started a fight and kidnapped me." It sidled sideways and leaned one flank against the wood stove. "That's nice." And pointed toward the outside. "But what is all that klab kak?"

Tinker sighed, turned, walked over and spun into his chair. "Worse and worse and worse."

Kartz joined him, sitting in his lap, one arm looped around his neck, fingers plucking at the buttons on his shirt. She tossed her legs over one arm of the chair.

"Most brazen a'wench," observed Chicken.

"Cruisin' for a brusin'," said Chantal.

"Gir dit dit," snarled R-Bar. "She knows that we are witch debt."

"Kan kak to," agreed Ran.

Rekel gasped. And stared at R-Bar.

Ranna stared at them both, Ran and R-Bar. "Is that where our niece learned such vile?"

"No," snarled Shitar. "I learned it on my own." She looked at R-Bar and Ran. "Really really crude, Aunts."

Tinker looked at them. "How about you all go somewhere and fill in Ranna about Kartz and compare your vulgarisms."

He waggled a hand. "And I will try to get better

information from these two."

Messenger walked over to the a'demon and kicked it on the side of one large warped foot. "You are drooling on our rug. And the hardwood floor. Stop that."

The knobby tongue slowly licked across thick lips and snaggled fangs. "All these tastes make me hungry."

Fair Morn hurried to the kitchen.

The a'demon crouched down, opened one door of the stove, fetched out a piece of burning wood and began to delicately chew upon it. "Not too bad."

"PUT THAT BACK!" yelled Tinker. "And close the stove door. You are smoking up the house." He glared at it.

The a'demon did as ordered. "Of course, Master Boss." And looked at the smoke floating grey streamer across the ceiling. "Pretty nice."

"Go home," said Tinker.

It shook its head, ears flapping loudly. "Can not. Demon block works both ways. No in. No out."

R-Bar grabbed Ranna by an arm and tugged her toward the hall. Ran and Shitar hovered around the still wobbly Rekel as she followed the others from the room.

Kartz tickled Tinker's chest. She had his shirt open to his waist.

"Stop that." He batted at her hand. "And send that thing home."

"Stays."

He craned his head around. "Princess, help?"

"Praps do thee this wench in private be'speak, Me'Lord. We will the ugly thing train."

He looked at Smoke. "Where did the mob go?"

"The common space in the Chamber. Take her up to The Den." Smoke smiled at him.

"Whoa," snapped Chantal. She glared at Smoke, "We are not getting into any more of that Vander behavior, are we?"

"No!" said Tinker.

"Good," said Chantal.

"Here," said Fair Morn, handing the a'demon a thick ham sandwich.

It popped it into its mouth and chewed slowly. "Not bad. Tastes a little like dab demon."

"Bet that she pounces first." Smoke smiled at him.

"No one is pouncing on anyone," grumbled Tinker. He shoved at Kartz. "Get off, so I can stand."

Kartz stood.

So did he.

"Come on. We are going to have a private conversation." He glared at Smoke. "With no interruptions. Of any kind."

"Better not be," mumbled Chantal as she watched Kartz and Tinker head down the hall. "Or she'll get her butt shot off."

Fair Morn banged the a'demon on top of the head. "Can you just sit there and be quiet? And not drool?"

"Of course." It mopped the floor, and rolled its eyes at her, mostly at her chest. "How about just a little nip?"

"No."

"Another of those things to eat?" Both ears shot straight up.

"O.K. Just stay where you are." She headed back to the kitchen.

The a'demon eyed everyone else. And panted at Messenger, who moved away and sat at the far end of one of the couches.

Chicken stepped over and sat next to Smoke. "This do be a'getting most complicated."

Smoke nodded.

"Damn witches," grumbled Chantal.

The a'demon nodded agreement. And carefully began to polish the other lower tusk. Witches always caused trouble. Any demon knew that.

He shut the door, walked over to the small refrigerator, and fetched out two bottles. And handed one to Kartz? "Here! Canadian."

He walked over to stare out the window at blue tinged evening turning night black. And twisted off the bottle cap. She watched how he did that, then did the same thing.

She stepped to his side. And looked out. "Tin Kar, it was best to come bring that beast chasrak. The winged ginktaa left a hole and will up pour. This must be not."

Around them things sizzled.

He didn't see anything. "Drink your beer." He took another long swallow. "So, how are things at home?"

Kartz smiled warmly at him. The sizzling stopped. "Nice nice. Six over, my sister sighs grateful." She handed him a ring fetched from somewhere. "Gift gift."

"Is it safe?" He carefully held the ring with two fingertips. It felt like metal. It looked like soft ruby gem. "What is it?"

"Safe keep Obto."

"If I put it on my finger will I be able to take it back off?"

She nodded. "Obey our savior you."

He slipped it on a finger and stared at the flame being forming in front of him. Kartz nodded at it, then at him.

"Can you see it?"

She nodded.

"Can anyone else?"

"Nowp."

"Go back into the ring," he said. The thing faded away.

"Obto."

"Guess so."

She slipped her free arm around his waist and

gently leaned against his side. "I am warm soft nice pleasant."

"I can tell." He sighed. "Not why we came up here."

"Goo duk." Her lower lip pushed out. She drained her bottle and sent it floating over to a corner.

"I suppose. Let's just sit and talk." He turned and sat on the floor, his back against a wall.

She sat next to him. And began to unbutton her blouse.

"Whoa, halt, stop." He frowned at her. "Just talk."

"Duk do duk." She pouted.

"All the same," he mumbled. "Just sit and talk," he ordered. And glared at nothing in particular. "All the same. Every witch in the universe of universes. Every one of them."

Kartz nodded. Everyone knew that.

Chantal settled at the dining room table and snapped the catches on the side of the battered and worn, ornate wooden box and opened it. And lifted out the long barreled revolver. And took it apart, carefully cleaning and inspecting everything. Then she began to reassemble it.

"Might as well get ready," she said to Messenger who sat nearby watching everything Chantal did. "Even if it is going to be a month or so."

Messenger nodded. "Does anyone really know

what those things really are? Or what is really going on, really really?" Round wide eyes stared at Chantal as she looked up. "Really really?"

"I would be surprised if they did," said Chantal, sliding the last round in and snapping the cylinder in place. Placing the gun back in the carrying case, she began to pack cartridge boxes full, making a stack next to the gun case. "Better take a lot."

"Think Kartz will come with us?"

"Wouldn't be surprised."

"Think it will also?"

"What?"

"The a'demon."

Chantal began to pack everything away. "Certainly hope not. It is bad enough having all those witches around."

"She seems nicer than the others."

"Who?" Chantal looked up again. "Others?"

Messenger leaned close and whispered, "Kartz, R-Bar's sisters."

Chantal laughed.

Chicken walked in and leaned against the back of Chantal's chair. "Most merry, Our Animal Doctor Self." And tickled one of Chantal's ears.

Chantal snorted. And laughed. "What a good idea. Thanks Princess." She gathered up the several boxes and shoved her chair back, gently. "Gotta make a phone call."

Smoke stretched out her legs and stared at the a'demon.

It stared back. Starting at her ankles and slowly working its way up. And licked its lips. And shifted one eye to see what Fair Morn was doing. And whispered to Smoke, "Wanna go somewhere and play?" It was rather loud actually. But for an a'demon it was a whisper.

"No. What do you know about those winged creatures?"

It smacked its lips. "Not too bad. As long as you boil them long enough. Tear their wings off first." Both ears rose straight up, twisting back and forth. "Want to know my favorite recipe?"

"No. That all you know?"

"Of course not." It hitched a little closer to her, still sitting on the floor.

Fair Morn stood and headed for the kitchen.

"Oooo," crooned the a'demon, watching her walk away. She looked so tasty.

"Tell me about those things. "

"Ak tasting. Hard to catch." It waggled bent and crooked fingers in the air. "Fly every all over." It gurgled wetly. "Akrazalb got 'em with a net zarkak. Right into the pot." One hand wiped across its lips. It hitched a little closer to her. "So?"

"What?"

"Trade for trade." It tapped her on the knee with one bent talon. "Just a little taste?"

"No."

"How about that bent and wobbly one?" It waggled one ear in Rekel's direction. Then wiped face, mouth, and lower tusks with a rag hastily yanked from another pocket.

"You have a one-track mind. Do you have a net zarkak with you?"

It nodded. "Thank you. Certainly." And wondered what she would taste like.

"So," he said. "You understand? And why I do not want to go out there again?"

Kartz nodded. And tugged her blouse from her trousers. And popped all the buttons free.

"Eight. Me."

He leaped to his feet, spun, bent over, and glared at her. "NO!" And backed away, straightening up. "No!" His back hit the door. "NO!"

Kartz stared up at him. "Tin Kar?"

"What?" he rasped.

"Just friendly friend. Not part part."

"Noooo." All harsh whisper. "No." He sagged to the floor. And sighed heavily. "This is really getting out of hand." And wondered, not for the first time, why none of them would ever pay attention.

Black grabbed her and yanked her away. *Just me and Ran, Tink. We will talk to her.*

The explosion boomed from the common space.

He lurched up, yanked the door wide and ran to the end of the hall, and leaned over the balcony, peering down into the common space. And saw Kartz as she shrugged off her blouse and threw it at Ranna. The soft material swirled around the tall witch's throat and yanked tight.

Kartz swung around. Ran leaped to R-Bar's side. A clear green sphere snapped around them.

Rekel backed into a far corner and huddled small.

Snarling loudly, Shitar hurtled Black Curse at the Nagar as she charged.

Kartz deflected the spell and tossed Shitar against Ranna who was crumbling to the floor, hands weakly tugging at the constriction around her neck.

"STOP THAT, KARTZ!" He leaned further out and pointed at her. "STOP THAT!"

Red flashed crackling around his finger. It snapped to the floor of the chamber and flowed over to Ranna, one glowing claw slicing through the stuff around her neck. Then it turned. And anchored Kartz to the floor, red bindings around her ankles. It expanded and seeped toward her.

"Merde," mumbled Tinker. "YOU, THING! GET BACK UP HERE." It flowed around her.

She screamed. "OBTO."

"OBTO, BACK!" It looked up at him. "BACK IN THE RING. NOW!"

Red flashed arrow straight, the ring glowed and faded.

Kartz threw her arms around herself and

shuddered.

"These witches require behavior talk," whispered faint soft as she tumbled over the railing, pushing past his shoulder. And turned, floating, standing, to face him. Throwing the hood back, she looked at him from great bottomless black eyes swallowing him. Alive. Expressionless face.

"Reep."

She nodded. "I will see to them. The children will stay with you." Feather soft smoke eddy she drifted down and around and settled to the floor of The Chamber. And spoke to Kartz. Who dropped to the floor, sitting on her legs, calling her blouse over and on, the parts shimmering back together.

The clear green sphere vanished as Reep beckoned over Ran and R-Bar. Who immediately sat near Kartz, shaping the circle.

In short order, Reep positioned the rest. And settled in the final spot. And began to speak to them.

Witches listened intently to this softest of soft voices. None dared not to.

Warm bodies leaned against his back and sides as they pressed against him and stared past his shoulders down into the common space. Arms circled his back and waist.

"They had better listen to that Aunt," said one soft gentle in his ear.

"We heard all about you, Uncle," purred the other, in the other ear.

"Yesssssss. The Black Knight who beds seven."
"And can even Love Charm witches."
They kissed the sides of his face.
"And takes Vander Magicians."
"And controls their Heart."
Their arms tightened.
He sighed.
"While they circle talk," breathed one, soft lips brushing his ear.
"You could take us," said the other.
Sighing even more heavily, he leaned on his forearms, draped over the railing. "O.K., who are you guys?"
"Reep daughter Faan magician Sha'gar," laughed one, ever so softly. "Uncle."
"Ripple daughter Faan witch Santar," laughed the other. "Uncle."
They released him. And stepped back, allowing him to turn and to see who he had been talking to.
"We were only teasing."
"Just that, Uncle."
"I am Sha'gar," said the taller one, brushing a finger over her light bronze colored skin, touching a jagged scar just by the corner of her mouth. "Training accident."
"Santar," said the other, pale skin seeming to glow in the dim hall light.
They were both tall, Sha'gar slightly taller than Santar by a few inches. Both were dressed in black

garments.

"We are finishing training," said Sha'gar.

"Aunt said that we must visit." Santar stepped closer. So did Sha'gar. Shoulder touched shoulder.

"Aunt said that we are new Faan," said Santar.

Sha'gar slipped an arm around her cousin. "Mage witch joined."

Santar's mouth twitched, small smile wrinkles forming, just barely. "Am I as beautiful as Mother?"

"And I." Sha'gar edged closer, soft warm voice, no expression stare.

He nodded. "Sure." And stared at them. "I don't understand how you guys do it."

They stared puzzlement at him.

"You were just born," he explained.

Heads shook. "We are eighteen of your year cycles old," snapped Santar, tugging down her blouse, pushing her shoulders back. "Young women."

"Not new born," added Sha'gar, slowly turning around. And grinning at him. "True?"

Santar lightly touched his chest. "I would meet my rangle sister. She was supposed to come and teach. But did not!"

Sha'gar nodded. "And all of your's. Is your daughter here? And your son?"

He laughed, gently he laughed. "How about we go downstairs and make some cocoa." He started down the hall, taking their arms in his. "Ladies."

Santar growled at him. "Not nice, Uncle."

"Forgot. Sorry."

"I do not mind being so named that," said Sha'gar, tightening her grip on his arm. "Uncle."

"Im dit," grumbled Santar. Then she quickly added, "Sorry sorry, Uncle."

He sighed.

They walked into the living room, carrying trays, laden with cups, cookies, and pots of cocoa.

"Sure," grumbled Chantal taking the tray from his hands. "What's two more? A little young, don't you think?"

Sha'gar whispered to him as Chantal began to pour into the cups being handed around by Messenger. "She, they, all, are as beautiful as tale told."

"Who is Shitar?" murmured Santar.

"The one sitting next to Reep with the sulky pout."

"Of course. Just like Mother." Santar handed her tray to Chicken and stepped quickly over to the couch. "I am Santar, sister." Bent and kissed Shitar on the forehead.

"I am Sha'gar," announced Sha'gar, setting her tray on a small side table. And looked around the room at all the ones not yet met.

"A magician," observed R-Bar, nudging Reep in the side. "You are done."

Reep nodded and looked at an open spot in the room. The birth of a magician stopped the Faan witch reproduction cycle.

J. C. appeared. "Oooop." He was wearing the bottoms of his pajama. "I just stepped from the shower. A moment ago."

Reep waggled a finger. He was clothed in his normal attire. Jeans, shirt, floppy shoes. She beckoned him over. And the young woman

"Hi," said J. C.

"I am Sha'gar. Father."

His head snapped to Reep. "Faster than the last time. Certainly going to be hard to explain." He looked back. "Ahhhhh, magician? Right?"

Sha'gar nodded. And frowned. "Not good?"

J. C. laughed. "No, no, no. Just making sure that I understand, that's all." He hugged her. "Another lovely daughter. You must take after your mother. Even if you are taller." And laughed again. "You meet Szaifeh yet?"

"No."

"Have some cocoa," said Messenger, standing there, holding two filled cups.

J. C. released Sha'gar and took one, handed it to her, then took the other and sipped. He looked over at Tinker. "Certainly have a full house all right."

Tinker dropped into his chair. And pointed. "Ranna. And Rekel. Sisters of R-Bar and Reep. And Kartz. She is a Nagar. Ummm, from a different layer of elseplaces. They are types of witches that split from the main bunch eons ago, apparently. I'll tell you all about that some other time." Then he indicated the thing next to the wood stove. "That is an a'demon. Kartz dragged it here."

"Ugly beyond belief." J. C. stared at it.

"Thank you," replied the a'demon. "You part of the A.P.'s? They seem to have gotten very witchy."

J.C. asked, "A.P.'s?"

"Avon Polymorph," explained the a'demon. "Getting very witchy." It shook its head. One long ear banged across the vertical stove pipe. "Horrid thing to do. Witches taste zark qat." And nodded at Smoke. "Doesn't matter what kind of seasoning you use, either. Just zark qat."

"I think that I will kill it." Ranna surged to her feet. She had heard just about enough demon witch remarks.

"NOWP," barked Kartz at Ranna.

"Sit down," snapped R-Bar.

"Bet that one is stringy," said the a'demon to Smoke as it lurched upright. "Two meals though." Talons popped into position. It watched Ranna.

Tinker leaped up. "All right, that's it!" He glared around the room. "I have had it right up to here." He indicated the top of his throat with one hand. "I have had it with all you guys and then some. This is my home. Not yours. MINE!"

Smoke yanked Chicken down as she started to rise.

He jabbed one finger at Ranna. She winced,

watching that red ring. "Get out of here," he snarled. "Go home. Go anywhere. Go!" She vanished.

He spun around. "And as for you. Over there, in that corner. Sit! Be quiet! Understand?"

The a'demon nodded. "Of course, Master Boss." It sat in the far corner and watched him, ears hanging straight down. Master Bosses could be so hard.

He spun and glared at Rekel. "Anything to say?"

"No." She didn't dare. He was in a very dangerous mood.

He whirled and stared at Kartz. "How about you?"

She shook her head and watched the ring on his finger pulse soft scarlet.

Loud humming started to come from another corner.

His head snapped around. He glared at the great black two-handed sword. "Goes for you too."

"Really rangle," whispered Santar to Shitar. "None told of this."

"Father?" hissed Sha'gar, clenching J. C.'s arm.

"Somebody really pushed his button," said J. C.

"True?" gasped Sha'gar, staring at Tinker, eyes searching for this thing.

J. C. laughed. "I'll explain after we get home. Speaking of which, we should probably do."

Ran leaned close to R-Bar. "Extreme witch bother."

R-Bar hissed softly back, "Worse case I have ever

seen."

Messenger stepped in front of him. "MyTinker, you are scaring them."

"Me?"

"Time to go home," said J. C. loudly. "Party's getting rough." He walked over. "Well, Bad Guy, after you get done beating everyone up, give me a call if I can do anything, O.K.? Like home sitting."

Tinker smiled. "Sure. Sha'gar, do come back and visit with us when we don't have so many irritating visitors. O. K.?"

"Yes, Uncle." A soft half-smile formed. And faded.

Reep slipped up to them. And nodded. "They will behave. Now." And twisted away. Home. Taking husband and daughter.

"Think that I will take a walk." He headed for the hall closet.

"Wait for me, Cowboy." Chantal hurried after him. "We need to talk."

Chicken looked at Smoke. Smoke shrugged. Chantal hadn't said anything to her.

"Do you have a good spell?" whispered R-Bar. Ran nodded.

"Let's go work on it in my room." They hurried away. Something had to calm him down.

Messenger gently touched Kartz on the arm. "Let's make some cookies. I will show you how." And took her to the kitchen.

"Where did Aunt go?" murmured Santar.

"Not long," replied Shitar. "Reach. Feel."

"How?"

"This."

"Hum."

"Exactly, Sister, exactly." Shitar kissed her. "Let us talk in private." They headed for the corner bedroom.

"Whoosh," exhaled Chicken, throwing open a cabinet door and grabbing out a decanter and several small glasses. "Most great a'storm t'were that." And handed around the filled crystal. She drank her's. And refilled it. "Happy holidays."

Chapter Five.

The Medicine Man.

Grandeville. Tinker's Place.

"You did what?"

They were standing on top of a snow drift, staring down into the great hollow, admiring winter's handiwork. The wind had carved sharp edged, blue shadowed waves up the slope.

Chantal had just told him.

"Yep," she replied. "Sure did."

"A medical doctor is coming out here? To do tests? On them?"

"Yep, yep, yep."

"Nope." He turned toward her. "No. No, no, no. He won't believe what he sees. And will start calling in experts. And then we will be overrun with medical curiosity seekers." His arms flailed wildly. His eyebrows pulled down.

She shook her head. "Not true, John. Raj will keep our secret, secret. And he is brilliant. And just relocated over here to Grandeville from the west side."

He glared from beneath his thick knit cap which

had a tendency to slip lower and lower over his eyes. "If he doesn't keep it a secret, I will let R-Bar or Ran do something to him. As horrible as that sounds."

"Won't be necessary," she grumbled at him.

"Him or us," he grumbled back. "Us comes first."

She hugged him. "I know." And kissed the tip of his nose. "But this way I will be able to pack a real medicine kit. And not have to worry that alien blood chemistry will kill them if I shoot them full of antibiotics."

"We are still alive."

"Lucky. And you know it, Mighty Protector." He was being stubborn. Again.

"Gumpf." He nodded. "O.K. What is Raj? Indian, from India?"

"Nope. British. Just a nickname. He hates his given name." She shook him. "So you will behave, right?"

"Sure." He grinned. "You figure out what kind of story he will believe?"

"Ummmmmm, Cowboy?"

"Oh, oh. What?"

"I think that we will have to tell him the truth."

The angry frown returned. "He will think that we are all bug nuts. Get us all locked up."

"No, he won't." She held her hand in the air. "Promise."

He sighed. "Reep can always get rid of the body for us." He laughed at her expression. "Just kidding."

And kissed the tip of her nose. "But this brilliant Brit better be all you say that he is."

She grinned. "You are just an old pussy cat." And shoved him over the edge, turned, and ran for the house. It wasn't all that much of a run, more waddle than run. Given the number of layers of clothing she was wearing. He caught her halfway across the pasture.

Fair Morn yelled at them from her balcony as they clumped their snow covered way up onto the rear deck. "I will make hot cider. There's new cookies just coming out of the oven."

They waved up at her. And threw snowballs. She kicked all the accumulated snow over the edge at them. Then backed inside, slamming the sliding door shut as more snowballs flew upward.

"Cider and cookies sound wonderful," said Chantal.

"Hot tub sounds even better."

"Or, all three." She yanked the side door open.

He followed her inside. And started shedding layer after layer.

They were feeling pretty relaxed by the time that Messenger and Kartz carried in two trays with cups, a steaming pot, and a large batch of cookies.

"Chocolate chip," said Messenger. "Kartz helped."

Tinker grinned. "I can tell."

Kartz had white blotches in a number of places, stark contrast to her black attire.

They set the trays within reach and left.

"Well, Rudolph, want some hot cider?" He slid the tray over and filled two cups.

"Do for starters. Your nose is pretty red also, Cowboy. And some cookies please?"

He shoved that tray along the edge so she could reach it and take what she wanted, and handed her a mug. "My pleasure, Doc." And smiled.

"Much better."

"What?"

"A happy Cowboy, Simba Leader."

He laughed. "Right. Nothing like being kicked down a hill into a snowdrift to take care of the grumbles." And slipped over to her. "And being in a hot tub with a real babe."

She grinned and set her cup and cookies out of the way. "What I thought."

A Week Or So Later.

It was past dinner time. Smoke and Fair Morn had cooked. Steak and fries. Lots of salad. And two pounds of hot dogs for the a'demon, who had been allowed to sit next to the stove again. It had been behaving.

And all were now in the living room, relaxing.

Chicken had decided that everyone should wear

pajamas.

So, Ran and R-Bar had waved in appropriate size for them all, including their guests, apologized for doing so, as trivial things were not supposed to be done. Acording to The Witches Code.

Santar leaned close to her sister and whispered, "For all those hard years of study, The Aunts certainly left out many many about Uncle and his." She plucked at her garment.

Shitar nodded. The Aunts didn't know everything.

Everyone was relaxed and relaxing. Even the witches. Which was an interesting thing for them to experience. Even if it was only a small amount of relaxation.

Smoke turned Messenger around and started to brush her hair.

Tinker slumped and disappeared inside the book he was reading. Chicken sat by his side, working on a complicated wire puzzle she had received for Christmas. Kartz sat and watched her.

Chantal had sprawled, feet in his lap, back propped up against one arm of the couch, reading her way through a backlog of professional journals.

Ran, R-Bar, and Rekel held a soft witch conversation in the dining room, the air crackling and buzzing now and then. Rekel was almost recovered. Kartz had done something to her.

Dat stood on the a'demon's shoulder and was

talking quietly into one long, bent over ear. She had taught it how to speak low.

Fair Morn had slipped outside, assuring Tinker that she would not be long. But the air was calm, the night was dark, and her wings itched from being folded too long and she needed some exercise. But not for too long. It was cold, after all.

Everyone was relaxed and relaxing.

Each in their own fashion.

The front door bell rang.

Chantal swung her legs around and down. "I'll get it." And did. Answered the door.

"Come in, Raj. Boots go there, coat hangs here. I see you brought your bag."

Moderate height on the slim side. Sandy brown unkept hair. He leaned against the wall and yanked one boot off, then started on the other. And froze. Staring. "Bloody hell, Chan."

Tinker looked up. "Merde. And damn."

Raj was staring at the a'demon. Dat had disappeared.

Chantal banged Raj on the shoulder. "This way, through this door. Bring your bag." She quickly led him into the interconnecting enclosed walkway between the two buildings after he hastily removed the other boot.

All eyes looked at Tinker.

"My Lord?" Chicken looked up, puzzled by what seemed to be going on.

The front door banged open. Fair Morn heaved herself inside, great butterfly wings still fully extended. "I need room. And warmth." Tears ran down her cheeks.

Smoke jumped over to her.

Fair Morn wiped her face with her sleeve. "Cold. COLD!" She jerked. "OUCH, OUCH, OUCH." The wings quivered.

"What can we do?" asked Smoke.

Tinker joined them, frowning darkly over Smoke's shoulder.

"Nothing. Ahhhhhhh, warming up." The wings waggled gently back and forth, their tips scraping the ceiling and the floor. "Never do that again." Then she folded, and folded, and folded them.

Tinker stepped around and grabbed her by the shoulders. "What happened?"

"They got so cold. And so stiff. Wouldn't fold." She blinked back more tears. "And it hurt."

He slipped his arms around her and held her gently. "O.K., now?"

She nodded. And slipped her arms around his waist.

"No damage?"

"No. Never gonna do that again."

"Ummm?"

"What?"

"You hafta fly?"

"Was getting very itchy."

He knew that if she kept them folded up too long, they started to get itchy. "How about just vigorous wing flapping instead?"

She hugged him.

"OOOOOF." His breath gushed from his chest.

"Sorry." She released him, a little. "Might be all right. Really dull, though. Where?"

"Just for the winter in the common space of The Chamber. Plenty of room there."

She kissed him. "I will try it tomorrow."

"Good." He kissed her back. "You sure everything is all right?"

"Yep. Who was the visitor?"

"Ummmm, Chantal will explain that. How about you go to the shower and run lots of hot water over everything?"

"O.K." She slipped from his arms and headed for the hall. "You care to scrub things?"

"Sure."

"JOHN," called Chantal. She was standing in the interconnecting door and waggled one hand at him. "I need some help, ahhh, explaining."

Smoke joined Fair Morn. "Let's go."

"I'll take a rain check," called Fair Morn as Tinker turned and headed over to Chantal.

"John Tinker, Doctor Ralfred Alfred-Smyth."
"Hi," said Tinker, shaking the proffered hand.
"Delighted, Mister Tinker."

"Tinker, just Tinker."

"Of course. I prefer Raj."

"Fine." Tinker yanked out a chair and sat. "So?" And looked over at Chantal.

She looked back.

"What?" asked Tinker.

Chantal cleared her throat. "I asked Raj to come up here and check, ahhh, blood chemistry and make a general physical so we could carry the necessary medical supplies, ummmm, in case of injury. To tell us whether these things might have an adverse effect. But he is balking."

Tinker slumped in his chair. "Hasn't met anyone yet."

"Exotic diseases are quite out of my line," said Raj. "Quite."

"So, who is diseased?"

Chantal cleared her throat, again. "He saw it."

"Oh," said Tinker. "Right." And nodded. And smiled at Raj. "Far as I can tell, it is perfectly healthy."

Raj stared at him, then at Chantal. "Chan?" Then he smiled. Broadly. "Right. This is some sort of rough hewn local humor of the rural sort. Break the city dude in." He nodded at them. And smiled even broader.

"No," answered Chantal. "I asked you to help us. And it is no joke." She frowned at the surface of the table. "We can not afford to lose any more parts." And glared up at Tinker. "We are not going anywhere until we are properly prepared. Medically."

Tinker sighed. And stood. "Stay. Back in a bit." And walked out, mumbling something to himself.

"Rather strange fella," observed Raj. And began to wonder what all this was about. "Parts?"

Chantal reached over and lightly touched his arm. "You are about to study beings medical science may not have prepared you for."

"Beings?"

"Yep. And let me restate what I said earlier." She grabbed his forearm. "Anything you do, anything you learn here, must remain more secret than any secret any agency, or government, ever tried to keep."

"Intriguing. Of course, you know that."

She tightened her grip. "More than intriguing, Raj. More than personal confidences. I really believe horrible things might happen to you if you blabbed."

"Most dramatic." Soft blue eyes watched her face.

She laughed. "Understatement of the new year."

"O.K.," said Tinker, returning. "Thought that we would start easy."

Smoke followed him in and sat down. She was wearing one of the thick white robes, hair obviously wet. "I was in the shower."

"Raj," said Tinker, "this is Smoke."

Raj stood and shook her hand. "Delighted. Rather interesting name." He sat. Then he looked again. "Quite different." And leaned back, his eyes dancing to Chantal and back to Smoke. "Do any other of your family members have eyes like that?"

Smoke nodded. "Everyone."

"Amazing." Raj hefted his bag to the table top, popped it open, and fished out a flashlight, clicking it on. "May I?"

Smoke nodded. *MindMate?*

Whatever he wants.

Raj stood, walked over, bent and peered into Smoke's eyes.

High curiosity.

Chantal laughed.

Raj jerked back and looked at her. "What?"

"Nothing," said Chantal. "Proceed."

"I require a blood sample." Raj looked at Smoke. "May I?"

Smoke nodded, and held out an arm. And gave no indication that she felt anything while he drew a sample.

He labeled the vial and put it away. "May I listen to your heart and lungs?"

Smoke nodded. And opened her robe.

Raj leaned forward and did. And sat. And stared at her.

"Is something wrong?" asked Smoke, tugging her robe closed, eyes shifting to Tinker's. "With anything?"

Raj shook his head. "Obviously not. Lungs are clear. Heart beat is solid, regular."

"But?" asked Tinker.

"Slow," said Raj. "Hibernatingly slow." He took out another instrument. "Body temperature." And after a short while sat back and stared at Chantal. "What did you say, initially?"

"I said, beings that medical science hadn't prepared you for."

Raj nodded. "Quiet right, quiet right." And began to poke and prod Smoke. And finished.

"Really would like to do much more, but I would require instrumentation. Don't suppose you would like to come hospital."

Smoke shook her head. And pulled her robe closed again.

"No? Too bad." He nodded to himself. "May I ask? About all those scars?"

"It was a bad accident. Unplanned. While we were traveling."

Raj turned to Tinker. "Um, I see. Next." And looked across the table.

"Me?"

"Absolutely."

Tinker sighed. And allowed himself to be poked, prodded, and have some blood taken. He wasn't as calm as Smoke about having a needle stuck into his arm.

"Seems perfectly normal," said Raj.

"Not surprised," mumbled Tinker.

Raj laughed. "Chan said that there were six women to be checked. Shall we?"

Tinker nodded. "Messenger."

Smoke smiled. *Kitten, come here, please.*

Coming, mom.

And in a moment, Messenger popped into the room. "Kartz is making more cookies. All by herself." And smiled at everyone. "What?"

Tinker explained.

And Raj did.

And this time Raj, when he finished his examination, just sat, quietly, for a long time. Then his eyes jumped over to Chantal. He nodded. "I see." And yanked a pad from his bag and began to make notes.

"Oh, my," said Messenger, looking at Tinker. "Is something wrong? With me?"

"Nope," said Tinker.

"I do not believe that there is," answered Raj. He looked at Chantal. "Could I have a cup of tea? Very strong, very black tea?"

Chantal stood. "I'll get it." And looked at Tinker. "Who's next?"

He slumped in his chair. "We better work our way up. Ummmmm, R-Bar."

Chantal nodded. And left. Followed by Messenger.

And in a moment, R-Bar walked in. "Tink?"

Raj looked at her, then at Tinker.

Tinker nodded. And explained to R-Bar what was going on.

She nodded.

So Raj made his examination.

Raj sipped at his tea and stared across the table at her. It had been another surprise.

"Im dik dik ptar tak," growled R-Bar.

"Medical science," said Tinker. "Relax kiddo."

"The Faan do not customarily allow others to do that," she snapped.

"Her clan," explained Chantal to Raj.

"Oh." He smiled at R-Bar. "Frightfully sorry, my dear. No one told me."

"Ran," said Tinker, when Raj finished his examination.

"I do not know about that," grumbled R-Bar. "She is Tanpak."

Tinker looked at Smoke. She winked. R-Bar left.

Raj stood. And began to pace back and forth, looking from face to face. Ran watched him carefully, sliding a small dark purple crystal sphere from hand to hand.

"More tea?" asked Chantal.

"Please," said Raj.

Tinker frowned at Ran.

She left the room.

And Kartz came in, carrying a basket full of still warm cookies. "Fresh fresh."

Followed by Messenger. "I told her to." She took the basket and shoved it at Raj. "Have some."

Kartz looked at the tall slim man, and smiled warmly at him.

Raj stopped in his tracks and gaped at her. "By George, it is Circe herself." He looked at Tinker. "Her also?"

"No." Tinker shook his head.

Kartz and Messenger left as Chicken came back, carrying two large tea pots. "We did make a'plenty." And set them on the table, slipping the cozies in place. "My Lord?"

"This should be interesting," mumbled Tinker as Raj started his examination of Chicken.

"Quite right, you know," snapped Raj. "Medical science did not properly prepare me for this."

"Most familiar a fellow this medico do be," frowned Chicken, seating herself next to Tinker, yanking her robe closed across the base of her neck. She slipped one arm through his.

"We had better get something useful out of all this," he grumbled.

Chantal watched Raj carefully. He had shed his jacket, his vest, and his tie. And had rolled his sleeves up to his elbows.

The table top was littered with the contents of his black bag. Pages of scribbled notes intermingled with everything else.

"Chantal," said Tinker. "Your turn."

"WHAT?"

"Tee hee."

"Bull crap."

"Your idea."

"Healthy as ever," said Raj as he finished his examination of Chantal. "Although you do seem to have lost that extra weight you were carrying around. Good for you." He looked around the table. "That the lot?"

"One more," said Tinker. "Saved the best for the last."

Raj looked even more puzzled.

Smoke called.

Fair Morn walked in. "One?" She was also wearing one of the thick white robes. And received all their memories. She stared at Tinker. "Are you sure? I do not want to be put on display."

Raj's eyes flew wide. He looked at Chantal. She shook her head.

"Never happen," said Tinker. "Ahhh, keep 'em folded. I think we can skip that for now."

She nodded.

Raj stared from one to the other, not understanding their conversation at all, wondering what they could be referring to this time. "Shall we start?"

Fair Morn nodded.

"Bloody be damned to hell and beyond,"

murmured Raj as he finished and dropped heavily into a chair. "Is there any brandy in the house?"

Chicken jumped up. "We will Us fetch great jug." She hurried away.

Raj looked at Chantal. "Beyond belief, you know. Quite."

"So much for that great idea," grumbled Tinker.

"Really now," said Raj. "Just have to see what the blood samples have to tell us. How did? Where did?" He wiped his brow with his handkerchief. "I mean, all in one place? Frightfully great odds."

Tinker looked around the table. "Why don't you all go into the living room and relax. I will stay here with Raj. And talk. And, ahh, and try to explain." He fingered the ornate ring he was wearing.

Chicken slipped back in and set a large bottle on the table top and glasses. "Me'Lord." She bent and kissed him. "Frown not, Our Prince. All will be well. This medico person pears most skillful though overly familiar in manner." She left, gently closing the door as she did.

Raj carefully poured. "Chin chin." And sipped. "Delightful."

"Hundred years old. A gift." Tinker hoisted his glass. "Here's to science."

"And to new frontiers." Raj refilled his glass. And looked sharply at Tinker. "Hundred years old, you say?"

"Umm," said Tinker. "I think that you need some

additional information. About them. It might help. Ready?"

Raj leaned back in his chair, keeping the bottle within reach. "As I'll ever be."

So Tinker told him.

"Believe me?"

"Rather outside my range of experience, old chap. Quite." Raj slurred his words and squinted at Tinker.

The contents of the bottle were close to the bottom. His face was rosy, cheeks flushed.

He nodded. "But, yes, I do actually. More or less." He waggled one hand loosely. "Now I understand what Chan was alluding to." He lurched upright. "Real challenge, that."

Then he leaned forward. And slowly shook his head. "But not demons and monsters and all that childhood fairy tale stuff. Your women friends are just rather rare cases, that's all, rather rare cases. The rest, Hollywood bush wallah." He smiled crookedly. "Sorry, old chap. But it is a bit of a strange thing to do, you know, to collect women with rare physical attributes."

Tinker nodded. "What I thought you'd say, sorta. Might as well go all the way, if you are going to be any help at all." He slid one arm out onto the table top, pointing the ring toward Raj. "Dat, go talk to the man."

The ornate ring flashed.

She stalked across the table top and glared up at

him. "It is not nice to not believe what my Great Master says."

Raj bent forward until his chin was resting on his crossed forearms, his face very close to hers. Pushing his glass aside with his free hand he carefully touched her with a cautious fingertip.

"Shades of something or other," he mumbled. "Either you are real or I am hallucinating myself into a padded cell."

Dat kicked his forearm. "I am Dat. I am real." She ran her hands over her bare torso. "And beautiful."

"Quite so," agreed Raj. "A tiny beautiful person."

"I am not a person." She kicked him again. "I am an indjinn. His indjinn."

"Oh," said Raj, slowly, carefully. "Of course. An indjinn. Never met one before, you know. How cha'do?"

"Fine," replied Dat. She looked over her shoulder at Tinker. "I think that he is going to sleep."

Tinker stood. "I think that we will just leave him where he is." And held out an arm. "Let's go, Dat."

"Morning, morning, morning, morning," bubbled Messenger as Raj wandered in from the other building.

"I, ah, slept in the bedroom in there." He waved one arm vaguely in the correct direction. "Eventually."

"No problemo, dude. Coffee?" She waggled the coffee pot at him.

"Please." He dropped into a chair and took the mug shoved at him. And watched while she poured and wondered at the strange dialect spoken out here in the eastern edge of Oregon.

"Special blend." She set the pot down and yanked a chair over. "Staying long?"

"Actually, no. I'd rather thought, last night, that I would be in and out quickly. Your, ah, Tinker has some rather powerful brandy. Dropped right off." He looked at her. "Funny though, I feel quite all right."

"Bright glow," said Kartz, smiling at Raj and Messenger as she walked into the room and look a seat.

"Morning to you, Circe." Raj refilled his cup. "Coffee?"

"Nowp Circe," said Kartz, shaking her head. "Kartz."

"Right. Kartz it is." He stared at her. "Was I supposed to check you as well?" He frowned. "Rather hard to believe. Not sure whether you were on the list or not."

"Nowp," said Kartz.

"Oh, no," gasped Messenger "Just us."

Raj smiled. "Good. Rather overdosed with new as it is." He nodded at Messenger. "That Tinker fella is quite a story teller." He shivered.

Messenger handed him a blanket. She and Kartz were wearing thick white robes, belts looped around their waists. The house was chilly in the morning.

Kartz was watching Raj and carefully allowing

the top of her robe to artfully fall open.

Smoke and Fair Morn joined them.

"Anyone eat yet?" asked Fair Morn.

Smoke reached down and yanked Kartz' robe closed. "Leave our guest alone." And nodded at him. "We are having ranch eggs with lots of onions and green chilie."

"Lovely," said Raj.

"With sausage," added Fair Morn.

"Wonderful," said Raj. "I do enjoy a large breakfast. Might I have tea?" He looked up at Smoke.

"Sure," said Smoke as she and Fair Morn headed for the kitchen.

"Lots and lots of toast and jelly, too," called Messenger.

"Sleep plenty?" asked Kartz.

"Quite," answered Raj. "What did you say your name was?"

"Kartz. Kartz of Nagar Tre Tzak." She shook her head sadly. "Few few."

"Gosh," said Messenger.

Kartz held up two fingers. "Dak sister." Then folded four down. And hissed, "Witch afar."

"Killed?" asked Raj.

"Yeel." Kartz nodded slowly.

"Horrid."

"Oh, my," said Messenger.

"Yeel."

"Toast," announced Fair Morn, setting a large

basket on the low table near them. "And several jams and jelly." She dropped knives and spoons in a heap and went back to help Smoke finish breakfast.

"I think that she is after him." Fair Morn shoved the sizzling sausage around in the cast iron frying pan.

"Who?" asked Smoke, ladling everything onto a large platter.

"Kartz. And Raj."

"Better talk to her. After we eat."

"Morn," mumbled Chantal, dropping into her chair, eyes mere slits. One hand reached out, dragged over her cup.

Messenger filled it. "We are having ranch eggs, want some?" she whispered.

"Bit," Chantal slumped and sipped. Her eyes grew marginally more open. "Still here?"

"Slept in your other building. Fraid I dropped off." Raj smiled. "Bit too much of that hundred year old brandy." He took another helping of the eggs. "Wonderful. But I must pop off. Hate to eat and run."

"Fair Morn," said Chicken as she sat and filled her cup. "One and all."

Raj stood. "Must go. Lots of work to do." He smiled around the table. "Many thanks for the bed and the food. And the drink. I will just get my things and let myself out. Ta."

"Bye," said Messenger.

"Phone," said Chantal.

"Of course." Raj turned and hurried away. And didn't feel the lightest of light touches as he passed Kartz. She smiled.

"O.K., now what's going on?"
It was after breakfast. Right after breakfast. And Tinker sat in his chair in the living room and looked around at all the others. "Well?"
Chicken shook her head. "Naught, My Lord."
"Oh?"
"Indeed. We do here but sit, most serene." She smiled at him
"Where's the a'demon?"
Her head snapped around to stare in the general direction of the wood stove. "GA'ZOOKS, tis missing."
"Yep." He slumped and glared at the wood stove. And sighed. "Just what we need. A little something to entertain the fair folk of Grandeville. An a'demon wandering loose across the countryside."
"Nowp," stated Kartz.
"Nowp?" echoed Tinker.
"Indeed?" asked Chicken.
He lurched more upright. "Where is it?"
Kartz held out one hand, thumb and forefinger almost touching. "Small small."
"Where is it?" demanded Tinker, wondering what she had done this time.
Dat stood on his lap and looked up at him. "In my home."

"What?"

"Thy ring house?" Chicken leaned forward and looked at the indjinn. "Great thing do be therein?"

Dat nodded. "Kartz and I did it." She grinned at Tinker. "That way, Great Master, that Raj person drunk would not see it."

"He is not a drunk," stated Chantal.

"Bleary-eyed dis-believer," grumbled Dat.

"Nowp," said Kartz. "Nice nice."

"Slept on the table," grumbled Dat, whirling around to glare at Kartz. "Called me a . . . person. And poked me."

"Enough!" He wasn't in the mood for this debate.

"Gimble, gimble," gurgled Dat, spinning back around and glaring up at him.

"Can we leave that a'demon in your ring for awhile? Save an awfully large amount of trouble if we could."

Dat fingered her necklace. It was now missing two gems. "As you wish, Great Master. But where will I sleep?"

"With me," bubbled Messenger. "You can sleep in my room. I will get you your own pillow and everything. Really really."

Dat leaped to the floor, ran over, and jumped up into Messenger's lap. "All right. But I will go somewhere else if he wants to come and play with you."

Tinker sighed.

Messenger giggled.

Smoke stood and stretched. "Lots of work to do. Outside."

Shitar and Santar went with R-Bar and Ran.

Kartz disappeared.

Everyone else headed for their assigned chores. Chicken did the assigning.

And they decided that they were going to have an early Spring from the look of things.

Grandeville. River View Hospital.

She appeared.

    She just appeared.

In the room.

    In the laboratory.

        Near the door,

He was hunched over, peering into a binocular microscope, scribbling notes all over a large sheet of paper, without looking at what he was writing. A radio was playing somewhere, hidden behind a jumble of equipment. It was the local station, playing what passed for the local taste in music. He thought that it was ghastly.

He mumbled, scribbled, and stared at what he saw, down there, in the slide. The blood sample slide. Other equipment was buzzing and crackling and spewing out a streamer of paper as it did other things to another portion of this same blood sample.

She slipped to his side, standing slightly back, and looked. And shrugged. His script was unintelligible. To her.

He worked on.

She waited.

A Nurse burst into the lab, clenching a report. It was the results of another test of the same blood sample.

"Doctor, there must be some . . . " And jerked to a halt. "MISS, no visitors are allowed in here." She pointed. "The main lobby is just down that hall. Information can tell you how to find where you want to go."

Kartz stared at her. "Nowp." And shook her head.

"Ummmm?" Raj sat back and swung around, the swivel top of his stool squealing loudly. "By Jove, it is Circe."

"Nowp," said Kartz shaking her head. "Kartz."

Raj shoved out one hand. "Report, Nurse. Please?"

As the nurse jabbed the folder into his hand, he said, "It is quite all right. She is a friend. Ahhhh, a colleague. Dr. Kartz."

"Oh," said the Nurse.

"We can discuss this report later."

"Yes, Doctor." The Nurse spun on one heel and burst back into the outside hall.

Raj smiled at her. "You are, aren't you?"

"Nowp."

"A friend?" He spun the folder around and began to read.

"Yeel." She smiled broadly.

"Astonishing. Really. Quite astonishing. These results." He leaned back, against the counter top edge. And laughed softly. "So tell me, Dr. Kartz, why are you here, trespassing in these guarded environs?"

"Visit . . . you."

"Splendid." He nodded. "Ah, Kartz, do you know much about that woman, Smoke?" He waggled one hand at the microscope and waved the unopened folder in the other. "It is her blood, you see. Rather peculiar. Most peculiar. Damned unusual, actually."

Kartz shook her head.

His eyes unfocused as he thought about what he had seen, then flicked open the folder and began to read it again.

Spinning around, he tossed it on the table among the other papers, on top of the scattered pages of notes, and carefully put away the slide. And turned back to her. "Would you care for tea? Doctor's lounge is just down the hall."

Kartz nodded.

Gently taking her arm, he led her out of his lab and down the hall. "She is not human, you know. Can't be."

Kartz frowned. And wondered why that was important.

>>> 238 <<<

Chapter Six.

It's A Full House, All Right.

Grandeville. Tinker's Place.

He looked around the room.

Slowly.

He looked around the living room.

Almost as slowly as he felt that time was passing. They usually didn't have house guests for weeks and weeks.

It was getting rather full, this room.

"You know," he said, frowning. "You guys are worse than rabbits, big black rabbits."

"Tink!" growled R-Bar, frowning back at him.

"Every time you turn around," he continued. "There they are, more of them." He sighed. And slumped deeper into his chair. "And they all seem to want to come here."

R-Bar was making gurgling sounds.

He rolled his head and looked over at her. "What sa'matta, kiddo? Don't you guys have any other place to hang out? That the problem, Faan need a club house?"

Better ease off, Cowboy. She looks like she is ready to explode. Chantal sat up, ready to leap to his rescue.

R-Bar leaped to her feet. "I AM NOT! Going to explode." She stalked over to bend and glare into his face. "Ik tik ptar gob zak!"

Every witch in the room sucked in her breath.

"AUNT!" choked Santar, hastily covering her face with both hands.

"HORRID!" gasped Sha'gar, who had come for a visit. "Even for a witch, Aunt."

"Feel better?" grumbled Tinker. "Now that you have grossed out your nieces and sisters?"

"If you weren't me, I would put a kantang on you," hissed R-Bar.

"You are not answering the question, shorty." He poked her with one finger. "Must be practicing to be a politician."

Something crackled and whipped around the room. Witches hastily pulled protection from every direction. The room grew noticeably dimmer.

Sha'gar lurched to her feet, clenched her waist with both arms, bent over, and ran down the hall for the toilet, moaning.

Ran carefully eased up to them, gently touching R-Bar on one arm. "Sister self, the environment is coming undone."

"Nik do," snapped R-Bar, unbending and looking around, waving the room clear. Then she tapped him on the chest with one knuckle. "Make a lap."

He did.

She occupied it. And plucked at his shirt. "You have something against witches?" she grumbled.

He blew into her hair. "Nope. Some are even kinna cute."

Santar peeked at them from between her fingers. And nudged her sister with an elbow, and whispered, softly, carefully, very carefully, "Mother did not tell of this, ever."

Shitar kissed her sister's cheek next to her hand. "I do not think that she knows." And said sternly, "She need not."

"Yesssssss," said Santar. She dropped her hands and nodded, once. And wondered about her Uncle.

Shitar sat up. "Uncle?"

"What?"

She nodded at him. "You are correct. But understand not."

"Oh, oh," said Chantal.

"Now what?" He sat up a little, and shifted around, rearranging R-Bar. And looked across the room. "So?"

"What?" asked Shitar.

"You wanna explain your cryptic remark? Or is this a new style of discourse?"

"Uncle, stop being so rangle." It was a demand.

"Sure. What is it?"

"Explain later," mumbled R-Bar, unfastening one

of his shirt buttons.

Shitar glared at him. "Your home, and this spot." She waved one arm. "It is an environment that is witch comfortable safe. We all feel it. Even the witch ba . . . Nagar felt it."

She nodded at him. "I suspect every witch you have come in contact with feels the same. You, Uncle, radiate comfort."

Chantal laughed. "So, that is what it is." She relaxed and leaned back. "And I thought all this time that it was his rampant sex appeal."

"Merde." He slumped, then hastily yanked up his knees to keep R-Bar from sliding to the floor. He looked around the room, frowned at Chantal who was grinning merrily, his eyes finally returning to Shitar's.

"You mean to tell me that we have become some sort of comfort zone for hordes of you guys? Just coming and going all the time?" He tickled R-Bar. "Think fast, kiddo. I am definitely not interested in becoming the hotel keeper to hard-nosed, grumpy, snarling and growling witches of every stripe and color making demands."

"Hum," said R-Bar. "This is going to take much thought."

He tickled her again. "It is bad enough that you have so many sisters. That is hard enough to put up with. But thousands and thousands is just beyond doing. "

"Braggart," snorted Chantal, relaxing even more

as she felt him relaxing.

"Tis a conundrum, My Lord." Chicken looked around the room at all the witches and stood. "Coffee? Cookies?"

"I'll do it." Messenger hurried toward the kitchen.

Chicken looked at the witches. "Me'thinks all ought this problem consider most seriously."

Heads nodded.

Sha'gar came from the kitchen, carrying two large baskets of cookies. "I was told to bring these." She looked around the room and nodded. "Much nicer in here." And looked at R-Bar. "Aunt, that was really ugly."

"Sorry sorry." R-Bar poked Tinker in the stomach. "I was him bothered."

"Hum," Sha'gar's eyes caressed his face, a soft half-smile tugging at the side of her mouth. The Chantal was wrong. He was very appealing. Along with being comforting. She set down the baskets and carefully touched him with one fingertip.

The cookies were demolished. Coffee and tea pots emptied. Everyone was relaxed. More or less.

He was staring into nowhere, visualizing his home as a bustling bus station, witches coming and going, demanding this and that, as they tended to do. And feeling more and more unhappy with that image.

Seven minds were carefully, very carefully

staying away. The rest sat and were just being witch or magician. Sha'gar talked quietly with Santar and Shitar.

And then, there they were.

Unannounced.

Just there.

Standing.

In the middle of the living room.

She had one arm tucked under one of his, the free hand clenching his arm tightly. He was holding a cup of tea in his free hand And looking very, very surprised.

"Oh," he gasped.

And looked around the room.

"Oh, I say!"

Tinker's eyes refocused. "Oh no . . . " He stared at them. Raj and Kartz.

"Quite," said Raj, "unbelievable."

"Merde," muttered Tinker. And a number of other things.

R-Bar tried to look surprised at his comments.

"Found," stated Kartz, looking at Raj, smiling.

All around the room witches hissed, most of them. Smiling witches were known to be close to mayhem. And this was a witch bane, a Nagar.

R-Bar and Ran knew better. In terms of Kartz, at least.

Raj took a sip from his cup and stared pointedly at Tinker. "Is that really you? Am I actually standing in the middle of your living room?"

Tinker sighed. And nodded. "Better find a seat, Raj." He indicated Kartz. "She did it."

"Circe?"

"Nowp," said Kartz, shaking her head. "Kartz."

"Of course, my dear." Raj looked down at his arm, still tightly held. "Perhaps if you released me, I might sit some . . . where."

Kartz towed him over, close to Tinker, beckoned in a chair from the dining room, and released Raj. And then stood behind him as soon as he had taken his seat.

"Tinker, I truly do not understand. Did Chantal slip a little something into my morning beverage?" He frowned and leaned forward. "You see, I was just now, then, standing in the middle of my laboratory, having just returned from the Doctor's lounge with Circe. Now, here I am." Raj looked at his wrist watch. "Only about thirty seconds ago." And looked up. "More or less." He frowned.

"Not possible, you know. None of it." Raj sat back and waved his empty hand. "None of it. This. Your women, except Chan of course. Everything else, not possible." He leaned back, really back, and closed his eyes. "Bloody mind is buggered up." He held the cup on his lap. With both hands.

Kartz frowned. Witches shifted uneasily. And carefully watched her.

Chantal slipped into the room from the hallway, and sat on the arm of Tinker's chair, sliding one arm around his shoulders, leaning against him, nudging

R-Bar. "Sorry, Cowboy. I would blow her ass away if I thought that it would do any good. But the damage has been done." She laughed. "Poor Raj."

His eyes popped open. "Chan?"

"Yep."

"You are really there, are you not?"

"Yep."

"And I am here, am I not?"

"Yep."

"Mass hysteria?"

"Nope."

"Psychedelic chemicals?"

"Nope."

"Soooooooooooooo?"

Chantal sat up, but kept her arm around Tinker's shoulders. "Kartz thinks that you are pretty special, Raj."

Kartz ran her hand through his hair and kissed the top of his head.

"Raj?" asked Tinker.

"Yes?"

"Find out anything, yet?"

"Quite." He sat straighter, waving one hand vaguely around his head, warding off Kartz. "Not human. The whole lot of them." He smiled. "Except Chan, of course. And yourself. Both quite normal, quite healthy." And nodded at them and pointed at Chantal. "In fact, Chan is in much better shape than the last time that I saw her. Much."

Chantal tickled one of Tinker's ears and murmured to him, "Guess being a Lady Lion is good for you, huh?"

Messenger came in with another pot, a tea pot, and refilled Raj's cup.

"Thank you," said Raj. "Really makes no sense at all. Must have botched the samples, somehow." He sipped and looked at Tinker. And shook his head.

"Welcome, welcome, welcome, welcome," giggled Messenger as she circled around, refilling the various cups and mugs held out. Then she set the pot on a table and looked at Kartz. "That was really really naughty. Really really."

Kartz threw her arms around Raj. "FOUND!"

Tugging at her hands, freeing himself, frowning, Raj looked from Messenger to Tinker and Chantal. "But I wasn't lost. Perhaps one of you might explain what is going on? If you would?"

"Sure," said Chantal, standing. "Let's use the conference room." She frowned and snapped at Kartz, "Get your hands away, Kartz. He is not going anywhere." And mumbling loudly, she headed toward the conference room. "Damn witches."

Raj stood and turned toward Kartz. "Just be next door." And hurried after Chantal.

"Bloody unbelievable."

"That is not the half of it," said Chantal. "But I think that you are getting the general idea."

"Witches? Magic using witches? Rather hard to accept that, you know. She is really quite beautiful though." He stared at her. "All of them, the ones dressed all in black?"

"Mostly," agreed Chantal. "Except for Sha'gar. She is a magician. You can tell them by their skin color. The witches are always a pale, pale color. Magicians are always sorta tan. Certainly is unbelievable all right. And I am really very sorry. If I had any idea something like this was going to happen, I wouldn't have invited you up here. It could have waited, I suppose."

Raj slipped way down in his chair, his hands linked together over his stomach. And stared in the general direction of his toes, somewhere out of sight below the table. "So. This Kartz . . . witch . . . person has decided that I am supposed to be her husband, or mate, or something like that? Correct?"

"Yep."

He nodded. "I see. And, um, she can just pop me back to my laboratory from here, um, if I ask?"

"Yep."

He nodded again. "I see. Um, do they ever give up, these witch creatures?"

Chantal laughed. "Haven't the foggiest idea. In the cultures they come from, it doesn't seem to happen. Ahh, that is, the males, ahhhhh, male magic users, or non-magic users, as the case may be, all seem to think that it is just a great idea. Having one of them. Around."

Her forehead wrinkled as she frowned. "I never

heard of anyone doing any different. When they pick someone it seems to be by some sort of mutual consent. I could ask R-Bar or Ran? They would probably know."

He shook his head. "Never mind. I shall just have a little talk with her. In private." He sat up. "Really quite strange, you know, knowing what you told me. And what he said that last night and all."

He laughed and smiled across the table at her. "You were quite right, Chan, quite right. Medical school certainly did not prepare me for all this." He waved one hand wildly. "Not . . . at . . . all. But it is a rather interesting problem."

They headed back to the living room.

He had gathered them all up in Fair Morn's room. All the rest of himself. For a private discussion, free of all distractions, meaning their house guests.

"So," he said. "Does anyone have any ideas, bright or otherwise?"

Smoke lay flat on the floor, staring at the ceiling, hands crossed over her stomach.

Chicken was watching him, chewing on one corner of her mouth, just a little.

Messenger sat in front of her. Both were on the floor.

Fair Morn was sprawled face down, along the length of her bed, head resting on crossed forearms, watching him as well. Her wings were out and draped over the sides of the bed and onto the floor.

R-Bar and Ran sat, shoulders almost touching, back against one wall, not looking at anything at all.

Then Chicken began to brush Messenger's hair.

Chantal, sitting on the floor, stretched out her legs, fully extended as she leaned back against the end of the bed, just to one side of where Fair Morn's head was. She shook her head. "Nope."

He looked from one to the next.

Chantal looked at R-Bar and Ran. "Ought to be some way to cut down the traffic. Don't the various clans have some sort of territorial boundaries?"

Ran nudged R-Bar.

"Well," began R-Bar. "It has been done, in some elseplaces, in the past." She frowned at Tinker. "Causes lots of grumbling."

"Too damn bad," grumbled Chantal.

"Amtar," said Ran, "we would have to include Tanpak."

"And Zwar," added R-Bar. "We are clan tied."

"Nagar, Me'Lord, as well." Chicken started braiding Messenger's hair.

"O.K." He nodded at each suggestion. "Faan, Tanpak, Zwar, and Nagar. Three out of four of them seem to be small groups anyhow."

Chantal glowered at him. "Better include all those Vander babes as well."

"Have to speak to Ramp," said R-Bar. "She would know whether magicians would honor a vicinabanlist."

"A what?"

"A place ward," explained Ran. "It tells everyone that a spot may only be entered by correct folk."

"Only correct folk do be those mentioned?" Chicken looked over Messenger's shoulder at the two witches.

Ran nodded.

"Umm?" said Tinker.

"None other would dare," stated R-Bar.

"Umm?"

Ran nodded.

"Can you do it?" asked Fair Morn.

"Ummm?"

R-Bar nodded. "Oh, sure. With help." She threw one arm around Ran's waist.

Ran nodded.

"Ummm?"

"My Lord?" Chicken looked at him. "Do speak thy question."

Messenger giggled.

"Ummm," he said. "What happens if non-correct folk come ahead."

"Pretty horrible," hissed R-Bar. Ran nodded.

"Horrible?"

"Yep." Both R-Bar and Ran nodded again.

"How horrible?"

"Bad bad," said Ran.

"Uh huh."

R-Bar held up three fingers. "Us, ah, Faan,

Tanpak, and Zwar. Strong, standard witch stuff. It would probably push anyone away."

"Nagar," said Ran, harsh voiced.

R-Bar popped up another finger. "The bane makes it mind paralyzing."

"Crash, crash, crash," chanted Ran.

"Then we add in Vander," droned R-Bar, lifting another finger, one on her other hand.

"Witch magician magic tangled," gurgled Ran. "Horrid."

"Gosh," gasped Messenger.

"Ummm?"

"Do sound most brutal," said Chicken.

"No middle ground?" asked Chantal.

Both witches shook their heads.

"Nope," stated Tinker. "I don't think we want dead witch bodies raining down upon us."

"Magicians also," stated Ran.

He looked up at them. From the spot on the floor at which he had been staring. "Can't we just warn them away? Incrementally? Or use something like the demon block that the a'demons created around the place?"

"Hum," said R-Bar.

"Hum, hum," added Ran.

Smoke rolled onto her side and propped her head on one hand and looked at the pair. "Yes?"

"Pretty tricky," said R-Bar.

Ran nodded. "Tricky."

"But?" asked Tinker.

R-Bar exhaled loudly. "But . . . I think it could be done." She frowned at him. "But . . . you won't like it."

"Why not?"

"Well . . . . ."

He sat straighter. "Spit it out."

"Everyone will behave," stated R-Bar, carefully stressing the word 'behave.'

"Yessss," hissed Ran.

"Oh, oh," mumbled Chantal.

"Now what?" It was a demand. He was starting to worry and to frown.

R-Bar sat up. Ran grabbed R-Bar's hand.

"We will have to have some help," stated R-Bar, firmly.

Now he was really beginning to worry. Lots. "What kind of help did you have in mind?"

"It is your fault," grumbled R-Bar, frowning at him. "And your idea!"

Ran nodded.

"Get to the point, short stuff." He was beginning to lean forward.

"It will require Ran and I working together," said R-Bar.

Ran nodded. "Tanpak Faan."

"And Kartz," added R-Bar.

Ran nodded. "Nagar."

"And Surlindar," added R-Bar.

Ran nodded. "Zwar."

"And Sa'ar," finished R-Bar.

"Vander." Ran nodded. "That makes it tricky, tricky."

"Merde," he grumbled at no-one in particular.

"Cowboy," snapped Chantal. "If it takes all those babes running loose in the place, panting after your bod, I am for it. Just as long as we get the job done."

"Five guys, huh?"

Fair Morn began to fold and fold and fold her wings. Then she stood and stretched.

"Right, Tink." R-Bar nodded.

"Must must, Amtar," said Ran. "A gradual ward takes much talent, many varied skills."

"And it is hard work," stated R-Bar frowning back at him. "So you are going to have to be nice to everyone involved."

Smoke rolled into a sitting position and tickled Chantal.

"Nice?" he asked, wondering what she had in mind.

"Absolutely," stated Ran, smiling.

"And when am I not nice?" He sat back and smiled at them. "I am always nice." And disappeared underneath the mob as they jumped him.

"To you guys," said a muffled voice.

"All right, where is she?"

Tinker strolled into the living room in the late afternoon and looked at them. They had mostly gotten there ahead of him.

"Who?" asked Messenger, sitting on the floor, surrounded by the kittens. She was playing with the entire herd.

"Kartz."

Chantal dropped a journal onto the pile on the floor and opened the last one. "Probably hanging around the hospital, panting after Raj," she mumbled, rapidly scanning the Table of Contents and turning to an interesting article.

"Needs a leash," grumbled Tinker.

"What do you want her for?" R-Bar spun around, watering can in hand. She had been taking care of the various plants sitting on the window sills. It was something that she had found was a pleasant thing to do. Most unusual for a witch.

"Nothing. Just trying to keep track of our house guests. Good hosteller that I am." He looked at Shitar and Santar. "I need some help." He grinned at them. "Moving fire wood. You can help." He spun around, headed for the back door.

Santar stared at her sister who was growling darkly. "Sister?"

Shitar surged to her feet. "'Uncle is being ragdag." She started after Tinker. "COME."

"Hee, hee, hee," cackled R-Bar as the pair walked past.

"Not nice, Aunt," muttered Santar.

Physical work was not something witches enjoyed. Or did. If they could help it.

Grandeville. River View Hospital.

A very stern Raj swivelled around on his stool and frowned at her.

"My Dear, you will just have to sit quietly when I am working. If not, then you shall just have to go home." He stood and stuffed the back of his shirt into his trousers.

"Time tea," stated Kartz very softly, crossing her arms over her chest.

His eyes flicked sideways to the wall clock. "So it is." He smiled at her. "Sorry. But I do not like to have someone interrupt when I am working, breaks my concentration. Tea time can always wait."

He stepped closer, and held out one arm, elbow crooked. "But. Shall we?"

Kartz slipped her arm through his. They headed for the Doctor's Lounge.

Grandeville. Tinker's Place.

She appeared.

Just after the other one.

She appeared.

Holding a Styrofoam cup.

Filled with hot tea.

"A bane!" loudly hissed the first one, whipping protection down and around.

"Nagar," snapped Kartz.

R-Bar jabbed young woman in the ribs. "They do not like being called that. They call themselves Nagar."

"Ahm."

"Kartz," said R-Bar. "This is Zwar witch Surlindar. Clan tied." She nudged Surlindar. "I called her. She is visiting. And stands in witch debt to us and as do we to her. And thus to you."

"Ahm, ahm," said Surlindar, watching Kartz carefully.

"Yeel," agreed Kartz.

"I called you. Both," explained R-Bar. "We must talk, spell talk." She spun on her heels. "Tink, may we use The Den?"

He looked up from his book. "Huh? Oh, sure. Hi, Surlindar." And went back to reading.

R-Bar yanked the Zwar witch toward the hallway. "This way." Surlindar had started in Tinker's direction.

Ran and Kartz followed them.

Santar nudged Shitar. "She is Zwar?"

"Yessssss. We are clan linked."

Santar nodded. "We were in class told of the three link. Faan Zwar Tanpak. No one mentioned Nagar."

"All your Aunt's work."

"Her?"

"Yesssssssss."

"No one told that small Aunt was so strong."

Shitar slipped an arm around a narrow waist. "Sister, never never test her. She is magic tangled." And leaned close, mouth near Santar's ear. "And she read one of the banned spell tomes."

Santar twitched. And softly asked, barely moving her lips, "How?"

"Found before they eliminated the Brn."

"Hum, hum, hum."

"And do not bother him."

"Sister?"

"What?"

"Let us do wander. I feel this place bothered. I thought it backward primitive not arcane twisted."

Shitar shook her head. "NO! I will rescue mine." One corner of her mouth puckered. "I believe that they will help." And pinched Santar. "It is just here, where they dwell. Not this elseplace."

Santar threw dark ugly. She did not like being pinched.

Shitar pushed it nowhere. "Getting better."

"Hum," said Santar.

She sat there.
      Late in the very late afternoon.
She sat there.
      Carefully not doing anything.
          Watching Chicken, actually.

Chicken had been fussing with the wire puzzle for the last three days.

She sat there.

Pressed against his side.
Carefully not doing anything.

It was all Smoke's fault. She had leaned against his other side. And shoved him into Surlindar.

So, as it turned out, he was pressing against her.

Tinker was only vaguely aware of them. He was deep inside the novel he was reading. And into the next to the last chapter of this very thick book.

"Where is that indjinn?" demanded Ranna, stepping into the living room, carrying a tray with two steaming pots on it. She had returned when he had begrudgingly asked her to come back.

Fair Morn was behind her carrying another tray laden with cups.

"What do you want?" Dat sat on the edge of one book shelf and kicked her legs back and forth.

"I made some of this cocoa stuff. Want?"

"YES." Dat leaped. She hit the back of Tinker's couch, rolled over Surlindar's shoulder and down into her lap.

"KARPOT!"

"Huh?"

"Ooooof."

"Damn."

These being the comments of Surlindar jerking wildly into Tinker, who snapped aware of something and shoved Smoke, who toppled Chantal sideways into another stack of reading materials.

Dat stood on the badly tilted Smoke and looked at the somewhat startled Tinker, and pointed at Surlindar. "That new houri of your's is jitter jitter."

"She is not my new anything. What caused this?" He nudged Surlindar. "You wanna let me up?"

She lunged the other way. Into Chicken.

"Be' damned wench." Chicken jerked and glared at Surlindar, having just lost her concentration and the idea of how to figure out the puzzle.

Tinker sat up.

"You didn't really have to," purred Smoke.

"Yes, he did," snarled Chantal, shoving at Smoke. "Sprawl the other way."

Ranna bend over and let Dat jump onto the tray. Dat dipped her cup into one of the pots.

"Thank you," said Dat, being very proper and polite.

"Cocoa," announced Ranna loudly as Fair Morn handed out cups. "I did it exactly as R-Bar formula explained." She nodded at Tinker. A very satisfied witch.

"Um," said Tinker, taking a cup. "Thanks. Didn't realize it was so late."

The air shimmered violet. Then cleared.

"Still adding," she observed. And began to count. "One, two, thre . . . "

"STOP!" barked Tinker. And shoved his cup at her. "Have some cocoa."

"A purple mage," gurgled Santar.

"Only your cousin, Sa'ar," explained Shitar.

"That is Sa'ar?"

"Yesssss." Shitar jumped up and hugged Sa'ar, carefully not sloshing her cup. "Hayou, cousin." And spun away and pointed. "Santar, my sister."

"Hum, hum," said Sa'ar, her eyes caressing this new one, this new cousin. "Hayou, new cousin Santar."

"Zwar witch Surlindar, clan tied," continued Shitar. "Ranna you met and Rekel, Aunts. Sha'gar, Szaifeh's sister."

"Strange gather," observed Sa'ar, looking around the room, nodding greeting to all and to Sha'gar and to Kartz. "You look well, Nagar. Hayou, new cousin magician Sha'gar."

Kartz nodded.

Sha'gar sat and looked mage proper.

Sa'ar sipped her cocoa. "Pretty good."

"I did it," said Ranna, proud of her new, rather strange, skill.

"Hello," said Dat, dipping her cup in the pot again.

"Nice necklace," observed Sa'ar.

"Nearly gone," said Dat. She stared pointedly at Sa'ar's blouse. "Yum, yum, yum, yum."

"Quiet, Dat," grumbled Tinker.

"Thanks, Dat," said Sa'ar, smiling at Tinker. "You also look well, Vander Lord."

"Sit somewhere. Ooooof!"

She had dropped into his lap. Now she kissed

him. "First Greetings, Lord." And took another sip.

"Aunt, is there more?" Sa'ar licked the brown line from her upper lip. "Wonderfully good."

Ranna reached over with the other pot and filled the held out cup.

Messenger carefully set a marshmallow into the cup. "Gonna stay awhile?"

"Perhaps. I hadn't planned on returning here, so soon. But the call had haste." She looked at Tinker. "Does something threaten harm." Her eyes bored into his. Something deep flickered.

"Nope. Relax. R-Bar will explain." He sighed.

She spoke softly, "Do I detect a certain amount of witch bother in that sigh, Vander Lord?" She smiled. "My Aunts and Cousins being witch witch?"

"Sorta."

Her eyes flew wide. "Worse than that?"

So he told her about Raj. And about Kartz.

She laughed.

"You look different."

"You noticed, huh?"

"Yep."

"Elend, a newer member has worked mightily on our archives. And found many things from before before." She kissed him. "And one of the things our ancestral Vander learned was how to stop Vander tinge. So, with a pair of exceptions, no more purple." Her eyes crinkled at their corners as she whispered, "But those decorations will have to be inspected in private, Lord of the Vander Heart."

Sa'ar smiled at Surlindar. "Never before met, Zwar."

Surlindar leaned close and carefully touched the tiny orange dot on Sa'ar's cheek bone. "Clan tied."

"We are."

"Ahm, ahm," said Surlindar, eyes flicking at Tinker and away.

"Special relationship," explained Sa'ar, tickling him.

Who grumbled at her. "Knock it off."

"Watch your word choice," ordered Chantal.

Tinker sighed.

"Behave," he said to Sa'ar while he frowned at Chantal.

"As you command, so shall it be," she replied, all solemn serious.

He sighed again.

And frowned.

At her.

She laughed. "Vander Lord, you are more fun to tease than anyone I know." And slipped from his lap. "It is late. May I help cook dinner? Who is cooking?"

Chantal stood. "You may. I am. With help." She started for the kitchen.

Followed by Sa'ar.

And Chicken.

"I will make salad, soon. Just lots and lots," called Messenger, tickling some furry bellies.

Sha'gar stood. "Having meal with my parents." She shimmered away.

Late The Next Day.

"Something attractive about my lap all of a sudden?" he grumbled.

"Yep." Messenger beamed at him. And nodded violently. "Really really."

"I don't think that I'll ask what is going on this time."

She leaned against his chest and murmured, "She really really likes you."

"Who? She?"

"Sa'ar."

"Good thing that she doesn't live around here. You guys would be figuring how to expand again."

"Well," stated Messenger. "She is awfully nice."

"So what are you all up to now?"

"Nothing." Messenger laughed, just a little laugh. "Other than Kartz."

"Right. Where is she?"

Messenger shrugged.

He reached out. *Anyone seen Kartz?*

In the common space, Tink. With us, Ran and I. Send Surlindar, please.

Messenger kissed him, a quick peck on the cheek. "I'll do it" She slipped from his lap, and stood. "Come on. R-Bar wants to talk." And waggled one finger at the Zwar witch.

As Messenger and Surlindar headed down the hall toward the Common Space, he poked Chicken in the side gently. "O. K., Slim, what are you guys up to this time?"

"Eeeek," she squeaked, looking at him. "Me'Lord?" And smiled. She had finally finished the wire puzzle.

"Up to? What are you, all of you, up to? Now? Collectively?"

"Naught." She waggled the puzzle at him. "Tis done."

"I was referring to Messenger comments."

She shrugged. "We do, Our Verra Own Self, hear naught as fierce puzzle do Our Own concentration most fully betaken." She frowned, just a little. "Pray tell this one, Thy Verra Own and Most Attentive and Most Sweet Queen, pon subject which Our Sweet Kitten do just now converse."

"Sa'ar," he mumbled. "She was telling me how nice Sa'ar was."

Chicken smiled. "Most true." She nodded. And laughed.

"Yes?"

"Think thee not?"

"Not the point."

"We do Ourself most fair confused be." Her hand slipped across his forehead. "Art thee ill?"

"Battle fatigue." He slumped.

"My Lord?"

"I think that I am wearing out."

"We do believe, We do, that she will fully understand."

"Who? What?"

She brushed his hair back from his forehead. "Most a'curved Sa'ar."

He sighed. "What are you talking about?"

"Most Fair Vander Heart will thy bed leave most vacant."

"Gumble glob gop."

She frowned. "Me'Lord?"

He went limp. And toppled over. Over Chicken. "I just gave up, Princess. Just no fighting it any longer. Females of every stripe are intent upon messing with my head and our lives. Don't you think that there ought to be some way to stop all this?"

"Mine Prince, thy Verra own weighty self do press Our Verra Own body pon wiry puzzle in most tender a'part."

He heaved himself upright. "Sorry about that. "

Chicken began to unbutton her shirt, to check for damage.

"STOP!"

And to tease him.

They gathered.
    All of them.
They gathered.
    And started the process.

It was a very tricky thing to do. Tangling witch magic and magician magic this way.

R-Bar coordinated their efforts. Carefully watching, making corrections, as the spell sang higher and higher.

They had taken over The Den, midst heavy duty grumbling from Tinker, who had none-the-less acquiesced. Although he was still worried about damage.

So, they stood in a circle in The Den and did this thing. Sa'ar, Surlindar, Kartz, Ran, and Shitar. R-Bar prowled around the outside, poking and prodding. Shitar was handling the Faan portion.

And the spell sang higher.
And higher.
And higher.

He slumped, deep in the couch. Deeper and deeper, he slumped. And worried, just a little. About The Den.

Fair Morn leaned over the back of the couch and tickled one of his ears with a finger. He grumbled at her. So she tickled his other ear.

"STOP IT!"

She tousled his hair. With both hands. Violently.

"KNOCK IT OFF!"

Messenger barreled into the couch, thumping down against his side. "I AM IT, I AM IT!" And then stage-whispered to him. "Or are we playing tag?"

Chicken stepped over and tickled the bottom of one of his feet. "We do believe tis it. Shall We run?" She grinned. "Or wilt thee grab Our Verra Own Self sans flee?"

"Pretty big," grumbled Tinker, slipping lower, swinging one hand wildly over the top of his head at Fair Morn.

"My Lord?"

"For a sand flea."

Chicken spun, toppled back onto the couch, next to his free side, grabbed his arm, and nipped him on the wrist.

"HEY!"

"Tis naught but some most small a'flea bite."

"Ouch!"

Messenger had nipped his other wrist. "Geep," she said. "Geep, geep." And grinned at him. "That is flea talk."

"Geep, geep, geep." Fair Morn leaned further and further over the couch back.

"Go away," he mumbled. "Before I get the bug spray."

Smoke joined them. "Is this a private banquet? Or may anyone join?" She shook her head. "Really a very strange looking appetizer." And clacked her teeth loudly. "However." She rolled her eyes at him.

"Don't you even think about it," he hissed.

"Geep, geep," laughed Fair Morn as she began to

topple over the back of the couch onto him. "Oooops."

"Bug nuts," he muttered as they all piled on. "If you will pardon the pun. Or whatever."

"Wrong gender," stated Smoke.

From far over head, it came.
A loud thump.
It vibrated through the house.
Things shook.
The group on the couch felt it.
That loud thump.

"Well, Tink," she announced. R-Bar stood there, looking witch proud, and stated, "We did it. That spell is really and truly cast. As requested."

He shoved bodies away, jumped up, and wrapped her in a hug. "Thanks, kid." And smiled past her as the rest of them filed in. "I owe all you guys."

"Hum, hum, hum," said Shitar, chewing, just a little on the corner of her mouth.

R-Bar hissed at her.

Santar looked up from her chair and stared.

Tinker cleared his throat as Sa'ar slipped up to his side. And grinned at him.

R-Bar frowned at her.

"Perhaps," said Tinker. "I ought to rephrase that. Let me think about it, see if I can find a less, ahhh, suggestive term." Then he frowned at R-Bar and Sa'ar and Shitar. "You guys know what I mean, meant."

Ran nodded.

Kartz beamed at him. And disappeared.

"Where is she going?"

"Pounce on Raj, I'd say," said R-Bar. "That witch is really focused." She whispered to him, "The bane, ummm, Nagar, are very strong. In a strange overtone. Never felt anyone do something like that before."

Ran nudged his free side. "Most true, Amtar. That must be what caused all the tale horror, that overtone."

Sa'ar tickled his ribs. "Vander Lord," she murmured softly. "I am staying for a few days. That spell and working for Aunt, was draining. I am going to bed." She faded away.

R-Bar yawned widely. "Me too."

Ran reached over and smoothed the hair back from R-Bar's forehead. "Most tired." And kissed him on the cheek. "Your Ran also." And threw an arm around R-Bar's shoulders, as the shorter witch headed for the hall, and walked out with her.

Shitar stepped close, eye lids sagging. "Hold me, Uncle. I feel nervous nervous tired. For just a little." He did.

She leaned heavily against him, slipping her arms around his waist.

"You guys are amazing, you know that, don't you?"

"Of course. How? What?"

"Well, witches are usually so hard positive

thorny direct."

"Of course, Uncle." Everyone knew that.

"Unless you are tired or ill. Then you are at the other end of the behavioral spectrum."

"Of course," she mumbled. Everyone knew that. Also. Her breathing slowed down and down and down as she fell asleep.

He looked at Smoke as the weight he held suddenly sagged and threatened to topple him over.

Smoke jumped over and casually scooped Shitar into her arms. "Sound asleep, MindMate."

Fair Morn smiled at him. "You are a real soporific, One. Couple of minutes in your arms and she is out like a light." She looked at Smoke as she stepped past. "Room three is open."

Grandeville. River View Hospital.

She appeared.

Just as he was turning from his work.

She appeared.

"Oh," said Raj. "Hello again." He stepped over and carefully looked at her. "Do you feel ill?"

Kartz forced her eyes open. And shuddered. "Tired."

"Quite."

"Home."

"Didn't you just come from that Tinker chap's place?"

Kartz nodded. She stared at him. "Home."

Raj stared at her. "My place? You want to go to my home?"

She nodded. And forced her eyes back open.

"Dear, dear," muttered Raj. "Can you walk? My automobile is parked just over the lot a bit."

She nodded. And grabbed his arm as he started to guide her toward the door. She stumbled. He held her up.

Grandeville. The Dwelling of Raj. On the Slope.

Raj removed a stack of books intermingled with journals and sat on the now emptied chair and punched in Tinker's phone number.

"Tinker please, Raj here."

He straightened another stack of journals that sat on the table next to the telephone. It was a small one bedroom apartment. Every horizontal surface was littered with notes, journals, and books. Raj hadn't decided whether he was staying here in Grandeville or not. Yet.

"Tinker? Raj here. Bit of a problem so to speak. Kartz turned up at my laboratory, falling asleep on her feet, and insisted that I take her home. So, she is sleeping in my bed, in my digs. You, ummm, want to tell the others, umm, in case they start worrying about her whereabouts. Or, ummm, whatever they do. Many thanks, old chap."

Raj laughed. "No room. I shall just have to sleep on the couch." He laughed again. "Rather reminds me of my graduate student days, actually." He nodded. "Right. I shall have a very stern and a very firm talk with her in the morning. Ta ta."

Grandeville. Tinker's Place.

Tinker hung up, laughed softly to himself, and walked back to the living room, and flopped into his chair. He grinned at Chicken, who was eyeing him suspiciously.

"Kartz is crashed in Raj's bed. And he is going to sleep on the couch. And he is going to have a very stern and firm talk with her in the morning."

Chantal sat on the arm of Tinker's chair. "Raj is rather straight-laced. That babe has her work cut out for her if she is after his bod." She nudged him. "And speaking of bods."

"We were?"

"I was, Cowboy."

"O.K. What?"

"Wanna mess around?" She burst into laughter at his expression.

Tinker sighed. "When's dinner?"

Soon, replied Messenger. It was her turn to do dinner. *Pizza, lots and lots.*

"Yum, yum, yum, yum," said Chantal, running one finger around and around in his hair.

I want anchovies, said Tinker.

Yuck, yuck, yuck. Just on your part. Messenger went into the pantry to get a tin.

Smoke returned and sat on the other arm of his chair.

"Oh, oh."

"I like anchovies," purred Smoke, tickling the side of his neck. *Me too, kitten.*

"Will you two quit it?" He banged at various hands doing various things to him. "You guys are making me nervous."

"I asked first," said Chantal to Smoke.

"Yum, yum, yum," announced Fair Morn, coming in from the hallway. She had been helping Messenger.

"Indeed," agreed Chicken.

Fair Morn sat next to her on the couch. "I meant the pizza, not him."

"In truth, t'was Our Verra Own thought as well." Chicken nodded at her. "T'was naught pon yon anchovy a'sucking lecher." She jerked a thumb at Tinker.

"Wait one moment." He sat up straighter. "Just hold on, Princess. What are you going on about?"

"Nay Us, Our Prince, that do grope and fondle most fair handfuls of Our Fair Niece just some few moments past."

"Ah, ha," stated Tinker.

Chicken nodded.

"She fell asleep," grumped he. "In my arms." And nudged Smoke "Didn't she?"

"Yep," agreed Smoke. "He never had a chance to

properly grab her."

"Whoa," he growled.

"Poor dear," cooed Chantal.

"Goofy , goofy, goofy," he mumbled.

"DINNERTIME," called Messenger from the dining room. "EVERYONE COME. NOW. SALAD TIME."

"Low blood sugar," muttered Tinker at one and all. "That must be the problem with you guys."

"I will have another slice, please." He shoved his dish at Chicken who passed it down toward Fair Morn who was serving the dessert, chocolate cake.

Chicken filled his cup. "Most logy a'look, Our Love."

"Stuffed, Princess. Relaxed."

"Thanks, Tink." R-Bar nodded at him.

He nodded back and smiled. "You are right. Thanks one and all. I really wasn't ready to operate Witch International."

"You are safe now, Cowboy." Chantal nudged Fair Morn and pushed her plate sideways.

"Just one big family," said Messenger.

"Not family," corrected Ran. "Clan linked."

Tinker nodded. And looked at R-Bar. "Now, if I can just keep you from linking any other bunch in, we are in good shape."

"Gib dip dip," suggested R-Bar, not liking his comment at all.

"Well, you are the guy that decided we needed Faan Tanpak Zwar, aren't you?"

"And who," growled R-Bar, "tacked on the Nagar?"

"Can't just keep killing people," he mumbled.

Chantal smiled at him. "Good thing Raj turned up or you'd be trying to add another one."

"No way, Cowgirl!" He sat straighter. And glowered at her.

"It was Szaifeh done," stated Ran.

"What?" He stared at her.

"Linked Faan Vander."

"Our very own Vander Lord," added Chantal, grinning at him.

"All right." He sighed. "I give up." He smiled at R-Bar. "We all did our part." His finger jabbed at the ceiling. "But no more. Right?" He looked from face to face. "Right?"

And received only very careful looks. Head nods. And smiles.

Sighing loudly, he slumped. "That is not very reassuring. Not at all."

"Fret thee not, Our Verra Own Sweet Prince. Do we ever in deed be frivolous?" Chicken gently kicked the side of his foot. Reminding him how they had come to be.

He nodded. And looked at R-Bar. "How come you are not tired and snoozing still?"

"The others did most of the work." She grinned.

"Never before has such a thing been attempted. And we did it." She yawned. She nudged Ran who had started to doze off and handed her something. "But I am somewhat tired." She yawned. Again. Wider.

Ran nodded at her. And slipped The Ring to Chantal.

Tinker tapped the table top lightly. "Tomorrow. After everyone is awake, we had better start deciding what we, that is, us, are going to do about those winged things." He stood. "And."

"What?" asked Messenger.

He looked at R-Bar. "Yank that Nagar back here. She can chase Raj after we are done. She needs to put all her energies into the more immediate problem." He swung around and headed for the living room.

Smoke kissed Chantal on the cheek.

Then the rest followed him.

Except R-Bar.

She went up to her room.

To sleep.

Followed by Ran.

"Never believed... and all this been attempted, I have did it. Everyone did. She muttered can we thin of how to doze off and happen we... something" Rao Lton "cooperation, the "she gestured, Area, Vada.

Ran nodded at her. And sell the, "The King, o Chanul.

Tinker in nod the Table ton lightly. "Tomorrow, I At the everyone is... that we're... believe the pace in what to finish that very easy, to run about have when of things?" he said.

Chapter Seven.

Once More Into The Breach, Dear Friends.

Grandeville. Tinker's Place.

Bright sunshine poured in the window.

Outside he could see the green on the front lawn.

Things were starting to pop out and up.

The snow was gone.

Mostly.

Spring.

As the saying goes.

Had sprung.

He pushed the breakfast dishes forward, and away, pulled his coffee cup over, and slurped softly. His eyes scanned the faces watching him, seated all around the large dining room table.

"Well, group, it is business time. Finally. It is time to decide what it is that we are going to do." He frowned at the glowering Kartz. "That goes for you too!"

Enough time had passed.

Everyone was healthy.

Again.

They had been resting, and healing, for week after week. All winter, more or less. Now it was finally the beginnings of Spring and he was really to solve the problem.

Witches on either side of Kartz carefully edged their chairs away. Just in case.

He looked down the table. "Smoke?"

"Everyone is rested. And healed." She grinned. "And in very good shape."

"Good." He sipped from his cup. Loudly. "Shitar and Kartz are coming with us. The rest of you get to stay here. Or somewhere." And laughed at the number of pouts and sulks.

"Shitar comes because it is her husband that got snatched. Kartz because she brought that a'demon and knows where the hole is that those things boiled up through. No one else is required."

He slumped deeper in his chair, and mumbled at the several kinds of grumpy witch expressions, "And I do not care how unhappy anyone is."

"Vander Lord?" Sa'ar rested her hands on the table top.

"What?"

"I wish to stay here for some small time."

He waved a hand. "Sure. Visit your folks, and your brother and his wife. You guys have the run of the place. Just behave if anyone should visit, ahhh, from around here."

Chicken reached over and snagged his cup, and filled it. "My Lord?" And shoved it back.

"Ummm?"

"Let us this day prepare all and on the morrow away."

He nodded. "Good idea." And looked at R-Bar "Kiddo, how about you four witchy types get your heads together and work out the whatever. O.K.?"

"Yep." She took them to her room.

Smoke stood. "Fair Morn and I will fix the packs with the necessary stuff." And headed out through the kitchen.

Chantal jumped up. "Going to town, get our medical supplies." And hurried to her room. To change her clothes. Raj had finally figured out what they would need. Even if he wouldn't say how well it would work.

Chicken tapped him on the arm. "We will, Our Kitten and Us, see to proper foods for to be a'camping."

The pair headed for the storeroom attached to the garage.

He looked at the last four, still sitting there. "Santar, you could go to J. C. and Reep's place and visit with Sha'gar until we return. It should only be a few days lapsed time for here."

Santar nodded. "Yes, Uncle." And reached out. And disappeared. The two cousins had been visiting back and forth.

"Not nice," grumbled Ranna.

"Gik tar," suggested Rekel, feeling rather unhappy about not being chosen.

"No," stated Tinker. "Go beat on someone else."

The room darkened.

He sighed. "Look, we do not need any more help, not with the four already going." He slumped even deeper in his chair. "Besides, if we do, R-Bar, or Shitar, can always contact you, right?"

Slowly the light in the room returned to normal.

"Surlindar?"

"Chosen One?"

"I suppose you could hang around as well, if you like."

She shook her head. "You are well protected." And vanished.

He looked at Ranna. "The Zwar different than the rest of you guys?"

"In what way?"

"She seemed more rational."

Rekel stared at him. Ranna nodded. "They are just not Faan." She felt that explained everything that needed explanation.

"So," he said, topping up his cup. "What are you two going to do while we rescue Shitar's husband?"

"Stay here," said Ranna.

Rekel slammed the table with the flat of her hand. "Tinker Lord, you are bekak angak."

"I suppose."

She glowered at him. "We are witch debt tied for all that you and your's did. You allow us no way to satisfy this. Most uncomfortable."

"Oh," he said.

"Yesssss," hissed Ranna, sitting straighter. Rekel was correct.

"Well, I will just have to think of something, I suppose."

Ranna began to unfasten her blouse.

"Hold it, hold it," snapped Tinker.

Looking puzzled, she lifted out the chain and the orange stone. "Take this."

He shook his head. "It is your's."

Ranna nodded, dropped it back, and fastened her blouse. "Then name your wish."

"Um," he replied.

"Two wishes," said Rekel.

"Ummm," he said. "How about after we return?"

They nodded.

    He exhaled.

        Softly.

    And stood.

"Well, I had better go see how things are coming along." He hurried away, out through the kitchen.

He stood and watched them sorting through the boxes of dried food.

"Most courtier be'spoken, Me'Lord." Chicken smiled up at him. "Thee do most cleverly ne'commit thyself."

"I get a lot of practice with you guys. Stand up, Slim."

She did.

He kissed her.

"Our Prince?"

"Felt like it."

Messenger bounced to her feet. "Me too, me too."

"Sure."

So he did.

And then he sighed and hugged them both. "I think that somehow we are making progress, as strange as that sounds."

"How now?" asked Chicken.

"What?" asked Messenger.

He grinned. "A while back we got the a'demons to block this place away from all of them. Now we are blocked out from all manner of witchy types and magician types."

He kissed each one again. "I am feeling better and better about that."

Messenger ran a finger up and down his ribs. "Meow, meow, meow." And giggled.

"What?"

"Wanna tickle my belly?"

Chicken pinched her. "Wench!"

Messenger jerked. "Nothing wrong with that." And grinned. "You are just grumpy because I thought of it first."

"Eeeek!"

Messenger had pinched Chicken back.

"Ahem," said Tinker, just to get their attention. "How's the packing coming?"

"Just fine," said Messenger. She nodded violently. "Really really."

"Until thee do come a'bothering, Our Prince." Chicken leaned against his side. And slipped one hand into his back pocket.

"Whelp," he said. "Time to go visit the rest of our crack team. See how they are doing." Chicken released him and he ducked out the door.

As he stepped into the common space of The Chamber, he was grabbed.

"No messin' with the workers, Pilgrim," said John Wayne.

"Not me whose feet are dangling in the air. Wanna put me down?"

She let him go.

"Oooof. Not drop. Put."

She kissed him.

Then Smoke tapped him on the shoulder. And reached over past his head and tapped Fair Morn. "Time."

"Goofy," he said.

"Not so," said Smoke tapping him on the shoulder again. And grabbed him as he turned inside

Fair Morn's arms. "My turn."

Fair Morn released him.

Smoke smiled. "Did you bring the coffee pot?"

Fair Morn tickled the back of his neck. "Obviously not."

He tried to slap her hand.

Smoke nodded. "Maybe we ought to cut cards?"

"Nope," said Fair Morn, laughing. "We got 'em, we keep 'em. Let's flip to see who gets to drag him into a dark corner."

"HEY!" She was tickling him again.

Smoke poked him in the stomach with one fingertip. "Certainly keep you out of trouble."

"Right," agreed Fair Morn, leaning her chin on his left shoulder. "Unless you've got her hidden somewhere handy and close by."

"Who?"

"Trouble."

"Coarse," he grumbled.

"Tee hee." Fair Morn slipped her arms around his chest. "Possession is nine-tenths of something."

"Hold it. Hold it," snapped Tinker.

"I am." She tugged at his shirt.

"You didn't flip," grumbled Smoke.

"Knock it off," he snarled.

"Wonderful idea," purred Smoke, leaning close. "Pick a number between one and two. We need a break."

"I am number two," breathed Fair Morn in his

ear.

"Vander influence," he mumbled. "Right?"

"Suppose you could," said Smoke, winking at him.

"She is staying behind."

Fair Morn kissed the back of his neck. "Be your last chance for awhile, Stud."

"Lemme go," muttered Tinker. "I need to go find the butterfly net before you two nuts cases go fluttering off."

"She doesn't have wings." Fair Morn released him, gave him a friendly pat, and stepped around him to stand by Smoke's side. "Grumpier than usual."

"Back to work," suggested Smoke. "Maybe the Lady Doc could shoot him in the butt with some anti-grump wonder drug."

"Goofier and goofier." He headed for the stairs up. Just to see what the others were doing.

"Hum, hum, hum," said R-Bar as he stepped into her room.

"Stay away," hissed Ran.

"What?" snapped Shitar.

Kartz stepped to one side and watched him.

"Now what?" He looked from witchy expression to witchy expression.

Shitar looked at R-Bar. "I could call Santar."

Ran growled at her.

Kartz stepped over and slid the palm of her

hand across the side of his neck, and looked at Shitar. "Nowp."

"Nowp what?" he asked.

"Hum," replied R-Bar, nudging Ran.

Ran frowned and rolled a small black sphere between her palms.

R-Bar's lower lip pushed out as she stared at him.

Tinker sighed and beckoned Ran over. "I think that everyone needs to be checked out. Maybe your super spell did something else. Also."

Ran smashed the sphere on his chest.

He looked down at the spot it made. "Now what?" And toppled forward.

He woke.
    Slowly, he woke.
Slowly he woke.
    And stared at the ceiling.

It looked familiar.
    That ceiling.
It was.
    He had painted that ceiling.
It was his.
    Bedroom.
        Ceiling.

He was warm. There were warm bodies on either side of him.

"Goomp," he said to the ceiling.

It didn't answer.

"Don't be such a grump," came a reply. "Or a goomp." It wasn't the ceiling. It was Chantal. "Don't see how you could be. Not with two luscious babes pressing their hot bods against your limp and uncaring inert carcass."

"Morning?" He thought that it looked like morning.

"Yep. Another day." She nudged him. "How you feeling, John? Had us worried."

"Worried?"

"Yes."

"Certainly did." Sa'ar rolled onto her side, slipping one arm over his chest. "Shitar saw it right. You are very comforting."

"And toasty," added Chantal, rolling toward him, stuffing her pillow under her head, and blowing into his ear.

"Even limp and inert," explained Sa'ar. "It was spell surge. Ran fixed you."

"And why," he asked, "are you here? In here."

"Who?" asked Chantal, who was echoed by Sa'ar's, "Who?"

"Goomp," he suggested, staring up at the ceiling again. "Two owls."

"We made a deal," said Chantal.

"An understanding," explained Sa'ar. "Not a deal."

"Oh?" It was a very worried comment. He didn't like the direction that this conversation was starting to go in.

"Right, Cowboy."

"Yes, Vander Lord."

"Oh? What kind of deal, or, umm, understanding do you have?"

"Well, Simba Leader, you old Honey Bunch." Chantal slipped her arm over his chest just below Sa'ar's. "We decided, given your rather tangled social relationships and all. And agreed."

With a certain amount of squirming he managed to get one arm around each neck, and sighed. "What? Decide what?"

"Taking all the stress away," said Sa'ar.

"What stress?" he grumbled.

"We, your Lady Lions," laughed Chantal, "accept unconditionally all your outside the group interests, all your lady non-Lion grabbing."

"I didn't grab anyone," he muttered.

"That's me," laughed Sa'ar. "And Imdar. The grabees."

"You were getting too sensitive to our feelings," stated Chantal.

"Spell blow back," added Sa'ar.

"So, there you are, Stud. No more worries."

"Goomp," he mumbled.

"And we didn't do anything at all," said Sa'ar.

"After all, it is a fairly limited population, Babe

Magnet." Chantal tickled him.

"What is?" He tickled her back.

Sa'ar tickled him from the other side. "There are only three Tanpak, three Zwar, three Nagar, twelve Vander, fifteen Faan, and seven of you."

"Lucky devil," chortled Chantal. "That is only forty-three, Tinker Pasha. Probably cause a whole lot of emirs to sulk in their tents when they find out."

He yanked his arms free and lurched upright.

They sat up and dragged blankets and quilts up and around themselves.

"Potentially," said Chantal. "We can reduce the number by four Faan, one Nagar, and probably ten Vander. That leaves a grand total of only twenty-eight."

"What?" He stared from smiling face to smiling face.

"Out Vandering the Vander," noted Sa'ar.

"What?" he said.

"Lay back and calm down," ordered Chantal, pushing him over.

"No one said you had to," added Sa'ar.

"I am calm. Crazy, crazy, crazy," he mumbled. "The whole thing. And everyone in it. Bug nuts."

"Nope," said Chantal. She tickled him.

"Not at all," said Sa'ar. "You are now spell protected. And all understand that it is not up to them."

"Absolutely," stated Chantal firmly. "It is just that now we will understand. Just like we accepted Imdar and Sa'ar. Just as you accepted Imdar and Sa'ar."

She kissed the side of his face. "Now, doesn't that make you feel better, knowing all that?"

"Nope."

Sa'ar kissed the other side of his face. "Sure you do. Now, no matter what they say or do, you know."

"Ummmmm," he said, glowering at the ceiling.

"Calming right down," snickered Chantal.

"Let's sleep. It is early," suggested Sa'ar.

They did.

And eventually he said, "Goomp," to the ceiling again. He was awake again. Only this time he was receiving radiant heat from only one side.

"You," he said.

"What is your wish, Vander Lord?" She tickled his ribs.

"Nuthin. I am getting out of the wish business." He tickled her back.

"As you wish," she laughed. "So will it be."

"Ummmmmm."

"Chantal said to say to you, grab it while ye may, we are leaving this afternoon. I assume that the it in her statement is me." She kissed his cheek. "Or some portion thereof." And sat up and stared down at him. "You certainly frown well."

He stopped frowning. "That is because my whole life doesn't make a whole lotta sense anymore, you know that?" He knew that it didn't to him. Not any more. Not any longer. It was just getting more and more strange.

She stroked his chest with soft fingers. "Vander Lord, you are healthy, well-cared for, independent in life style and economic standing. I do not understand."

"Permanent culture shock," sighed Tinker. "Every value that I grew up with has gone out the door. I am a fairy tale being living with fairy tale beings doing fairy tale things in fairy tale worlds. But I live here, in a very non-fairy tale place in a very non-fairy tale community, and in a very non-fairy tale world."

She leaned over and kissed his forehead. "There are elseplaces beyond counting. Move."

"I like living here. Most of my friends, non-fairy tale friends, live here. And look what is happening to them. Hard, J. C., and even Raj, ummm, maybe."

He sighed and stared past her at the ceiling. "I think that I do not know who I am any longer."

Sa'ar yanked blankets and quilts around until she could sprawl comfortably alongside and on top of him. "Perhaps the problem is trying to force your out-of-date John Tinker image onto today's John Tinker self."

She hitched a little higher. "You are a changed man. Self-changed. Mostly. Think of your many names. Each is you, each is some aspect of your person."

She stared into his eyes, and chanted softly, "John Tinker. The Chosen One. Center of Your Group. Vander Lord. Slayer of the Brn, and the Mad Magician, and the Vander Great Enemy, and Dram, the Evil One. Friend of Big Red, of Macabre, of Bahn Duhr Tohr, and of beings in many elseplaces besides the one you live in. Father of Sedeem, of Rorx."

She held him, pressing herself against his body. "All of these are you, a tale among tales. And above all else," she laughed, a soft deep in the throat laugh, "a nice, warm, comfortable male."

He laughed with her. "That's me. Everyone's security blanket." And hugged her.

"That is what the witches said." She kissed him. "And more than just that." And smiled. "Much more."

Chicken grabbed her as she stepped into the kitchen, hair wrapped in a towel. And kissed her.

"Princess?"

"Sweet Doctor Self, thee do be most clever a'person indeed."

"Well, I thought that a medical kit was a pretty good idea."

Smoke and Fair Morn joined them, giving Chantal a friendly pat and an extended hug.

"Not that," said Fair Morn.

"What?"

Smoke hooked one hand behind Chantal's neck, tugged her close and kissed her. "Sa'ar is making him understand."

Chantal snorted. "Making him, I'll accept."

Messenger hopped across the kitchen giggling. "Bounce, bounce, bounce, bounce!" And grinned widely, and squirmed inside all those arms just so she could hug Chantal too. "And understand. You can feeeeeeel it."

"Get out of the way," snarled R-Bar as she and Ran joined the group. Everyone did. The witch pair grabbed Chantal and hugged her and beamed at her.

R-Bar looked up, made carrot munching noises, and said. "Yaaaaaah, what's up, Doc?"

Then everyone laughed at the image that flashed through Chantal's mind.

"Most crude," laughed Chicken. "Most true."

"Let's eat," said Chantal.

"I made waffles, just lots and lots." Messenger spun away to get the syrup and jelly.

And then they smiled at each other, and laughed, and enjoyed breakfast. They noticed that Ranna and Rekel also appeared relaxed as well. At least for witches.

And eventually, as it usually happened, he arrived, slumped in his chair, took a sip from his cup, ate his breakfast, and then looked around the table.

Finally breakfast was demolished, and everyone looked ready. They were all there, locals and visitors. A sea of female faces. He looked around the table with new eyes.

He smiled, and started to laugh.

Some frowned.

Some looked puzzled.

Chantal was one of the frowners. "Thoughts like

that will get you in deep trouble, Cowboy."

In between bubbles of laughter, he managed to burst out, "Wasn't my idea, Doc."

Chicken rapped his arm with the handle of her dinner knife. "MY Lord, there do be most great a'crevice t'ween what do be possible and what do be permissible." She kicked the side of his foot. *Cease thy ogle pon Sweet and Young and Fair and Silky Sha'gar.*

Finally regaining control, he nodded and gasped, "Ah, ha."

"You betcha," snapped Chantal.

"Heh, heh, heh," he commented.

Seven breakfast rolls hit him in the chest.

Everyone else was watching them closely, very, very puzzled.

Santar leaned close to Shitar and whispered, "Sister?"

"I do not know," hissed Shitar.

Sha'gar watched him over the top of her hand, clamped with the other one over her lower face and mouth. Then dropped them. "Uncle?"

He shook his head. "Nothing. Ummmm, private joke. Hard to explain."

"Hum," said Sha'gar, staring intently at him.

Tinker looked at Chicken, then Smoke. "We ready?"

"Indeed." Chicken nodded.

"Packed and ready." Smoke smiled, just a small smile, flickering her eyes at Sha'gar and back.

"Don't even think it," grumbled Tinker.

"Right," agreed Chantal.

Messenger slumped in her chair. She leaned close to Smoke and whispered behind her hand, "What's going on?"

"Nothing," replied Smoke, shoving her chair back. "Shall we go?"

"Sure," said Tinker. He stood. "Let's get our travel clothes on and do it." He indicated Shitar and Kartz. "You ready?"

"Yeel."

"Yes, Uncle."

"Then we are ready. Back in a bit."

He spun and headed for his room. The rest headed for their rooms.

Shitar leaned sideways and kissed Santar on the cheek. "Stay, do not wander."

"Yes, sister."

Kartz walked into the living room.

He stepped from his closet, traveling clothes half on. That is, he was wearing the trousers but carrying boots and shirt jacket in his hands. She wrapped her arms around him, stopping all motion. "Princess?"

"Most agitated was Our Chantal."

"Her own fault."

"Thee do lech pon fair silky Sha'gar."

"I did not. Lech."

"Thy thought t'was most rapacious."

"It was not."

"Praps despoil?"

He sighed. "You guys are all getting gross."

"T'were not Our thought, Great Prince."

He smiled. "It was Chantal's. She is the one that suggested that there was great mob out there, free, single, and willing, if not over, ahh, urged."

He banged her on the hip with his boots. "So, I just sorta looked over and wondered. Chantal caught the thought and got all huffy. So, it is all her fault." He swung his other arm around her. "Never would have crossed my mind otherwise."

"Praps," conceded Chicken.

"Slim?"

"Me'Lord?"

"How come you don't have your shirt on?"

Her hands rubbed up and down his back. "We do wish for to direct thy attentions back to the proper few pon which thee ought think thy most randy a'thoughts."

"Ah, ha."

"Indeed."

"We in a hurry to leave, to start this trip?"

"Nay."

The boots made a heavy thud as they hit the floor. The shirt made a soft slither.

"Most rapacious thy thought now, Our Love."

"Your fault. No shirt, bare feet, and all."

Smoke nudged Chantal as they carried their gear

into the tub room and set it near the outside door. "She is a sneak."

"Sorry," said Chantal. "I was just trying to get him to stop fussing about all those witches."

"And grumbling because he looked at one."

"Magician." Chantal frowned. "You heard his thought."

"It didn't mean anything."

Chantal leaned back against the wall. "Just because I am part of the gang doesn't mean that I am completely happy with it. After all, I didn't volunteer to be made one of the Lady Lions. Ripple just made a mistake."

Smoke leaned against the wall next to her side. "Should I try to undo it?"

"NO!" Chantal's head jerked around. "It would be horrible. You can't go back, you know."

Smoke slipped an arm around Chantal's shoulders. "Being a single being is hard for me to feel and understand. The Velvetmist never are."

"My culture, John's culture, do not do things like this. It is very hard. For both of us."

"I can see that. I thought that we were finally complete, a whole of parts. Something is missing, something subtle." She set her minds to the problem.

Chantal glanced at her. "Not another babe?"

Smoke shrugged a shoulder.

"Let's get the coffee pot started. We might as well wait in the living room, get comfortable."

"Others are there."

They started for the kitchen, cutting through the shower room.

"When we get back," said Chantal, filling the coffee maker. "We need a new room, a sort of a smaller cozier room for us. The living room we have has all the feel of a hotel lobby."

Smoke nodded. "I will think about that. Also."

Chapter Eight.

Into the Wilds, So To Speak.

Wintl. The Home of Kartz. Afternoon.
"Home."
Kartz smiled. She strode across the square to her house. As she walked she met and talked with various of the town folk. Many of them nodded greetings to Tinker and his group.

The town folk remembered them from the last time, the time they had brought Kartz home. And had made peace between the Nagar and the witch clans.

Everyone settled in front of Kartz' home, sitting on the benches that lined the fronts of most houses as they faced the great open town square.

"Seems peaceful enough." Tinker looked around the square. He didn't see anything that indicated excitement.

It was just a quiet, serene village, basking in the bright sun of a lovely blue sky day. All the houses were white, neat and tidy.

So, they waited for Kartz to return.

He sat on the pavement and leaned back against

the wall, and idly watched the passing scene.

Chicken joined him. "Me'Lord?"

"Ummm?"

"Tis most peaceful a'place."

"Yep."

She nodded. "Pears not a'place do winged furies attack."

"Nope."

She grabbed a wedge of his side and pinched.

"OUCH." He banged at her hand. "What are you doing?"

"Thee do be most uncommunicative, Our Prince."

"Wasn't a whole lot to communicate about," he grumbled, wondering what the problem was, this time.

"I like being this size," said a very happy voice from his other side.

Both heads snapped in that direction.

"Dat!" He jerked sideways, banging into Chicken.

"In the flesh." Dat smiled at him. "Great Master."

"Indeed," observed Chicken pushing him back.

"Put a shirt on," growled Tinker. "And explain what is going on. What are you doing? This big? Here?"

"Gimble, gimble, gimble," grumbled the indjinn, yanking on a translucent silk garment, all soft folds. It matched her trousers.

"Like our's," grumbled Tinker.

"Gimble, gimble, gimble," she added, changing the garment into a bright pink corduroy shirt

"Jeans," ordered he.

It happened.

"Button up your shirt."

It happened.

"You are not nice," muttered Dat.

"Well?" He stared at her.

"Just did. Something about coming to this layer of elseplaces. It is what happened the last time. And The Princess houri thought that I should be with you on this trip." She looked past him at Chicken. "Mighty Warrior Queen?"

"Fair Dat?"

"Would it be all right with you, and the rest of his houris, if he played with my body, now that I am large enough that he can? For a little. While he is just sitting around, waiting?"

Chicken snorted.

Tinker leaped to his feet, spun, and glared at the indjinn. "Knock it off. Just knock off that talk! Stop!"

He stomped out into and across the square, and sat on the edge of the three foot high central fountain surround, a very ornate wall.

Dat looked from him, sitting over there, to Chicken. "Well, I get tired just sitting around in that ring and being little all the time." Her hands stroked over her shirt. "And I am beautiful."

"Beautiful Dat?"

"Yes?"

"We must ourselves bespeak pon this thy request, else he does banish thee into thy ring forever."

Dat sat close to Chicken, and they began to talk in soft tones.

Chantal joined him. "What'sa matta, Cowboy?"

"You know damn well what the matter is."

Chantal banged him on one shoulder. "Don't swear at me, damn it." And laughed.

"Ha, Ha. Ha."

"Poor dear is lonely."

"Gonna have to stay that way." He glowered at the pavement. "This trip has just started and already it is going to pot. Fifteen minutes old, if that, and it is going to pot. A new Olympic world record in the Going To Pot event. And that is not a good sign."

Messenger looked across the square at Tinker and Chantal, then over at Dat and Chicken, and said to Smoke, "She is pretty. Really really."

"Yep. Nice claws and fangs."

"Her canines only show a little when she smiles. I think that it is cute. Really really." Messenger plucked at one of her shirt buttons. "And her fingernails aren't all that long."

"Kitten, he does not need that kind of distraction now."

Messenger looked up at Smoke through her

eyebrows. "I suppose."

Ran nudged R-Bar. "Let's put her back inside the ring."

R-Bar shook her head. "Just make things worse."

Shitar stared at them. "You would share with her?" And hastily added "Aunts" as two pair of jet black eyes stared back.

"The indjinn is his," stated R-Bar.

Shitar leaned close. "Uncle is strange."

"Hum," said Ran.

R-Bar nodded. "It is his upbringing in his primitive elseplace." She lightly touched Shitar's knee. "But we have pushed on that."

"He is very sensitive," added Ran.

"In some areas," expanded R-Bar.

"Hum," replied Shitar.

Her Aunts nodded.

Fair Morn joined the pair at the fountain. She sat on his free side. "How's things, Big Stud?"

"Don't you start," he growled.

"Certainly touchy."

"I do not need any more female . . . persons deciding that they can just do any old thing that happens to pop into their minds." He waved one arm. "They can all just go back to fairy tale land and take care of their own problems on their own." He sighed. "If it isn't witches or magicians, it is something else."

"Like indjinns," said Fair Morn. She held up one hand, thumb and forefinger almost touching. "Tiny, tiny indjinns."

"Right."

"Saved my life," said Chantal.

"Certainly did," agreed Fair Morn.

"So what?" asked Tinker.

"Least you could do," added Chantal.

"What?" His head snapped right, then left. "Now what?" Then he glared at Chantal.

"Whoa, Cowboy." She slid away from him.

"That it?" he snapped. "I pay your debt?"

"What?" asked Fair Morn.

"Well," he snarled at Chantal, glaring darkly. "You going to talk to Hanred, see what Ripple is up for? She saved people's lives. Let's see, who else? Does Gyre count? Lady Chen? Plum Duff? There is a whole lot of folk out there!"

"Whoa, whoa, whoa," barked Chantal, jumping to her feet and spinning to face him. "You don't calm down, you're gonna get punched." Her hands were balled into tight fists.

"Tough guy, huh."

"Damn right." She spit the words at him.

Fair Morn gently tapped him on one shoulder. "I don't know what you are getting so excited about. All she did is ask you an innocent question."

"Right," agreed Chantal. "M. C. P."

"Huh?"

"Male chauvinistic pig," stated Chantal. "Oink, oink, oink."

He stared at her. "Piffle."

"Don't you piffle me," growled Chantal.

"Chauvinistic," stated Fair Morn. "A person unreasonably devoted to his sex and contemptuous of the opposite sex."

"Right," agreed Tinker. "That is you guys. You are chauving over me all the time."

"Piffle," hissed Chantal.

"Aaaaargh," gurgled Tinker, looking wounded.

"Oh my goodness gracious," announced Fair Morn as dramatically as she could, using her rolling radio announcer tones, "He has been piffled."

"Deserved it." Chantal nodded at her.

"Probably," agreed Fair Morn. "After all, all Dat did was to ask him a perfectly innocent question vis a vis her pulchritudinous person."

"Acres and acres of beauty," said Tinker. "Saved!"

He had just seen Kartz coming their way. A young woman walked by her side. She was watching them carefully.

Kartz stopped and smiled at them, at him. "Sister Paktz. Gratefull."

"Ahhhhhhh?" said Tinker, beginning to worry.

Paktz held out her hand, palm up. A gleaming golden ring lay there. She smiled at him. "Gift."

Carefully, gingerly, he picked it up. "Thank you.

But it is not necessary."

"Nowp," stated Paktz.

"Must gift," said Kartz.

He nodded and looked across the plaza where the others where sitting. *Messenger?*

Nagar magic. Looks safe.

He smiled at Paktz. "Thank you." And slipped the ring on a finger.

She shook her head, took his hand, and slipped the ring off and handed it to Fair Morn.

Fair Morn slipped it on. "Very nice."

"Yeel," said Parktz. She turned, kissed Kartz, and disappeared.

"We ready?" asked Tinker, wondering what that had all been about.

"Yeel," replied Kartz.

And took them.

To the hole.

They stood and looked at it. It was a hole. Sorta. They could see the other edge about thirty feet away. It was a round out of focus place. Just sitting there in the middle of the grass covered area.

Kartz pointed at it.

"Do you have any idea what is in there?" Tinker backed up. Looking at the thing made him dizzy.

"Nowp." Kartz shook her head.

Everyone was edging closer together.

Ran whispered in R-Bar's ear. She nodded. And

touched Tinker's arm. "Ran will wrap us in a clear sphere and have it take us in."

"We will be protected," added Ran, rolling a deep green sphere over the knuckles of one hand.

"Ummmmm?"

"Amtar?"

"You gonna be all right if you do? This is not one of those energy draining things, is it?"

Ran shook her head. "No."

"O.K. Guess that it is the only way. Everyone ready?"

A chorus of yeses and one yeel started them on their way.

Into the hole.

Inside the green clear sphere.

The sphere sank gently.

Downward. Through the hole.

"I feel like the good witch from the Wizard of Oz," said Tinker.

Ran, R-Bar, Shitar, and Kartz gave him strange looks.

Antar Dak Tak. Noon. More or Less. Bright Day.

The clear sphere settled lightly on the soft greenery. And disappeared.

R-Bar kissed Ran on the side of the face. "Nice nice."

"Now what?" Tinker looked around as the group spread out, holding weapons of various kinds.

"That way, Great Master." Dat pointed. "There is a building."

Tinker squinted. "That black speck on the skyline?"

"Yes," said Dat.

He looked at Kartz. "Been here before?"

"Nowp."

"This where those winged things live?"

Kartz shrugged. "Here. End of hole."

"Ah, ha," said Tinker, looking at his group. "It is the usual problem. We have no idea where here is. No idea what we are doing. No idea what is here. No idea!"

He stepped sideways and threw his arm around Chicken. "Talk to me, Princess. Tell me that everything will be just fine, and that we are going to live happily ever after."

"Most ferle, My Lord." She turned and faced him, swinging her arms around his waist "Praps dwellers yonder mayhap know answers to these, thy questions?"

He gave her a quick kiss, and stepped back, turning to face the rest. "O.K. Let's go visit. And we do not mess around. Kiddo?"

"Tink?"

"Can you take us home from here if we want to?"

"Yep."

"All righty, let's take a hike."

"No need, Great Master." Dat took them.

They were there.
    Standing.
        Not too far away.

From.
    The structure.

The edifice was all black stone jagged spines and turrets poking up from multi-layered wandering extrusions. Many angled roofs stretched steep peaked at random spots. Windows and openings dotted all visible sides. Dark streamers fluttered from every available point, furring the thing in soft waves of ripple.

"Well," said Tinker, looking at Dat. "That was interesting."

"It was easy." Dat smiled at him.

He tilted his head way back, cupping his hands around his eyes. "I know that we have never seen this place before. How about you, Kartz?"

"Nowp."

He sighed. Loudly, he sighed. "I think that I am beginning to detect a pattern, an all too familiar pattern, an all too familiar pain in the butt pattern."

He looked from her to Shitar. "Do we have any way to know where those things went? Any little witchy trick tucked up those baggy sleeves to track them with?"

Shitar stared at him

"Your mouth is hanging open," he said.

"Uncle?"

"What?"

"I have never tried to do something like that."

"Like what?"

Her eyes jumped to R-Bar, and back.

"What?" he repeated.

"It was Reep told," she whispered.

He stepped closer to her. "What?"

"Mate tracking," she gasped.

Ran hissed loudly.

Kartz leaped sideways.

R-Bar yanked in a long blue wand. It crackled and sparked blue fire.

"What," he demanded. "What is that?"

Smoke stepped over and wrapped Shitar in her arms. "Relax, relax." And looked past Shitar's head at Tinker. "Very, very nervous."

"Umm, anyone?"

R-Bar stepped to his side, and cleared her throat. Twice. "Tricky tricky. He might die."

"Who ?"

"Her mate-for-life."

"How?"

Ran joined them. "Energy drain. She will have to pull his energy to her. The streamer will stretch and stretch and stretch until it touches her."

R-Bar cleared her throat again. "And she will see it. Then we will have to hurry. To follow it back to him."

Ran nodded. "Very, very fast."

"Can we do that? Hurry?"

"Hum," said Ran.

"Hum," agreed R-Bar. She wasn't sure either.

"I will try," gasped Shitar.

Kartz circled around them, keeping a safe distance, and came up behind Tinker. "Dangerous."

Dat walked over. "I will move us down the energy path."

The witches stared at her, disbelief written on each face.

"It is easy," stated Dat. She pushed past Smoke and Shitar to stand in front of Tinker, and smiled at him. "For an indjinn." She had thought that everyone knew that indjinns could do anything that they wished to do. But, after looking at all the staring faces, she decided that apparently this was not so.

"What do you think, Smoke?" *How is Shitar doing?*

"If she wishes." *Very strong niece, MindMate.*

Shitar nodded and gently pushed Smoke's arms away. "Witches protect," she commanded, and paused to give the others time to do that. Then she started her cast.

Smoke stepped further away.

And it came.

    A thin, tenuous streamer.

Stretching and stretching.

Flaming gossamer vague.
Around, and over, and around, and up.
It came.
Toward Shitar.
It came.
Reaching, reaching.
It came.
Reaching.
And touched her.

"It's pale green," gasped Messenger.

"Can you see it, Dat?" Tinker couldn't see anything, except Shitar swaying from her effort, eyes closed, sweating forming and running down her face.

"Yes, Great Master."

"Then take us there," snapped Tinker. "Now!"

Amittle.

It was mostly flat to the distant horizons. Green. Flat. Punctuated by truncated pyramids. These were wide-based, four-sided, grey squat things.

"That way." Dat pointed. "Not far. Too close to take." She strode off, rapidly, following the ever weakening streamer.

Messenger grabbed Tinker's arm. *MyTinker, he is dying. Fast. Hurry hurry.*

"RUN!" he shouted, yanking his arm free and swinging down the great two-handed sword. He charged after the indjinn. "RUN, DAT, RUN!"

The rest yanked weapons out, or in, and hurtled after the rapidly moving pair.

Not all that far away, The Fit swirled into the sky. Monsters, terrors, horrors were attacking. The barely conscious meal, carefully saved, mumbled something. And twitched. It was almost ready to eat.

Tinker stared at the distant swirling cloud pouring up into the sky, pouring up from a cluster of the flat-topped pyramids. "This must be the place that Ranna and Rekel visited. It certainly looks like what they described."

Then the group charged into the open central space.

"HUSBAND!" Shitar grabbed and violently yanked at the body lying draped and dangling from one of the stone structures.

Smoke joined her, shoved Shitar aside, and grabbed him, easily holding his weight as he slid free.

"Alive, still alive," she said. "But fading fast. Do something."

Shitar nodded, sagged, and collapsed.

"Spell drained," cried R-Bar, running up to them. "Ran, help. Kartz, help."

The witches gathered and bent over the body as it was gently laid on the ground by Smoke. And started.

The Clutch dropped from the sky.

High-pitched screeching turmoil intermingled

with the electrical crackle of magic, punctuated by the loud thump of two guns, Smoke's and Chantal's. Pieces of the environment disappeared as Fair Morn fired.

The Nesery swarmed over them.

Everywhere he looked all Tinker could see were snapping clawing monstrosities. He saw Kartz go down under the assault of a large clump of the things.

Spinning in a circle, he hacked a clearing with his weaponkin as it took control, and then tried to force his way to her. The red flame being from his ring protected him as he slashed at everything within reach.

"Dat!" bellowed Smoke. "DAT!"

The indjinn casually strolled over toward Smoke's calling voice, smashing monstrosities to the ground with either hand.

"Yes?"

Smoke broke something's neck and grabbed another, crushing its windpipe. Her gun was empty with no time to reload. "Release the a'demon from your ring. Your Great Master commands it."

Dat nodded.

And did.

The a'demon stretched and yawned and looked at the turmoil swirling around them. "Rather cramped in there. Are we having a party? Those winged things are really not all that tasty."

Smoke lurched to her feet, snapping something's wings backwards. "Cast your net. We have to contain them."

It did.

Far and wide.

Tinker charged over, raging mad, through the suddenly vacant space, sword flashing in a high, overhead, downward cut. And managed to direct it sideways before it sliced through the startled indjinn. The sword buried itself in the tattered grass and churned ground.

Dat stared at him. "That was not nice."

"WE WERE BEING BUTCHERED AND YOU WERE JUST STANDING THERE! GAWKlNG!"

"You do not have to yell," said Dat softly.

"MERDE!" yelled Tinker. His mind flashed wide, seeking the rest of himself. He was still . . . there. But? He wobbled sideways. Everyone still felt alive.

The a'demon staked the net to the ground far to one side and ambled back, chewing and swallowing. "A certain delicate flavor, none the less, raw." He ogled Dat and indicated Tinker. "He giving you trouble? Master Bosses are like that."

Ran staggered over and fell against him, wrapping her arms around him. "Amtar, we require help."

"You look very tenderized," observed the a'demon, licking its lips, admiring the parts of her that it could see. Her clothes were badly ripped and shredded. Then it flapped one ear to the side. "May I have that one?"

"No, you may not." Tinker looked at Ran.

"What?"

The a'demon walked away.

"Help," she gasped. "Shitar is closed. Her's is near far. Your R-Bar and that Kartz are badly drained. And Kartz is almost far as well, badly hurt."

Tinker tightened his left arm around Ran and looked at Dat. "Well?"

"Your houris are soft stuff."

"Why they are mine." He glared across the open space at the a'demon. "And don't you touch anyone."

The a'demon looked up and dropped Kartz. She thumped loose-limbed to the soft green rust red stained grass.

"There first." Tinker waggled his sword at R-Bar. She was kneeling next to Shitar who was lying on top of Mantara, arms tightly wrapped around the still form.

Dat walked over and tapped Shitar with one fingertip and then rolled the unresisting form over and off her mate. Dat knelt next to them and stared at the pair. "Very very messy."

"Him first," gurgled R-Bar, slowly toppling onto her side.

Dat nodded.

And began.

Tinker slowly settled to the ground, lying his sword to one side, still holding Ran. His head jerked sideways.

Chantal was wobbling their way, one arm supporting Chicken. They were supporting each other actually.

Fair Morn lurched from the other direction, from between two of the flat topped pyramids, tears running down her cheeks. Her left wing set dragged on the ground behind her as she stumbled toward them. Her shirt on that side hung in tatters.

Swinging her cannon to one side, she fired. A great sector became flat, sterile bare soil.

Then he looked around and realized that there were a number of bare wide paths radiating out from where they were, each one representing a cannon discharge.

She dropped to her knees in front of him. "One," she cried. "They tore my wings. It hurtzzzzz . . . "

The a'demon sat and looked around at the carnage and destruction surrounding them, admiring the mess. "Pretty nice. You A.P.'s are just what we had heard." It looked over at Tinker. "You A.P.'s are pretty good. Not as crazy as we thought."

Dat turned from Shitar and shoved R-Bar onto her back. "While I am at it, shall I make you larger?"

"No," growled R-Bar. "Stay same." And fell into a deep sleep as Dat's hand touched her.

The a'demon inched closer, stretched out one long arm, and poked Kartz with a bent talon.

"Leave her alone," snarled Tinker.

"Pot ready," observed the a'demon, smacking its lips.

"Amtar," mumbled Ran "Your Ran does not feel

good."

He kissed her forehead. "Feel pretty good to me."

She slumped loosely against him.

He looked sideways. "Smoke?"

"We are still alive." She indicated Kartz. "The Nagar almost isn't." She pushed Fair Morn's pain deeper and deeper, and shuddered. "This much injury never happened to a Velvetmist group." The great orange gold eyes blinked away tears. "Never."

"DAT!" called Tinker. "OVER HERE! HURRY!"

She stood and walked over, knell next to Kartz. "Who has been nibbling on her?"

The a'demon hastily scooted backwards. "I didn't do it."

"She needs new parts." Dat looked at Tinker.

"Do it." He sagged and stared from Dat to Fair Morn to Smoke and tightened his hold on Ran.

"All this because two witches were looking for magic. Those two have a lot to pay for.

"Zum pdak zig gam," mumbled Ran. On the far horizon a great gout of flame shot into the sky. Then they all heard the dull rumble of distant thunder.

"My Lord?" gasped Chicken, staring at the far distant roiling column of fire streaked black cloud surging ever upward.

"Beats me," he said.

R-Bar managed to crawl over. She banged Ran on a shoulder. "Ran, stop."

"Cowboy," said Chantal as she and Chicken dropped to the ground nearby. "You surely look a mess. Is she going to make it?" She nodded toward Kartz lying where Dat had placed her.

The indjinn was hunched over the body, facing away from them, obscuring their view.

Finally Dat sat back and turned and stood. She stepped over to Fair Morn, ripped the remains of her shirt away and smiled. "You must have indjinn ancestors." Dat slid one hand over Fair Morn, slowly, gently.

"Dat!" snapped Tinker. "It is her wings that need repair, not her, ahhh, ummm, chest."

The indjinn glanced at him and stood behind Fair Morn, and carefully lifted the top wing by its upper edge. "Not too had." And released it. "We require more room to spread them out." She stood, lifted Fair Morn to her feet.

The pair walked to a clear spot where Fair Morn could lay face down.

"My Lord," said Chicken softly. "Me'thinks thee do owe most Fair a'Dat many thanks and heart felt apology."

Chantal smiled at him. "Certainly do, Simba Leader. She is saving our butts. And then some. Almost literally. The medical kit that we have wouldn't have helped with all this damage. Not at all."

"Oom zag pak," muttered Ran. "Zig diptar kakgon." Something violent whirled past them and attacked the struggling, snarling mass captured in the a'demon's net. Body parts blew in all directions.

R-Bar struggled to sit up, managed to do it, and dumped dark green on Ran. The destruction stopped.

"Umm GUM," growled Ran, her eyes snapping open, staring at him. "Hold me, Amtar, for your Ran is going far."

He hugged her tighter. "I am holding you. No, you are not. Dat? R-Bar?"

"Witch shock," observed R-Bar, handing Ran a small earthen dirt grey jug. "Drink it," she ordered.

Ran did. And belched and hiccuped. "That was mug dug taste." And sent the jug somewhere.

Dat turned away from Fair Morn and looked at Tinker. "This houris is fixed. Of course, if you wish some changes made, I could do it now."

"No changes," gasped Ran as Dat approached her.

"Leave her physique alone," snapped Tinker. Dat nodded.

"She is fine, as is." Tinker brushed the hair back from Ran's face. "Right?"

He eased Ran to the ground so she could lie flat and looked at Smoke as Dat began doing something to Ran. "How are we? All?"

Smoke sucked in a deep breath and exhaled nosily and slowly. "Alive. Healing. Battered beyond belief." She stared around them at all the others and at the a'demon and at Dat. "MindMate, we should go home. We need to den up." Muscles in her face jumped and twitched. She jerked.

They all felt it. Her nervousness at losing control.

He looked at R-Bar. "Can you do it? I don't think anyone else is capable."

R-Bar frowned.

"I will help," stated Ran, pushing at Dat as Dat sat back. Ran grabbed one of R-Bar's hands.

Grandeville. Tinker's Place. Afternoon.
They came down.
    Onto the front lawn.
        They came down.
Frightening a flock of red-winged blackbirds.
    They had been hunting.
        On the front lawn.
    On the over-due for mowing lawn.
They came down.
    They had been gone longer than usual.

He started crawling for the front deck and the front door to the house. He was certainly glad that it was Spring and not Winter like that last time.

He was crawling. That was all the strength that he had, to crawl. Ever so slowly.

Someone grabbed him by the back of the shirt and lifted him up, chest free of the ground, and dragged him into the house, feet bumping along. And dropped him near one of the couches. She collapsed into a chair.

"Best that I can do, MindMate."

He rolled over, turned his head, and gave her a wan smile. "You are beautiful," he rasped.

Tears were trickling down her cheeks, leaving clean lines on an otherwise grimy face. "The Hub is strong," she sobbed. "The strongest of the group." She blinked and stared at him.

"If you were down here, I could hold you," he croaked.

She leaned, very slowly she leaned, and collapsed, out of the chair, thudding down next to him.

He shoved at the limp body, pushing and pulling. "Smoke?" And rolled onto his side and looked at her slack jawed face, staring eyes.

Smoke? You in there? Somewhere?

MindMate? It was a faint question. And far away.

Hang on, Big Cat, we need you. He kissed her.

"My Lord, we do not be well, one and all." Chicken lurched into the room, one of Messenger's arms thrown around her neck, more or less dragging the shorter younger woman along. She shoved Messenger into one of the couches and dropped to the floor and leaned back against it, mostly sitting up, facing him and Smoke. "We do require assistance."

Snarling and growling, R-Bar stumbled in, one arm around Ran's waist, the other clenching an angry flashing green wand. Ran sagged into the chair just vacated by Smoke and nodded at R-Bar.

R-Bar swayed from side to side, slashing

violently with her wand. "Sisters!" she commanded. "SISTERS!" Dark exploded in all directions. She sagged and sat next to Chicken, dropping her free hand on Tinker's chest. "They will help."

Two hissing, snarling witches appeared. Ranna and Rekel.

"QUIET!" snapped R-Bar before they could say anything. "Front lawn. Go help. DO IT!"

The pair stared at the bodies, nodded, and hurried outside.

Those inside heard Ranna's surprised gasp as she saw the others. "Dik dik ptar nar."

"Wonderfully vile," commented R-Bar.

And soon, the two sisters had the living room littered with bodies.

Sha'gar shimmered in. "I heard Aunt R-Bar call." She stared around the room. "ZHAK TAK!"

"Where did you learn such vile speak, young magician," hissed Ranna.

"Ripple," stated Sha'gar, kneeling next to R-Bar. "What do you wish, Aunt?"

"Healing," mumbled R-Bar.

Sha'gar nodded. And called.

Reep, then Ramp, popped in.

"A bandak mess," observed Ramp.

Reep looked and drifted over to Shitar, beckoning for Sha'gar to come.

Ramp directed Ranna and Rekel, who grumbled at being ordered around by a magician even if it was their youngest sister, but both did as instructed.

Fair Morn stood and wobbled toward the kitchen. "Food. We need lots of food." She banged into the end of the dining room table, then lurched into the kitchen.

Chicken heaved herself up and followed her. "We will thee assist."

And after a long time, Tinker opened his eyes and stared up at the ceiling. "Well, how are we doing?" he asked it. He hugged Smoke with the arm she was lying on. *You still there?*

Yes. The answer was closer, louder, stronger. *We are still whole.*

Chantal crawled over and sat next to them. "Cowboy, I am going to reload my gun and blow the butts off those two witches. When I have the strength to do it."

Dat walked up Tinker's chest and stared into his face. "Great Master, I am small again."

He blinked at her. "Thanks for everything, Dat. You almost became unemployed."

"Gimble, gimble, gimble," grumbled the indjinn. She walked down and across and up and over Smoke and sat on her chest And bounced gently on the soft swelling. "This houri is gaktle."

"Sounds bad to me," said Tinker.

"Not good." Dat poked at Smoke with a fingertip and leaped back onto Tinker. "Here she comes."

Smoke coughed, snorted, jerked violently, and

snapped into a sitting position, eyes rolling wildly. Then they focused. She smiled and bent and kissed Tinker. "I'm back," she intoned. And sat back against the front of the couch. "Thanks, Dat. I needed that." And licked her lips. "Food."

Chicken and Fair Morn had returned. Chicken carried a tray littered with bowls, spoons, and a ladle.

"We made thick soup," announced Fair Morn. "It's got lots of everything in it." She held a very large kettle with hot pads.

"Indeed," agreed Chicken. "We do fair empty cans a'many in it."

And so it went.
Day after day after day after day.

Actually, it was almost two weeks.

"Well," he said as he looked around the dining room table at the rest of himself and at their dinner guests. "It appears that we are all feeling pretty well recovered."

Everyone nodded, including Dat. She was sitting on Chantal's shoulder, smiling, one hand buried deep in Chantal's hair for support. She leaned closer to Chantal's ear and whispered, "Is our Great Master going to play with your body? He keeps staring at . . ."

"Quiet," whispered back Chantal, cutting off any further discussion Dat might have along those lines.

Tinker crooked a finger at their end of the table.

"Now you did it," hissed Chantal.

"Come'mer Dat."

She leaped to the table top and strolled around the serving dishes to his end of the table. And stood looking up at him, hands on hips.

"I think," said Tinker, "that Ranna and Rekel owe us a great deal for all the trouble they got us into, don't you?"

Dat nodded.

"Yeel," agreed Kartz. Parts of her still felt new.

"And," continued Tinker, "we all owe you a whole bunch for keeping us alive."

Dat nodded.

"Yeel," breathed Kartz.

"So," finished Tinker, "why don't you just stroll on down there and tell those two whatever you might want." He stared pointedly at Ranna and Rekel. "I am sure that they will try and do whatever you might ask for."

Dat laughed softly, spun around, and scampered down to the two witches and beckoned their heads down to her level, and told them.

"Hum," said Rekel.

"Hum, hum, hum, hum," agreed Ranna, eyes twinkling.

Then the pair sat back and nodded agreement.

Dat walked back and leaped onto Chantal's shoulder and laughed silently.

Ran leaned sideways and nudged R-Bar.

"I do not know," whispered R-Bar. "But I do not like their expressions." Whatever it was that her sisters had decided to do had a certain witch look to it. And that look was a look of intense witch devious.

The living room air shimmered and Sedeem and Farth stepped out and strode into the dining room. Bending over, she kissed Tinker on the cheek. "Hi, Pop." And straightened up and looked slowly around the table.

She smiled. "Hi, Moms. Hayou Aunts. Hayou Cousins." And looked at the tall young woman, rising to her feet, clasping her hands in front of herself, being very mage proper.

Dark eyes looked across the table into soft blue eye glow. She nodded. She had heard tales of this daughter of his. And introduced herself again.

"I am Sha'gar, magician" she said. "Of the clan Faan. Sister to Szaifeh, Cousin Sedeem." It was the most formal of formal magician greetings.

Sedeem laughed happily. "Hayou, Cousin." And looked around the table. "Where's Szai?"

"Not here," said Shitar, sitting more erect. "Deem, this is mine, Mantara."

Sedeem nodded. "Very nice. What are you?"

Farth fizzled softly. That question didn't sound polite to him.

"Grenzanr," answered Mantara.

Sedeem slipped an arm through one of Farth's.

"This is mine, Farth, a Silver Ranger."

"Imm," replied Mantara.

Farth disengaged his arm, and fetched two chairs. And bowed to Tinker. "Noble Lord, may we visit?"

"But of course," said Chicken, smiling, waving him toward one of the chairs.

"Sure," added Tinker.

Sedeem leaned against him. "What have you been doing, Dad? Everyone looks strange, very strange. Well, most of them do."

"Long story. Tell you later."

"That bad, huh?" Then she looked carefully and laughed. "OH. Hi, Dat. Almost didn't see you there."

Dat waved and leaned close to Chantal's ear. "She should have a sister."

"Forget it," grumbled Chantal.

"I think that the other witch houri could."

"Maybe she is not interested in doing something like that. Either."

"I will go ask."

Chantal's arm swung up and around, her hand trapping the indjinn in place. "Don't be such a busy body."

"Gimble, gimble," grumbled Dat

"Gimble, gimble, yourself," softly growled back Chantal. "We are just barely recovered. Least thing we need to start worrying about is having children." She released the indjinn.

"Don't you think that the Nagar is be-u-ti-ful?"

"Sure," agreed Chantal. "What did you do?"

"She required many new parts."

"What did you do? To her?"

"I just emphasized this and that, a little. Just a little."

"I think that I would not mention this to anyone if I was you."

"Think so?"

"Yes, I do."

Dat nodded. And admired her handiwork. Kartz was stretching and yawning.

Kartz looked at Tinker, then at his daughter and her mate. And said something soft, near silent.

Raj appeared. He stared across the room at the crowded table. He was standing in the kitchen doorway. "BY GEORGE!" His eyes danced from face to face. "You are back." Then he rocked forward and glared at Kartz. "Circe, where have you been? Do you realize that it has been a fortnight?"

Kartz stood.

"Damned inconsiderate just popping off like that."

Kartz slipped up to his side and clenched one of his arms lightly.

"Are you all right?" he asked, his voice going soft and considerate. "You look . . . different."

"Yeel."

They disappeared.

>>> 331 <<<

"Who was that person?" asked Sedeem. "Dad? And what was she?"

"Ask Chantal."

Chantal stood. "Let's go to my room." She headed out through the kitchen. Sedeem followed, patting Farth on the shoulder as she left. Dat went along for the ride.

Sha'gar leaned close to Shitar. "Our cousin does not look or feel what I had expected. From all that we were told."

"Who?"

"Sedeem."

"And what did you expect?" Shitar tapped Sha'gar on the forearm with her fork.

Sha'gar shook her head. "Different. Much different. I could hardly feel." She grabbed Shitar's arm. "Nervous, nervous, nervous. Anyone with that great a control."

Shitar kissed her on the cheek. "Just a cousin, cousin. Deem and I are double debt tied. Let us sit on a couch and I will speak that tale."

They did. The three of them. Mantara wanted to hear the story as well. After all, it concerned his mate-for-life. He walked slowly after them, not yet fully healed from his ordeal.

Grandeville. River View Hospital.

Kartz was sprawled flat on the examining table.

"Wider," ordered Raj as he bent over her. Then

he nodded. "All right, you may close your mouth." He straightened up. "You may sit up, if you wish."

Kartz did and smiled at him. And buttoned her blouse.

Raj leaned against the wall of the small examining room and folded his arms over his chest. "Far as I can tell, quite healthy." He looked at her. "You do feel quite right, correct?"

She nodded. "Yeel."

"Care for a cup of tea, My Dear? The lounge is just down the hall. Oh, of course you already know that." Heaving himself away from the wall, he gathered up his notes, threw everything into his bag.

Kartz dropped lightly to the floor and opened the door.

As they stepped into the hall, Raj called, "Nurse, we are done in there." He guided Kartz down the hall, one hand gently holding her by the elbow.

After getting two cups of tea, he selected a table in a far corner.

"Now My Dear Circe," he said as they sat. "We have to come to a decision."

She sipped and watched his face.

Raj cleared his throat. "Ahem. Ahem. Chantal told me all about you witches, and I . . . "

"Nowp," snapped Kartz. "Nagar."

"Oh. Sorry." He started again. "Ahem. Ahem, about you, ah, Nagar, and all that." He took a quick sip of his tea. "And, ah, I have been thinking these past few weeks, and, all, well, damn it all, I did miss you frightfully." His hand flew up as he saw her start to speak. He shook his head.

Then he stared at the table top. "Really do not think that I could live in your world, dear Circe, not really my cup of tea." He looked up and smiled. "In fact, rather thought that I would stay in this, um, quaint village." He nodded. "Hospital is quite nice, you see."

She watched him, absolutely still.

"And so, you see, I, ah, well." Raj took another sip of his tea. "That is, ahem, there is a rather nice place for sale not all that far from here, this hospital." He paused. "Actually, only two blocks away, actually. Oh dear, repeating myself."

Raj shoved his tea cup aside. He leaned, reached across the table, and took her hands in his.

"Circe dear, think you might like living here, ummm, with me, stuffy old medical doctor that I am." He hastily added, "Get married of course." And cleared his throat. "AHEM. Or whatever it is that you Nagar folk do."

She sat and stared into his eyes.

"Um," he said, very, very softly. "Well? My dear?"

Kartz looked around the room. It was empty. "Yeel." she whispered. They disappeared.

Grandeville. Tinker's Place.

They were mostly in the living room,

comfortably lounging, here and there.

Doing things.

One of the things was Tinker.

Ran was doing the doing. To him.

She had curled up next to him as he sat on the couch and pressed herself against his side.

One of his arms was swung over her shoulders. He was reading. She was fiddling with the buttons on his shirt. It was a thing that they all felt was the thing to do, to him. Fiddle with the buttons on his shirt

And then.

There they were.

Standing there.

In the middle of the living room.

Kartz and Raj.

Tinker looked up. "Uh." He smiled at them. " Hi, guys."

"Mine," announced Kartz.

"Really really?" Messenger stared at them.

"Yeel."

"Quite," stated Raj. "Popped the old question to her. Does appear that she has accepted." He smiled.

Kartz beckoned R-Bar and Ran from the room.

Raj joined Tinker on the couch.

"Wonder how she will adjust," said Raj.

"Huh?"

"We are staying here. In Grandeville. I shall buy

the large place close to the hospital. Walk to work. No need to pop in and out. She agreed." Raj frowned and looked at Tinker. "Do these Nagar have some sort of special rites, ceremonies, rituals, all that sort of thing?"

"Haven't the foggiest. I suspect that is why she and R-Bar and Ran went off together." He slumped further down. And said to no-one in particular. "Place is getting littered them."

"Who?"

"Magic folk."

"Really."

"Yep. There is R-Bar and Ran up here. Reep with J. C., and their daughter. Ramp, she's a magician, with Hard, and their son who is also a magician. And now you have Kartz." He laughed. "There goes the neighborhood."

"Not nice. Uncle." Shitar glowered at him from another of the couches. Mantara looked blank. Sha'gar looked carefully innocent.

"Just kidding. I think." Suddenly his eyes flew wide. He swivelled his head sideways. "Dat!"

The indjinn appeared, sitting on the edge of the shelf of bookshelf. "Great Master?"

"Come over here."

She leaped, bounced off the back of the closest couch, over Sha'gar's shoulder, and slid down the front of her blouse. Standing on the startled magician's lap, Dat smiled up at her. "Very nice. Are you going to become one of his houris?"

"DAT!"

She spun and leaped to the floor and scampered over and sprang onto his thigh. "Great Master?"

"Leave her alone."

"Who?"

"Sha'gar."

Dat smiled. "Very nice."

"She is Szaifeh's sister."

Dat nodded. "You want me to do something to her?"

Tinker sighed. "No. I want to know where that a'demon got to. And that net full of horrors it had."

"The Nagar and I send it home." She smiled at Raj. Then climbed swiftly up Tinker's shirt and sat on his shoulder. "We closed that hole also."

"When did you do all this?"

Dat kicked her legs happily. "Yesterday. The Nagar was healthy enough then." She edged sideways and whispered into his ear. "Did you know that she has three sisters?"

"Yes," he sighed. "I did, I do know that. Sorta. I wasn't sure exactly how many sisters she had. I thought that it was only two."

"Do you see how that magician looks at you? She would let you play with her body, I'll bet."

"One more comment like that and you get to stay inside your ring."

"Glimble, gimble, gimble," grumbled Dat.

Raj cleared his throat. "Ahhh, umm, Tinker?"

"Umm?"

"Is, ahh, this sort of thing going to, ahhh, go on with, umm, ahhh, Circe and me?" He waved his hand around the room, frowning and looking unhappy.

"I doubt it." Tinker sighed heavily. "It seems to be a rather centralized pain in the butt. My pain, my butt."

A soft hand reached from behind him and tickled the ear on the Dat free side. "Nice butt." It was Chantal. "What are you guys up to?"

"Nothing," mumbled Tinker, vigorously waving a hand around his ear.

She walked around and sat by his side as Raj made room.

Dat relocated onto her shoulder, and grumbled softly.

"He giving you a hard time?" asked Chantal.

"NO," snapped Tinker.

"Gimble, gimble, gimble," grumbled Dat.

"Pretty bad." Chantal pinched him on the side.

"Ouch! She is trying to recruit."

"What?"

"Houris," answered Dat.

"We do not, he does not, need any more." Chantal reached up and poked the indjinn with one fingertip.

"Coffee on?" asked Raj.

"Yep," said Chantal, and watched him head for the kitchen. Then she said to Dat. "You are getting to be an awfully busy little body."

"Oh," said Tinker, half turning. "What else has she been doing?"

Dat ran around Chantal's head and sat on the far side, and peered past Chantal's face at him.

"What?" demanded Tinker.

"Thinks Sedeem needs a sister," mumbled Chantal.

"You?" gasped Tinker, staring at Chantal.

"Or Ran."

Tinker leaned forward and frowned at Dat, and growled, "You are going to be inside that ring forever."

Chantal grinned and kissed the tip of his nose. And gave him another peck on the cheek. "Messenger is baking a batch of fresh cookies. Why don't you go and help? I will talk with Dat." Chantal stood and headed for the front deck.

Tinker headed for the kitchen.

And from there, he was borrowed by Chicken to help her, Fair Morn, and Smoke work in one of the flower gardens. He was given explicit instructions of what, and where, and how, to plant this and that.

Halfway through their activities, Smoke sat back and said to him, "She is a very silky animal."

"Ummm," observed Tinker, shoving his almost empty flat of bedding plants sideways. "Huh?"

Smoke stared at him. "She is a very silky animal."

He swiped his hair back into place, leaving a line

of dirt on the side of his face and one side of his forehead. "Who is?"

"Sha'gar."

"Don't start," he cautioned.

"Prithee, Me'Lord?" asked Chicken.

"What." He stabbed his gardening trowel deep into the soft soil.

"Fair Sha'gar."

He sat back, looked around, and glowered at them. "All right, now what's going on?"

Fair Morn glowered back. "I didn't say anything, grumpy lech."

He sighed, a very long, a very loud heavy sigh. "You guys are all ready to add another one, aren't you? In spite of your promises." He sagged. "Bigger and bigger and bigger and bigger. I thought that seven was it."

Then he smiled at Chicken and Smoke. "O.K., let's do it." And held up one finger. "But we get rid of one to compensate for the addition." And went back to work, satisfied in the belief that this ought to terminate that conversation. He hoped.

Chicken looked at Smoke who shrugged one shoulder.

Fair Morn reached inside and asked them what they were up to, this time. And the conversation expanded outward, drawing them all into it, inside their collective mind net, swirling around and around him.

Tinker worked on.

They carefully stayed away.

He finished. "All done."

And so were they.

He gently patted the soil around the last plant, sat back and admired his work. And listened to the silence. And sighed.

Chicken moved over and leaned against his back. "Sweet, My Lord?"

"What?"

"No more."

"Sure?"

"Indeed."

"Glad to hear it."

"But."

"Oh, oh."

She started laughing. He looked sideways. Smoke and Fair Morn were restraining themselves.

"What? Spill it!"

"We do decide, we do, that . . . " Her laughter overrode her sentence.

"I am going to be grey-haired and feeble before you get to the point."

Chicken hugged him tighter. He could feel her silent laughter against his back.

"We," said Smoke, pushing aside her grin, "decided what to do."

"Yes?" He watched her very carefully.

"Thirty day free home trial," said Smoke, smiling broadly.

"Or double your money back," laughed Fair Morn.

"What are you comediennes carrying on about?" He banged at Chicken's hand.

She stopped tickling him. "Me'Lord, we do naught but borrow most clever idea from this thy Verra Own culture."

"What exactly did you borrow?"

"Try before you buy, so to speak," explained Fair Morn.

He squinted at Smoke. "Try what?"

"Sha'gar."

"OH. Well, Madame Smoke, around this part of the elseplaces procuring is a crime. Or have you guys decided to make this place into a bawdy house? Now? Utilize all those witches?"

Chicken released him. "Most crude." She twisted around and glared at him.

"Me," he gasped. "I am not the one wanting to start luring young women into a life of crime."

"We didn't lure anyone," stated Fair Morn with great indignation.

"Right," agreed Smoke. "We did not."

"Indeed." Chicken jabbed him in the side.

He jerked around, partly to keep an eye on her, partly to protect his side. "I suppose that she just decided to volunteer then? Looking for a new career? Tired of the magician business already?"

"Nay," stated Chicken. "We dinna ask."

"What?"

"Yet," added Smoke.

"I am gonna get the water checked. Something is affecting you all big time."

"Just most tender affection for thee, Our Verra Own Bonny Prince," cooed Chicken, batting her eyes at him.

"And she could probably have a daughter," suggested Fair Morn.

"Ah, ha!" He stared from innocent appearing face to innocent appearing face. "The cat is out of the bag." And lurched to his feet, and headed for the house, grumbling loudly, "Worse and worse and worse and worse."

Fair Morn ducked her head as she looked at a glowering Chicken. "Well, he would have found out sooner or later."

Chicken reached out and warned everyone.

Ran and R-Bar yanked all the witches up to R-Bar's room before they had a chance to protest, including Sha'gar. It wasn't safe for them to be anywhere around him, not when he was like this. It was an automatic witch reaction to an extremely agitated mate-for-life.

It was a tomb silent house that he walked into and through.

As he washed his hands in the kitchen sink, he felt the quiet. Seven minds were shuttered tight. All were keeping their distance from him. "Worse and worse." Taking a handful of cookies, he poured a cup of coffee, and headed for the living room. "Worse and worse and worse."

In the empty living room he dropped into one of the couches, sighed, and slumped, and grabbed up his novel and began to read, and eat, and sip.

Ranna grumbled dark at R-Bar and hissed, "Why are we pulled here?"

"Keep you out of harm's way," replied R-Bar.

Ran sat on the floor, against one wall. "He is fiercely bothered."

"Who, Aunt?" Sha'gar looked at the black swirling around Ranna, then at Ran.

"Tink," snapped R-Bar.

"Uncle?"

"Yessssssss." hissed Ran. "Bad bad."

Sha'gar jammed her hands on her hips and stared down at them. "Why should I hide? I have done nothing to you. Or to your's." Her eyes flared red fire.

So R-Bar related their conversation in the flower bed to her.

"ANDAK DIT! Warta!" Sha'gar yanked out a gold and silver wand and snarled at them all. Angry bounced around the room.

"Most vile coarse, Niece," stated Rekel, swatting at something nearby.

"PAK PTAR GANDAT!"

Ran threw protection around R-Bar and herself

This young magician was near danger flash.

The explosion blew the windows out of the room. Sha'gar was gone.

Smoke leaped to her feet. "NO!" And grabbed as many of their minds as she could, clamping them tightly together. Tinker wasn't there.

She hurtled toward and inside the house, raced up to Chantal's room, leaped through the doorway and dragged Chantal to the floor just as Chantal spun and fired. A lamp base exploded into dust, a large hole appeared in the wall behind it.

GOTCHA. Smoke banged in calm, her arms and legs clamping the writhing woman into a tight bundle. She held her until she felt Chantal begin to relax.

"Sorry, sorry, sorry," murmured Smoke as she kissed the tears from Chantal's face. "I missed."

Chantal sobbed and gasped. "Smoke?"

"Yes. It is me."

"I felt myself rip apart." Chantal rolled onto her side and stared at Smoke. "My mind was not right." She sat up. "Where is he? I can't feel anything." Her eyes jerked wildly.

Smoke sat up and hugged her. "I do not know." And kissed her. "I got everyone but you. You went down too fast."

Chantal dug her finger's into Smoke's back. "Is this what it feels like to lose a part, what he felt that time?" She slumped and felt warm comfort pushing in.

"Upstairs," said Smoke. "We need to go upstairs

and talk with the witches." She stood and gently lifted Chantal to her feet. "Come. And yes, it is, and it was."

They slowly made their way up to R-Bar's room.

He leaped to his feet, staring into grey out of focus mist swirling around and around and around. Something in his mind clamped down. It was something that Smoke had placed deep. Although he didn't know that.

"NOOOOOOOOOOO...," he screamed into the vagueness. The mists muffled the cry.

Lurching sideways, he slowly spun around and regained his balance. And knew. They were gone. All of them. It was just him. Here. Alone.

"Somebody is going to die," he snarled. And looked around. The light flickered on and off, dim to bright. Someone unseen was cursing wildly. At least that is what it sounded like to him. But he couldn't quite make out the words. He kicked off his slippers and slipped on silent bare feet in that direction.

Smoke kicked open the door and staggered into the room, one arm around Chantal's waist.

Ran sat in a corner, arms wrapped around R-Bar who sat slumped against her. Tears oozed down Ran's face.

Rekel and Ranna stood back to back, wands held in their hands. The wands sparkled angry flame.

Black shapes shifted around Shitar as she cast

wildly.

"What happened in here?" demanded Smoke.

"Mage flare," hissed Shitar. "Sha'gar."

A soft breeze blew into the room through the remains of the shattered windows.

Ran looked up. "R-Bar told her of . . . your conversation . . . down below."

Chantal stared at her and at the mess and the shambles of the room. "Sha'gar did this?"

He could see someone, vaguely, walking back and forth, three steps one way, three steps back, snarling and cursing, waving a wand that threw red flame around her. Then he recognized her. He thought.

"Sha'gar, that you?"

"Kan kak to," she snarled. Something orange exploded nearby. She glared in his direction.

"Whoa! Hold it, hold it!" He waved his arms wildly. "Calm down, take a deep breath. And then you can tell me. WHAT THE HELL IS GOING ON?"

She jerked, straightened up, and sizzled at him. And kicked a dark thing creeping past her leg at him. It bounced and scampered away.

"Where are we?" He took another look around. The air seemed just a little bit more transparent here.

"Dar space," she snapped. "Many twisted."

"Your's?"

"Yesssssssssssssssss."

"Why am I here? Why are we here?"

"I came. You were dragged."

"Huh?"

"You," she gurgled, jabbing the crackling wand at him. Its fire matched the flaring of her eyes. "Are an accident."

"Oh." He edged a little closer. "Can I, may I, go home?" And sagged. "I think that this accident of your's may have killed me."

"WHAT?" Something flashed past their heads and exploded not far away. "Uncle?"

"Separation," he rasped, leaning heavily, somewhat toward her, somewhat to one side. "It is deadly. Breaks the mental linkages, major trauma, start coming apart." He thought that he could feel himself going.

The air exploded.

The dar space imploded.

He toppled sideways and knocked them over. Then he shoved himself into a sitting up position, a sitting up on the floor position. He smiled at them. "Hi, gang, fancy meeting you here." And slumped over Smoke. "Where is here?"

Chantal heaved herself up and over him, wrapping him in her arms. "Home, John, you are home."

And after some small struggle, he managed to sit up again and kiss Chantal, and stare down at Smoke.

She smiled up at him. "We are alive," she whispered. "MindMate. All alive." And blinked back the tears welling up.

Then he could hear all of them, the growing louder thud of people's feet running up the stairs.

Chicken hurtled through the door first, crashed down in front of Tinker, throwing her arms around him. "Ohhhhhh, My Lord, we do be most sorely a'feared."

The rest dropped around them.

Messenger bent over and kissed Smoke, again and again. "I thought that I was dying. Again." She huddled on Smoke's chest, weeping.

Smoke gently pushed at her. "Let me up, kitten, You are dripping on me."

Then everyone tried to hug and kiss everyone else.

The air in the room settled down as the witches settled down.

Wands disappeared.

    Things disappeared.

Witches relaxed, as much as they ever did.

Messenger stood and leaned out the window, wiping her eyes with one sleeve. "All over the rear deck and into the flower beds."

Chicken sat on her knees, legs tucked in, back straight, and faced him, warrior-faced, grim.

"My Lord, t'were Our Verra Own fault and none other." She paused, gathering her strength.

"That great terror do rain down pon us, this do

We Ourself cause." She stood. "Therefore, We do Ourself expel into exile and do command Great Smoke for to disconnect Us, We from thee."

She bowed formally, clicked her heels together, spun smartly, and headed for the door.

He tackled her.

Helped by Smoke and Chantal

"Release Us," she demanded. "For We do Us near kill all. Most horribly."

"Nope," he said.

"Nope," they all chorused.

But they did release her.

Sitting in a circle around her.

Chicken leaped out of the group, yanked a blade from her boot, clamped her mind shut before Smoke could reach inside. "Fair thee well, Sweet Prince. And sweeter Sister Selfs." She yanked the knife in.

Sha'gar slammed Chicken's arm numb with a sizzling green wand and banged deep sleep over her. She caught the crumbling body, as the knife tumbled from a limp hand, and gently eased her to the floor. Stepping over Chicken she knelt in front of Tinker.

"Had to be done, she will sleep until I chose to release her." Her head snapped around as she snarled at the others. "Do not try anything, Aunts, Cousin." And looked back at Tinker.

"Great foregiveness, forever debt." She slumped, and waited.

"Ummmm." He looked sideways. *Smoke?*

The Princess sleeps unharmed. Sha'gar waits nervous, fearful.

"So, how about we all go downstairs and get a cup of coffee and relax." He stood and looked around the room. "All of us." And turned and walked from the room.

Fair Morn scooped up the sleeping Chicken and laid her on the bed, dragged a blanket around, and carefully brushed the hair from her face.

Chantal picked up Chicken's blade and wondered why she had been carrying it around like that to begin with.

Soon, things were completed in the kitchen, and things were taken into the living room. He stopped Sha'gar with a gentle hand, a light touch on her shoulder. "Let's go sit on the rear deck, just you and I." And headed that way.

"As you will," replied Sha'gar, magician humble.

He sighed, not liking that response at all. *Smoke. check everyone, please? For injuries, damages, or whatever?*

Everyone?

Yep. Whatever it was that Sha'gar did, it seems to have been extremely violent. I think that she surprised everyone, especially the witches.

Smoke nodded, grabbed a second cookie, and sat in one of the large chairs. And reached out. With her minds.

On the rear deck, he sat at one of the tables. She

sat across from him and waited, watching his face carefully.

"Ummmm," he grunted. And stood. "Let's take a walk." And headed out through the flower beds and into the first pasture.

"What do you think he is going to do?" whispered Messenger to Smoke.

"No idea. He is clamped down tight."

The pair sat on the edge of the great hollow, legs poked out and over the edge. Around them, towering over their heads, waved the native grasses. They sat in the quiet, broken only by bird song and an occasional cow noise.

"You really frightened them, you know."

"Sorry sorry," she replied softly.

"Was that stuff that you learned in school?"

"No. I studied small time with Vulparqua Mage Handan Andan."

"How'd you manage that?"

"I slipped out after all slept, for a few hours each night." She tried a small half-smile in his direction. "Not even Ripple noticed."

He smiled back. "Much better."

"What?" Her smile jumped away.

"When you smile."

"Oh." Her soft half-smile slipped back.

He slipped over the edge and down, just a little, and leaned back on the slope, looking up and out, chewing on a stalk of grass.

"Ummmmmmm?"

"What?" She slipped down and reclined near him, but not too close.

"What exactly happened? Back there? I don't really understand." He waited. And admired one of the clouds as it changed from this to that.

"Sorry sorry." She sat up, and looked down at him. "No one does that to me." A ripped handful of grass flew downslope. "Unless I want."

"What?"

"My body is mine."

"Sure."

He waited.

"All your's."

He waited.

"Pretty nice."

He waited.

And nodded at the cloud that he had been watching. Now it looked like a cow. Sorta. A very warped cow.

"What?" she asked.

"Your bod."

More grass flew downslope. She looked at him. "True?"

"Yep."

"Hum."

He suppressed his smile. The cloud cow was now mostly a lump of mashed potatoes. He wondered what it was going to be when it grew up.

"R-Bar said that the Princess wanted me to mother you a child daughter."

"Ummmm." The cloud just looked like a cloud. It was being stubborn.

"Don't you want to?"

"Nope." He thought that it might be an incipient dragon floating up there.

"Un dak lak." A section of grass puffed into smoke and floated away.

"Ah?"

"WHAT?"

"Where did you get such a foul temper from? Not even the witches behave like this, and certainly not Reep or J. C."

"Do not know." She poked him with a finger until he turned his head and looked at her.

"Kiss me," she demanded.

He sat up and did. Then he released her. "Sorry. Habit."

She smiled her small half-smile. "It was . . . nice. I did not mind your hand doing . . . that."

He stood. "Let's walk back. Before they start worrying."

They did.
     And he talked to her.
          About the rest of himself
They walked.

He threw his arm over her shoulders.
She slipped her arm around his waist.

As they climbed up the steps onto the rear deck, he said, "So, no more blown out windows or anything?"

"Yessssssssssssssss."

"Let's get a cup of coffee."

They headed for the kitchen.

In the living room, Sha'gar bowed to each one in turn, most meek young magician proper. And said, "Sorry sorry." To each one. And kissed each on the forehead.

Tinker settled on the couch next to Chantal. "How we doing?"

All are fine, MindMate. Smoke nodded at him.

Chantal kissed his cheek, and said softly in his ear, "Love ya, John."

Me too, he said to each of them. He slumped as much as he could and sighed.

Sha'gar sat by his free side.

"Boy," he said, "do I need a vacation."

Shitar stood, pulled Mantara from a safe place, and said, "We are leaving to our home. To rest." She felt that it would be much safer there.

They disappeared.

Ranna stood. "We will be visiting Ripple soon."

Rekel looked surprise at her.

Ranna nodded.

They disappeared.

He looked over. "Smoke?"

"Right away." She hurried from the room.

He sipped from his cup and waited. So did the rest of himself.

Ready. Smoke was upstairs, standing next to the bed containing the sleeping Chicken.

"Sha'gar," he said. "Wake the Princess up, please."

She nodded.

Chicken popped awake.

Smoke grabbed her.

And they become one, soothing, calming, comforting.

Messenger jumped up and headed for the kitchen to fetch one of the coffee pots and a cup for Chicken.

Fair Morn followed her, having decided that they could all use a snack. Besides, there were a large number of doughnuts left.

Chantal stood, walked over, and hugged Chicken as she stepped into the room. Then nudged her over to the couch and down next to Tinker.

He slipped an arm around her. "My, my. Nice and warm."

Chicken leaned against his side and sniffled, just a little.

"All our house guests are gone, save one."

"Indeed," she replied, shrugging off his arm,

standing and turning. "Stand up, magician."

Slowly, carefully, she did.

Chicken wrapped Sha'gar in her arms and patted her back. "We do be Ourself most sorry."

Sha'gar hugged her in return, and murmured softly, "Sorry sorry, Princess. Sorry sorry."

"Snack time," announced Fair Morn, carrying in a large basket full.

"I brought the coffee pots," said Messenger. She nudged Chicken in the back with the tray. "I brought you a cup, also."

The group settled down, around him, mostly on the floor.

    Laughing.

        Talking.

            Eating doughnuts.

                Drinking coffee.

Chapter Nine.

So, It's A Cure.

Grandeville. Doc's Home.

She drifted ghost silent into the library and over to the figure hunched over the desk. He was writing, consulting this and that piece of paper, and shoving things from here to there, as he found this or that bit of information.

A tall stack of books, rested near one edge of the desk, multiple pieces of torn paper poked out from the pages in a number of directions. He was working on a project for Doc.

She poked him in the side. Just to get his attention. Nothing happened.

She waited, knowing that he would eventually notice her presence, and her sharp finger, jabbing his ribs with a steady rhythm. She was very patient. A most unusual skill for a witch.

Then, finally, it happened, He sat back and turned his head.

"Hi, there. What's up?" He smiled happily and swung one arm around, drawing her close.

Reep poked him again. This time in the center of his chest. "Our daughter is making trouble."

"Which one?"

"Sha'gar."

"Pretty fast. She hasn't been around all that long. What kind of trouble and to whom? Hard to believe that anyone could give any of you trouble."

"Him. Them."

"Sure." He nodded. "Who? Them?"

"The Chosen One."

"Oh." He shook his head. "Pretty hard visualizing anyone giving him and that group trouble either."

"We must visit."

"Sure."

"Now."

He looked around. The library door slowly closed itself. "Sure."

Grandeville. Tinker's Place.

They were there.

"Wow," said J. C. "A party."

The group was just finishing the last of the doughnuts. Almost.

Messenger had joined the couch group and was busily tickling Chicken who was squirming and toppling Tinker sideways into Sha'gar who was not all that sure what to do about it. She hung onto her jelly doughnut and sent her cup to a small table.

"Sha'gar," said the softest of soft whispers.

"Mother," she replied, trying to look daughter dutiful as she was crushed into the mass of pillows filling her end of the couch, one arm now sticking straight out, hand holding her jelly doughnut.

Fair Morn banged a basket into J. C.'s knees. "Have a doughnut. There are a few left."

He took two and handed one to Reep. "No one looks very bothered to me."

Chantal was brushing Smoke's hair and trying to convince her to let it grow long.

Ran and R-Bar sat talking quietly and spell working some new things that they thought might be useful.

"Hum," whispered the sunlight to her daughter.

"NOT!" barked Sha'gar. "Mother," she added softly.

"Off, off, off," ordered Tinker. He had felt a sharp electric jolt in his side from the Sha'gar side as she had answered her mother.

Messenger yanked Chicken upright and peered around her at Tinker and Sha'gar as he straightened up.

"OOOOOOOPS," giggled Messenger. "Did you get jelly on, ummm, anything?"

"No . . . kitten," replied Sha'gar.

J. C. sat on the floor. "Got another cup?"

Fair Morn shoved over the appropriate tray. "Here." And looked at Reep.

Reep nodded and settled gently next to J. C. and

looked at her daughter, tilting her head slightly to one side. Her cast was lightening fast.

The silver bolt struck Sha'gar in the center of her chest and blew her up and over the end of the couch. The doughnut fell to the floor and bounced. Darkness surrounded the crumpled form.

Reep waggled a cautioning hand at Ran and R-Bar, warning them not to interfere. The air around the pair settled down.

Everyone stared at her. Even J. C.

"What?" he asked.

"Healing, Husband," sighed the sunlight. "Our daughter was . . . mage ill, subject to dangerous flaring. It is what I told in the library."

He nodded. "Is she . . . will she, be all right?"

"I am well." Sha'gar rolled over and sat up, then stood. "Father. Mother."

Tinker leaned forward and stared at Reep. "She was sick?"

Reep nodded. "Dangerously so."

"Oh, My Lord." Chicken leaped up and hurried around the couch and wrapped Sha'gar in her arms. "We knew not, understood not."

"I did not know." Sha'gar hugged Chicken in return.

"Stay for dinner?" asked Smoke, tapping J. C. on the thigh.

"Who's cooking?"

"I am."

"Steak and fries, right?"

Messenger bounced up and headed for the kitchen after handing Sha'gar her doughnut. "And lots and lots of salad."

J. C. stood. "I'll help."

Smoke uncoiled in one smooth motion. "Come with me, cutie."

J. C. laughed as they headed after Messenger. "Careful, you will get me in trouble."

Reep drifted over to Chicken and Sha'gar. "Bend down, tall daughter."

Sha'gar did.

Reep kissed her on the forehead. And nodded. "A very strong magician. A very lovely daughter."

Sha'gar crushed her mother in her arms. "You too, Mother." And released her. "Let's go out back and talk." She finished eating her doughnut on the way.

As they headed down the hall, Tinker stood, stepped up behind Chicken, and wrapped his arms around her, nuzzling the side of her neck. "So, how ya doing, Princess?"

"Well, My Prince, well."

Bahn Duhr Tohr. The Quarters of the Royal Advisors.

It was a quiet evening. For them.

He was reading. A large tome.

She was lounging. In his lap.

Someone knocked, ever so gently, on the hallway door.

He dropped the tome, closed, on the floor. The thick volume puffed dust in a soft cloud.

He winked at her. "Can't be anyone you know, Dusky Delight. Much too polite."

Grumbling soft comment, she stalked to the door and threw it open, stared, leaped backward, and hurtled her mate-for-life elsewhere. Then she stood and watched the pair enter their quarters as she prepared as best she could for her death.

"Most sorry to startle you," said the man, an obvious mage of some sort or other.

His companion drifted silently, softly, into the room. "This one is Lady Fairdeath. That one is the clever Ransapal, Sluba mage. This one means no harm. May this pair sit and talk?"

Ripple stared at them, sucked in a deep breath, and indicated the table, now decorated with the appropriate number of mugs and a jug. She pulled Hanred back to be with her.

He looked at their visitors. "My." And wondered, really wondered how come his wife was still breathing, and joined the trio at the table.

Lady Fairdeath gently touched Ransapal on one arm. "He will tell all that we now know. He will tell all that we have learned and explain."

Ransapal cleared his throat. "This is a tale of ancient history from long before long before."

He swallowed loudly. And cleared his throat again. "This knowledge will unsettle most clan's and guild's and phylota's belief systems." He took a sip from his mug. "But what I am about to explain is true, very, very true."

Ransapal told them the history that they had discovered.

Many of the witch groups, whether the Witch Clan, the Sorcerer Phylota, the Nagar sort, and the Divineal have a tale from a time long before long before, and long before written records, of fleeing their homeland before it was destroyed by an event that no magic could prevent. This tale was passed member to member as an oral tradition and eventually was written down. It appears that this event happened.

But, as the magic users scattered into the universe of universes, their knowledge and identities became unique, group to group, and most felt that they were different than all the others.

However, all the groups so far mentioned are witch, even though some felt that others were not and needed to be hunted down and destroyed.

What none of them knew, or understood, is that the magicians were also from this same single event. Witch and magician fled from the same homeland, although, in some manner not understood, the magicians lost the remembrance of that past happening.

The witch and magician groups on that homeland attempted to cast a great spell of prevention. It failed and they fled. None knew that the failure of that spell caused a great change in their magics, with witch and magician forces becoming polar opposites of each other, hence the great danger, now, of mixing, one with the other, magic or personal, most of the time.

Ransapal nodded at Ripple. "It has taken the Divineal generations to gather all the bits and pieces of knowledge and put this account together."

Then he smiled at her. "So, Faan witch Ripple, we are actually distant cousins. That means: Witch; Sorcerer, called Shadow Witch; Nagar, called Bane; and the Divineal, called The Sisters of Death; and all the varieties of magicians out there is the elseplaces."

He folded his hands together on top of the table and looked at her shocked expression. "Isn't that interesting?"

Chapter Ten.

So, What's Another?

Grandeville. Tinker's Place.

Another few weeks had passed.

And it was another day.

It was morning.

Not too long after breakfast.

She stomped into the living room and glared at them. Just stood there and glared at them.

Them were sprawled, more or less, lounging about, just being lazy, taking it easy, and causing Tinker to worry.

It had been a quiet time of weeks since Sha'gar had flared and now everyone was feeling healthy and relaxed and well and rested.

It was the latter parts, the well and rested, that was causing Tinker to worry. As far as he was concerned, well and rested and lounging in languid poses indicated that they were up to something. And in as much as he hadn't a clue as to what they might be up to that there was plenty of cause for him to worry. So he did. Worry. A Lot.

She glared at them and stomped one foot. The stomp lost a great deal of its dramatic potential as she was bare footed and the rug that she so dramatically stomped upon was thick.

"Cease and desist," she demanded.

"Huh?" He snapped from his internal musings and stared up at her.

"We do Ourself be most healthy and do Ourself require ne'care." She stomped again.

"Sure," agreed Tinker. "Look pretty healthy to me."

"Patronize Us not, Sirrah!" she growled, glaring, leaning in his direction.

"Wasn't," he grumbled back. "So what is your problem, healthy but grumpy Princess?"

So she explained, glaring at each one of them in turn. She was never alone. Someone was always nearby being helpful. She strode over, dropped to her knees and leaned on his. "My Lord, We do Us require nursemaids not."

Fully recovered, said Smoke in his mind.

"Right." He leaned forward and tousled Chicken's hair. "Absolutely." And did it again. "Sho nuff and without a doubt, Kimo sabe."

She grabbed his arm. "Leave off thy villainous assault not Ranger Lonely."

"What?"

"Thee do Our Verra Own fair hair drive to fair state of disorder."

"Oh." He winked at her. "Pretty cute when it pokes out every which way." He looked around, too late.

They mobbed him.

"Damn," he mumbled from somewhere in the heap on the floor, from somewhere on the bottom.

And then.

Slowly.

After awhile.

The pile rearranged itself.

On the floor.

"Meow, meow," said Chantal, resting her head on one of his shoulders, pinning his arm in place.

"Now what?" he grumbled.

"Just making Lady Lion noises," she explained. "Seeing as we are all on the floor being in one big friendly heap."

"You sure that it is friendly?" He grunted, trying to free his other arm.

Fair Morn was sprawling over that side, aided and abetted by Smoke.

"Most friendly a'pride, indeed," added Chicken, sprawling on top of him, peering down into his eyes. "Think thee not?"

"Right." He decided it was best to agree. It was safer. "Friendly, friendly."

Chantal tickled someone.

Someone laughed, a soft husky laugh.

He stopped moving. And stared up at the ceiling.

"All right, who was that?"

R-Bar sat up and stopped tickling his ear. And tapped him on the forehead with one knuckle. "Nasty, nasty."

"STOP THAT!"

"Nasty! Nasty, nasty," sang Messenger, tickling the bottom of one of his feet. "Really really." She was draped across his legs, and giggling as he twitched.

"KNOCK IT OFF!"

"Probably what she is referring to," suggested Chantal.

He mumbled to himself.

"Sly clutcher," sneered R-Bar at him.

"Grabber," said Ran, tickling a few ribs.

Someone sat up, leaned over Ran, leaned on Chicken, and looked down at him.

"Sha'gar," he gasped.

She nodded.

"Child abuse," suggested Smoke.

"I am not a child," stated Sha'gar.

"Most fully grown," grinned Chicken at Tinker.

"You?" he asked. "Laughed?"

She smiled a soft half-smile at him.

"What are you doing here?"

"Being fondled would be my guess," laughed Chantal.

"Visiting," said Sha'gar. "I have been on long wander. Mother sent me. One week ago here time."

"And?" he asked.

"I asked her to," giggled Messenger.

"Do what?" growled Tinker.

"Pounce," laughed Messenger. "When we did. She is really good at it. Really really."

Smoke sat up. "Not too bad, for a beginner."

"Now what?" he asked.

"Naught." Chicken kissed his cheek.

"I am now twenty-four years old, as you reckon time and age in this elseplace," stated Sha'gar firmly. "It was a long and convoluted wander. I trained with many many."

"Thought that your face looked different," said Tinker, trying to sit up, trying to free an arm or two. Trying to redirect the conversation into what he felt might be safer topics.

"Or other things," laughed Chantal. "Watch it, sneak fingers."

Sighing heavily, he gave up, and lay there, inert.

"I would stand back, if I was you," said Chantal to Sha'gar. "We are about to release this crazed male animal."

They readied themselves.

Chicken shoved Sha'gar sideways.

And they all rolled away.

    They tumbled.

        Off and away from their victim.

    They jumped.

        To safety.

Their victim just lay there, looking up at the

ceiling. "Crazier and crazier," he muttered. "You all are just getting crazier and crazier." And sat up. "We have any coffee left in the pot?" He glanced sideways and saw Sha'gar being hauled behind one of the couches by Chantal and Fair Morn. For protection.

He stood and headed for the kitchen.

"HEY," called a small voice. It was Dat, standing on a book shelf.

"Come on," he mumbled, holding out one arm.

She ran up it and sat on his shoulder. "Yum, yum, yum."

"Suppose that means you want cocoa," he grumbled.

"That also, Great Master."

In the kitchen, he rounded up the necessary stuff and started making cocoa. "What? Also?"

Dat jumped down to the counter top, walked over and leaned against the side of the pot, and kicked one bare foot back and forth through the blue flames licking up the side of the pot as she waited. "Your new houri. Yum, yum, yum, yum, yum."

"Quiet." He gave the cocoa another stir. "Not my new anything."

"Certainly is. Quiet."

"Indjinn Dat, answer me true."

"Of course. Isn't it done yet?"

"No."

"What?"

"When you were fixing everyone, did you do

anything?"

"Of course."

"What?"

"Kartz required three ribs, a lung, a piece of thigh, and . . . "

"Not that."

"What? Then?" Dat dipped her cup into the swirling brown liquid and took a sip. "Almost as good as when Messenger makes it."

"Other than physical stuff, you mess with anyone's thought processes, things like that?"

"Of course not. That would not be proper. You going to take her upstairs and play with her body?"

"Drink your cocoa," he snarled, and walked away to start one of the coffee pots.

"She is almost as beautiful as me," called Dat. She told the burner to turn off. The cocoa was done, and she didn't want it to burn. She walked over and sat on the edge of the counter top. "Are there indjinns in her ancestral line?"

He took a cup of coffee, let the machine finish, and walked back to Dat. "You gonna share your cocoa? Is that possible?"

"Yes," replied Dat, "to both." She ran up his arm as he grabbed the large cocoa pan. "I would produce a beau-ti-ful daughter. Get someone to cast a large spell on me."

"Change the subject."

"The pair of witches owe me. They could do it."

"Shhhhhhhhhh."

"Gimble, gimble, gimble," she grumbled, hanging onto his shirt collar as he headed for the living room. She smiled brightly at Sha'gar as they walked over and began to serve the cocoa, to the cocoa drinkers.

Everyone was watching him carefully, very carefully.

He emptied the pot, took it back to the kitchen, and returned. "Coffee is almost done." And sat in his chair, slumped, and looked at them. "How did you guys infect even Dat?"

"My Lord?" Chicken frowned at Dat as she scampered down, over, and then up onto Chantal's shoulder. "Be fair indjinn ill?"

He slid lower. And sighed, heavily he sighed. "Maybe we could just go to rent-a-kid. Get one with a warranty."

Messenger looked at him. "From downtown?"

He looked from face to face to face. "Or we could just drive over to Portland and snatch some homeless waif off the mean streets?"

Chicken sat straighter. "Could this be done?"

He waggled a hand at her. "Between Smoke and the rest of this motley, I suspect anything is possible."

"Oh boy," bubbled Messenger. "Let's get two."

R-Bar frowned. "They would just be people."

"I suspect," said Chantal. "That he is just being sarcastic."

Smoke smiled at her. "It would be easy to do. Sarcastic or not."

"If we got seven," suggested Fair Morn. "Then we could each have a daughter."

He lurched upright. "You guys can't be serious. We would all wind up in the jail for sure. Kidnaping is a serious crime. It upsets the FBI. Not to mention the people being snatched."

"Piffle," offered Chicken.

"Definitely something," he mumbled. *Smoke?*

It was your suggestion.

"We are not," he stated firmly. "I will repeat that, not, not filling this house with kidnaped children."

Dat leaned close to Chantal's ear. "I offered my beautiful self. Indjinns produce wonderful children."

"Beautiful? Right?"

"Of course. And smart too.""

"How about we do something else," suggested Tinker. "Like go outside and run around. You guys are all getting goofy. Must be logy brains."

Smoke sat up and stretched. Lots of exercise sounded like a good idea to her. "First one that catches the rabbit, gets it." She leered at him. "You are the rabbit. Give you a five minute head start."

"What?"

"Four minutes and forty-five seconds," she intoned.

He leaped up and hurtled down the hallway.

"Guess we don't change clothes first, he is still

wearing pajamas." Messenger smiled.

They waited the allocated time and then boiled out of every door and a few of the windows.

And hunted for him.

All minds were clamped shut. No peeking was allowed.

He squirmed into a comfortable position, closed his eyes, and dozed, confident that they would never think to look here.

He was almost correct.

Soft warmth woke him.

From his deep doze.

She was snuggled against and on top of him. Her hand lightly pressed over his mouth. She shook her head, and breathed softly soft. "Shhhh, wouldn't want them to find you." And fastened her lips over his as she settled onto him.

The huntresses fanned far and wide.

And circled around and back.

And began to mumble.

"Our Prince do be most devious, a'times," grumbled Chicken.

Messenger charged up. "He is really really hidden this time."

They walked up onto the rear deck and sat at one of the tables to compare notes. And one by one by one, the others joined them.

The conversations were animated and twisted seven ways around.

Suddenly Chantal banged the table top with one fist. "O.K., where is that Sha'gar?"

"Hum," said R-Bar.

"Hum hum," replied Ran.

"Oh my gosh," gasped Messenger. "Do you think that he has dragged her somewhere?"

"Bet that she did the dragging," suggested Fair Morn. "Somewhere. Pass the cinnamon rolls, please." She had carried two pans full from the kitchen.

"A strong pouncer," commented Smoke, taking a roll, and shoving the pan towards Fair Morn.

She held him tight and kissed the sweat from the joint of his neck and shoulder. And smiled, a soft half smile at the conversations going on just above their heads.

And then she drifted the thought lightly out and touched Smoke. Who grabbed another of the remaining rolls and took a big bite just to disguise her reaction. And asked, very carefully, very guarded, *Are you sure?*

Yessssssssss.

Smoke? It was Tinker.

MindMate?

Did it again, didn't we?

Not yet. Smoke refilled her cup. *But she wants to. Badly.*

What about the rest of us?

Didn't ask, yet.

I am really nervous about the idea.

We know that. But you'll cope if we do. We will give

you all the tender loving care you can stand. Especially her.

They all heard the loud sigh.

"He is under the deck." Fair Morn sprawled flat and pressed her face against the boards, one eye peering through the narrow crack between two deck planks.

"Damn sneaky," snarled Chantal, staring at the deck. "I didn't know that there was enough space under there for anyone."

Fair Morn sat up and spun around, and winked at her. "Anyones."

Chantal stomped on the deck and growled at it. "You fink, Cowboy. You dragged that mod bod under there."

"Really really sneaky," giggled Messenger. "Really really."

Smoke shared her memories with them.

"By George!" Chicken stared at Smoke. "That silky magician do be some fair sneaky her own same self." She looked from face to face. "What say all? Dare we do this deed?" She refilled her cup and stared, blank-faced across the flower beds.

"Thought that this mob was done expanding," grumbled Chantal.

"Does he want to?" whispered Messenger.

Fair Morn sat next to Chicken and slipped one arm around her waist. "If it happened, would he, ahhh, stay, ummmmm, together?"

Everyone looked at Smoke. She nodded. "I think so." And smiled. "We have an extra room, the one we added for Sedeem, which she didn't use. A little minor reconstruction would make it private."

"I do not like it." Chantal frowned at the table top. "Too damn casual, the whole lot of you." She banged the table top with the flat of her hand. "You guys just keep tossing him at whatever happens to come by."

"Hum," said R-Bar.

"Hum hum," replied Ran.

"Oh dear," said Messenger, holding her hand in front of her mouth.

"Hum," said R-Bar.

"Well?" Chantal waved one arm at the pasture. "Why don't we just build a nest of condos out there. Just house the whole load. Save some time. One or two a week and we will see him maybe two, three times a year."

"Very agitated," observed Ran.

Two loud splashes broke into their conversation. Sha'gar had moved them into the pool.

They had been rather dusty.

She cautiously peered up and over the pool edge at the group sitting around the table.

Tinker paddled out to the deep end. "Safer out here, I think."

Smoke swivelled around. "MindMate?"

"What?"

"No more."

Sha'gar surged higher, glaring at her.

R-Bar threw protection around everyone. Ran layered on. And held a deep purple-green sphere in her hand. Just in case. And watched Sha'gar carefully.

The air at the pool edge shimmered. Reep stood there. A baggy Hawaiian shirt hung over crimson shorts. She was also wearing bright pink sunglasses.

"Daughter," sighed the breeze. "Into the house. We must talk, you and I." Reep turned and drifted through the side door.

Sha'gar scrambled out of the pool, dressed in proper black magician attire, dry, and hurried after her mother, looking neither to the right nor to the left.

"Well, Cowboy," growled Chantal. "Get out of there and get over here. It is decision time, Big Simba Stud."

Messenger ran inside and back out again, flapping open a heavy white robe, and held it out for him.

"Ummmmmm?" said Tinker, sitting on the bench, wiping wet hair back from his face. "Thanks, kitten."

"Not too close, Rat Fink," snarled Chantal.

"Wasn't my idea, you know," he mumbled.

"Didn't realize you had brains down there."

He sighed and looked around the table. "Once upon a time, my life was so simple and easy. But look at it now. Now I have a harem. Only they do not pay any attention to me. Not at all. All it is, is nothing but grumping and mumbling."

"Oh, you poor dear," cooed Chantal, looking not exactly understanding or pleased.

"What I meant," muttered Tinker.

"Me'Lord?"

"What?"

"What do we with fair silky wench?"

"Who?"

"Your new baby doll," snapped Chantal. "Filthy trick, Stud Butt, us running all over the place looking for you while you are under the deck wrestling with the young stuff."

"I was by myself napping," he stated loudly, firmly. "And then, there she was." He frowned at Chantal. "And I did not do anything."

"Ho, ho, ho."

"Wrong gender for Santa Claus." He slumped and sighed. "So, what are we going to do about her? Huh?"

"Amtar?" Ran leaned on the table and looked at him. "I think that we shouldn't think or do anything. Not until Faan witch Reep decides."

"Ummm."

Fair Morn looked at the witch pair, sitting side by side. "Do witches have much control over their daughters?"

"No." Ran shook her head. "Not much. Most of the time."

"Wouldn't want an angry mother, though," stated R-Bar. "Fiercely protective."

"Takes care of any gonadinally oriented ideas," said Chantal.

"Not me that was suggesting that she ought to produce a daughter, a sister for Sedeem," grumbled Tinker. "Was it?" He frowned at Chicken.

"When are we going to Portland?" Messenger interjected, and beamed at him.

"What? Who said that we were?"

"To get a daughter." She smiled at him. "You did."

"No! We are not!""

Her face fell. "Not even some poor homeless orphan waif slowly starving on the mean streets?"

"No. Definitely not. We do not need that kind of problem either."

"What either?" suggested Chantal.

"Keeping seven out-of-control babes happy and content."

"I am never out of control," said Smoke.

He nodded. "O.K. One exception."

Reep drifted from the house, tapped Messenger on the shoulder, and settled in the space between her and Tinker. Her hand rested lightly on his forearm.

"Sorry about all this," said Tinker.

Reep nodded. "My daughter, Faan magician Sha'gar, four-folded and double-twisted, many trained, is zartap i'indir a'am."

R-Bar grabbed and squeezed one of Ran's hands and stared at her sister.

Ran whispered, "How?"

"What?" asked Tinker.

"Flare hook," breathed Reep.

"Ummm?" said Tinker. "What?" Nothing she had said made any sense to him at all.

Reep clenched his forearm. "When she mage flared, you were pulled along. Hum, hum. Sha'gar was already focused upon you. As a, hum, mate type. Most strange for one of our clan."

She nodded at R-Bar. "The flare drove this, hum, hum, need deep. Now it is her zartap, her must. Her i'indir, her absolute. Her a'am, her reason for life."

"Oh my goodness," gasped Messenger.

"Damnation," mumbled Chantal.

Reep shoved her sunglasses to the top of her head. "It is your choice, John Tinker, friend of J. C. mate, friend of myself. Only your choice, none else."

"Ahhh?" sighed Tinker, looking around the table.

"What happens?" asked Fair Morn.

"Do we decide not?" finished Chicken.

Reep set her hands in her lap and looked at them, one by one, great black eyes pulling them all in. "Then my daughter," whispered the soft breeze, "will go far."

Smoke looked at her. "There is no way to stop her from dying?"

"No."

Tinker exhaled loudly and looked at Chantal. "Ummmmm, ahhhh, welllll . . . "

Chantal slipped her arm around him and pinched him ever so gently. "Guess we have no choice, do we?"

He looked sideways. "Smoke?"

"MindMate?"

"There has to be some limit we can put on this. We just can not keep adding and adding, regardless of the reason." He stared at the table top. "Don't you guys, the Velvetmist, have some way to do that? To stop adding?"

He sighed and stared even harder at the tabletop. "There are all kinds of people out there, dying. Or something." He looked up at her. " We can't help them all. Can't we stop?"

Smoke nodded. "Among my folk, adding Sha'gar would be what you would call maxed out."

"Then what happens?" asked Chantal, leaning on her arms, both forearms now draped on the table top.

"Oh, oh." Tinker frowned at Smoke. "Spit it out!"

"Then we become disinterested. Or perhaps it is more appropriate to call it, disinteresting."

"Gosh." Messenger stared at Smoke. "That is terrible. Really really." She nodded violently.

"To others. Outside the group."

Messenger blushed. "Oh."

"And," added Smoke, smiling at one and all.

"What?" asked R-Bar, beginning to relax. A little. As much as a witch ever did. Ran nodded.

"And others stop being interested is us."

"Hallelujah," stated Chantal. "And amen. Will that work for us?"

Smoke nodded. "I think so." She shrugged.

"No matter who, or what?"

Smoke grinned at her. "He will be safe."

"Ummmmm?" said Tinker.

"She seems like a nice person," said Fair Morn, looking at Reep.

"Ummmmm?" said Tinker.

"Really really nice," bubbled Messenger.

"Ummmmmm?"

"Risky having a magician," suggested Ran.

"Most," tacked on R-Bar.

"Oh, I can fix that," gushed Messenger, bouncing slightly.

"Ummmmmmmm?"

"Sweet Prince?" Chicken frowned at him. "Thee do ummmm muchly."

"Sure does," grinned Fair Morn.

"How come," began Tinker. "How come this number eight size wasn't made plain long, long ago?"

"Right." Chantal stared at Smoke. "Would have saved him a lot of trouble. Just grab eight and relax."

Smoke stared at Tinker. "You were not ready."

"Are we ready now?" He sighed. "Really?"

Chantal smacked the table top with the flat of her hand. "Enough discussion. I call for a vote!"

All eyes stared in his direction.

Tinker stared back. "I suppose that we can't let

her die."

"Just topped up his tank," observed Chantal.

Tinker looked at Reep. "Is it all right with you?"

Reep grabbed him and kissed him.

R-Bar stared at her sister, mouth dropping open. And whispered to Ran, "Really strange behavior for her."

Reep sat back and stared deep into Tinker's eyes. "Debt beyond debt, all that and more." She stood and stepped clear of the table. "I will tell J. C." And faded away in a soft puff of black.

"Go talk to her, Smoke."

Smoke winked at him, and headed inside the house.

Chantal leaned sideways and kissed his check. "Well, Simba Leader, that solves that problem."

"Let's have lunch." Fair Morn stood and headed down the deck for the kitchen.

"I'll help, I'll help." Messenger ran after her, laughing happily.

"Merry belated Christmas, Pasha John," said Chantal. "You want us to wrap her for you. Just being the present that she is?"

"All right, all right," he grumbled. He wasn't really sure how he had gotten into this fix. Again.

"Well, what do you give a man who has everything?" She laughed. "Don't look so glum and solemn, Cowboy. All's well that ends well, so to speak."

He looked at her. And sighed. "Certainly hope

so."

"Happy Holiday," she said.

Chapter Eleven.

Settling Down, Nicely.

Grandeville. Tinker's Place.
It was a week later.
Another week later.
It was a loud, noisy, and mess making another week later.
The contractors, and the carpenters, and the plasters, and all the other noise makers and mess makers, had come and gone. A new door had been installed where none had been before. A wall had been modified. The new room had been fixed, prepared, painted, and finished.
Smoke had slowly fitted Sha'gar into their collective being, into their complex unity, and they had slowly merged, and blended, and became a new slightly larger being. She had Sha'gar sleep with her as much of the work was done when the other's mind was sleeping. But now, she was finished.
As were the house revisions.
And the contractors were gone.
And it was quiet and serene again.

In a manner of speaking.

They were in the living room, a slightly rearranged living room, being quiet.

Tinker was on one of the couches, slumped, reading. He was flanked by Chicken and Messenger, who were taking turns fiddling with the buttons on his shirt, and grinning past him at each other.

Ran and R-Bar sat on the floor nearby doing something with a short, squat, black cylinder.

"Hee, hee, hee," cackled R-Bar.

Silver streams curled lazily toward the high ceiling.

Ran nodded.

Fair Morn, Chantal, and Smoke were cooking a Supper Dooper meal to celebrate the state of their final being. They had yanked Sha'gar with them, insisting that she had to learn how to do this cooking thing.

"Merde," mumbled Tinker.

"How now, Foul Lord?" Chicken tickled his sternum with one finger tip poked through his shirt.

So did Messenger "Tickle, tickle, tickle." She giggled.

He wacked each of them on top of the head with his closed book. "PESTS! That is how now, Brown Cow."

Chicken frowned darkly at him. "We be naught but Thy Verra Own Sweet Queen, bovine slur cur."

"Yah," agreed Messenger. "Moo nasty guy."

He looked over at the witches. "What is that?"

"Private," replied R-Bar.

"Private," agreed Ran. She set a black clear sphere in the silver streamers and watched it drift upwards.

Fair Morn popped into the room and announced, "Time." And smiled at Tinker. "Dinner in half an hour or so."

She headed down the hall. The room emptied. They all went with her. Except for Tinker. He picked up his book and found his place and started to read.

Somewhere, sometime, deep inside Chapter Five, they came and got him.

Chicken kicked the bottom of one of his feet.

"Huh?"

"Our Prince, tis time."

"Oh. Time to eat?" He closed his book over a book mark, dropped it on the floor, and followed her into the dining room.

She dragged his chair around, set it just so, pointed at it. "Seat thyself just there."

He did.

"Shudder thy orbs, nay peeking."

He shut his eyes. Then he heard the soft sounds of them all entering the room. And wondered, now what?

"You may look now, MindMate."

His eyes popped open. "HOLY COW!"

They had outfitted Sha'gar in various bits and pieces from the several wardrobes. Chicken had set the jet black hair in an ornate style, a silver filigree diadem was set in the dark mass that was framing her face, neck and shoulders. The color of her garments reflected and enhanced her soft bronze skin tones.

Tinker cleared his throat. Twice. "Sha'gar?"

"Yessssss," she said, soft tone, soft half-smile. "They insisted. Said it was a birthday treat. Not magician garb."

"What?"

"Her birth, Tink." R-Bar slipped around and behind him. "Just now, she has become."

"Very nice," murmured Ran, tickling the back of his neck, and kissing his ear. "For a magician."

"CHOW TIME," called Chantal. "SIT UP, SIT UP."

Messenger tugged Sha'gar to her seat around the dining room table. "You are really beautiful, really really." And kissed her as soon as she sat down. "And don't worry about touching the witches, I fixed that even more than the way you were."

Messenger sat, filled her glass with red wine, then Sha'gar's. "Your magic is that color, dark wine red burgundy."

"True?"

Messenger nodded. "Oh yes." She leaned close. "There were some really tangled areas." And smiled broadly. "But everything is straightened out now."

Then Chantal and Smoke served while Fair Morn carved. It was a large roast.

"Me'Lord, a toast." Chicken held her glass high. They all did.
"To Smoke, for all that we do now be."
    They drank.
"To thee, Our Love."
    They drank again.
"To Silky Sha'gar, our last, our final."
    They emptied their glasses.
    Then they passed around the jugs. And had a jolly good time.

    Chicken poked his elbow with her fork. "Sweet Prince, for dessert do leave some room."
    Chantal looked around the table and yelled, "DAT, GET OUT HERE!" And smiled at Tinker. "She might as well be here, join the party, meet Sha'gar, and all that."
    The tiny figure scampered under the table, up Chantal's pant leg, over her blouse, and sat on her shoulder.
    "Watch those claws," ordered Chantal.
    Dat grabbed a handful of Chantal's hair and leaned forward. "Aren't you supposed to being wearing something underneath?"
    "Do I make comments on how you dress?"
    "Yum, yum, yum," observed Dat. "You trying to entice him?"
    "Quiet."
    "Gimble, gimble," grumbled the indjinn. "His

new houri is beautiful. Almost as beautiful as me. Told you so."

Chantal laughed. "No false sense of modesty here."

And eventually, as was usual, they headed for the living room, to watch a movie, or two.

Messenger tossed a number of pillows to one end of a couch, shoved the couch around, and beamed at him. "Comfy, comfy, comfy."

"I'll say," said Tinker.

"All your's," added R-Bar, banging the pillows into shape.

"Ummm?"

"Don't be a pill, John." Chantal gave him a shove toward the couch. "Lie down, lie back, get comfortable." She turned and tugged Sha'gar over. "O.K., numba eight, sprawl next to him and look goo-gaa into his eyes."

"What?" snapped Tinker

"Eh?" asked Sha'gar.

"You wanted him, now you got him." Chantal shoved Sha'gar toward the couch. Then onto Tinker.

"Hey," grumbled Tinker.

"Hum." Sha'gar rearranged herself.

Smoke let Ran pick the first movie. It was a vampire movie with lots of action and blood.

Ran thought that it was a comedy.

Halfway through the movie, Messenger rolled over and started to read a book. "Yuk, yuk, yuk, Ran."

Ran laughed. A vampire had just grabbed another victim.

Suddenly Tinker lurched from the couch and stood. "All right, everyone up, on your feet."

Everyone stared at him from everywhere.

"Oh, my," gasped Messenger. "What did she do to him?" She looked over at Smoke just uncoiling from the floor.

Smoke shrugged and watched Tinker.

"Line up, line up," he demanded.

They did.

    Frowning.

        Looking blank.

    Looking worried.

He started at one end of the line.

    And kissed them.

One by one by one by one by one by one by one.

And stepped back and beamed at them, laughing happily. "I really feel good. You know that, really good." He winked at Messenger. "Really really. Just wonderful.

Then he stepped back over to Smoke and wrapped her in his arms. "It is all your fault, you know." And kissed her again. "Thanks."

He disappeared.

    Under the mob.

"Is this really necessary?" grumbled someone from the bottom.

They all thought so.
And told him so.

So life went on.
In its usually disorganized, more or less, way. And then it was several weeks later.
It was several weeks later.
It was several relatively quiet weeks later.

She tossed her arms around him from the back and kissed the side of his neck. "Mate'mer, I am now one with us."

They had just finished lunch. And were heading in different directions, depending upon what each had decided to work on.

Smoke stepped around him. "Everything is in there, MindMate. All the memories." She spun close and kissed him, and winked. "As long as you are there."

Back late. Chantal headed out the back door. *Jon Johnson's horse needs tending to.* She jumped into her car and roared down the driveway. Out, and into Grandeville. Out of their sensenet.

Smoke looked over his shoulder at Sha'gar. "I think that something about living here allows that type of separation without core shock." She shook her head. "I do not understand it." She headed outside and onto the front lawn. It required mowing.

"I could have fixed that grass," grumbled

Sha'gar. "But she wouldn't let me."

"Likes the exercise," explained Tinker. Then they could hear the sound of a hand propelled lawn mower clattering across the front lawn.

He tugged her to come along to the rear deck. He wanted to see what Messenger had been doing to the flowers gardens out there.

So they stood and admired everything.

Her arms tightened, just a little. "Mate'mer?"

"What?"

"Tiny Dat wishes to be taken."

"Not interested in traveling out there."

"In bed."

"Huh?"

"It is your solemn gift, freely given." She kissed his neck again.

"What is?"

"You did tell Dat that she could ask for anything from the Aunts Ranna and Rekel as they did owe the indjinn much."

"And?" He tugged at his arm. She wouldn't let go."

"The beautiful indjinn wants you to treat her just like one of your houris. Thus spake tiny Dat. For two long nights."

"Damn difficult thing to do."

"Hum, hum, hum."

"Oh, oh. What?"

"The powerful Aunts, Ranna and Rekel, gave me

the spell."

"Ahhhhhhh?"

"Dat will be as big as you. For two days."

"Merde," he grumbled. "You gonna let go?"

"Not yet." She laughed, soft soft. "Hum, hum."

He sighed. "Now what?"

"Everyone agreed."

"Oh they did, did they?" He reached out and felt minds banging shut. "Cowards," he mumbled.

She released him. And stated firmly, "A debt owed, a gift given."

He turned and glared at her.

She smiled, a small half-smile, and fiddled with the buttons on his shirt. "For two days."

He swatted at her hands. "O.K. Two days."

Dat stepped from the house and smiled at him. And threw an arm around Sha'gar's shoulders. "Thank you, Houri Sha'gar."

"Put some clothes on, Dat. You are not running around dressed like that."

Dat frowned, glared, and grumbled. But her clothes changed. "I want to go to town, see it, eat at Chen's, drink some of that beer stuff at that bar, and then return home." She nodded at him. "Just like one of your houris."

He stared at her. "Now?"

"Yes. I do not have much time."

He pulled his lips one way, then the other. Then he sighed. "What I get, I suppose. O.K., let's go. BUT!"

"What, Great Master?"

"You will do whatever I tell you to do, right?"

"Of course. I am your very own beautiful indjinn after all."

"Good." He pointed at her bare feet. "Shoes or sandals and socks." And looked at her eyes. "And sunglasses."

"Gimble, gimble, gimble," grumbled Dat. But she wore sandals and socks. And sunglasses.

He headed for the parking space and their truck.

Dat slipped one arm through his. "Just like one of your houris." She smiled.

"Oh well," he grumbled. "It was a quiet few weeks."

The entire gang met them out in the driveway. And kissed and hugged Dat.

They waved gaily as the pair drove into town.

Dat waved back at them, all the way down the driveway.

Grandeville. Greater Downtown, Such As It Is.

"Not all that much to see," he said as they walked back the way they had come. "Want some ice cream?"

Dat nodded.

So they ordered through the outside window and then wandered up the main street of town. He pointed. "That bay window is Sandy's place, her office. My, our, attorney."

"Let's eat. Dinner." Dat turned him toward Chen's Chinese.

"Now?"

"Yes."

Chen met them at the counter near the entrance.

"This is Dat," said Tinker.

"Very beautiful," observed Chen, smiling at her.

Dat bowed to him, very properly.

"And well mannered." Chen waved over his numba one waitress. "Booth one. Numba One Special Dinner for two."

And soon they sat, munching on egg roll appetizers, and drinking tea.

Tinker took another. "I thought that indjinns didn't need to eat."

"We do not," replied Dat, crunching loudly as she ate a sweet and sour pork rib, bone and all. "But it is fun. Sometimes."

And then, after all the dishes had been set on the table, just so, and the booth closed, Dat shoved her sunglasses to the top of her head.

"Really disconcerting. Purple eyeballs."

"Lovely color." Dat took some shrimp. "Are you angry, at all of your houris?"

He shook his head. "Nope." And shoveled several things onto his plate. "I just figured that you would ask for something else, that's all."

"Don't need anything else." She poured tea for them. "Get's lonely being that size. Even for an indjinn."

"Didn't realize."

"Have some of this." She shoved a dish across the table. It was one of the chicken dishes.

When they were finally done, she happily filled a number of small cartons and carried them back to the truck. "They will enjoy the rest for lunch tomorrow."

He relocated the truck and parked. In front of the bar. "Well, here we are."

"Let's see a movie first. We have plenty of time."

So they did.
See a movie.

And then they walked back.
To Big Darlene's.

The pair sat on stools at the bar.

Dat beamed happily at everyone and everything in the joint.

And ordered. A big bowl of chili.

"Smoke told me to," she said as she ate it after pouring lots of hot sauce all over it. Then she ordered a stein of beer. And drank it. "Smoke told me to." She smiled at him.

"I think that I will have a talk with Smoke," he grumbled.

Finally, they headed for home.

On the drive back, Dat sat very close to him, and

slipped an arm around his waist, and leaned her head on his shoulder.

"Don't tell me," he mumbled. "Smoke told you to."

As they slipped silently inside the house, he whispered, "You are a nice person, Dat."

"I am an indjinn. Not a person."

"Forgot." He tossed her sunglasses on the counter top and wrapped her in his arms and kissed her.

"Yum, yum, yum," she said after awhile, yanking his shirt free.

"You are pretty yummy yourself."

Morning.

It was really mid-morning before they straggled into breakfast. He slumped in his chair and reached for his coffee cup while Dat remained in the kitchen to talk with Chantal who was making breakfast for Tinker.

"Want something to eat? Cocoa?"

"Cocoa." Dat kissed Chantal on the cheek. "I like being large. I like being one of his houris."

Chantal wacked Dat lightly, with the wooden spoon she held. "Don't mess with the cook."

Dat stood next to her and watched the breakfast preparation. "He is nice. And warm."

"I know."

"He is very nice."

"Already said that."

"For a Great Master."

"Oh." Chantal gave the cocoa another stir. "Bout ready. Get a cup?"

Dat did. And held it out.

Chantal poured. "You want a marshmallow?"

Dat nodded.

Chantal pointed. "In there." And watched as the indjinn found the bag and dropped one into her cup. "You have a good time?"

Dat leaned back against the counter and smiled. "Yes."

"Canines are really noticeable when you smile."

"Beautiful."

"Like a cat." Chantal smiled at her. "That is it, you know."

Dat sipped. "What?"

"Cat. You have a lot of our domestic cat-like behaviors. Are all indjinn like that?"

"Far as I know." Dat looked at the pot on the stove. "Is there more?"

Chantal nodded. "Sure." And slid the breakfast from the cast iron skillet onto a plate and handed it to Dat. "Here. Take this in. He is just about awake."

Dat did.

Chantal headed for the back and the washing machine. It was her turn to do the laundry. He was next on this assignment list.

"Here." Dat slid the plate in front of him and sat in Chicken's chair.

"Thanks." He sat up and began to eat.

Dat sipped and watched.

Fair Morn leaned in one of open windows. "Need some help. Come on, Dat."

"Gimble, gimble, gimble," grumbled Dat as she stepped out through the opening and followed Fair Morn.

"What happens when you are large," laughed Fair Morn, leading her around to the Corporate Headquarters building. And to a row of shrubs still in containers that required planting.

It was late, very late afternoon by the time they were finished.

"Let's shower before dinner," suggested Fair Morn, heading for the house.

Sha'gar was in the kitchen being taught by Messenger all about pizza.

"And we need lots and lots of salad."

Sha'gar nodded. "Yessssssss. Mother and Father are coming for dinner."

Messenger gasped, "Oh my goodness. We will have to have more pizza as well."

So they did.

    Make lots and lots.

    Of salad.

    And pizza.

When dinner was over they all headed for the living room.

J. C. caught Tinker by an elbow and held him back, and asked in a very, very low whisper, "Is she a vampire?"

Tinker smiled. "Dat is an indjinn. They just have canines like that. She is, ummmmmm, only here for a short while, a very short visit."

J. C. smiled. "Just wondered. Ready to believe anything any more." He swung an arm around Tinker's shoulders. "Father-in-law." And laughed. "Reep told me everything. Kind of hard to believe that also."

"Right," agreed Tinker. "It is. But." He laughed. "Father-in-law. But I think that everything has finally settled down. And we all love Sha'gar very much. Did Reep tell you about her, ahhh, skills?"

"A little. Not much. Doesn't seem to be a thing that they want to talk about. Why?" J. C. frowned.

"Relax, Dad." Tinker nudged his close friend. "Sha'gar did a very J. C. thing. She studied everything. And with everyone that she could find and convince to train her."

J. C. laughed.

So did Tinker, who said, "She spooked two of her aunts and impressed R-Bar and Ran. And that takes some doing."

"My Lord," called Chicken. "Do come and join us for we do all most patiently wait for to start."

J. C. and Tinker hurried to their seats and Chantal started the movie.

Dat snuggled against Tinker's side and

murmured into his ear. "Just like one of your houris."

Reep slipped up against J. C.'s side and poked him in the ribs until he slipped one arm around her and one around his daughter, Sha'gar, who had claimed his other side.

"I am very happy," she whispered to her parents.
"Good," said J. C.
"Hum," sighed the shadows.
"Mother!" snapped Sha'gar.
"Hum, hum," replied the darkness.
"Father?"
"Ssssh," said J. C. "Watch the movie."
"Stop picking on your daughter," he said to Reep, hugging her against his side. "And leave my ribs alone."

The group watched two movies and ate lots of popcorn, and sat around and talked after the movies were over.

Then all retired for the night. J. C. and Reep returned to Grandeville.

She sat up and peered into his eyes. "You are the best Great Master that I have ever had."
He smiled up at her. "Is that a pun?"
"I was always tiny."
"Really?"
"Yes." She leaned closer. "I like being large."
He sighed.
She kissed him. "I understand. Winged houri

Fair Morn, who is almost as well formed and beautiful as I am, explained." She wiggled, just a little. "I have a nice form, very enjoyable for male people human play."

"Uh huh."

She stretched out and hugged him. "Great Master, may I breach indjinn code?"

"Do what?"

"Ask for a favor?"

He stared into those strange eyes and held her gently. "Sure."

She pressed against him, getting as close as she could get. "I would like to be big every now and then and be treated like one of them, your houris, and not just be Dat, the tiny indjinn."

"Ahhhhh . . . . "

"Gimble, gimble, gimble."

He sighed heavily. "Do you have any sisters?"

"I do not know. I have never met another indjinn."

"Really?"

"Yes. I have been around almost before ever. And it is so. Please?" She gasped. A loud, sudden gasp.

"Dat?"

She hugged him tighter. "Be not angry. I shouldn't do that."

"What?"

"Ask for favors. And beg."

He gently kissed her. "I am flattered. Ahhhhh, would you settle for every other month, something like that? Two days? Like this time?"

She rolled over, dragging him with her. "And Christmas and Thanksgiving." And wrapped her arms and legs around him. "And New Years."

He laughed. "O.K. But you get to explain it to them."

"Your houris will understand."

Morning. Again.

They felt him drift through the kitchen and into the living room. And waited.

He stared at the watching faces and mumbled, "Now what?"

Chantal filled his coffee cup and then the others held out in her direction, and then set the coffee pot on a low table. "John, you are just an old softy."

"And we all agreed," bubbled Messenger. "Really really."

"Yep," added Fair Morn.

"Right, Tink." R-Bar nodded.

So did Ran. "Yessssss, Amtar."

Chicken sat next to him and patted his thigh. "Indeed, Our Prince. We did Ourselves agree."

Smoke settled by his other Side. "As long as you agree, we agree."

Sha'gar tucked her legs up and nodded. "Yesssssss, Mate'mer, we all agree."

He looked around the room. "So, where is she?"

"Sleeping, My Lord."

Smoke nodded. "Pummeled into exhaustion."

"Don't start," he growled.

"Bounce, bounce, bounce," laughed Chantal. "You ready for breakfast, Cowboy?"

So, he had breakfast, amidst a certain amount of laughing and giggling.

And then, everyone dispersed to do chores of one kind or another.

It was later.

Much later.

And all were in the living room, relaxing.

And it happened.

With a silence as quiet as a long abandoned tomb, they faded in and looked around the room.

Two witches and a magician dumped every protection that they knew over everyone, knowing that it was probably a waste of effort. But, perhaps, someone could run fast enough to escape before the layers were ripped away.

Tinker stared at the pair who stared back.

"How did you get in here, past the ward?"

She drifted soft silent over to him and swept the hood of her green almost black robe back from her face and down and off the back of her neck. Magic users gasped.

"Nothing may keep death from entering, Chosen One." Her companion looked nervous at the others in the room.

"Huh?"

"This one is The Lady Fairdeath, Divineal of Thantala." She gestured. "This one is the very clever Ransapal, Sluba mage, consort."

R-Bar's mouth dropped open. Ran nudged her with an elbow. Sha'gar stared at this mage. No one had ever heard of one of the Divineal traveling with a companion, especially a magical user.

Tinker noticed the several shocked expressions and really began to worry about what ever was going on this time.

"This one has traveled far and far and has studied much. In our long ago long ago it was told of a Dark Warrior who was The Lady of Death's companion. The Shadow Wrapped Male was told to some day come once again into the elseplaces."

She drifted closer to Tinker and held out the short gold staff, eyes watching his very carefully.

Equally as carefully he reached out and took it. He turned it over in his hand and smiled at her. "Very nice." And handed it back.

Lady Fairdeath took the staff and slowly sank to her knees and looked up into his face. Tears glistened in her eyes as she whispered to him, "The Lady tells us these things. The Face of Death is rarely seen. Which is as it should be. The Voice of Death is but a passing whisper. Which is as it should be. The Touch of Death is but a light caress. Which is as it should be. The Passage of Death is but a soft shadow. Which is as it should be. Beginning and ending are but a whole."

Slowly she rose, reached out and tapped him in the center of the chest with the gold staff.

R-Bar screamed.

Ran collapsed.

Sha'gar glared red fire.

Lady Fairdeath leaned forward and kissed Tinker in the middle of his forehead and straightened up. She drifted back, slipped her arm under one of Ransapal's, and said to Tinker, "The mere whisper of my name will call me to your presence. All will honor your name, Dark Knight of The Lady of Death."

She faded away, taking her companion with her.

Tinker stared around the room. "Anyone have any idea what that was all about?"

R-Bar, now sitting up, cleared her throat. "Tink, how do you feel?"

"Fine. Just fine. Why?"

"One gentle tap from that gold staff and everything dies. When she handed it to you, seeking release from this life, she gave her life to you. And you gave it back." She sagged and leaned against Ran who had pushed herself upright. "Some of them even use a shadow. No one ever knows what the Divineal are doing. And no one would ever dare ask them."

"Mate'mer, you should be careful in ever mentioning her name. The Divineal are feared by everything with any sense at all." Sha'gar stood and headed for the kitchen. "I need something to eat."

Kantor's Spot. An Ice World.

He lurched into the large room, dragging the body along by the hair. His robes were white, trimmed and decorated in red and green twisting curving designs.

It was obvious from the way he moved and the way his body was bent and twisted that something terrible had happened to him, some long time in the past.

Releasing his burden in the center of the room, he beckoned over a throne-like chair and dropped into it just after kicking the body in the side with one sandal clad foot.

"Revenge should be slow, sooooooo slow."

Her eyes watched his face. It was the only thing that he was allowing free movement. Anything else was much too dangerous.

He nodded at her. "Surprise, surprise. Never that you would ever see me again, did you?"

Stretching out his legs he shoved at her shoulder with one foot and watched the body slowly flop back and forth, a soft noddle wobble.

Jerking himself into a more comfortable position, he stared down at his prize. "Thought that I was a wreck forever?" He shook his head. "Narrow mind, narrow vision. Should have looked wider. But your type is much too head strong, not subtle at all. But here you are, subtle caught."

He yawned widely, mostly for her benefit. "Nap

time." And lurched upright and stumbled jerked from the room, singing softly to himself. "Dirkle, dirkle, dirkle."

Grandeville. Tinker's Place.

He shoved back from his desk, swivel chair squeaking loudly. Yawned. And stretched.

It had been a full week. Finally a rather quiet full week. In fact, it had been a very comfortable week that had just passed. And he felt really very good. He leaned forward and shut everything, computer, etc., off. Then he headed downstairs. It was time for tea and cookies.

Filling a cup, he grabbed a handful of cookies, and headed toward the living room, crunching loudly.

They all sat there, smiling at him as he entered the living room.

He flopped in his chair and smiled back. "Hi gang, what's up?"

"My Lord?" Chicken sat straighter.

"Ummmmm?" His mouth was full.

"We must a'town go."

Sure. It was easier to answer this way, mind to mind, than hastily chewing and swallowing. *How come?*

Messenger beamed at him. "Buying presents."

"For Raj," explained Chantal.

"And Kartz," added Fair Morn.

"Big wedding," said Smoke.

"On a small scale," amended R-Bar.

"This your Saturday," said Ran.

Sha'gar looked at him. "Why didn't we do that?"

"Let's take Dat," bubbled Messenger. "To the wedding."

"Who's going to be there?" asked Tinker to Chantal, after swallowing his cookie. "I don't know, except we didn't do that for anyone except R-Bar because of Sedeem, our daughter," he said to Sha'gar.

"Just us, Cowboy. Raj doesn't have any friends over here. And he isn't planning on inviting anyone over from the coast either. He doesn't like big happenings like that anyway."

Chantal smiled at him. "Let Dat come. Large. After all, she repaired Kartz, and a bunch of us. Might as well let her see her handiwork getting hitched."

"A real wedding in a real church," gushed Messenger.

He looked at her. And swallowed another cookie piece.

"The small stone outfit at the corner of Pott's Road and Hay Lane," explained Chantal. "Raj knows the minister. It will be very, very British."

"We are the wedding party," said Fair Morn. "Almost."

"Almost?" He stared at the last cookie.

"Fair Kartz' sisters do come," explained Chicken.

"Should be interesting," mumbled Tinker around the last cookie.

Sha'gar sat on the arm of his chair. "I want to do this wedding process also."

"Can't," stated Tinker, gulping down the last part of the cookie. "Only allowed one at a time. I married R-Bar a couple of years ago." He frowned at the floor. "Thought I was going to raise a daughter."

R-Bar looked up from tickling one of the cats that sprawled in her lap, "We could get a divorce. Then you could marry Sha'gar."

"Never mind," he grumbled. "Not going to start something like that."

Messenger beamed at him. "Do we really get to throw uncooked rice at them? Really, really?"

"Yep."

"Oh boy! I'll bring just lots and lots."

"HOLD IT!" Tinker looked from happy face to happy face. "Everyone gets two handfuls and that is all."

"Gosh," said Messenger.

"It is just a gesture, not an assault."

He tickled Sha'gar. "I suppose we could go on a honeymoon, someplace."

"Hum," said Sha'gar.

"Where you figuring on going, Stud?" Chantal slumped in her chair.

"Doth Lamex," suggested R-Bar. "Good place."

Ran nodded. "Hum, hum."

Tinker stood. "Let's go shopping." It was time to redirect their interest, for a moment at least.

They trooped outside.

And headed for town.

Grandeville. The Dwelling of Raj and Kartz.

Saturday afternoon.

It was after the ceremony.

And they were all in the backyard.

Kartz was holding an animated conversation with her three sisters in one corner of the yard.

Chantal gave Raj a very comradely hug. "Congratulations, I suppose."

"Suppose?"

"Yep. Her culture is really different."

Raj nodded. "Quite." He smiled. "Wonderful person."

"Uh huh."

He nodded. "She is, you know. Been telling me all about the Nagar, their history. Rah-ther ghastly."

"I know. But that is all over." Chantal indicated the group in the far corner of the yard. "What's that all about?"

Raj shrugged one shoulder. Then he held up his right hand. "Chan, you ever see a ring like this?" On his forefinger he wore a wide band of deep crimson. The soft burnished surface appeared translucent.

"Nope."

"She insisted. No idea?"

"Ummm," replied Chantal.

"What?" Raj tugged at the ring. "Won't come off, you know."

Chantal smiled. "Given who she is, I suspect that it is some kind of magic thing. I have a hunch that you are being heavily protected."

She indicated R-Bar, Ran, and Sha'gar. "When it comes to their mates, they get very protective, fiercely so."

She laughed softly. "So if some big city mugger ever decides to give you trouble they are going to be in for a big surprise. Probably lethal. So, how's work?"

"Jolly good fun. Circe has been helping me."

"Helping?"

"Quite." Raj shook his head. "Although I had to stop her from curing people. One or two spontaneous cures might be all right, but we can't have a rash of them. Place would be overrun in no time. Bit of a problem, that."

"Yep," agreed Chantal. "Other than that, how you doing?"

"Fine. Fine. And fine." He tugged her over to an empty space, as far from everyone as they could get. He nodded at Dat, who was trying out various of the food stuffs on the large table, just to see what they were like.

"Kartz told me about, ahhhh, that Dat, ummm, person and all." He frowned darkly at Chantal and spoke very softly. "Your group can't keep doing things. like that."

"Like?"

"Being rebuilt all the time." He cleared his throat. "Ahh, having body parts replaced." He stared into her grey-green eyes. "Chan, I do not believe that kind of trauma can be ignored. I really do believe that there must be some unseen and unfelt damage. If it is not physical, then most certainly it is psychological."

"I think we retired from that kind of action out there." And then she described how they had managed to bar all kinds of visitors from ever coming in. She skipped over the Divineal visit.

And then.

Everyone joined everyone.

To celebrate.

They partied.

Just a little.

And waved goodbye to Kartz' sisters.

And went home.

It was a kind of a holiday.

Chapter Twelve.

Offspring.

Bahn Duhr Tohr. The Quarters of the Royal Advisors.
Soft knocking woke her.
Soft cautious knocking.
She looked out and spoke, not too kindly. It was late at night, after all. "What do you want?"
"Talk."
"Dir dit," she grumbled.
"Please?"
Her eyes flew wide. This strange word seemed to be creeping into too many vocabularies.
She rolled from the bed, and stalked into the main room, waving on clothes. "Enter."
Rekel sat at the table and poured two mugs full and slid one over to her sister.
Ripple sat, and glared, and drank. "What?"
Rekel gulped from her mug. "Ranna is eyereach lost."
Ripple leaned back, eyes narrowing. "Explain."
Rekel unfastened the high, severe military-style collar of her shirt and yanked out the thin chain with

the orange glowing stone. "These eyereach, one to one." She swung it gently back and forth.

"Ranna and I always vision know feel the other, allplace."

"Hum," said Ripple.

Rekel frowned at her. "Not nice."

"Speak tell."

Rekel nodded. "Ranna suddenly was not there."

"How?"

Rekel refilled her mug. And shook her head. "Just lost."

"And?" Dark vague hovered around Ripple.

"Seek find." Rekel looked up from the table top at her. "Our sister was on Dark Gabe, spell seeking. Then she was . . . not."

The ceiling grumbled softly.

Rekel shook her head. "Alive. The eldest is alive. Soft touch feel. And you know it. We all can feel our sisters." She shoved her chair back and stuffed the orange stone back inside her blouse, fastening the collar.

"A long twisted journey," stated Ripple.

"Ask Raft."

"Hum," said Ripple.

Rekel nodded.

Kantor's Spot. An Ice World.

He ordered the clatka beast to throw the body on the low couch-like device. And frowned.

He supposed he ought to let her eat. Otherwise.

It would end to soon.

So he decided.

He ordered food.

He made sure that her vocal cords still were frozen. No words could she speak. Then set a sakto beast to feed her. Her arms and hands were not allowed to work. Either.

"Eat! Or be forced to eat."

She chewed slowly, black eyes boring into his. And tried to form the words.

He watched carefully. Then, satisfied that she was incapable of spell casting, he left the room. The food smells had made him hungry. And he didn't like being stared at like that.

Dark Gabe.

The elseplace name was really a misnomer. It was a land of bright sun, warm and pleasant.

Medium sized towns were widely scattered, a combination of agriculture and arcane arts. Users of all magical varieties passed through. Some seeking special ingredients. Some seeking unique spells, or some other bit of arcana. There was a brisk market for all commodities.

The inhabitants paid little attention to any of their visitors. Strange was strange. And usually did strange. And none of them bothered the local folk. It wouldn't do to be barred entry to Dark Gabe.

Raft appeared in Tar Tor, a town often visited by

the witches. And went to the main food place.

One moment she stood in the market place talking to a short witch. The next she was standing inside Pook's Gar, tapping Pook on the chest.

"Has Faan witch Ranna lodged here?" She handed Pook a gold coin.

"Tall piece?" asked Pook, touching his cheek with one fingertip. "Mark here?"

"Yesssss."

"Room paid." Pook held up four fingers. "Came two brights back" He shook his head. "No see."

"I will see her room."

Pook nodded, puckering his lips. "Your health." He knew that the witches often set wards on their doors. If this short one wanted to chance that, it was no business of Pook to worry. He pointed up the staircase. "Two up." And gestured. "Three on that side. Brown door."

She was gone.

Pook blinked. He had never met one that moved like that before. Instantly.

Raft cautiously touched the door with a light light fingertip. Ranna was subtle vicious.

The door swung inward. She stood next to the table and looked. And nodded. Ranna was not gone long. Raft turned and headed for that primitive elseplace.

Grandeville. Tinker's Place.

He looked up from the book, and grumbled loudly. "O.K., now what is going on?" And frowned at her.

R-Bar stuffed the video back into the cabinet and whirled around. "What?" She looked through him and chewed on one corner of her lower lip. And wandered out and down the hall.

He reached out with his mind. *Smoke?*

What? She dug in her heels and pushed her back harder against the bedroom closet door.

Heavy thumping and cursing was coming from the other side. Chicken had dropped a water-filled balloon on Smoke as Smoke had walked through the common, open area of the Chamber. The banging and cursing was a Royal Statement about being tossed inside the closet roughly.

Check on R-Bar, will ya? Something is suddenly not right.

Sure. Part of Smoke's mind reached out, seeking that part of their intertwined being that was the short witch. She smiled to herself and vigorously shook the can of whipping cream. And then spun away from the door, flattening herself against the wall, opposite the hinged side.

Ran leaped from her chair. "Amtar! Visitor!"

He jerked "Who?" He hadn't heard a car coming up the driveway. "Where?"

"AN DAK DO!" snarled someone. "Let me in."

Ran looked at Tinker.

He nodded.

She appeared.

"Raft!" He smiled at her. "Been a long time."

"R-Bar mate," she acknowledged. "Where is my sister Reep? Your ward block mesh spell would only let me come in here." The air crackled around her.

Sha'gar slipped silently into the room. "Fast Aunt," she announced. "I am Reep daughter Faan magician Sha'gar. Come." She crooked one finger. And disappeared taking Raft.

Smoke hurtled into the living room from the hall, skidded and slid, and shot into the dining room.

"FOUL DARK WENCH," bellowed Chicken, as she charged into the living room from the hallway. "STAND AND FIGHT US, WE DO DEMAND THIS!"

She stood, sucking in deep breathes, angrily shaking the can of whipping cream. A thick white stripe ran from her forehead down to her waist. She had a smear where she had wiped her face. Another large patch had been rubbed across and over her left eye and into her foam matted hair.

"WHOA!" shouted Tinker. "HOLD IT!"

"My Lord," stated Chicken in her most royal and regal tone of voice. "Most just King, We do demand Us justice, We do, for We, thy most Ever Humble and Ever Obedient Queen, do have been most grievously ill-treated."

"Oh?"

Chicken threw her shoulders back. "Indeed! We, thy Verra Own Queen, do be most foully assaulted by that grumpish grimalkin."

"Really?"

She nodded. "T'was most cruel an assault, Fair Prince."

He grinned. "Grumpish grimalkin?"

She nodded agreement. "We do Us think pon other terms, but do then decide t'were most uncouth for those thy own most gentle ears for to be a'hearing."

Smoke leaned in, just past the doorjamb. She had circled around and had slipped silently up the hallway. "Skinny started it." And jerked back as a hiss of white spurted into the hallway.

"CEASE FIRE," yelped Tinker, leaping to his feet and shoving out one hand. "Let me have that."

She did.

Coating him from the nose to the belt buckle. And ran laughing wildly toward the kitchen.

"Murgle." He looked around the room at the several laughing faces. And demanded angrily, "What's going on? This time?"

"Party time?" asked Messenger, looking hopeful. "Can we use that white edible goo stuff also?"

"NO," he snapped.

"Don't ask me." Fair Morn smiled broadly at him. "I am just an innocent butterfly."

Chantal strolled into the room. "You are a mess,

Cowboy. What were you doing?" She pointed at the hall floor. "And I am not cleaning up after you."

"Chicken did it."

"Faan witch upset," explained Ran.

"I'm lost." He headed down the hall, to clean up, to change clothes.

Chantal flopped into a chair and frowned at Ran. "That damn bunch is a pain in the butt."

Sha'gar shimmered in. "Aunt Raft and Mother have gone to search for Aunt Ranna. She has disappeared. All are very disturbed and bothered."

As Tinker passed near the door to the tub room he heard Chicken graphically describing Smoke's ancestry.

Smoke had just dumped Chicken into the hot tub.

He leaned in through the door. "What's going on?"

"Dropped her into the tub," explained Smoke, kneeling next to the edge and shoving Chicken back under the water. "R-Bar is bothered and this one is reacting to it."

Chicken surged to the surface, sputtering and blowing. "A curse do be upon thy house, wench."

"Piffle," commented Smoke, yanking Tinker sideways and tossing him in on top of Chicken. She waited for him to come snarling to the surface. "You were pretty messy as well. Stay in there and calm down the Royal. We will clean the tub later."

He grabbed Chicken as she started to clamber out of the tub. And watched Smoke head into the Chamber.

"Be thee angry, My Lord?"

"Nope. Why should I be?" His arm circled around her and tugged her back against his chest.

"We do thee coat."

"S'all right, Princess. We can clean the tub. Later."

"R-Bar do be most bothered."

"Uh huh."

"Me Lord?"

"What?"

"Thee do Us fondle most outrageously."

"It's cause you are there. Sorta like a mountiain."

"Gosh," gasped Messenger, blushing.

"Hum," said Sha'gar.

Ran nodded at her.

Fair Morn winked at Chantal. "Let's make something to eat. She'll be hungry."

Dark Gabe.

Pook jerked nervously. He had heard of this witch, The Silent One.

He began to sweat.

And to shudder.

"Sh . . . sh . . . she hasn't re . . . re . . . returned."

Raft stood at the top of the stairs and beckoned.

Reep drifted shadow soft quiet, following her sister.

Inside the room, Raft stood in a corner and asked, "See anything? Pook said it has only been a few days."

Reep slowly scanned the room, great dark eyes taking in everything.

"Yes," whispered the softest of soft voices. She carefully anchored the strand. "Wait." And then she wasn't there. Following the magic strand.

Raft grumbled to herself. She hated waiting.

Kantor's Spot. An Ice World.

Finished with his meal, he wobbled lurched toward the door, and back into the other room.

And saw that she was finished with her meal as well. He stared at the floor. Bits and pieces of food were strewn all about.

Waggling one hand, he ordered the floor clean. "Next time, I will use something else to feed you."

He ordered the table and the beast away, and lurched closer. "I am really having trouble deciding what to do. To you."

Reaching out, he slid the fingers of his good left hand over her face. "So lovely." And smiled. "Now mine to enjoy in any way that I might choose."

His fingers slowly fluttered lower.

Touching.

Enjoying.

Staring into her eyes, he could see the flicker fire

deep down, far far deep inside those black black eyes.

Tugging the fastening loose, he slowly, ever so slowly slipped her blouse from one shoulder. The dark material made stark contrast against pale white skin.

"Moon caressed," he sighed, leaning forward, kissing the soft hollow where neck joined shoulder. He breathed deeply, leaned back, nodded to himself. "Mustn't rush. We have all the time I need and more."

He beckoned over a chair and sat. And sighed. "All the time needed." He nodded, this time at the dark eyes watching him.

Grandeville. Tinker's Place.

Chicken took another sandwich.

"See," said Fair Morn, nudging Chantal.

Tinker eyed them, carefully looking from face to face as they sat around the dining room table. "Anyone care to talk?"

"Pon?" asked Chicken.

"Weirder than usual behavior."

"Most bothered, Fair Prince."

"Uh huh."

"R-Bar do be most a'bothered, Our Leige, and this do bother all."

His eyes rolled sideways. "Yo, kiddo."

"Tink?" She looked up, great black eyes, staring eyes, looking at him.

"What's the problem?"

She blinked.

"Tell me, tell us." He nodded at the rest of them. "Your bother is getting to them all, to all of us. What's up?"

R-Bar shoved her forearms onto the table top. "Ranna disappeared. Rekel felt her disappear. Raft and Reep are searching."

She sat straighter. "Something got her, Tink. Witches just do not disappear."

"Ummmmmmm. Any idea?"

She shook her head.

"You wanna stop worrying so much?"

"I will try." R-Bar looked at Chicken. "Sorry sorry."

Tinker cleared his throat. "Ahem. I hate to ask this."

"What?"

"Anything we can do?"

She shook her head. "Not until we hear from Raft or Reep."

He slumped and sighed. "Well, I suppose we ought to start getting things ready."

R-Bar frowned at him. "We do not know that."

"I have a hunch." He didn't like that hunch. Not at all.

Fair Morn stood. "Smoke and I will get the gear ready." They headed for the correct hall closet. Chantal followed them.

"Gumble gob glob," grumbled Tinker.

Sha'gar stood, walked over and laid a carefull

hand on his forehead. "Mate'mer?"

"I feel fine. It was just an editorial comment."

Chicken nodded. "He do grumble so. Be'times."

Chantal stepped back into the room and set an fancy ring on the table top in front of Tinker. "Don't leave home without it."

A small figure appeared and stared up at him. "We going somewhere?"

Tinker managed to slump even deeper in his chair. "Probably."

"I get to come along?"

"Sure," answered Chantal.

"In the ring," added Tinker.

"Gimble, gimble, gimble," grumbled Dat.

"You are our secret," said Chantal. "We may need one."

"Well," said Dat. "I suppose. If you think so."

"Either in the ring," explained Chantal. "Or you get to ride around in someone's shirt pocket."

"RING!" snapped Dat. "Might as well be comfortable." She scampered across the table and ran up one of Sha'gar's sleeves and sat on her shoulder. After shoving one hand into the jet black hair, Dat leaned forward and peered down. "Yum, yum, yum, yum. I'll bet that he really enjoys playing with you."

"Dat!" snarled Tinker.

Dat huddled close to Sha'gar's head. And then whispered in her ear. "Right?"

"Quiet, Dat!" snapped Tinker. "Don't need one

of those conversations right now."

Dark Gabe.

Raft was suddenly there, standing in the main room. Right in front of Pook. She smashed him in the chest. With one fist. And stood in a far corner and watched as he started to sag to his knees.

Reep drifted over, grabbed a handful of hair, and kept him from going any further down.

"Pook," whispered the shadows. "Do you know the spot where Ranna was taken?"

Pook snapped his eyes closed and mumbled that he did.

"Who?"

"I do not know."

"What did you see?"

"Nothing," he mumbled.

Reep lifted his head. The rest of Pook followed.

"Pook sees everything," breathed darkness close to his face. "Speak tell."

"He will come."

"No." She jerked his hair. "No, he will not. Who?"

Pook felt his eyes being opened. He didn't want to open his eyes.

But they opened.

Midnight peered in.

"Who?" it asked.

"Not who. Just white. Swirling white. It wrapped

around and around and around and around and took her. Away." Pook's knees banged against the floor. They were gone. Both witches were gone. He crawled to a chair and finally managed to sit in it, thanking various things that he was still alive.

Grandeville. Tinker's Place.
 Traveling gear had been readied for two days.
 It was now mid-afternoon.
 Tinker sat slumped on one of the couches editing a final draft.
 Sha'gar sat on a chair and watched him. She enjoyed watching him.
 Smoke was lying on the floor, flat on her back, on one of the rugs, eyes open, staring at the ceiling, both hands, fingers intertwined, resting on her stomach.
 Dat had been sitting on Smoke's hands. Now she walked up Smoke's chest and nudged a soft swelling with a toe. "I could make these much more beautiful."
 Smoke stared past her nose at the tiny indjinn. "I am already beautiful."
 "Not to bad," observed Dat.
 "My anatomy does not require changing."
 "It wouldn't hurt."
 Smoke smiled. "If we were all as beautiful as you, he would be bored. There would be no variety. And he would then, probably, leave you tiny all the time."
 Dat crossed her arms over her chest and thought

about that. And nodded. "Guess you are correct. May I remove the scar on your cheek."

"O.K. But no other changes."

Dat walked up and did. "He shouldn't beat you."

"It was an explosion."

"Oh." Dat walked down, and sat, and bounced, just a little. And poked with one finger. "Could be just a little fuller."

"No, Dat. Don't you have anything else to do?"

"Just trying to make his houris irresistible."

"We already are."

Chantal stepped over, bent, and snatched the indjinn. "Come on, busy body, I am going to make cocoa."

Dat squeaked.

Fair Morn was stretched out flat, forearms curled around, face resting on one hand. Messenger looked up. She was sitting in the small of Fair Morn's back massaging Fair Morn's shoulder and neck muscles. "With marshmallows."

Chicken jumped to her feet. "Nay. Whip'd cream. We do some have yet in goop can."

"Ran out of victims, huh?" Smoke smiled at her.

"Piffle," commented Chicken, following Chantal toward the kitchen.

Grandeville. River View Hospital.

"Quite amazing, you know."

Raj leaned back in his chair· and smiled across

the small table at her.

Kartz smiled back.

They were sitting in the Doctor's Lounge, having just finished lunch.

She was dressed in whites and looking very Doctor. The white of the material made the jet black of her hair all that more startling. Raj was dressed in his usual rumpled clothes.

"Yes, Doctor," she said. She had been practicing saying that word, yes.

Raj laughed. "I was referring to you."

Kartz shook her head. "Nowp."

"Absolutely. You are the most amazing person that I have ever met." He stood. "Shall we? We have patients to see."

Kartz stood, slipped around the table and kissed his cheek. "Yes, Doctor."

They headed out of the room and down the hallway.

Bahn Duhr Tohr. The Quarters of the Royal Advisors.

Raft and Reep shimmered into the room.

Their entrance brought Ripple snarling to her feet. She had been in the process of having her blouse snuck off by Hanred as she sprawled across his lap.

It wasn't much of a sneak as she was, as always, a willing participant in that game. She was not happy at the interruption.

Ripple waved on her blouse, glowering at Raft,

and said very gently to the slight figure with the great staring dark eyes, "What did you find?"

Reep nodded at Hanred, who smiled at her. Then she touched Ripple lightly on the arm.

"I think that we shall have to ask The Chosen One for help."

Ripple dropped into a chair at the large table, ordered something to drink, and cups, and poured. Everyone joined her at the table.

"What did you find?" she asked.

"Little," breathed the soft shadows. "Much. Enveloping white magic took Ranna. And left no trace to follow. The one trace went nowhere."

"Hum," said Ripple.

"Hayou, Hanred." Raft leaned against him, pushing her chair against his.

"Hayou, Raft." He threw a comradely arm over her shoulders.

"Husband," cautioned Ripple, frowning at Raft.

"I was not," pouted Raft, now sitting across the table from Hanred. His arm dropped into the empty space.

"Why?" asked Ripple, looking at Reep.

She shrugged. "His urh-witch wears a white magic ring gifted by Ranna.

"White magic ring?" hissed Ripple. "Gifted by Ranna?"

"Yessssssssssss."

"Shall we come?"

"No need." Reep faded away.

Ripple crooked one finger, yanking Raft back in. "You stay. And tell me everything that you two did."

Hanred filled their cups. And sat and listened attentively.

Kantor's Spot. An Ice World.

Reaching out with a long white wand, he hooked the blouse further down. "As well formed as I always imaged."

He poked at an irregular grey green splotch. "The clatka beast must think so also. Did you enjoy that? All those tiny teeth and that ever so rasping tongue?"

The chair slid back until he had sufficient space to hitch himself into a standing position.

"Have to go. Pook sent a message. Nosy visiters poking around. I left no trace."

He jerked across the room and lurched through the opening door, saying back over his shoulder, "I left not a trace."

Grandeville. Tinker's Place.

R-Bar, Ran, and Sha'gar sprawled comfortably.

On him.

Him was on the floor.

On the bottom.

Sha'gar had first started it. On the couch. But somehow, as things usually went, everyone wound up on the floor, Tinker on the bottom.

"Hum, hum, hum," whispered nothing at all.

"Come in," said R-Bar, tickling some Tinker ribs.

"We were not," stated Sha'gar gently, watching Reep shimmer in. "Hayou, Mother."

Ran nodded. And tickled him behind a knee.

"Knock it off," he growled, pinching someone.

"Hum," observed Reep.

Messenger bounced into the room and stopped and stared at them. "Gosh! What is he doing to you? All?"

"Nuthin," grumbled Tinker.

Messenger beamed at Reep. "Want some cocoa? We made just lots and lots."

"Off, off, off."

R-Bar, Ran, and Sha'gar released him and stood.

Tinker sat up. "You look tired."

Reep nodded. "Going home. Sleep." She kissed R-Bar on the forehead. "Your ward works very well." And disappeared.

Chantal walked in carrying a tray with two pots of cocoa. Messenger filled the cups.

Chantal smiled at him. "Pretty gross behavior, Simba Leader."

"Huh?" He stood.

"Three at a time."

"Don't start," he growled, taking a cup, sitting in his chair, holding out the empty cup. "Please."

"Wonder what she was doing?" said R-Bar,

taking a sip from her cup.

"I am not supposed to ask," answered Chantal as she filled his cup and watched Sha'gar stuffing her shirt back into her trousers.

"Reep," said R-Bar.

"Oh." Chantal dropped a marshmallow into Tinker's cup and winked at him.

Kantor's Spot. An Ice World.

He lurched back into the room. Over to the couch like device. And beckoned a chair over, and sat, facing her.

"Have a pleasant night?" He ordered the clatka beast off and allowed her to sit up.

Angry dark eyes glared at him. Patches of her clothes were missing, places where the beast had been busy.

Food appeared. And a food server to feed her.

He nodded at her as she chewed. "Have to keep your strength up." Leaning back, he fingered a ring on his other hand, on his other misshapen, badly warped hand. Something had fused that hand into mostly a lump. Only the thumb and forefinger were free. The ring glistened bronze blue. On his thumb.

The chair slid forward until his knees touched her knees. He leaned, reached with the good hand and snapped off the next two buttons on her blouse.

"What is this that dangles so tantalizingly erotic here?" He carefully tugged at the cording, pulling carefully, pulling the object from her blouse.

"Orange? Orange magic? What are you doing with orange magic?" He stared at the stonecast orange blush on her pale skin.

"Strange strange for one of your clan. So conservative. So black."

He released the orange, jerking his hand away. It fell and hung outside her blouse.

"Wouldn't want to spell burn ourselves now, would we?"

Grandeville. Tinker's Place.

It was mid-morning.

He could tell from the position of the strip of light on the ceiling. And the numerals on the face of the alarm clock.

She gently stroked a tickle touch finger across his stomach, leaned over and kissed the center of his chest. And murmured softly, softly, "Mate'mer, you taste pleasant salt mate male nice."

"Huh?" Then he laughed. "You don't taste too bad yourself."

She twisted the ornate ring on one of her fingers so that the jewel was on the palm side of her hand and tapped him on the forehead with it. Gently. She smiled soft smile at him. "Mine," she whispered. "Our's." And bent over until she rested on him, head twisted around to look into his face.

"Do you know," he asked. "That you are a very

warm person?"

"Your's."

"Body heat." He gently tickled. "You are much warmer than any of the others, even Fair Morn."

"Hum." She twisted and stretched along his side. "I will ask Aunt Ramp."

"What?"

"Magician."

He cleared his throat. "Ahhhhh, I don't think so."

"What?"

"Ummmmmm. Sa'ar is a magician."

She breathed warm into the junction of his neck and shoulder. "It is told that the Purple Ones are smoothly soft pleasing. True?"

"Ummmmmmmmm, yes."

Her fingers tickled his ribs on the far side of his chest. "Erotic warm pleasant?"

"I suppose." He kissed her forehead. "But not as warm."

"Hum, hum, hum."

"Soooo, I do not think that it has anything to do with being anything in particular. Ummmm, in the genetic sense, that is." He decided not to mention The Tark demons.

Bahn Duhr Tohr. The Quarters of the Royal Advisors.

Reptar appeared and sat in one of the chairs. "I received your call."

Ripple looked up from the large open tome lying

on the table. "Ranna has been taken."

Reptar hissed. Dark swirled down and around.

"Calm, sister, calm." Ripple turned one of the thick pages and glanced down, then up.

"Who?" grumbled Reptar.

"Know not. Reep went to ask The Chosen One for assistance."

"Um." Reptar stood. She felt that witches should handle their own business. But Ripple was the clan head so her decision was binding.

Hanred walked from the other room clenching two large tomes in his arms. "Make room, Dark Hearts."

The pair stepped away from the table. He dropped the books. Dust eddied in grey waves from them.

"Powerful ugly lives in these ancient collections." He reached around and slid one hand around Ripple's waist, leaving a dusty streak.

"Hum, hum," she murmured.

"Dusky Delight, I would prefer not being in the room when you open this pair of arcane horrible. I do not think that it would be safe for a mere Illusionist such as I."

Reptar touched a careful finger to one book cover. "Sister?"

"You will help," snapped Ripple. "He will go shopping." She handed Hanred a list. "Clever mate, we will require these items. Bang loudly and wait until I, only I, open that door."

Hanred snatched the list from her hand, gave her a parting pat on the hip, and waved a jaunty goodbye as he headed out the door and into the main corridor of the castle. He was headed down and out to visit various shops and booths in the main market square where he could find the required items.

Ripple ordered the door to close and to be held tight. Then she opened the first book of the pair. "Now, sister, let us find something . . . suitable." Dark began to gather across the ceiling.

Grandeville. Tinker's Place.

She leaned over the back of the couch, the one where he was slumped and reading, and tickled one of his ears with a long goose feather. One of the geese had donated it, so to speak.

He grumbled.

"Your Messenger said to do this."

He grumbled something.

    At her.

"Not nice."

"Goes for people who jab other people in the ear with bird remains." He tried to slump deeper into the couch. And to not lose his place. Unsuccessfully.

Placing a bookmark where he thought he had been, he dropped the book on the floor, sat up, turned to check her position, and lunged.

Up and over the couch, dragging her down,

between the wall and the couch back.

"An gak!"

"What happens to feather wielding attack witch wenches."

"Your Ran is not a wench!"

"Where did that feather get to?"

The leather was floating up near the ceiling. It headed for a higher area.

"UNKIND . . . UNKIND!"

The couch started to slide away.

"Leave that couch alone."

"Ammmmm . . . tarrrr."

"Certainly ticklish."

Messenger crashed onto the couch and carefully peered over the back. "GOSH." And shot him. Right between the shoulder blades.

"Hey!"

Leaping away, she hurtled through the dining room and into the kitchen where some of the others were doing things. "Quick, more ice water."

She quickly filled her small water pistol. And headed down the hallway.

As she slipped stealthily into the living room, Messenger saw the victim walk from behind the couch, stuffing her blouse back into her trousers.

He stood and glared at them from behind the couch. "And exactly what is going on this time?"

Messenger stuck her tongue out at him. "Our sister Ran was being pulled asunder by a monster so I shot that body creep fiend." She smiled at him. "That is you, the body creep fiend."

"I think that we need a tredmill, some way for you guys to work off excess energy."

"May I enter," asked soft dark shadow.

"Yessssssss," said Ran.

Reep stood there. She eyed Ran's clothes. "Hum, hum, hum." She looked at Tinker.

Sha'gar slipped into the room and stood quiet proper. "Hayou, Mother."

"Tall daughter." Reep looked back at Tinker. "She looks happy well."

R-Bar walked in from the dining room. "Of course."

"We must talk."

R-Bar nodded. She and Reep went to R-Bar's bedroom.

Sha'gar stepped over to Tinker as he came from behind the couch. "Mother wants help. For something dangerous. I could feel it."

"Oh, my." Messenger looked at her. Something flickered around Sha'gar.

"Calm down," said Tinker.

Ran edged closer.

"You too," he grumbled, throwing an arm around each waist and tugging them against his sides.

"We will just have to wait and see. Then we can say no." He nudged them in the general direction of the kitchen. "Let's go get a cup of coffee." And nodded at

Messenger. "You too, squirt."

She shot him.

"Hey!"

"I am taller than R-Bar," stated Messenger. "Let's make cocoa." She stepped over, patted the wet splotch on his stomach. "What you get."

"You guys are really making me worry, you know that?"

They headed for the kitchen. And met Smoke and Fair Morn making sandwiches.

"We felt hungry," explained Smoke.

"Right," said Tinker. "What are we having?"

"Grilled cheese," said Fair Morn.

"With onions," added Chantal, entering from the back door carrying a bowl full.

"Picnic time," announced Messenger as she hurryed off to arrange plates and things on the floor in the living room.

"Most wonderful an idea. Think you not, Our Prince?" Chicken joined them, carrying a gallon of red wine up from the storage area below the kitchen.

"You non-workers wanna get out of the way," grumbled Chantal at Tinker, Ran, and Sha'gar, and Chicken.

They headed for the living room.

Bahn Duhr Tohr. The Quarters of the Royal Advisors.

Hanred banged on the outer door. Standing in the hall, arms filled with packages, he banged on the outer door. With one boot tip.

And waited. And eyed one of the Queen's Attendants as she passed by.

He smiled. She smiled back.

Then he turned and booted the door again.

It opened, did that door. Slowly it opened.

Vague shadows peered out through a narrow of narrow spaces, eyes fluxing yellow. "Enter, tasty man."

"Pahn Tahn Dahn delivery, as ordered. Witch Ripple in?"

The door slammed shut.

He heard a soft thump from the other side. Then the door flew open. Green fumes billowed out and up towards the high ceiling of the hallway.

Ripple leaned out through the opening. "Clever Mate. Set all that on the back table."

Hanred nodded. But didn't move. "Step out here, Midnight Delight."

She turned and popped back inside. "Sister, hold this door." And spun and stepped outside. "Husband?"

"Turn around."

She did.

Hanred smiled. "Let's go inside."

The air in the room was hazy. Streamers of green blue orange drifted on soft currents. Just over the tops of their heads thick layers of green billowed gently back and forth.

Hanred dumped his burdens on the table and swung an arm around her. "Sounds like Ripple, looks like Ripple." He grinned. "Feels like Ripple."

"Sneak," she purred.

"Hum, hum," murmured Reptar.

"Are you Dark Hearts sure that you should be doing whatever it is that you are doing?"

He looked carefully around the room and at them. Their clothes were splash marked in a number of colors. And as far as he could tell so were the walls and the floor. He suspected that it was true of the ceiling as well.

"Of course."

"What answered the door?"

"Spell wierk."

"Something new?"

"Not nice," said Reptar.

"Husband, go teach the Young Royals some clever thing or things. When we finish I will come there."

He wrapped his arms around her and peered into those dark dark eyes. "Careful, Please?"

She nodded. One quick nod. "Go away."

He stepped back and smiled at her. "You will require several baths." And spun and hurried out into the hall.

The door banged shut.

Ripple spun and handed Reptar some of the things from one of the bags. "Start step two."

Kantor's Spot. An Ice World.

He hitched into the room and flew into a chair. And ordered the chair over to the long furniture thing. He flailed at the clatka beast with a long bronze wand.

"Get off, get off!"

He leaned and stared at the open eyes, his chair sliding closer. "You are not dead. Yet."

Her eyes rolled in his direction. Dark eyes surrounded by darkening flesh. Deep lines etched into her face.

He nodded, mostly to himself. "Slowly draining away. Then what?" He nodded again, this time to her. "We will have to do something special."

One hand jerked up, beckoning the beast over. "Get her up." He waved food in. "Feed her." His chair slid toward the door. "And do not do anything else."

Grandeville. Tinker's place.

The picnic was getting very relaxed.

Chicken had fetched another jug.

They were sitting and sprawling in a loose circle on the floor.

He was leaning back against one of the couches.

Ran was leaning against his side. His free arm was around her waist. The other hand held a mostly eaten sandwich.

She beckoned another sandwich over. Grilled cheese sandwiches were exotic cuisine to her.

Relaxation and comfort surged through them in soft waves. All left R-Bar in her own private space. She was still in her room with Reep.

Fair Morn relocated and sprawled by his free side. And enticed one of the cats over with a piece of grilled cheese.

"Teach them bad habits," said Tinker.

"Too late." Smoke fed the black male a piece of her sandwich.

He looked around the room and smiled at them. "It is true, you know."

"Spoiled cats?" Messenger slipped the small white female a piece of bread.

"Males are attracted to healthy young females."

Chantal nudged Sha'gar. "That's you, Silk." And refilled her glass. "Of course, he might be referring to the cats."

Chicken nodded. "Pears so, Me'Lord. Thee do fair fill thy house." And laughed. "Protesting most loud as one and all t'were seduced mightily."

"Another psychological principle twisted beyond all recognition," he muttered. "Be a lot quieter if they weren't all so healthy," he grumbled, mostly to himself.

"Any special reason for that sage comment?" asked Chantal. "Or are you just trying to justify a floor full of babes."

"Just something that I remembered. Thought that it sorta explains this mob." He handed his glass to Chicken. "As long as we are already on the floor. Fill it, please?"

"Can not count your Dat, Amtar." Ran twitched

another of her shirt buttons open.

"Huh?"

"The indjinn is eons old."

"Certainly well preserved." He grinned at the tiny figure standing with one arm thrown over the back of the grey female cat.

"We do not age," stated Dat. "We just are. Always. But we are very healthy."

R-Bar and Reep joined them.

"We will discuss it in the morning," R-Bar nodded at her sister. "Come for breakfast? Please?"

Reep looked at the group. And nodded. And went home. In a small puff of black.

R-Bar found an open spot and sat. And grabbed a just filled glass and a sandwich from the tray. And looked over at Ran as she popped another button open. "Hum, hum, hum."

Ran tugged one corner of his shirt loose. "He likes us because we are young and healthy."

Dat walked over to R-Bar and looked up. "And not too bad looking either. For non-indjinns."

"What did Reep want?" he asked.

"Talk in the morning," mumbled R-Bar around her sandwich.

Later in the day. Next Day.

She stepped into the living room and glared at him. Until he looked up from the book that he was reading. He was taking a break from editing.

"Yes?"

"He needs killing," she hissed.

"Oh, goody, goody." He smiled into her glower. "Who? He?"

She gurgled, deep in her throat she gurgled.

He nodded. "Nice sound."

Messenger jabbed him in the side. "You are not being nice."

"Uuuump!" He batted at Messenger's finger, her still threatening finger. "Knock it off." And indicated R-Bar. "She is not making a whole lot of sense, or haven't you been paying attention?"

"Parquor the White," snapped R-Bar.

"Him?" asked Tinker.

"Oh, My Gosh." Messenger looked at the white ring on her finger.

"Yesssssssssssssss," replied R-Bar.

"How come, short and agitated?"

She leaned forward. "I am not short."

He reached out and toppled her into his lap. "One out of two ain't too bad," he sang.

"Zwar witch Trozindar heard from a Tanto Mage. She told her sister, Surlindar, who sent a message to Ripple who sent one to me. He grabbed Ranna."

"Parquor?"

"Yessssss. The White."

"Anyone know how to find this guy?"

"Hum."

"Knew it! We are staying home!"

"Din do kaktar," she suggested.

Sha'gar gasped. "Coarse coarse." She was sitting on his other side, R-Bar's legs sprawled across her lap.

"He deserves it," explained R-Bar, growling at Tinker.

"Hum," observed Sha'gar.

The small figure bounced and jumped into R-Bar's lap. "Where are we going?"

"No where," grumbled Tinker.

"I am coming. Also."

"Ahhhhh, O.K." said Tinker. "But you stay in the ring as we agreed."

"Gimble, gimble," grumbled Dat.

"Or stay home."

She looked up at him. "Do you know what tomorrow is?"

"Nope."

"Mine. I am large." She smiled. "For two days. Kickle, kickle, kickle."

"That's new."

"What, Great Master?"

"I never heard you go kickle, kickle, kickle before."

"It is a gay, infectious laugh."

"Oh?"

Dat nodded. "All indjinns have gay, infectious laughter."

He nodded. "When they laugh."

"Yes." She frowned. "I just did not have much to

laugh about before."

"Ohhhhhhhhhhh," sighed Messenger.

Dat nodded at her. "Great Masters are a terrible burden." And grinned up at Tinker. "Except for you. And your understanding houris." She crawled up his shirt to his shoulder and stepped over and onto Sha'gar's shoulder.

Dat leaned forward and peered down. "Does he drool when he gets your blouse off?"

"Hum," replied Sha'gar.

"Quiet!" demanded Tinker.

"Just curious," mumbled Dat.

Chantal strolled into the room, stopped, and stared at them, smiling broadly. "Not bad, Cowboy. You are covered with three and one percent beautiful babes."

"Bouzel bak bak," snapped Dat, not liking the one percent part of Chantal's observation.

"What's your problem, dinky?" Chantal glared at the indjinn.

Tinker managed to slump while still retaining R-Bar on his lap.

"He told me to be quiet," muttered Dat.

"Brute," suggested Chantal.

Tinker sighed. He knew it was starting again. Another one of those conversations.

"Just because I asked an innocent question," added Dat.

"What?"

"Never mind," he grumbled. And off they go, he thought to himself.

"I just wanted to know whether he drooled when he got her blouse off."

"Forget it," mumbled he, still trying to interrupt the conversation, such as it was.

"Who's blouse?" asked Chantal.

"Sha'gar's," replied Dat.

"No!" stated he.

"Certainly doesn't drool on me." Messenger nudged R-Bar. "You?"

"No!" restated he.

"No," said R-Bar.

"Change the subject," he suggested.

"Lots to drool about," observed Dat.

"You are gonna loss two days bigness," growled he.

Dat leaped to the bookshelf and disappeared into her ring.

Chantal began to unbutton her shirt,

He frowned at her. "What are you doing?"

"Thought that we could run a little scientific experiment, Dr. Pavlov. See whether your salivary glands have been conditioned instead of us dogs, so to speak."

"HA! Ha! Ha! Ha! Stop!" He nudged R-Bar. "Get up."

"Nope."

"Da Tovarishch," snapped Chantal as she

dropped into a chair, grinning at him. "Or something like that. Dribble, dribble, dribble."

"Witch little," stated he, "wants us to go out there and kill Parquor the White."

"WHAT?" Chantal snapped upright.

"He grabbed Ranna," explained R-Bar. Taking one of the Faan clan was not to be allowed by anyone.

"Oh." Chantal leaned back in her chair. "That all? Send Ripple."

"Can't go," hissed R-Bar.

"Why not?"

"Sook."

"Huh?" asked Tinker.

"A cousin," replied Sha'gar.

"Oh my gosh," gasped Messenger.

"Certainly fast," suggested Chantal. "And fecund."

"What?" he asked.

"John," laughed Chantal. "Sometimes you are really slow. Ripple is having another daughter and motherhood takes precedence over killing bad guys."

"We do not require assistance," grumbled R-Bar.

"Another daughter?"

"Sook." R-Bar nodded. "Wonder where she got that name from?"

He slumped, just a little more. "Does that mean that we are going to have another one hanging around here, causing trouble?"

Chantal laughed. "Relax Cowboy. What's one

more witch?"

"Or magician," added Sha'gar.

"Hum," said R-Bar.

"She could be," added Sha'gar.

"Hum," said R-Bar.

"She could be," restated Sha'gar.

"What if it is a boy?" asked Tinker.

"Could happen." R-Bar nodded at him. Her eyes unfocused as she looked elsewhere.

He poked her. "Forget it. Whatever it is."

She poked him back. "Shem is the only Faan male in his generation name group. And he took Tajaar."

"So?"

"Another male could cross-tie to another clan." R-Bar smiled. The air crackled. "Maybe with the Crusjur."

Sha'gar jerked away. "Aunt! Self!" Loud crackling bounced from the ceiling.

He tried to sit up. "HOLD IT!" And tumbled R-Bar to the floor. "Hold it!" And sat up. "Who, or what are Cursjur?"

"Pakak kak," spit Sha'gar.

R-Bar hissed at her. "All the better reason," she snapped, sitting up.

"Well," he stated. "They aren't coming here. They are not on the A-list, the list you guys put on the ban thingee."

"Hafta change it." R-Bar pushed into the space

between Tinker and Sha'gar.

"Aren't you just jumping the gun, a little?"

"Maybe."

"You haven't explained Crusjur."

"Twisted shadow magic users," grumbled Sha'gar. "They ate Patander the Grey Mda warlock and his sister witches."

"Cannibals?" Tinker stared at R-Bar.

"Sucked them inside out," whispered Sha'gar. "And no one saw them. The Grey Mda were two layer many protected."

"Child tell tales," stated R-Bar firmly.

"Um do tik tik," suggested Sha'gar under her breath.

R-Bar growled at her.

Tinker grabbed R-Bar. "O.K., O.K., enough discussion, such as it is, about whatever they are, or might be. New subject. What's for dinner?"

"SANDWICHES," called Fair Morn, from the kitchen. "BEAT YOU TO IT."

They stood and headed for the dining room table.

"Me too," called a small voice from the book case. Chantal stepped over and let Dat leap onto her shoulder.

"Just be quiet," cautioned Chantal. "No conversations about anatomy or reproduction."

"Those are favorite indjinn topics."

Chantal moved around to her chair and sat.

"Maybe you ought to become a sports fan."

Everyone else filtered in and joined the bunch for sandwiches.

Halfway through the meal, Dat asked loudly, "Didn't anyone make cocoa?"

Chicken nodded. "We will Our Verra Own Self fetch it here." She did

Dat walked down to Chicken's place and dipped her cup in the pot. "Thank you, Pretty Princess."

"Most welcome, Lovely Dat."

Dat leaned against the pot and looked up as she sipped from her cup. "What do you think of Parlin as a girl's name?"

"Most strange."

"Zindir?"

"Also."

"Kakenpa?"

"Odd."

"Je'leel?"

"Say again."

"Je'leel."

"Fair exotic."

"You like it?"

Chicken frowned at the indjinn, then nodded. "Indeed."

Dat spun around and looked up at Tinker. "Do you like it?"

"Sure. Cocoa is pretty good stuff. OUCH!"

Chicken had kicked his ankle.

He nodded at Dat. "Right. Nice name." And glared at Chicken.

Dat hurried down the table and reclaimed her perch on Chantal's shoulder. "I like it also."

"Cocoa?"

"Je'leel."

"Friend of your's?"

"Nooooooo. Just something that I wanted to know." Dat leaned close to Chantal's ear. "I am big tomorrow."

"We know."

"For two days."

"That too."

Tinker stood. "Work to do. I'll be upstairs."

And they all scattered.

As they always did.

Kantor's Spot. An Ice World.

"Get off, get off."

He glared from the doorway and watched the clatka beast slip to the floor.

"Bring her into this room."

Taloned paws hooked into the jet black hair and dragged the limp form thumping to the floor and over to the doorway and into the next room. The beast left its burden in the central spot and cringed next to the wall.

He lurched close and nudged her with one toe.

Dark eyes glared up at him.

"Good. Still alive." He prodded her with the end

of his staff. "Lovely, just lovely. In spite of everything."

He smiled down at her. "Do you enjoy what the beast is doing? You must. You are still sane."

Slowly he indicated the walls of the room. Covered with mirrors. "A special place." And slowly settled to the floor until he could rest one hand on her, palm slowly sliding back and forth over soft velvet skin.

"I have heard that something called a Tinker is coming to fetch you away, my lovely witch. Never heard of anything like that before." Caressing fingers tightened. "Does it want your body also?"

His head snapped around. "Help me up. Then feed her. She is the bait for this Tinker thing. Whatever it is, you can eat it. After it dies."

As the beast hauled him upright, he poked her with a toe. "If you survive, I think that I will take you to my bed." He lurched for the doorway, snarling at the beast, "Do not touch her."

Grandeville. Tinker's Place.

The bedroom door banged open.

And bounced from the wall.

It was early morning.

"Carpenters are here." Smoke leaned in through the opening and smiled at them. "Just thought that you ought to know. In case you hear the banging, etc."

She backed away, pulling the door closed.

He rolled onto his side. "Why are there carpenters here ready to begin banging, etc.?"

"Your Smoke is having things added to your house."

"Uh huh?"

"Yes."

He reached over and gave her a little tickle. "Do you know what sorts of things?"

"Yes." Ran nodded. And wiggled. She tickled him back.

"Well, Witch Number Two, you gonna tell me? Or are you guys up to something? Again?"

"Yes." She hitched just a little closer.

"Well?"

"Your Chantal wanted a small, a smaller, more cosy living room, just for us. Not for visitors."

"Cosy living room?"

Ran kissed him. "It is what she called it."

He kissed her back. "And?"

Her hand slid gently up and down his ribs. "Very nice." She smiled. "Your Smoke said that it was just for you." And laughed.

"Yes?"

"And for us." She tugged him over.

Later Morning.

Steam billowed in soft waves through the room. The shower was going full tilt.

Dat finished rinsing her hair under one of the many nozzles and smiled at him as the other stepped close.

"Great Master, I am large again. For two days. Would you like to play with my body before breakfast?"

"I noticed, Dat," he mumbled. "No."

"Smoke has an army of men terrorizing the structure." She wrapped her arms around his chest and leaned against his back. And looked over his shoulder at Ran. "Is bouncing around in the grass filler in the barn building fun?"

"I do not know." Ran headed for the tub room to towel herself dry.

"Let go, Dat."

She did and followed him into the tub room.

Ran handed him a large towel so he could dry his hair. He did. And nodded. "O.K., Dat, your turn." He dried her hair.

Dragging on heavy white robes, they headed for breakfast.

The rest were already eating.

Chicken served the latecomers.

Ran handed the ornate ring to Messenger who slipped it over her thumb and took another piece of toast.

"Where's the Cat?" Tinker dropped into his chair and reached for his coffee cup, just filled by Chicken.

"Directing great hordes of artisans, My Lord." She shoved a filled plate at him, then another at Ran.

"Getting a new living room, Cowboy." Chantal poked Messenger who shoved one of the coffee pots over and nodded at him.

Someone kissed the top of his head and draped her arms around his neck. And slipped one hand inside his robe. "Just for you."

"Your idea?"

"Nope. Chantal's."

Dat took some breakfast. Just to be polite. And smiled down the table at Tinker. She was sitting next to Chantal.

Smoke gave him a friendly pinch and headed back outside.

"What are all the grins for?"

"Your houris are very, very nice." Dat smiled. "Very, very nice."

"Right." He shoved his cup toward Chicken, who filled it. "I always thought so." He looked around the table. "So what else is going on?"

Messenger bounced upright. "We are going to town and buy just lots and lots of flowers."

"Oh?"

"I am going also," added Dat. She stood. "As soon as you get properly dressed, Great Master."

He shoved his chair back. "I am going too?"

"Yep." Messenger bounded from her chair and headed for the back door. "We are adding to the rear flower beds."

Chapter Thirteen.

Another?

Grandeville. The Burger And Bowl.
It was the third game.
The third game in the series of three.
The losers of game two had just paid the waitress for the liquid refreshments and were watching the winners of game two take their turns, starting game three. The losers each held a large pitcher from which they took an occasional sip. The third pitcher was for the winners.
"She look taller to you?" Green took a thoughtful sip. In his hand the pitcher didn't look all that big.
"Sure does." Red nodded, took a sip from his pitcher. The one he held didn't look all that big in his hand either.
"Used to be tall to just about here, right by this button." Green tapped the appropriate button on his shirt. It was right in the center of his sternum. "Now the top of her head comes to right about to the tip of my nose."
He took another sip and admired one of their

opponents. "I thought that people stopped growing when they grew up."

"Beats me," said Red. "Sorta looks different, ummm, here and there."

"Sure does," agreed Green. "She kinna fills her shirt differently."

"Did you ask her?"

"Partner, questions like that can get you shot, for sure, for sure."

Red nodded. "Meant being taller, not, um, the rest."

Their opponents came over to where they sat. The slightly shorter of the pair patted Red on the stomach.

"Your turn. The full pitcher our's?"

"Sure, babe." Red's eyes jumped from one to the other. Then he took a sip, set his pitcher down, and headed for the appropriate lane. It was their turn to bowl. "Come on, Partner. We have a game to win." He ambled over and grabbed his bowling ball.

The slightly taller turned to her friend. "How come your moose was staring at our chests?"

Sandy poured two glasses full. "Beats me. But it was definitely a cop look, not the usual lech type of thing."

Janine laughed "Well, I didn't steal them from anyone. Think that he wants to do a body search? Make sure everything is firmly attached?"

"Cool it, Streak," snapped Sandy. "Or I will cut

off your liquid refreshment."

"O.K. Shall we let them win this game?"

"Sure." Sandy filled their glasses. "Better. Or they might find some other sport. One that isn't co-ed."

Janine emptied her glass. "Our turn. I'll shave it close." She smiled up at Green as he walked past. "Order us some food. Or are you two trying to get us too drunk to shoot straight?"

The pair shoved past the two gigantic men and headed for their bowling lanes.

Red nodded at Green. "She definitely grew. Taller. And, ummmm."

Green grabbed his pitcher. "Certainly ummmm all right. Think we will win this game?"

"Might. If we get lucky."

Grandeville, Tinker's Place.

"Certainly got lots and lots of flowers all right."

Tinker stood and stretched. They had worked through the day and were fast approaching dinner time.

Everyone had worked on the project. Except Smoke. She was overseeing the building reconstruction activities. Messenger had talked with and planned the new arrangements with Tiny Rosebud, the Garden Gnome emissary, who visited every once in awhile.

Messenger directed the flowerbed overhaul. She sat back and beamed at him. "It will be really really neato."

"I need to soak in the hot tub." Tinker arched his

back and slowly twisted.

"We can finish tomorrow." Messenger stood and began to water everything.

People scattered.

Mainly for the house.

"Ahhhhhhhh," sighed Tinker as the warm water lapped up around his neck.

Dat dropped into the tub and slipped up to him. "This is a wonderous device, Great Master. When you are big."

"Yep."

"Drive me into panting ecstasy."

He laughed. "Not sure that I can do that."

Dat leaned against him. "You could try."

He looked into those strange purple eyes. "I came here to try and loosen up."

She slipped both arms around his neck and then gently raked her claws down his ribs. And smiled.

"What?"

Her lips brushed his. "Your houris told me." She settled just a little. Her arms tightened.

"Careful," he gasped. "I don't want any broken ribs."

Chantal joined Messenger as she sat on the edge of the swimming pool and kicked her feet in the water. "That indjinn is certainly forward."

Messenger giggled.

"I wasn't referring to her anatomy," grumbled Chantal.

"She only has two days."

Dat lurched and smiled.

"What?"

"I think that Je'leel is a beautiful name for a daughter."

"I suppose."

"Indjinns have beautiful offpring."

"I suppose."

"Won't have claws."

He kissed her gently. "What are you talking about?"

"A daughter, Great Master."

"Sedeem?"

"Je'leel."

"What?"

She kissed him. "OOOOOK!" Blue smoke puffed from her nostrils.

"What's going on?"

"I have to leave."

He was by himself. Just gentle waves sloshing back and forth in the tub.

But not for long.

Sha'gar slipped into the hot tub and sank up to her chin, smiling a soft half-smile at him. "Mate'mer?"

"Beats me."

"That Dat creature has heart given."

"What?"

"Not servant. Nor ring gift." She half closed her eyes. "In never never told is there such a mention. When we are one mind I see no such skill power. From where does it come?"

"What?"

"Your power."

"I don't have any."

"Hum, hum, hum." She slipped closer and said ever so softly. "You took her. And lived."

He sighed and stared at the water. "We owe her our lives. She wanted to. Debt payment, of a sort." He grumbled at her, "As bad as the Vander."

Sha'gar sank just a little deeper, water almost touching her nose, eyes watching. Dark pools stared at him, red spots flickered deep down inside.

Chantal and Messenger dropped in. Sha'gar stood, clearing her face from the sudden waves.

"Where's Dat, Cowboy?"

"Dun know."

"Gosh." Messenger looked at Sha'gar. Sha'gar shrugged.

Kantor's Spot. An Ice World.

He dropped heavily into the large chair, stared down at her lying on her back, on the floor.

"Something killed Pook. Perhaps, just perhaps, we should relocate." He nodded at her, to himself. "You are still alive. I am not done with you. Yet."

Dark bottomless black eyes watched him. And deep deep down far inside, he saw the flicker.

He smiled. "Now," he said, as if speaking to a child, "where did your blouse go?" One sandaled foot reached out and pushed, not too gently. "Very nice. Your clan certainly is noted for their beauty."

His foot slowly slid back and forth. "Yesssssss, very nice, Even now."

In a more or less controlled collapse, he slumped from the chair and thumped to the floor next to her. And ran his left hand over soft flesh.

"Ahhhhhhh. Just as I always thought."

Her eyes tightened.

"Just very soft silk pleasant." He sighed. His head snapped up as he gestured toward a dark corner of the room. "Drag her into the tartak room. And do not do anything else. She is mine, This body is mine."

Resting the lump shape right hand on her stomach, he shoved and managed to heave himself upright.

Her breath gasped from her mouth.

"And feed her. Much! Her ribs are starting to show."

Weaving his usual tortuous way toward the doorway, he laughed. "I shall find a comfortable spot for us. Far from here. You are too nice to waste."

He lurched through.

The door slammed shut.

The clatka beast watched, bent over, and took a

taste. Then it slowly dragged her into the ordered chamber.

Grandeville. Tinker's Place.

"So, it is decided?"

He looked around the living room and saw in each face, agreement.

They were going.

Out there.

Again.

He nodded at Reep. "Looks like we are going. We will take a couple of days to put our gear together. And rest a bunch. So, how does Thursday sound?"

Reep nodded. And said soft shadow soft, "A great debt."

"Umm, ummm. Let's worry about debt afterwards." He wasn't really interested in debts, especially after the problem he had previously had with the Vander magicians. And now Dat. Every time someone mentioned debt, he winced.

R-Bar poked Reep on the shoulder, gently, and cautioned, gently, "Sister."

Reep nodded. She faded away in a puff of soft dark.

"Strange strange," said Sha'gar softly, mostly to herself. She was beginning to wonder about her mother's behavior.

"Hum," said Ran.

Sha'gar gasped.

"Shhhhh," hissed R-Bar at Ran.

Chantal dropped onto his lap.

"OOOOOOOOOOF!" he grunted.

Chantal threw an arm around his neck. "For such a grumbly butt, you are just an old pussy cat, John." She kissed his forehead. "And before you start, yes, we will be careful, etc., etc., etc."

"Just us. Right?"

"And Reep," added R-Bar, leaning against the back of his chair, running a hand through his hair. "To guide us."

"And me," called a small voice as the tiny figure clambered up his pant leg and then across Chantal.

"Of course," said Chantal.

"All right," he grumbled. "You also. Where have you been?"

"Big?" asked Dat, ignoring his question.

"Ummm."

"Big," she demanded.

"Getting kinna bossy."

"Sure," said Chantal, wacking Dat not too lightly on top of the head.

The indjinn was standing with one hand shoved through the gap between two buttons on Chantal's shirt.

"Stop all that messing around!"

Dat jerked her hand out. "Yum, yum, yum."

The loud sigh was Tinker.

"Little pest," grumbled Chantal.

"Pookle, pookle, pookle," replied Dat.

Tinker grabbed her.

Dat squeeked.

"What'sa matta, Cowboy? Jealous?" Chantal winked at Dat.

"Bug nuts," he murmured as he dropped Dat back into Chantal's lap.

She banged into the room.

From somewhere. In angry black.

Snarling and grumbling.

"What pak tak dir dir created that kak tak ward set?"

Dark stuff swirled around and across the ceiling. And rumbled mumbled down at them.

Hanred smiled at Tinker. "Any of that coffee stuff around?"

Messenger hurried off. "I'll get it. And two more cups."

Chantal joined her in the kitchen. And poured some golden liquid into a tall cup for Ripple. "I think that she requires a little Irish in her coffee."

R-Bar looked at her sister and grumbled, "I did."

"Hum," said Ripple. "Might have realized. It has a certain touch." She dropped into Hanred's lap. He had taken one of the larger overstuffed chairs.

"We shall make some adjustments," stated Ripple, taking her cup from Chantal as Messenger handed another to Hanred.

Hanred nodded thanks. And quickly counted everyone as they scrambled into the living room. And looked a question at Tinker.

Tinker smiled. "R-Bar can explain."

Reep shimmered into the room, in front of where her sister slumped across her mate's lap and looked at Ripple. "I felt you arrive."

Ripple nodded and took another sip. The air overhead cleared.

"Hum," said Reep.

"Muchly bothered," whispered Ran to Sha'gar.

"Aunt is very rangle," whispered back Sha'gar.

Ripple looked from Sha'gar to Reep and back again. "Hum, hum, hum."

Reep tapped Ripple on the forehead with one fingertip. "My daughter is very happy."

"Of course," said Ripple very gently. She drained her cup and held it in Chantal's direction.

Chantal grabbed it and headed for the kitchen.

Dat was sitting on the edge of the counter, next to the stove top, swinging her legs, and smiling happily.

"Yes?" said Chantal, filling Ripple's cup, adding another dose of the Irish to it. A much large dose this time.

"I have a surprise for My Great Master." Dat stood. "Are you going to make cocoa?"

"Patience. Be right back." Chantal hurried away. And quickly returned.

"O.K. One pot of cocoa coming right up. What surprise?"

"Je'leel."

"Who? What?" She poured the milk into the pot and added sugar and cocoa powder and began to stir.

"Mother?" asked the silken voice as she faded in.

Chantal spun around and stared.

It was a young girl slightly shorter than herself. She was dressed in translucent billowing trousers and blouse.

"Hello, Chantal. I am Je'leel."

Chantal stepped sideways and half-turned. "You called Dat mother?"

Then she nodded to herself. It was obvious. The same narrow waist. The same overall development. Of course, Je'leel was much younger. She was a more junior, senior high school version of Dat.

"Of course." Je'leel smiled at her.

"Beautiful," said Dat.

"Certainly a strong resemblance all right."

"No claws," said Dat. "Or fangs. Human eyes."

Chantal checked. It was true. Je'leel had bright blue irises surrounded by white eyeball.

"He will be very happy," said Dat.

"Who?" Chantal stirred the cocoa.

Je'leel stepped next to her and watched.

Dat leaned on the pot and kicked one foot back and forth through the blue fire flickering up along the edges of the pot.

Je'leel stared and poked one finger next to Dat's foot and waggled it back and forth through the flame.

Chantal gasped.

Je'leel laughed. "It tickles."

Chantal grabbed Je'leel's hand and looked at the finger. "You didn't burn." She let go and stirred the cocoa before it did.

"Of course not," said Dat. "Is the cocoa ready yet?" She smiled. "Indjinns do not burn."

"In a moment. So who is going to be happy?"

"My Great Master," explained Dat.

"Father," added Je'leel.

Chantal stopped stirring. "WHAT?" And looked at Je'leel. "What did you say?"

"Father."

Chantal stared her. "Him? He? John?"

Je'leel frowned and looked at Dat. "Mother? Is something wrong?"

Chantal turned off the burner, grabbed a high stool, sat on it, and stared at the pair. "You had better explain."

So Dat did.

Then she smiled at her daughter. "This is houri Chantal. He has eight. They will all mother raise you the rest of the way."

Je'leel nodded and looked at Chantal, and smiled. "Hello, Mother. Shall I make more cocoa?"

"No." Chantal looked at Dat. "She better dress in something else. He is going to be shocked enough as it is."

Dat nodded. Je'leel now wore jeans and a soft corduroy shirt. And sandals.

"This should be interesting," mumbled Chantal. "We will just wait here." She reached out with her mind. *John?*

What?

How about coming to the kitchen.

O.K

And in a moment, he walked in. "What's up?" He looked at this stranger, and then at Dat sitting on the lip of the counter.

"This is Je'leel," said Dat

"Oh. Hi, Je'leel."

"Hello," said Je'leel. "Father."

"Huh?"

Chantal watched his face very carefully.

"Ummmm, what do you mean?"

Dat took another sip from her cup. "This is Our daughter, Great Master. Isn't she beautiful?"

"You?" He stared at her. "Daughter?"

"And smart also," said Dat. "Just like me."

"Are my daughter," gurgled he. "Daughter? Our Daughter?"

"Lots of indjinn," added Dat.

"Yes," agreed Je'leel.

Chantal stood and shoved the stool against Tinker. "You had better sit down, Daddie. Your face is going pale."

He did. "I, ummm, am sorta surprised." He looked at Dat. "How old?"

"Eighteen of your years," stated Je'leel.

Dat tapped her own forehead. "Much older than that, in here."

Je'leel stepped close to him. "May I hug you, Father?"

"Sure. Of course."

So she did. And he did.

"My mother is beautiful."

Tinker nodded. "I know. She keeps telling us."

"So is Chantal."

"Thanks," said Chantal. "Well?" she said to Tinker.

"What?" He blinked, looked from Je'leel to Dat and back again.

"Let's go to the living room," suggested Chantal. "Our daughter ought to meet the rest of us."

Tinker stood as Je'leel stepped back. "Right."

Chantal held out an arm. Dat scampered up and sat on Chantal's shoulder. And beamed as Je'leel and her father walked ahead of them.

"This should really be interesting," murmured Chantal.

Tinker only wobbled a little bit.

Bahn Duhr Tohr. The Quarters of the Royal Advisors.

Raft wove a many protected, many layer, three twisted, and waggled a glowing red wand in front of her sister's face.

"And how do you propose to control that kanka dit ptar qat?"

"Grossly vile ugly," snarled Reptar, backing up, referring to her sister's language.

"Indoo dik tik," snapped Raft.

"Watch your mouth, younger sister!"

"Speak tell," demanded Raft, banging something ugly on top of its head with her wand. And leaning closer to her sister.

So Reptar did. Whispering all the secrets told by Ripple into her sister's ear.

"Ripple is rangle over rangle," gurgled Raft.

"Hum," agreed Reptar.

Grandeville. Tinker's Place.

"Oh my gosh."

Messenger looked all round eyes at them. "A daughter!"

"Mother." Dat, of course, had told her daughter all about them, many many times over. And Je'leel was indjinn aware. She kissed Messenger on the forehead.

Messenger could see the awareness sparkling around her. It looked just like Dat.

"Boy, do we have a problem," said Tinker, after everyone had hugged and kissed their daughter. And after Je'leeI had sat by his side, between him and Sha'gar.

Chicken had claimed his other side. "A beautiful Princess, My Lord." Chicken smiled at her daughter. Je'leel smiled back.

"What problem?" asked Smoke.

"No room at the inn," replied Tinker.

R-Bar looked at Ran who looked at Sha'gar who shrugged. She kissed this new daughter on the cheek.

"Certainly not Faan," mumbled Ripple against Hanred's chest referring to Tinker's behavior and his new daughter. Chantal's coffees were finally working.

"It is new to me, Dusky Delight," whispered Hanred. He had never heard of such a thing, in any elseplace. Never. Ever. He began to wonder exactly how powerful Tinker really was.

Chantal tapped Chicken on one knee. "Gimme room."

Chicken edged away, allowing Chantal to sit against Tinker.

"Ahem," she said.

"What?" he asked.

"There is a room. Free, so to speak."

"Umm?"

"Take deep breath. And relax." She could feel his muscles tense. *Smoke?* His mind was jittering.

Ready when you are.

Chantal slipped one arm over his shoulders. "The Den."

"What?"

Sha'gar wrapped her arms around Je'leel. She had felt his emotional surge.

Chantal leaned heavily against him. Smoke got ready to pounce.

"We can always build other one," suggested

Chantal.

"I can always have one built. Somewhere," added Smoke.

"Corner room," said Fair Morn softly to Hanred. Ripple was asleep.

Hanred nodded, stood, and carted his prize toward the door to the hall. The prize woke but decided that it was all right, being carried away.

"Ummm," said Tinker.

"O.K.," said Tinker.

"But she will need furniture."

Chapter Fourteen.

Now This Is Some Kind Of Surprise.

Grandeville. Tinker's Place.
"Sooooo, are we done messing around?"
He sat on the couch. He slumped deeper and deeper into the couch, He carefully scanned each of the smiling faces.
It was mid-afternoon of yet another day.
"Huh? Are we?"
Chicken sat straighter and stared all blank face at him. "Praps do thee, Our Verra Own Lord and Master, with some fair precision greater do define a'Us this messing around thing so that We, thy Verra Own Most Obedient and Ever Pliant to thy fierce will, Daughters of Eve, could most swiftly to thee give fair answer to this thy most peculiar query?"
The loud hiss of breath was Tinker sighing and sinking even deeper in the couch. He frowned and looked worried, more worried.
"As far as I can tell," observed Chantal, looking

around the room, suppressing her grin. "Everyone's shirt is still buttoned and there is ample free space on either side of Mister Super Grumble Butt."

Yah," agreed Messenger, taking another cookie from the tray as it was passed to her by Smoke. Messenger munched loudly at him. "You betcha."

"Merde," grumbled Tinker, crossing his arms over his chest and wondering, not for the first time why it was so difficult to get a direct answer from this crowd. He thought that he ought to be able to do that. After all, they were all himself.

Fair Morn took several cookies and handed the tray to R-Bar. "We could always cut cards."

"Rumpf," mumbled R-Bar around her mouthful of cookie.

Ran nodded.

Sha'gar nudged Ran. "Some arcane trick?"

Smoke shook her head. "Quick way to decide who goes first."

"Just what are you-all going on about now? Huh?" He threw the question out into their conversation, seeking enlightenment, perhaps even an answer.

Messenger giggled.

Chantal laughed, and leered at him. "We are just trying to decide who gets messed around with first, given that there are eight of us and only one of you. The messees and the messor."

Fair Morn snatched a deck of cards from the drawer in the end of the low table and quickly shuffled, cut, and dealt one card to each.

Sha'gar tossed her card on the floor and began to tug her shirt from her trousers. "High card wins this peculiar child play. Correct?"

"HOLD IT!" Tinker thrashed upright. And glowered at them. He thought glower might work as frown certainly wasn't having any effect. "You know that is not what I meant."

Sha'gar pouted at him.

"Keep it on," he grumbled.

"Sneaky wench," hissed Chicken, tossing her card next to Sha'gar's. "Thee be too fast."

Chantal filled coffee cups. "Looks like he either attacks two at a time or the winners cut cards again."

"KNOCK . . . IT . . . OFF!" He surged to his feet. "And put the damn cards away too."

"Most crude, Our Prince." Chicken tried to look demure and innocent. Her smile ruined the attempt.

"Burgle! I am hungry. What's to eat?"

Eight pair of eyes watched him stomp away.

Chantal nodded at Chicken. "Certainly pushed his button that time."

Sha'gar stared at Chantal.

Chantal flopped back in her chair. "Smoke?"

Smoke nodded and lifted Chantal's idiomatic language skills and passed them to Sha'gar.

Sha'gar smiled her half-smile and nodded. "He may not have a button, but we certainly do. And he does push them."

"He is returning," cautioned Smoke.

"Never heard them called that before," said Messenger as Tinker walked back in and dropped into the couch, holding a large sandwich in his hand.

Messenger popped two buttons open on her shirt, yanked it forward and peered inside. "Certainly do not look like buttons to me."

"Huh?" Tinker took a large bite from his sandwich.

"Well . . . ," began Messenger.

"Whish, kitten. Do make us coffee more." Chicken nodded at her and leaned back as Messenger bubbled toward the kitchen, singing mostly to herself, "Buttons buttons, who's got the buttons?"

"What?"

"Naught, My Lord."

"Well?"

"A deep, dark, damp hole in the ground," offered Fair Morn.

"I put hot mustard on it," said he, once again resigned to his fate, waggling the sandwich at them.

Messenger returned and filled every cup that needed filling.

"Naughty, naughty," she whispered to Sha'gar. "Your buttons are poking out."

R-Bar glanced over. "Hum, hum, hum."

Ran looked and nodded. "Hum."

"I think she wants her buttons pushed," giggled Messenger.

"What?" asked Tinker as he stuffed the last of his sandwich into his mouth.

"Better use one of the bedrooms," suggested Smoke. "Or should we relocate elsewhere?"

"Er gern t'ker," rumbled Sha'gar. Yellow smoke drifted from her nostrils. Her eyes flared red.

"WAR PAK PTAR!" shouted R-Bar, leaping away.

Ran jumped in a different direction.

Sha'gar lurched to her feet.

Ran tossed mage clamp. It anchored Sha'gar's left ankle to her chair leg. She lurched toward Tinker, smoke puffing from her clothes. And halted, the anchored leg stretching behind, dragging the heavy chair.

Smoke snatched Tinker from the couch and tossed him into the dining room.

"HEYYYYYYYYYYY . . ."

R-Bar spun and swung. Dark slammed into Sha'gar and pulled her down, wrapping her in tight midnight folds.

Tinker charged back into the room. "WHAT'S GOING ON?"

Red roar ripping away black. Sha'gar surged to her feet and spun in Tinker's direction.

Fair Morn shoved Chicken to one side, grabbed the tall magician by the shirt front and punched her between the eyes. And held her tight as the mage slowly sagged. "What do I do with her now?"

Chantal scooped the limp body into her arms. "What is wrong with her?"

"Mage blight," said Ran, hugging R-Bar. "I think."

"Kik ter tak tak," mumbled R-Bar, struggling against the back-shock caused by Sha'gar's breaking of the black bonds.

"Oh, my," gasped Messenger.

"What?" asked Tinker.

"Most strange." Chicken directed Chantal to set her burden on one of the couches.

Smoke walked over and looked over the back of the couch at Sha'gar's forehead. "Already turning black and blue."

Fair Morn walked over. "Can you keep her asleep?"

Smoke nodded. "Her mind is seething."

"What," asked Tinker. "Is going on?"

Messenger wrapped her arms around him and wept into his shirt front. "Something is wrong with Sha'gaaaaaaaaaaar."

Dat stood on the edge of one of the book shelves, stretching and yawning. "Who is making all that noise? I was sleeping."

Chantal walked over. "Sha'gar is throwing fits."

"Really?"

"Puffing smoke," added Chantal.

"Fits are ugly things," said Dat. "I didn't know that they lived around here." Her eyes scanned the room. "Where are they?"

"She is sick," explained Messenger, pushing back from Tinker, wiping her eyes on his shirt sleeve.

"What?" asked Chantal.

"I am not," stated Dat, glowering at Messenger. She leaped onto Chantal's shoulder. "Fits eat holes in clothes."

Chantal walked over to the couch and pointed. "What do you think, Dat?"

"I didn't think that he beat his houris. Smoke said that he didn't, but that certainly looks like a beating to me." She jumped and landed on Sha'gar's stomach and walked up to her neck. "Never saw anyone ooze smoke like that before. Very poor taste in colors." She reached out and touched Sha'gar's neck. "There."

The dark spreading bruise on Sha'gar's forehead faded, the swelling went down.

The indjinn turned and jabbed a soft mound with one fingertip. "Certainly aroused. Did he drug her also?" She glared up at Tinker. "I thought that you were a nice person."

"I did not drug her. Or beat her."

Ran stepped to his side. "Mage blight, I think."

"Certainly looks like it." R-Bar joined the group standing, staring down at Sha'gar.

"What do be this illness?" Chicken sat and gently stroked the jet black hair back from Sha'gar's forehead.

Tinker nodded. "Right."

"Hum," said Ran

"It is like witch fever," explained R-Bar.

His head snapped around. "She is pregnant?"

"No," stated Smoke.

"Only different," continued R-Bar. She shrugged one shoulder. "Magicians are . . . different."

The air shimmered in the middle of the room. Ramp stared at them. Then at R-Bar. "Sister, you sent a call?"

R-Bar nodded. "Sha'gar is dar dar kak."

Ramp stepped over, her eyes darting over the slack form. "Hum, hum."

Ran nodded.

R-Bar looked down, then up. "Can you fix?"

Ramp smiled at her. "Of course. Wonder what?" She looked at him. "It is unusual in one mated, ahhhhh, to behave so."

She pulled her lip with two fingers. "Might be a side effect of her mage spell flare." She leaned forward and tugged Sha'gar's shirt loose, then slipped one hand inside.

"Hum," said Ran.

"Hum, hum," replied R-Bar.

"Ker ger tek zer," mumbled Sha'gar, dribbling green smoke from the corner of her mouth.

"Hum," said Ramp. "Strange."

"Indeed," agreed Chicken. "Most."

"Fix cure," said R-Bar.

Ramp looked up. "The green batz fruit of the female Hakpur plant."

Ran nudged R-Bar, who shook her head. And asked her sister. "Where?"

Ramp shrugged. "Qanaar. An elseplace. Of

unknown location."

R-Bar hissed and reached out, yanking in Reep.

"Sister," whispered the shadows, chilling the room with black menace. The slight figure tugged her wildly decorated shirt back up and over one bare shoulder. She was also wearing very baggy shorts of a bright red that almost glowed.

"Sorry sorry," said R-Bar. "Qanaar, an elseplace."

"Unknown." said Reep. She faded away, never looking at anyone except R-Bar.

R-Bar growled.

Ran slipped a comforting arm around R-Bar's shoulders.

"DAT!" called Tinker.

"Great Master?" Dat walked along the top of the couch and stood near him.

"You know where Qanaar is?"

"Sounds demon layer to me."

"How can we find out?"

"Ask one."

"Huh?"

"Demon." Dat frowned up at him. "Can't do that from here. You blocked them all out."

"Ummmm."

"Get Kartz here," snapped Chantal.

R-Bar nodded.

Kartz appeared, took one look at Sha'gar, and said to Tinker, "Bad bad."

"Ever hear of Qanaar?" asked Fair Morn.

"Nowp." Kartz leaned forward, pinched Sha'gar's nostrils shut, and poured an oily red liquid down her throat.

Ramp took a hasty step backward. "It is good that Reep did not notice her daughter."

Kartz clamped her free hand over Sha'gar's mouth and held firm as the magician heaved and thrashed. Only after the last muscle spasm had faded away did she release her grip.

"So how do we find this place?" Tinker looked at the Nagar. Then at Ramp.

Ramp shrugged. "I will ask Shem." She was gone.

Kartz stepped over and kissed him, and murmured, "Help."

The Core Pair suddenly stood in the center of the room. Kartz vanished.

The two stepped over to Tinker, smiled and licked their lips. Pointed teeth glittered. They both eyed the body on the couch. Red eyes glowed brightly.

"It's them," gasped Messenger.

"Forget it," snarled Chantal at the pair. "She belongs to us."

"Hello Ladies," said Tinker, slipping an arm around each waist as they crowded close to him. He smiled. They were exactly where they appeared to be.

"Thanks."

Each nuzzled the side of his neck.

"Better get my gun." mumbled Chantal.

Tinker cleared his throat. "Do you two happen to

know of a place called Qanaar?"

Heads jerked away. Each looked into the other's eyes. And after a moment, they smiled at each other, then at Tinker.

Chantal cleared her throat. "You better ask them if this place is a burger spot for them. We are looking for veggies."

"Right." He nodded. "Ummmm, ladies, is Qanaar a, errrrrr, hunting place for your group?"

The pair licked their lips and edged closer. They were now as close as they could get.

Pretty warm.

Don't get excited, Cowboy. Chantal frowned at him.

"Real pouncers," observed Smoke.

"We have to find green batz fruit of the female Hakpur plant," explained Tinker.

The Core Pair made clearing noises in their throats and shook their heads.

"Not good to eat, huh?"

Two more head shakes.

"We need it for medicine to help Sha'gar." He pointed. "She is very sick."

In one smooth motion, Amamaedur stepped over, bent, and tossed Sha'gar over her shoulder, straightened up and looked expectantly at him.

He shook his head. "Not yet. We have got to get ready." Amamaedur nodded and dumped Sha'gar on the couch.

Tinker sighed. "This is gonna be a long couple of

days."

Smoke headed for the kitchen. "I will make dinner. Steak and stuff." She beckoned at the demons. "Come with me."

"I will help." Fair Morn went with them.

Messenger hurried toward the kitchen as well. "I will make just lots and lots of salad. For us."

Chantal stepped over and banged him sharply on a shoulder. "I am sleeping with you for the duration. And I am bringing my gun."

"Ummmmm."

"Some warm bodies are going to get their butts blown off if they decide to make any nocturnal visits."

"Oh."

Chantal nodded. "Damn right."

He kissed the tip of her nose. "Smoke said us being eight had changed all that."

"Taking no chances, Stud. Those babes are demons. Of some sort or other. It might not work on them."

"No gun is going to sleep with me."

"It will stay on the floor." She grinned. "You do not require another addition to the group."

He frowned.

"We are all the warm bodies you need."

"Didn't say anything."

"Grumble, grumble," she replied.

"How about we start getting our gear put together?"

Chicken flapped a blanket loose and tucked it around Sha'gar. "We will Us Ourself aid Fair Chantal, Me'Lord."

They headed into the hall. Chantal called back over her shoulder at him, "I will contact Raj, see about a medical kit. Given the way things seem to go, we will probably need one."

Tinker dragged over a chair and sat and looked at the slack face.

R-Bar leaned against the back of his chair. "Never knew that magicians were that different. Must be the drift that happened in their magic."

"Hum," agreed Ran.

"Think she will be all right?"

R-Bar rubbed her cheek against the side of his head. "If Ramp said so, I am sure."

"Your Ran agrees," said Ran, tickling his free ear.

R-Bar moved around and sat on one arm of his chair. "I do not like going to demon elseplaces."

Ran kissed his ear. "Neither does your Ran, Amtar."

He sighed. "Goes for me too. Think we could send that pair by themselves?"

"Hum," said R-Bar.

Ran growled.

"What?" asked Tinker. "Never mind. I don't want to know."

Then he wacked at R-Bar's hand. It was tickling his ear.

"Strange strange," said Ran.

"Certainly is," agreed R-Bar.

"What?" He slumped. He wasn't sure that he wanted to know about this either.

"A demon helped us rescue Shitar's," explained R-Bar. "Now two demons are giving us help to fix Sha'gar."

"Strange strange," repeated Ran.

"Ummmmm," mumbled he.

"Tink?" It was a very gentle question stated with a very gentle tone of voice. And that was strange strange for a witch.

"What?"

R-Bar leaned against him and whispered, "Maybe not all demons are horrid kak an tak."

Ran gurgled and gasped, "Faan witch R-Bar!"

"Sort of culture shock. Kinna like learning about the Nagar, I suspect."

"Qat dur dur," grumbled Ran, leaning against his other side, that part of him that she could lean on.

He had slowly managed to slump deeper and deeper in his chair. Both witches now leaned at rather steep angles.

"Let me up," he grumbled at them. "Before we have a problem."

He tried to sit up.

And somehow.

Wound up on the floor.

With two witches.

"Hum," said Ran.

"Hum, hum," agreed R-Bar.

"Bug, bug," added Tinker.

"It must be you," said R-Bar, slipping one hand inside his shirt.

"What?"

"Nagar and demons. Something that you do."

"Hum." Ran tugged his shirt loose.

"Stop that! I do not do anything. Things are always being done to me. Like now. There are now eight of you. Ummm, of me."

R-Bar whispered into his ear. "It is you. She can not help herself."

"Bull cheat! Nothing makes you guys ever do anything." He managed to heave himself into a sitting position. "Bug nuts. Both of you."

"Reprobate." Chantal kicked the bottom of one of his feet with her boot. "One on the couch and you drag two to the floor."

He looked up. "We are packed, right?"

"Yep. Raj can't come until tomorrow evening." She kicked his foot again. "Maybe I will ask him for a gonad deadener."

The thud was Tinker flopping back onto the rug. "Worse and worse. Every day in every way my life just keeps getting worse and worse."

"Dinner time, Cowboy." Chantal whirled away and headed for the dining room.

Smoke smiled at him as they ate dinner.

"What?"

"They like steak," she said, cutting a large chunk from her's.

He nodded. "Figures." And watched the pair as they rather delicately cut and ate their dinner. Including the french fries and the salad.

"Most well mannered, Our Prince," murmured Chicken.

"Uh huh. Life is just full of surprises."

Chicken winked at him and filled his wine glass again.

"Ah ha," stated Ahamaezur, emptying her glass. Amamaedur followed suit.

Fair Morn shoved the jug toward them.

Chantal filled the glasses of the demon pair. "You two can sleep in the hall bedrooms."

Ahamaezur nodded and delicately crunched and swallowed the steak bone.

Smoke pushed the platter in their direction. "I cooked much." And started on her second.

"Good," said Fair Morn, reaching out and hooking another large piece of meat onto her plate.

Tinker slumped and sipped from his glass and looked around the table and thought to himself, once again, that no-one would really believe him if he told them about things like this.

"I am hungry." Sha'gar dropped into the empty chair to Tinker's right.

Chicken jumped up and fetched dishes and utensils.

Smoke hurried around the table, heaping the plate full, setting in front of her. "You should eat much."

Leaning heavily on her left elbow, Sha'gar began to eat. Smoke had cut everything into small pieces. "What are those?" she mumbled to Tinker.

Those had emptied their plates and were now eyeing the rest of the food on the table.

"Have some more." Chantal shoved the salad bowl over. "We are used to big appetites. One or two."

"Couple of demons of some sort that we once met," whispered Tinker. "They are going to help us find some stuff that Ramp needs to fix you up."

"Hum, hum, hum."

"Friends," stated Tinker. "They are sorta friends, helped us with the Dark Emp."

"Dumpf Empf," mumbled Sha'gar.

"Don't talk with your mouth full," he replied.

Something deep in her eyes flickered. She swallowed.

"You O.K.?"

She sat up straighter. "NO." And burped green fumes.

"Want something for your stomach? Glass of water?"

Sha'gar shook her head. Red flickered brighter in her eyes. She emptied her glass. "Bed, Mate'mer, bed." She lurched to her feet.

Shoving his chair back, he leaped to his feet and grabbed her. "Careful."

"Bed."

As he guided her through the kitchen, Chantal called, "Gun's under my pillow. I'll get it later."

Late night.

Bright moonlight shot silver shaft across the polished wood floor, ran over their legs, and splashed against a wall.

The door eased open as she slipped inside the room on near silent feet.

"It's on my side," he said. "What are you doing up so late?"

The alarm clock glowed bright red figures at them through the dark where it lived.

12:02.

Oh," she said, coming around to his side and siting on the floor next to him. "Nothing. Reading."

Something metallic scraped over the floor. "Here."

She took her revolver, leaned forward to kiss him. "How's she doing?"

"Beats me. Sleeping. Puffing smoke. Really high body temperature."

"Bak tak tak," mumbled Sha'gar in her sleep, rolling onto her side, throwing an arm over his chest.

>>> 500 <<<

"Saying whatever."

Sha'gar coughed a bright flash of light.

Chantal gasped.

"That's new," he said.

Chantal kissed him. "Night, John. We plan on leaving right after breakfast."

"Night."

Chantal slipped from the room, eased the door closed, and wondered whether there really was anyway to keep him from worrying so much. It was bothering them all. She headed up to her room.

Mid-Morning.

They gathered on the rear deck. Everyone wore packs except Sha'gar and the two demons.

Fair Morn carried Sha'gar's pack.

He looked around. "We waiting for something?"

"Sure are, Cowboy. Raj." Chantal pointed at one of the wooden benches. "Park it."

"Bak tak tak," he mumbled as he sat.

Ran and R-Bar both sucked in quick breaths.

Sha'gar's eyebrows flew up.

Chicken settled next to him. "Be this most coarse, Our Prince?"

"Dun know. Just something that I heard."

Messenger hurtled around the corner and down the deck toward the group. "Raj is coming." She dropped onto the bench by his free side. And kissed his check.

Then they heard the car enter the parking area and stop.

And, in a moment, Raj walked toward them, accompanied by Kartz.

"Which one?" he asked Chantal. He stared at the Core Pair. "BY GEORGE!" And looked at Tinker. "What?"

"Lady demons. It is Sha'gar that requires checking."

Dropping his bag on the table top, Raj rummaged through it. "Probably nothing that I can do from what Chan explained." He handed a packet to Chantal. "Here, keep this. It might do some good. Let me know if you use it."

He spun and stepped over to Sha'gar, felt her forehead, peered into her eyes, watched the pale orange fumes seep from the corners of her mouth. And nodded to himself.

"Not much for western medicine here." He smiled at Sha'gar. "But you should probably drink lots of water."

Then he turned to Tinker. "Circe told me about your medicine hunt. May I watch, take notes, when, ummm, the cure is applied? Maybe have a sample or two for analysis?" He leaned close and whispered, "Do you think that they would mind if I took a closer look?"

Tinker shrugged. "You'll have to ask them."

Raj straightened and slowly approached the pair. Kartz stepped sideways and watched carefully.

"Ladies," asked Raj. "May I examine your eyes and teeth?"

The pair looked at each other, then at Tinker, then at Raj. And smiled.

He stepped closer, peered into Ahamaezur's eyes. And reached out to hold her head steady. His hand jerked back.

"What?" Tinker leaped from the bench.

Raj looked at his hand, then at Ahamaezur. "There was nothing there."

"Stop that," Tinker said to the pair. "Protective behavior," he explained to Raj. "Try it again."

Raj very carefully did. "By George, she is there this time."

"Ah ha," said Ahamaezur. She allowed Raj to peer into her eyes with some small instrument, and then to check her teeth.

"Rather like sharks," mumbled Raj. "Not filed at all. Good set of molars in the rear though."

"They are predators, of a sort," said Tinker.

Raj stepped away. "Thank you, my dear." And bumped into someone. "Oooooops."

He stared as Amamaedur turned him around and smiled at him.

"Better check her as well," suggested Tinker. "Then we can be on our way."

Raj did. And thanked her. "Amazing."

"We will talk when we return," said Chantal. She stepped down the deck stairs and walked toward the open patch on the far side of the flower beds. "Let's go."

Everyone waved at Raj and Kartz.

Ran and R-Bar took them to the demon elseplace.

Raj slipped one arm around Kartz' waist and headed back toward their car, after packing his bag.

"While I drive, do tell me all about those demon folk. They were quite pretty. Not at all like that other thing."

Chapter Fifteen.

Isn't It Fun Doing Medicine?

Qanaar. Dry and Sere.

The small group stood and looked at their surroundings. Dust brown and rust red soil and rock. Scrub, widely spaced brush grew from knee-high to chest-high. The vegetation's green-purple glinted metallic spot color in the bright suns. There were two, large and red-gold.

Overhead the sky was blue with a slight tinge of red and cloudless. Close to the horizon they could see the brown-red stain of atmospheric dust.

The demon set, reduced in number, members selected for this trip, had taken them here from their own elseplace.

The set stood in an enveloping circle around Tinker and his group, moving here and there, always close, a Brownian movement of predators.

It dawned on Tinker that toward the outer edge there were younger females, watching the command pair, nudging this young male or that one, but always remaining out on the edge.

"Ah ha," said Amamaedur.

Ahamaezur clacked her teeth.

Both looked at Tinker. The surrounding mass froze in place.

Waiting.

Staring inward.

"Which way?" he asked.

Both slipped closer to him.

"Now what?"

Both shook their heads and pointed in different directions.

"Doesn't matter, does it?"

Soft lips brushed across both sides of his face. Razor sharp pointed teeth delicately touched soft flesh.

He stepped back and pointed. "Let's go that way."

The pair swung away from him and waited.

Tinker looked around.

His group looked at this and that and waited.

Fair Morn had one arm swung around Sha'gar's waist as she leaned against the slightly taller Fair Morn.

He looked at R-Bar. "Kiddo, you know what to look for?"

"Yes, Ramp told me. Look for a bright red one. They are rare."

Tinker nodded. And they started walking.

And they walked.

And walked.

And walked.

Half a day.

They walked.

How ever long a half a day was in this elseplace.

"Lunch time," announced Tinker. "Time to rethink what we are doing."

He dumped his pack on the ground and sat next to it. And began to rummage around in it for something to eat. He crooked one finger at R-Bar. "Come'mer, kid."

She tromped over and sat next to him. "Tink?"

"What's the rest of this mob going to eat, for starters?"

"Hum."

"Yep. Bet they are not going to be interested in munching on the vegetation."

She stood, walked over and poked Ran on the shoulder. Ran nodded.

The pair walked over to talk with Ahamaezur and Amamaedur.

Then they waved in an appropriate meal.

And while the demon band was eating, Tinker beckoned Fair Morn over.

"One?" She sat near him, munching on something.

"I have had a thought," he said.

She smiled and nudged him. "Can't you wait until we get home?"

He sighed. And stared at his food.

She threw a comradely arm around his shoulders. "Other than that, what is on your mind?"

"Umm."

"Not in the mood for jokes, right?"

She received another long sigh. So, she bumped herself against him, just a little. "What?"

"We are on a wild berry chase," he grumbled.

She helped him finish his lunch. "What else can we do?"

"Glad that you asked."

"Oh, oh."

"I thought," he said, wacking the hand tickling his side. "That we could ask the Core Pair if there are dangerous things flying around here."

"Wonderful idea." Fair Morn stood and lifted him to his feet. "I could use some exercise. Like that." She winked.

They walked over, sat, and joined the Core Pair for lunch. At least, Fair Morn did. Tinker watched. And talked with the two Tark.

Eventually, the Core Pair made him understand that there was nothing around here that flew through the air. Their snickering and hissing also made him realize that they thought he was either being funny or was crazy.

"Better get some help." Tinker stood and waved for Ran and R-Bar. And then he explained.

"When Fair Morn takes to the air, I want you two to make sure that she is safe from them if they get excited. O.K.?"

Ran nodded. She rolled a glittering silver crystal

sphere from hand to hand.

"Ready." R-Bar reached in a long golden wand with red banding.

"You three stay here." He walked back and talked with the pair again. "... and you keep your bunch under control. I don't want anyone hurt."

"Ah ha," said Amamaedur.

"Ah ha," agreed Ahamaezur.

He nodded, turned and faced Fair Morn and the witches. And smiled at Fair Morn.

"Fly high, beautiful butterfly."

She nodded and slowly, ever so slowly, unfolded and unfolded and unfolded her great butterfly wings. The sun sparkled and danced from their multi-colored design as she pumped them back and forth.

"Ahhhhhh, feels so good."

Amamaedur and Ahamaezur barked commands at their agitated troop. All froze in place. The young females on the outer edges hunkered down and whispered softly to the nearest young males.

All eyes watched Fair Morn.

And stay out of trouble. Tinker watched her rise lightly into the air and take a gentle soaring circle around the group below. Then she lifted higher and soared outward. *Stay in touch.*

I am watching, MindMate. Smoke cast her sensenet far and wide.

I will. Fair Morn drifted off. But not out of range of Smoke's ever watching minds.

The demon pair slipped silently toward Tinker, approaching from either side, eyes focused upon him.

"Ummmmmm?" he said.

They came closer.

"Ladies?"

They came closer.

"Something wrong?" He waited. And could only watch one at a time.

Steady, Cowboy. Chantal slipped her revolver from its holster and eased the hammer back. It made a soft click as it cocked.

R-Bar called in something dark as Ran stepped to one side. The silver clear sphere floated upward.

He could feel warmth radiating against him from either side and knew that they had to be there. But he couldn't see anything from the corners of his eyes.

"What's up?" he asked. "If you will pardon the pun."

They gentle bumped against him. He could feel their breath on both sides of his face and throat.

Carefully, ever so carefully, he lifted his arms and reached. They were right there. So he slipped his arms around their waists and pulled them closer. And said very, very softly, "For us, Fair Morn flying here and there is perfectly normal."

He hugged the pair and felt their rippling muscles relax.

"I just thought we could speed up the search, that's all."

And then they were there, gurgling soft deep in their throats.

"Had me worried, you know." He laughed. "After all, we really do not have any idea of your cultural values."

Amamaedur waggled one arm. Ahamaezur did the same. And all around them the troop unfroze and began making small movements again. An outer male suddenly disappeared, dragged down by a fringe female. The Core Pair pretended not to notice. But the other females were growled at.

Giving each of them another hug, he smiled. "How about we all sit and relax while our bat is flitting about?"

Grandeville. River View Hospital.

"So, My Dear, those, umm, women belong to a race of predators?"

Kartz nodded. "Demon hunters. Fierce fierce."

They were finishing their lunch. In the Doctor's Lounge.

Raj frowned. "If they return with Tinker, do you think that they would allow me to do a look see?"

Kurtz pursed her lips. And shrugged. "The Tinker could tell command."

"Err ah? Tell command?"

"Yeel . . . yes."

He patted one of her hands. The other held her lunch. "Actually I rather enjoy yeel." He smiled happily at her.

She nodded, and said, ever so softly, "Yeel."

"What sort of people are those . . . ummm, ahhhhh?"

"Demon hunters." She took another bite from her lunch. It was a large hamburger dripping sauce. "Tark, they call themselves."

Raj handed her several napkins. And waited.

Kartz wiped her lips and chin, eyes twinkling. "They eat demons. They are demons. Fierce fierce."

"My dear?"

"They eat . . . every. . . thing."

"My dear?"

She popped the rest of her hamburger into her mouth and chewed happily. And admired his face.

"How is it, My Dear Circe, that you could bring two of them here, ahh, to his place?"

She smiled broadly. "Fierce fierce." And patted one of his hands. "Me. Your's."

"We really do have to speak about all these things. Your worlds are rather frightening. At least they are to a rather simple doctor like me."

He hooked his tea cup closer. "It was rather hard accepting Tinker and his, umm, ladies, ahhhh, female companions. And you, ermmmm, as a witch."

She shook her head. "Nagar."

"Quite. Nagar. Sorry."

She stood, walked around the table, wrapped her arms around him, and kissed the top of his head. And blew warm air into his hair. "Mine."

"We will speak about this later. It is time to return to work."

Kartz stepped back and waited until he stood. She hugged and kissed him again.

And then.

They went back to work.

The doctor and his assistant.

She looked like the doctor.

Qanaar. Dry and Sere.

She floated along enjoying the sun warmth. It felt so good. Here, in this strange land, she didn't have to worry about anyone seeing her. So she enjoyed the freedom.

To swoop.

To soar.

To make wide happy circles in the air, in the warm air, heated by the ground below, that poured upward, giving her all the lift she required.

So, most of the time, she just coasted along. The Big Red joke. A pinup person with gigantic butterfly wings. She laughed. A very happy laugh. It was fun being like a bird, having bird-like abilities.

And as she drifted here and there she felt the soft mental touch that was Smoke maintaining contact.

Not much here, mom.

Strange place, agreed Smoke.

Far to one side she saw something different.

Tilting that way she slipped over to take a look.

Then she swooped low, whipping along, just above the tops of the highest bushes.

And up.

And around.

It watched.

The Picnic Spot.

Chicken sat behind him, leaning her back against his. "Me Lord?"

"Ummm?" He had been almost dozing, trying not to notice the direct stares of a pair of flaming red eyes. The Core Pair sat facing him, shoulder touching shoulder.

"Me'thinks we do owe this pair some small token when we do return a'home."

"Ummm?"

"We did Us think some of most fair blue stone they do so highly prize."

"We could do that."

One, I found one of those red bushes.

Good. I was getting tired of sitting. And being stared at. Smoke?

Ready when you are. That bush is just beyond that slight rise on our left. Ten, fifteen minutes if we walk fast.

"Up, Princess. Let's walk fast."

They stood. The pair uncoiled. And Smoke pointed.

"That way," said Tinker, pointing. "Fair Morn has

found one of those red bushes. It is in that direction."

The Core Pair bounded to their feet, whirled away, barked commands, and raced into the brush, the troop hurtling with them, fanning outward as they ran, forming a great crescent, the outer points forward.

"Now what?" Tinker hurried after the rapidly disappearing horde.

"Excited," said Smoke. "Very excited."

"I'd say so," agreed Tinker. They left Smoke and Sha'gar behind, knowing that Smoke would see anything in time to warn them, if necessary.

And she did. *NOT THERE!* Her warning blasted into their minds, staggering them. Then they realized that the call was for Fair Morn as she coasted downward.

AAAAAAAAAA . . .

They felt her struggle, yanking herself free, lurching, wobbling upward, fighting for altitude.

Smoke pushed Fair Morn's pain deep and kept her awake.

Far below, Fair Morn could see the demon pack hurtle themselves into the squirming mass that had surged to the surface, snapping one tentacle into her.

Clenching her hands over the wound, she struggled to stay airborne, lurching violently in the direction of Smoke.

As she passed over Tinker and the rest, she shouted, "GET THE BERRIES, GET THE BERRIES."

She thudded into a heap, rolling and tumbling across the ground not far from her target, Smoke and

Sha'gar.

Smoke hurried to her side and lifted her up. "Fold your wings, fold your wings. They are in the way."

Fair Morn smiled at her and did. Smoke eased her to the ground and quickly checked for damage.

"We need Dat." Smoke unfolded the medical kit and took out the packet labeled for Fair Morn.

"Move your hands out of the way," she ordered. Then she plunged in the needle and pushed the plunger. "Present from Raj."

Tears welled into Fair Morn's eyes. "I am fading, mom."

"NO," shouted Smoke, leaping away and slapping Sha'gar across the face, again and again.

Something flashed deep red in Sha'gar's eyes.

"Help her, magician." Smoke's mind slipped inside and pushed.

Sha'gar grunted. "Smoke?"

"Fair Morn needs help. Do something to keep her alive."

Sha'gar nodded, reached deep inside for strength, and threw the spell.

Black tinged red surged over Fair Morn. And disappeared. Sha'gar collapsed.

In the few minutes it took Tinker and the rest to arrive, the demon horde had ripped the thing into shreds. They were happily munching on the remains. They had only lost one secondary male and one fringe female. The Antak usually inflicted greater damage than that.

Amamaedur led Tinker to the remains of the red bush and indicated that the thing used the bush as a lure. From somewhere she yanked free a small sack and began to fill it with the green fruit from the bush. She handed the sack to him as soon as it was filled.

MindMate, we must return home. Quickly.

Tinker tied the sack top closed and stuffed it inside shirt. "We have to get home. In a hurry. Can we do that?"

"Ah ha," said Amamaedur, turning and racing away, barking at Ahamaezur, who started the horde running back the way they had come.

"Let's go. Smoke wants us to hurry."

They ran after the demon set.

As soon as all stood around Smoke, the Core Pair took them to the Tark elseplace. Then R-Bar and Ran yanked their group away, including the Core Pair.

They crashed into the living room, tumbling in every direction.

"Dat! Get up, wake up. Get out here."

The tiny figure stood on the edge of the bookshelf, stretching and yawning.

"Gimble, gimble, gimble," she grumbled. "I was supposed to go along."

Tinker stepped over. "Sorry. Fair Morn needs repair. Hurry, please?"

"Big," demanded Dat, leaping to the couch, then

to the floor.

R-Bar nodded.

And Dat was.

Big.

The indjinn knelt and rolled the limp figure over onto her back and began to tear Fair Morn's clothes further open. Then she leaned over and peered at the wound. Looking up, she glared at the demon pair. "You do this?"

"It was a monster in the elseplace where we went," said Chantal.

"Very messy. She is put together strange."

"Fix her," said Tinker.

"There is mage stuff in the way." Dat nudged the crumpled Sha'gar. "Her's."

Undoing his shirt, he yanked out the sack. "Start with her first, then."

"Cannot," said Dat. "Mage sick."

"What?"

Chicken stepped over and wrapped her arms around him. She had felt the emotional pulse, the sudden mental jitter. "Steady on, My Lord."

The air in the center of the room shimmered. And Ramp looked at them.

R-Bar jumped over, snatched the sack from Tinker's hand, and jabbed it at her sister. "Hurry. Sha'gar's spell is keeping Fair Morn from being fixed."

Suddenly Smoke lurched sideways, tears streaming down her face. She gasped and growled,

"Slipping away."

"Noooooooooooooooooo . . . " Tinker thudded to the floor. Sitting, staring. Chicken wrapped herself around him.

Ramp grabbed the sack, waved in a bowl, and poured the berries into it. Then she shoved everyone out of the way and added other things to the bowl. Black flames boiled over the edge of the container and flowed down and over Sha'gar, sinking into her chest.

Sha'gar coughed. Her fingers flexed.

Ramp leaned over and said something, gurgling deep inside her throat, and plunged her fist into Sha'gar's mid-section. And ripped upward.

Sha'gar's leg jerked up, her arms wrapping around them, as she screamed and screamed and screamed and screamed

Ignoring the tortuous sound, Ramp turned to her sister. "Fair Morn should be released. Do whatever you wish. I must finish Sha'gar."

Spinning away, Ramp yanked her hood up and over her head. Black shadow peered out and down at the twitching body at her feet. Taking berries from the bowl floating in the air, she knelt and poked them one by one into Sha'gar's mouth, holding her jaws open with her free hand.

Dat grabbed Fair Morn by one leg and tugged her into the middle of the room. She knelt and began to work.

Something, an ever changing shape, hunkered

nearby, great orange gold eyes watching, watching, watching.

It was Smoke, her minds thrashing wildly, trying to retain herself as separation shock smashed against her mental control. She felt Fair Morn fading, fading, fading.

Dat began replacing, rebuilding, healing. And as she worked she began to finally understand the strange structure that was Fair Morn. Now she understood the nature of what Big Red had wrought when he had called his mythological jest into existence.

The monster clacked its teeth together and licked its lips. And eyed the meat lying on the floor. And from far, far, far, far away, it heard the faintest of faint voices speaking inside its minds.

Mom?

? The shape shifted. And looked more human.

I did't die?

NO. Smoke crashed back against the front of the couch. "You didn't die."

Red flame poured toward the high ceiling. "ANTAK TAK TA!" bellowed Sha'gar.

Ramp leaped away and fell over Dat and Fair Morn. Strong arms dragged her away. And hugged her.

"In dik dik," hissed Ramp.

"We owe you our lives," said Smoke, releasing her.

R-Bar knelt and began to carefully check her sister.

"I am uninjured," said Ramp, sweeping her hood

from her face and down her back.

"Just tired." Deep fatigue carved lines in her face. Dark smudged under her eyes. "Our sister's daughter is cured. Now she requires comforting. And rest. As do I." She heaved herself to her feet.

"Home." Ramp disappeared.

Dat patted Fair Morn's stomach. It was a very self-satisfied gesture, and looked over at Tinker. She smiled. Her canines glittered. "She is almost as beautiful as me." She patted Fair Morn's stomach again. "You will have to introduce me to the stuff that made her."

Je'leel ran into the room and knelt next to Dat and hugged her.

"Thank you," whispered Fair Morn. Tears glittered in the corners of her eyes. "It is good to be alive."

"Ah ha," murmured Amamaedur. The Core Pair had been standing to one side watching everything as it transpired.

Chantal hurried from the kitchen carrying a large tray with two pots of cocoa and cups.

Messenger held a large bag of marshmallows.

Lightly kicking Tinker, Chantal mumbled at him, "Thought we all could use a cup."

Chicken released him and nudged him up and into the couch. And handed him a filled cup. "Me Lord." She sat next to him. "We must gift the demon pair and Ramp and fair Dat."

He nodded. And slumped deeper and sipped,

eyes focused somewhere else.

"Our Prince?" Chicken leaned against his side. "Do come back. For us? For this thy Verra Own Queen."

He shuddered. And sighed. And turned and kissed her. And blinked back the tears that refused to blink away.

"Shhhhhhh," murmured Chicken. Her eyes darted from face to face to face, warning them all to stay away. For now.

Chantal having finished handing out cups to everyone, including the demon pair, who gingerly tried this strange liquid, set her tray aside and knelt next to Sha'gar. She gently brushed the hair back from the damp forehead and leaned over and kissed her. "Welcome back, sister self."

"Nervous nervous," mumbled Sha'gar, grabbing one of Chantal's arms.

Shoving her arms under the limp form, Chantal heaved herself to her feet, and carried Sha'gar to a couch and gently set her down, leaning her back against the soft cushions. Grabbing a comforter, she pulled it up and around them both and held Sha'gar in her arms. "You are safe, you are safe."

Fair Morn looked up at Smoke's face. "I am really hungry, mom."

Smoke nodded. "Me too." She stood and hurried to the kitchen. Messenger went with her.

Je'leel sat by his free side. "Mother is very talented."

He turned his head and smiled. "And beautiful as well." He surged to his feet and wrapped Dat in his arms. "How did you stay large?"

Dat shrugged and rubbed her hands up and down his back. "But it is nice." She whispered in his ear, "Would like another daughter?"

He jerked. "No!"

"Oh." She smiled at him. "Would you like to play with my body anyway?"

He released her and flopped back onto the couch. Chicken and Je'leel bounced. Just a little.

Dat watched him, carefully she watched him. "Great Master?"

"Me'Lord?"

"Father?"

He shook his head. "Nuthin. Too hard to explain." He looked at her. "Ahhhhh, Dat?"

"Yes?"

"Seeing as you are large."

"Yes?" She grinned.

"Do you know what turquoise is?"

Dat nodded. "Not very good tasting."

"Ummmm, we need two sacks of ornaments made from that stone to gift to the Core Pair. I think that they will appreciate it."

"I will return." Dat headed for the front door. "Shouldn't take long."

Smoke returned with a large kettle of soup. Messenger carried bowls, spoons and crackers.

Everyone, almost everyone, ate soup and crunched crackers.

Smoke fed Fair Morn while Chantal saw to it that Sha'gar ate.

By the time that they were finished with the soup, the demon pair had steak, rare, Dat returned and handed two small sacks to Tinker. They were soft leather tied with blue drawstrings.

He crooked a finger at the core pair and watched until they stood in front of him. He stood.

"Many thanks. For everything. Here." He held out his hands, one sack in each. "A small gift."

Amamaedur carefully took one sack and waited until Ahamaezur took the other. Then she opened her sack and poked one experimental finger inside. Her eyes flared bright. She grabbed him and buried her face into the joint of his neck and shoulder.

Ahamaezur opened her sack and peered inside. And grabbed him. "Ah ha." She breathed hot breath against the side of his neck on the other side.

"Careful, ladies," gasped Tinker. "Those teeth are sharp."

They released him and smiled. It seemed to Tinker that they were radiating much more heat than normal. For them.

"Ummm, are you both all right?"

Amamaedur ticked her lips and nudged Ahamaezur.

Ahamaezur removed a segment from one the

rings she wore and handed it to Amamaedur who removed a different segment from a ring she wore and fitted the two pieces together. They stepped close to Tinker.

Amamaedur reached out, lifted his right hand, and slipped the ring onto one of his fingers. And kissed his hand. Then Ahamaezur took the same hand and kissed it as well.

Each laid one hand on one of his shoulders and gurgled soft sounds at him. And backed away.

"If that is what I think that it is, someone is going to get their butts shot off," mumbled Chantal.

The core pair stepped into the open part of the living room and looked expectantly at him.

"Ummm, time for you to go?"

They both nodded.

"I will do it. Great Master."

He nodded. "O.K., do it. But wait a minute." He stepped over and hugged and kissed each of the pair. "Bye. And many, many thanks." And smiled.

Dat took them.
   Out.
      Away.
   Home.

Tinker rejoined his couch and slipped his arms around Chicken and Je'leel. "Whoosh." He laughed and held out his hands, looking at the many rings. "I am beginning to feel like a gypsy, no insult intended to any gypsy who might he listening."

"Our Prince?"

"Look at all the rings."

"Most Royal appearing, Sweet Prince."

He indicated the new one. "Messenger, come and take a look at it, please?"

She crawled over, she had been sitting next to Fair Morn, and sat and blinked at him.

"Well?" He held his hand closer to her face.

"Oh my gosh!" She blushed.

"Now what?" He grumbled, and frowned at no-one in particular.

"MyTinker, I am not sure, not exactly." Messenger clamped a hand over her mouth. Laugh wrinkles formed at the sides of her eyes.

"What?"

Chicken rubbed his back. "Calm thyself, Fair Prince."

Tinker tugged at the ring. "Ooop! Damn thing won't come off." He stared at the ring. "Another one that sticks."

Azure flame crackled around it, wandering through the ornate carving on the outer surface.

Je'leel reached over, took his hand, and slipped the ring free. "What do you want to do with it?"

"Gosh." Messenger stared at Je'leel.

"Better keep it, Cowboy," suggested Chantal. "Wouldn't want to irritate that pair."

He took back the ring and slipped it on the correct finger. And winked at Je'leel.

"Nice to know you can do things like that. What does it do?"

Je'leel looked at Messenger.

Messenger giggled. "It states that you, umm, have, ummmm, sort of, ummmmmm, license, umm, freedom, ahh, so to speak." Her face flushed brighter red.

R-Bar joined them and sat by Messenger's side. "To do what?"

Ran sat next to them, stared at the ring, and gurgled deep in her throat.

"What?" demanded Tinker.

R-Bar reached past Messenger and poked Ran in the side. "Speak tell."

"Demon mated," rasped Ran.

"Kan tak tak," snapped R-Bar.

"Not exactly," corrected Messenger "He just may, if he, umm, feels like it. It says that he is a Prime Male."

Chantal stood, walked around, leaned on the back of the couch, and swung her arms around him. "Still branching out, huh, Stud?"

"Must have been our gift," he grumbled at her.

"Of their species," finished Messenger.

"Turquoise seems to get them excited," he mumbled.

"You are a one man naval attachment." Chantal tickled one of his ears. "You have babes and babe-things in every port."

"How about," he suggested. "That we watch a

movie, and rest, and relax, and heal? Huh?"
 Soooooo . . .
  That is exactly what they did.

Chapter Sixteen.

Once More Into the Breach.

Grandeville. Tinker's Place.

It was a very cluttered room. Stacks of paper covered most of the horizontal surfaces. The stacks cuddled up to the computer gear.

It was his cluttered office.

He was hard at work.

Editing.

And mumbling.

Rewriting.

She slipped into the room, crept in on silent feet, and poked him in the side.

"Tink?"

"Go away," he grumbled, lifting and moving a chunk of text from here to there. The wonders of computer technology.

"Dir dit," she hissed.

Dat sat up. She had been lying at the edge of a shelf above the terminal. The books had been shoved back so that she had room. She looked down. "He is working."

"My sister is still missing," snarled R-Bar.

"Umm?" He leaned back and swung around in his swivel chair, which screeched loudly. Somehow oil never seemed to effect that noise. Not at all.

"Oh. Hi, kiddo. What's up?"

"We are all healthy and rested."

"Guess so."

"We have to find my sister."

"Guess so."

"Soon!"

"Guess so."

"Gir tak tak!"

"Guess so." He reached out, hooked his arms around her waist, and tugged her close.

"Pretty nice." And tugged her shirt loose.

"Better take her somewhere else," advised Dat. "There is no room on the floor."

He sighed.

"When are we going to go?" insisted R-Bar.

"Well." He slid his hand up her back. "Nice smooth skin." He winked at her. "How about . . . in two days?"

"Hum, hum," said R-Bar. "Fair Morn has The Ring."

"Oh." He leaned forward and stood, scooping her up in his arms at the same time. "In that case I guess we will just have to settle for a cup of cocoa." He started for the door, jouncing her up and down.

"HEY!" yelled Dat.

So he came back, swung around, and let Dat leap down. She landed on R-Bar's stomach. Dat leaned one one hand and looked up. "You going to drag her into some dark corner?"

"Quiet, Dat." He twisted out the door with his burdens, large and tiny.

"Watch what you are poking," hissed R-Bar at Dat.

Grandeville. Red and Sandy's home.

He was up early, sitting at the kitchen table, drinking a cup of coffee. She was gathering together the ingredients for his breakfast. Later she would eat dinner.

Red, and his partner, Green always had the night shift, a rather unusual split night shift.

"Your buddy ever tell you what happened?"

"Who? To what?" She whipped three eggs in a bowl and added something else.

"The jock babe. The one Green likes a whole bunch."

She tossed in some chopped parsley. "What do you mean?"

"She is taller for one thing."

She dumped in some cottage cheese. "For one thing?"

"Attorney babe, you are being lawyer evasive." He reached over and grabbed the coffee pot and refilled his cup.

She dumped everything in a pan and set it on the

front burner and put the lid on. And turned and wrapped her arms around his neck. "I am not. What one thing?"

"Confidential?"

"Sure."

"Both Green and I agree that her anatomy is different. Besides being taller. And don't tell me that you didn't notice. Babes always notice."

She smiled at him. "O.K. So I noticed. But I do not know why. And I didn't ask, either." She tightened her hug. "You two are right. Taller and different. Beat's me."

"Really unusual."

"It is that."

"Guess that we will never know. Right?"

"Not unless she decides to say something. And I am not going to ask her, either."

"Neither is Green. He doesn't want to get beat up. How's breakfast coming?"

She laughed and began to ladle everything onto a large plate. She shoved it front of him and winked.

Red sloshed hot sauce on everything and began to eat. "I know. He likes her a whole lot."

Tatok. High Mountains. Stark and Bare.

He lurched and pointed. "Drop her in there." He staggered over to the window and peered out at . . . nothing.

The clatka beast heaved the body onto the bed.

"Do not touch her. She is mine, all mine."

Jerking around, he waggled a short grey wand, summoning a servant. It would be one better suited to taking care of his prize.

She hurried into the room and bowed low.

"Clean her. Feed her. New clothes." He hitched toward a side door. "Do it! Now!"

The young woman straightened up as she heard the door slam shut. She stepped to the bed and kicked the beast in the side. "Leave her alone. Or die." She smashed it on the back with a short, thick staff of wood.

The clatka beast hissed and ran for the other door. The servant straightened out the limbs of the woman sprawling across the bed, and frowned. She spun away and hurried from the room to gather the necessary supplies.

Grandeville. Tinker's Place.

They sat on the new, soft, curved couch. It was set close to the large bay window. In the new and smaller living room.

Just Tinker and R-Bar.

And a pot of cocoa and a plate of cookies on a small table.

She was curled up in his lap. He kissed her on the temple. "Stop worrying. She'll be found."

R-Bar grumbled.

"Won't she?"

"Yesssss."

"So then?"

"I am worried."

"Guess so."

"It has been long long."

"Uh huh?" He took a sip from his cup and set it down. And gave her a little tickle. She was now leaning against one of the arms of the couch, legs stretched out.

She hissed.

"Just doing my job."

"Hum."

"Being comforting." He winked at her. "And all that kinna stuff."

She slid her hand over his chest, having already unbuttoned his shirt, starting at his belt and working her way up. "Hold me." She had moved back to his lap.

"Thought that I was." He swung his other arm around and held her as her arms wrapped around his chest.

It was a very long and heavy sigh.

It was Tinker, slumping into a more comfortable position. It was Tinker getting more worried than ever.

"Be'damn'd secrecy!" Chicken thumped across the living room, making soft dull sounds.

She was wearing thick fuzzy slippers.

Smoke leaned against the dining room archway, and watched her.

"What do be a'foot?" demanded Chicken.

Smoke shrugged. "Is all our gear packed and ready?"

"INDEED!"

Ran joined them. "Princess?"

"Agitated," observed Smoke.

"Hum."

"Vile hummer," grumbled Chicken.

Ran looked at Smoke.

Smoke nodded.

Ran reached down a clear blue sphere and mashed it against Chicken's chest.

For a moment there was a large blue splotch in the center of Chicken's shirt. Then it was gone.

Smoke smiled at Chicken. "Feel better?"

Chicken nodded.

Smoke leaned forward and kissed her on the forehead. "You worry almost as much as he does."

Chicken frowned at her. "Tis mission most hazardous."

Smoke shrugged.

"This Parquor fella pears most powerful do he grab fair elder sister witch of R-Bar witch."

Ran leaned close to them and whispered. "Ripple sent a tell and told me of the special spell that she and some of her sisters were raising." Ran frowned. Dark swirled around them. "That spell is frightening, terrible terror promising."

"Yucko," said Messenger, pushing black stuff aside as she joined the group.

Ran waved it away. "Sorry sorry, kitten."

"What is he doing in there?" Messenger stared in

the direction of their new room.

"He is comforting R-Bar," explained Smoke.

Messenger gasped. And blushed.

Fair Morn joined them. "We holding a meeting?" And gave Chicken a poke and looked at Smoke. "What did you do to her?"

"Naught," snapped Chicken.

Messenger nodded. So did Ran.

"Nothing," said Smoke.

Fair Morn threw a comradely arm around the shorter Messenger's shoulders. "Let's make some more cookies, then."

They headed for the kitchen.

Chantal clumped in from the back door dressed in coveralls and high rubber boots. "Yum, yum, fresh cookies."

"Peeeeeee you." Messenger wrinkled her nose and pointed at the floor. "You get to clean it up."

Chantal smiled and yanked off her boots. "Just old barnyard." She carried the boots to the back porch and wiped the floor. "Yes, mother. All clean."

"First batch is almost ready," said Fair Morn as she peered through the glass fronted door into the one of the ovens.

"Shower time." Chantal headed for the shower room.

Je'leel looked over Messenger's shoulder. "May I learn this art? Mom?"

"Oh," gasped Messenger, startled by her silent approach. "Sure. Really really quiet."

"Indjinns do not clump. Nor do their daughters." Je'leel stepped back and watched everything carefully as Messenger prepared another batch of cookie dough.

Fair Morn began dropping lumps of dough onto another cookie sheet.

"We are making just lots and lots," explained Messenger.

Je'leel pointed. "What are those brown bits?"

"Chocolate chips."

"Everyone's favorite cookie." Fair Morn exchanged cookie sheets with the oven and scraped the finished cookies onto the cooling rack.

"So, how ya doing?" He gave her a tickle here and there.

"Not ticklish," she mumbled, squirming a little.

"O.K."

"We are leaving her home when we go."

"Who?"

"Our daughter."

"Je'leel?"

"Yep."

"O.K. She is too young for that kind of thing anyway."

R-Bar kissed his chest.

He stroked her hair and shifted around, just a little. "Not too bad."

"What?"

"For a little, short witch." He laughed.

She straightened up and frowned at him. "I am not little, or short."

"Relatively speaking." He gave her a gentle poke with one finger.

"TINK!"

"Just checking."

"For what?"

"Wads of paper, sponge rubber. Things like that."

"Bik tik pak pak," she snapped. "Witches do not do things like that." She tugged her shirt the rest of the way from her trousers. "Check!"

"Naw," he said. "I'll take your word for it." And undid the last button. "But if you insist."

"Well?"

"Yep. Just you. No artificial ingredients. One hundred percent natural."

"Hum, hum."

"Wanna go get a cookie, cookie? Fresh. Chocolate chip." He had peeked out just to check on what might be happening. He and R-Bar had been clamped shut from all the others.

"Yessssssssss."

"Good." He kissed her. "Button your shirt, show off, and let's go."

Chicken met them as they entered the large living room. She grinned at him and began to unbutton her shirt.

"What are you doing?"

"Me'Lord, We would be comforted as well." She burst into laughter.

"Ha. Ha. Ha," stated Tinker. "Ho. Ho. Ho."

"Not funny," hissed R-Bar.

"Pretty tricky," said Smoke as they all headed for the kitchen sniffing the wonderful odor drifting from there. She nudged his shoulder with her's. "Sneaking her shirt open."

"Don't start," he grumbled.

Chantal met them in the kitchen. She was wearing one of the thick white robes. And was munching on a cookie. She glanced down, up, and winked at him. "All natural."

"Now what?" He looked at eight happy faces.

"Don't pay any attention to them," he said to Je'leel. "They get cabin fever."

Je'leel jerked and blanched and hastily searched each of the smiling faces for signs of this terrible disease.

"It is nothing," whispered Messenger. "I will tell you later."

Sha'gar handed him a cookie and eyed R-Bar.

"Bik bik," suggested R-Bar.

"Witch pootak," observed Sha'gar, handing her a cookie.

"Hum," said Ran.

R-Bar ignored her and poured a glass of milk. "What's for dinner?"

"Steak and fries," said Smoke. "Eat lots. We are leaving in the morning." He looked at him. "Reep came by while you were . . . comforting her. She found his home."

He nodded. "O.K. Big dinner, big breakfast. Lots of sleep in between."

"Spoil sport." Fair Morn twisted the ornate ring on her finger.

"Je'leel, this is J. C., one of my very best friends, and his wife, Reep, one of R-Bar's sisters." Tinker threw an arm around Je'leel's shoulders. "My Daughter."

They had been waiting on the rear deck, waiting for Reep to show up. J. C. drove them over so he could talk with Tinker before the group left. And to be able to get back to Doc's place without walking. Popping in and out was frowned upon and he didn't want Doc to start asking questions.

"A very pretty daughter," whispered the morning breeze.

J. C. smiled at Tinker. "Certainly is." He lifted Reep up and kissed her. "Be careful out there."

Reep nodded. And kissed him again. Then she slowly settled to the deck and looked from Tinker to R-Bar.

"We are ready," said R-Bar. Ran nodded.

Reep floated out into the first pasture just beyond the flower beds. They all gathered around her.

And waved goodbye to Je'leel and J. C.

And disappeared.

"Ahhhhhhhhh?" said J. C. "Want me to stay up here until they return?"

Je'leel shook her head. "No, I will be safe."

"Sure?"

"Oh yes. I am well trained."

"I suppose."

"Mother did it."

"Oh. Which mother?"

She smiled at him. "Dat."

J. C. sat on one of the benches with a thump and looked at her teeth. "Her?"

She nodded. "Yes, Uncle."

"Just J. C., please. Dat? But . . . . "

Je'leel sat next to him. "I am half-human. Mother made sure that I would appear correct for your kind. No fangs, no claws, and eyes just like his."

J. C. nodded slowly. "He, your father, continues to amaze me." He smiled at her. "You sure you don't want some company up here?"

"Oh, no, I am safe."

He stood. "O.K., then I'll see you later. Give me a call if you need anything."

"I will."

Je'leel walked with him out to his battered van and watched him drive away. She headed back inside the house and wondered why her uncle worried so much.

Kantor's Spot. An Ice World.

They appeared.

In the large room.

Everyone held weapons.

Reep was holding a small box in her left hand. She hadn't been holding it when they twisted out from home.

"What's that?" Tinker indicated the box.

"Ripple's gift," sighed dark shadow. "Her gift for Parquor."

"Smoke?" He scanned the empty room. Not much to see. One sorta large throne, one sorta large couch.

He walked over to check the furniture. He poked the sorta couch with one finger, gently, carefully. There were some very ugly stains on it.

"No one around, MindMate. Just us."

"Uh huh." He walked back and stood next to her. "Just like always." He sighed, and sucked in a deep breath. "O.K., everyone gather around. It is strategy time."

Once they had all moved close, he said to Fair Morn, "Big Bird, have you ever fired that cannon of your's at full strength?"

Fair Morn shook her head. "No. I was afraid to do that. Macabre said that it would punch holes in anything."

He grinned. Three witches and one magician sucked in their breath. And looked uneasy

"Set it. Full strength." He exhaled loudly. "I am

really tired of getting beat to pieces." He smiled at them. "Boy, do I ever understand Macabre's approach to life. Now." He looked from face to face. "Whatever you use, I want it to be as big and bad as it can be. All right?"

Everyone nodded.

The air crackled around witches and magician.

"Sounds like we are ready. Reep, take us where ever we need to go from here."

Tatok. High Mountains. Stark and Bare.

The young woman smashed the clatka beast across the snout with the thick wooden staff. Then broke several of its ribs, and drove it wobbling from the room.

She had washed and bathed this person and clothed her in new garments, carefully selected. And had left the room to fetch a meal. And returned to the sight of the caltka beast lying on top of her, feeding.

She set the staff next to the bed. "I will kill it, if it dares to return," she snarled to herself and the woman as she set the tray on a small table. After propping up the limp figure with large pillows, she began to gently feed her.

"I would kill him also but I am unable to do that." She indicated the staff. "All I have is this. And he guards too well."

She brushed the woman's hair back gently and watched her chew slowly. "He took me from my elseplace just before his accident."

"I am Zinjak Gurkta, level one trained. To kill him

would be a joy." She began to feed her patient again.

"You look witch to me, all pale moonlight skin and black eyes and hair." She gently touched the scar on Ranna's cheek and then raised the cup to silent lips. "Drink deep. It is a curative. He will not know."

She wiped the lips after removing the cup, and leaned close. "He must hate you deeply." She kissed her patient. "Sleep now." And hurried from the room, clenching the thick wooden staff in one hand.

"So, where are we now?"

They stood in the middle of a large room with doors all around the walls. The ceiling curved high overhead.

"Where the warlock came to," whispered the deep shadows at his side. "He left a small strand. Almost everyone does. I followed it. Rekel felt a faint orange magic touch as well."

"Smoke?"

He looked around the room. It was just a large empty chamber.

Smoke's minds reached out. Then she pointed. "A very angry young woman, that way." She swung her arm. "A number of things that way." Then turned and pointed. "The one we seek, that way." The arm shifted. "Ranna there."

"Hold it." Tinker waved his arms wildly as people started moving. "Slow up, let's do it this way. Smoke, Chicken, you guys go see to the angry young woman. Reep, Sha'gar, and Ran can look in upon Parquor. R-Bar, Chantal, and I will find Ranna. Fair Morn will remove everything in the direction of the things. Messenger will stay here with her." He looked around. "O.K.?"

Everyone nodded.

He reached up and swung down the great black sword. It began singing a soft song of destruction, taking control. "Right. And remember. I do not care what kind of destruction or damage we do to this place just as long as it is not to us."

He nudged R-Bar and Chantal toward the door that Smoke had indicated would lead them to Ranna.

As everyone burst through their assigned doors, Fair Morn waved Messenger to stand behind herself. "Back, kitten." She raised the muzzle of her space cannon and fired.

"GOSH!" Messenger peered around Fair Morn.

The cannon had made no sound as per usual.

One moment they were standing in a large circular room with many doors. Now a third of the room's wall was missing in the direction that Fair Morn had fired.

Beyond the opening there was nothing in an ever widening fan shaped space, far out there, to the horizon. The intervening mountains were now truncated pyramids. Cold wind gushed in through the opening.

Structural elements of the building crackled, bent, tumbled down, loosened from above by suddenly missing lower support.

Fair Morn and Messenger hastily backed up until they stood with their backs pressed against the wall between two of the still closed doors.

"Guess that we will just have to wait here until someone calls," said Fair Morn, adjusting some levers on the side of her device. "Certainly a Macabre weapon all right."

Three doors and two halls in, Smoke skidded to a halt and pointed, cautioning Chicken to get ready.

Chicken nodded, jerked the knife from her boot, and stood, sword in one hand, knife in the other, waiting for Smoke to open the door.

Smoke smashed it open and hurtled in.

The young woman whirled to one side, her staff cracking Smoke on the side of one shoulder. She danced further back, eyes dancing from face to face.

Chicken inched sideways, weapons making little flicking motions. "Yield, or die, wench."

"Kesh tunk," spat the woman, slipping away. Then she leaped backwards, eyes flying wide.

A Carkant rose from the floor. It drooled in her direction. The beast spread itself sideways forcing her to move toward the killer dressed all in yellow.

Screaming the battle-die oath, she hurtled herself to quick ending, attacking the beast.

Smoke grabbed the arm wielding the stave and threw the young woman to the floor. Smoke's minds punched through her war drive. The woman crumpled loosely.

Chicken hurried over. "Dark sister, what manner of beast t'were that?"

Smoke shrugged "Something that she knew. I thought that she would move in your direction. We can leave her here." She pointed. "We go that way."

Chicken knelt next to the body and pried the stave from still tightly clenched fingers and then straightened out arms and legs. And laughed. "Most curvaceous a warrior do be this one."

"Warrior Queen, you may inspect our prize later."

"Dark One, peer you here. This wench do be fair decorated." Chicken's fingers lightly ran across the colored pattern. "Passing strange this do be, tis textured."

Smoke leaned over and ran one finger down the decoration. "Yep." She headed for the door. "Come."

They charged into the room.

"Empty! Check that bed looking thing, I'll watch the doors." He swung around to face the three doors in the one wall. Chantal did the same thing, revolver in hand.

R-Bar stepped to the only piece of furniture and began yanking bed clothes in all directions.

"Sister!"

Dark swirled in all directions. Lightning crackled across the ceiling.

Tinker spun, ran over to see. "Ranna?"

R-Bar growled and began testing the magical bonds.

"She alive? Looks pretty bad to me."

"Kak tak! It will not loosen." She screamed.

Flapping the sword onto his back, he grabbed her.

"He cast slow die on her. If we can't break those bonds, it will eat her alive. Slowly. It was a spell bond break ward."

"Worse and worse." *Smoke?*

Coming. Kitten, come to us. Now!

Coming mom.

Reep, Ran, and Sha'gar slipped into the room.

"Are you the Tinker thing?" asked Parquor. White flare smashed them back against the wall.

Red flame boiled around Sha'gar, igniting the wall coverings, melting the white away.

"A MAGE! A red mage!" howled Parquor. "What is a mage like you doing with two witches like these?" He twisted white around and deflected a silver globe that blasted past his head.

He glared at Ran. "What are you doing here, Tanpak?" He reached out to call in the beasts but found only empty space.

Staring at them, he created a veil between himself and Reep. "I will wear your eyes as ear ornaments, Faan spak tik."

Reep pitched the box to his feet, slipped sideways

casting Ripple's protection over herself and the others.

The box bounced, rattled, and came to rest again his left foot.

The top popped open.

And something oozed out.

"THREE LEVELS PROHIBITED," screamed Parquor, lurching away, freezing the thing in place.

Crackling loudly, it expanded and licked his foot. The foot turned black.

Banging down white, he repaired and staggered back.

Reep looked at the veil. It began to decay and crumple to dust. She drifted sideways and said to him, voice soft as death. "You are no more, Warlock called Parquor the White."

She urged Ran and Sha'gar toward one of the doors. And triggered the releasing spell Ripple and her other sisters had wrapped around the box, many layers deep.

For an instant, space and time cracked open, and it slipped through.

Shoving everyone outside, Reep slammed the door shut and bound it and the room beyond in multilayers, in the deepest of silences. No one needed to hear the sounds coming from that room.

She gently touched Sha'gar on one arm. "Calm calm, fierce Daughter Magician. That one is paying for his evil deed and life." She looked at Ran. "Settle, Tanpak witch, settle. We must find my sisters."

Ran nodded and pointed. "That door! His Smoke directs us that way."

Messenger hurtled into the room. "MyTinker?" Her wand crackled and buzzed. She hurried to his side.

He pointed at the slack form lying on the bed. "Can you loosen her bonds? R-Bar tried and couldn't. She triggered something called a slow die."

Messenger stared and stared. "Ooooooooooh. It is going to kill her."

"What?" snapped R-Bar.

Messenger wiped her eyes with her free hand. "She is all tangled in white, all tied and tied. I can't see or find an end to it."

"Can't you just break it?" Tinker handed her his handkerchief.

Messenger shook her head. "No. It has to be untied." And wiped her eyes again.

Reep, Ran, and Sha'gar crashed into the room. Ran and Sha'gar ran. Reep drifted. They stood and stared at the bed.

"Trapped trapped," said Ran. She walked around the end of the bed and threw an arm around R-Bar. "Sorry sorry."

Sha'gar looked at Tinker and shook her head.

Reep leaned forward, frowned, touched Ranna's forehead and hissed softly. "He deserved Ripple's gift." Dark swirled around her.

Smoke, Fair Morn, and Chicken charged into the

room.

"Oh my gosh!" Messenger blushed and whispered, "'I forgot."

"What?" He stared at her.

"His ring. Ranna's gift to me." Messenger slipped it from her finger, lifted one slack hand, pushed the ring over and down one of Ranna's fingers. She ran around the bed and shoved him backwards. "Make room, everyone make room."

Loud sizzling buzzed from the bed as white mist began to form and drift from Ranna and to pour fog soft streamers over the edge of the bed. The bonds uncoiled and shattered, a cacophony of rupturing piano strings.

Messenger clapped her hands over her ears and looked at R-Bar.

Ranna's eyes fluttered, and popped open. She coughed, cleared her throat, and rasped, "Dak dak kak pak to."

R-Bar stepped close, leaned over and kissed her sister. "That is worse than anything I have ever heard from you before."

Reep drifted over and hugged Tinker. Soft shadows whispered in his ear, "What ever you would ever wish, that I will do."

Ranna's eyes swivelled in his direction. "Chosen One, witch debt. Again." She managed a weak smile. "When I heal. Again."

Reep released Tinker and drifted around to kiss R-Bar. "Our sister needs quiet quiet."

R-Bar nodded. So did Ran.

He backed away, made a quick check of everyone, and sighed. "Well, that went easier than I thought that it would go." He nodded. "O.K., she can stay with us. Again."

A door slammed open and smashed back against the wall as she charged into the room, clenching the wooden staff, screaming, "KAAAAAAAAAAA!" And attacked them.

"GA'ZOOKS!" yelled Chicken, parrying a blow to the head. "Tis most fair decorated amazon."

"Who is?" The great black sword sliced the staff into two pieces.

"Pretty strong." Smoke dodged away from a wild kick in her direction.

Fair Morn grabbed the back of the young woman's blouse, yanked, and spun, material ripped as the woman was hurled across the room to slam into the far wall.

"Whooops." Fair Morn stared at the piece of cloth, the large piece of cloth she held in her hand. "Flimsy stuff."

Lurching to her feet the young woman snarled and leaped at Chantal. Who punched her in the gut, two quick jabs to the jaw. She shoved the bent figure to the floor and sat on her stomach and grabbed her by the throat. "One more move out of you and I am going to break your face."

"Who is that?" He glared at everyone in the room.

Most of them looked blank back at him.

"She was in one of the rooms, several over that way." Smoke pointed.

"Most fierce a'warrior, Me'Lord." Chicken smiled at him. "Do attack one and all. Pears most crazed."

Reep drifted close and gently touched Tinker's hand. "We must leave. This elseplace is soon to die."

R-Bar snatched one of Ran's hands and grabbed one of Sha'gar's.

Grandeville. Tinker's Place.
They thumped down into the middle of the open space in The Chamber.

Fair Morn ran over, scooped Ranna into her arms. "Where?"

"Couch," grumbled Ranna. "I do not wish to be alone."

Fair Morn headed for the large living room.

Reep bowed to Tinker and disappeared. In a puff of black.

"Great King," gasped Chicken. "Fair warrior woman tis here."

"What?"

Chicken pointed. He spun. She lay in a crumpled heap against one of the walls.

"Merde."

Chantal stomped over. "I'll take her to the living room. You can admire her bod there." She straightened out the body, heaved her into her arms, and headed out and down the hallway.

He glared at Chicken. "I thought that we were done adding?"

Chicken stepped close, kissed him. "Fret thee naught, Sweet Our Prince. Tis healing, nay bedding, do that wench most require."

She tugged him toward the door to the hall. "Come, let us away go, and rid thyself of thy most fearsome blade."

They went.

He did.

Smoke, Messenger, and Ran brought cocoa and coffee to the large living room.

Ranna was propped up in one of the couches, a number of pillows stuffed behind her back. She sipped her cocoa and nodded at Tinker as he dropped into his chair.

"I make better brown liquid," she said.

"How are you feeling?"

"Alive. You may have anything that I have to give." She held up her free hand. "How did I get this ring back?"

Messenger dropped into the couch next to Ranna. "I put it there. It freed you from your bonds. He used another ring to make the bonds. It knew how to untie them. And did." She smiled at Ranna. "That ring is very, very nice."

Chantal finished stuffing blankets around the

young woman, tucking a thick comforter up around her neck. She peered into eyes that were slowly focusing. Then turned and looked at Ranna. "Who is this babe?"

Ranna shrugged, and winced at the sudden pain. "She was there. Taken by Parquor from some elseplace somewhere. A warrior type, I think."

Soft mumbling swung all the heads in one direction. The person under discussion was trying to sit up.

Sha'gar leaped to her feet and hurried over, to peer into pale yellow eyes. "If you attack any one of us I will kill you horribly." She tapped the young woman on the forehead with the glowing blue tip of a flaming red wand.

The pale eyes wandered from face to face, stopping on Ranna. She smiled. "You live."

Ranna nodded. "The Chosen one, and his, did it. Saved me, saved us."

Sha'gar jerked.

R-Bar sucked in a quick breath.

Ranna's sentence was twisted wrong. Proper Faan form was always cast to refer to her mate as her's, never marking the mate as having the witch as his.

Sha'gar stared at her Aunt and wondered whether her captivity had caused brain damage.

Ranna smiled witch wicked at R-Bar. "It is true."

The young woman stared at Tinker. "You are him?"

He sighed. "Yes?"

>>> 555 <<<

She forced herself into a sitting position. "I am Anjan Trap Zahan, first level Zinjak Gurkta!"

Tinker smiled at her. "Pleased to meet you. What is that?"

"No-fear weapon." She pointed at Smoke with her chin. "That kazan your's?"

"Yep. All mine."

Anjan looked at them, one by one by one by one. "All? Yours?"

"Nope. Ranna is just a visitor, sorta."

Anjan frowned.

"That beat up one on the couch," he explained. "Is Ranna. She is R-Bar's sister." He indicated the short witch.

Anjan smiled at Ranna. "A not-tied?"

Ranna shrugged.

Tinker stood. "How about you two rest. We have things to do."

He headed from the room. So did the rest. They had gear to put away, chores to do. It would be dinner time before they were all once again back inside the house.

Very late in the day some headed for the shower room, some headed for the kitchen.

He headed for the large living room, coffee cup in hand.

Anjan was sleeping with Ranna, their arms wrapped around each other. The kittens had joined the pair, nesting in various hollows.

"Hum," said R-Bar, coming in, waiting until she had a proper lap to sit in.

"Certainly freed up one couch," he mumbled, taking a sip from his cup.

She plucked at a button on his shirt. "I asked Ramp to contact Sa'ar and ask her to see whether the Vander have anything in their archives that talk about this zinjak gurkta group."

"Did you try to contact Mirf. I'll bet that Monetary Control has something in their files."

"I sent to Ripple. She said that Hanred was checking."

"Busy, busy, busy." He bumped the tip of her nose with his cup.

"Tink?" She undid another button.

"Who cares?" He handed her his cup. "Hold this."

She did.

He quickly unfastened all the buttons on her shirt, and yanked it free from her trousers. And took back his cup. "Thanks."

She growled at him.

He laughed. "Well, one arm is holding you, one hand is holding my cup." The holding arm snaked a hand around and tickled her, just a little:

"Hum, hum, hum," she murmured as she wiggled into a more comfortable position.

He nodded. "Pretty nice, you know."

"What is?"

He ran his thumb, still holding his cup, down her sternum. "You."

She slipped her hand inside his shirt and tickled a rib or two. "Of course."

"Not too bad," commented a small voice from the other couch. It was Dat, standing on top of the back. "You going to take her shirt off in public?"

"Quiet, Dat." He frowned in her direction.

Anjan's eyes popped open. She rolled and saw Dat, then the kittens. She began to shake Ranna.

Ranna's eyes flew open. "Dik dik." she snarled.

"Ran'na, we are beset by tzin and bakan."

Ranna looked up and smiled. "That small person is Dat, his indjinn, and a friend. The fuzzy things are called Kit Tens. They are friendly pet beasts belonging to them." She looked over at Tinker and R-Bar. "Hum, hum, hum."

R-Bar hissed at her and buttoned her shirt. "You are sounding better, sister."

Ranna nodded. "I heal fast fast. It is the white ring."

"How about you?" He nodded at Anjan.

She sat up, the cover falling to puddle soft folds around her waist. "Much well, Great and Mighty Warrior."

"Where's your shirt?" he grumbled.

"Napata." She pointed at the jumble on the floor.

"Very nice." Dat sat cross-legged on the couch back and admired Anjan's torso.

"Most pleasing for the eyes," said Chicken as she walked in from the hall and stood behind his chair. "Think thee not, My Lord?"

"Right," he mumbled. "Get her a shirt."

"To hear is to obey." Chicken laughed as she yanked off her shirt and tossed it to Anjan. "Do hide your charms tall and most fierce warrior else he do be greatly distracted becomen."

"Princess!"

Chicken headed back into the hall, and called back over her shoulder. "We will Ourself put on a'new."

Anjan shoved her arms into the sleeves, the shirt hanging half down her back, and stared at the buttons.

"Nice design." Dat smiled at her and indicated the marking that ran from her left shoulder diagonally to her right hip. "An'gurkta'dark."

Anjan's head snapped around. "You read?"

Ranna reached over and yanked the shirt into place and began to button it.

"Of course." Dat nodded. "Death Warrior Society." She stood and stretched. "You have reached the upper grade."

Anjan sat straighter. "Top."

Ranna brushed Anjan's hair back from her forehead. "Fierce."

"DINNER TIME!" announced Fair Morn from the dining room.

Anjan helped Ranna stand.

All through the meal, Anjan saw to it that Ranna's food was cut just so and that she ate a goodly amount.

R-Bar watched them and looked at Tinker.

He winked at her. *Looks like your sister found a guardian, so to speak.*

Most not witch.

Hum, interjected Ran.

Smoke shoved the platter of roast beef across the table toward Ranna and Anjan.

Chantal winked at him, using the eye on the far side, away from Ranna and Anjan. *Looks like that is one witch that you won't have to worry about, Babe Magnet.*

That is over. Remember?

"Pass the coffee," said Chantal.

After dessert, Ranna shoved back her chair and stood. "We are going to Doth Lamex. To rest. To finish healing."

Anjan stood. Ranna slipped an arm around her and smiled, a witch sly smile at Tinker.

The pair disappeared.

"Gosh," said Messenger.

"Let's watch a movie." He stood.

They filtered into the large living room.

"Hit the sack early," he added.

Messenger giggled.

Fair Morn nudged him. "That's me."

"Huh?"

"Your friendly sack."

He sighed. "Sounds like everything is back to normal around here."

She kissed him.

It was.
> Back to normal.
>> More or less.
> For awhile.
> For them.

Individuals Of Note

Grandeville.

Tinker's Place
John Tinker -- the individual used as an intermediary by Big Red in his ongoing activities to maintain the balance of the universes. During his initial time on Mirk Wild Weald, Tinker was told by The Thought that he is The Chosen One of legend. Now merged telepathically into an entity with the rest following the cultural values of Smoke's people.
Smoke of the Velvetmist - a gigantic, telepathic carnivore, now transformed into a human shape by Big Red. She was selected from her home, a hidden and never visited elseplace, to be one of the original companions to aid and journey with John Tinker. Now MindMate to Tinker, Chicken and the rest.
Princess Chicken - an Easter Season fluffy chicken toy from an Easter basket, transformed by Big Red and placed as a traveling companion and aid for John Tinker.
Messenger - Once "The Messenger" of her people but joined with Tinker and the rest when she began to fold inside herself believing Tinker and crew were monsters and demons from her folk's mythology come alive.

Fair Morn - a one-time mythological jest created by the magical force, Big Red. Messenger severed her magical bonds changing Fair Morn from jest to an alive person.
R-Bar - a witch of The Faan clan, now joined into the polyorganism of Tinker and the rest by Smoke.
    Sedeem - her daughter, a magician.
        Farth - her mate-for-life, a Silver Ranger.
Ferrelden - of the Risshar, a Night Runner from Zhorndar'h. (Deceased).
Flar - one time owner of a Magical Items Shop. (Deceased.)
Chantal Baire - a Veterinarian with a clinic near Grandeville.
Ran - witch of the Tanpak clan. Prefers to be called Ran.
Sha'gar - Faan magician, daughter of Reep and J.C.
Dat - an indjinn, gifted to Tinker when they bought a ring, The Eye of Dat.
    Je'leel - her daughter.

Chantal's Friends
Frederica Hensler - "Freddie" - lives in Portland.
    Ralph Andervante - her husband
Sandrew Sherl Sandermeyer now **Anderson** - "Sandy" - Tinker's Attorney.
    Red - her husband, a member of the Grandeville Police Department.
Janine Teacate - "Streak" - Sandy's secretary.

Chen's Chinese - The Building.
Adam Lieu Chen - Master Chen owns and operates *Chen's Chinese,* a restaurant located in Greater Downtown Grandeville. He also trains Tinker in the martial arts.

Dragon Ranch - not far from Tinker's Place.
Prince Goose - a windup plastic toy transformed by Big Red into a traveling companion for John Tinker. Goose commands The Guard, a number of warriors vaguely reminiscent of Grenadier Guards. He is a brother of Chicken.
Chen Gum Lung - The Golden Dragon of the House of Chen. She is a sometimes amulet gifted to Tinker by Master Chen.

Doc's Home
Kappa "Doc" Heckmann - anthropologist and adventurer. A friend and neighbor of John Tinker's.
J. C. Smith - one of Tinker's close friends. He works for Doc in many capacities.
> **Reep** - of the Faan witch clan, married to J. C.
> > **Szaifeh** - her daughter, a witch.
> > **Sha'gar** - her daughter, a magician.

Membrane - one of Doc's "associates." He run Doc's stores, *Cactus Spine*, specializing in cacti and succulents.
Badnews Treefalls - another of Doc's "associates." He is Doc's constant companion.

The Hardcastle Residence.
Alandale Fredrico Hardcastle IV, known as "Hard" by all his friends.
> **Ramp** - of the Faan witch clan, a magician, his wife.
>> **Sa'ar** - her twin daughter, a magician.
>> **Shem** - her twin son, a magician, also known by his parents and grandparents as Alandale Fredrico Hardcastle V.
>>> **Tajaar** - his wife.

Grandeville Police Department (GPD)
Red and **Green** - two very large men who once played football together on the local college team. They function, usually, as the late night patrol. They are good friends of Tinker, J. C., and Hard.

The Elseplaces

Paradise.
Big Red - a pure force of magic personified. He is primarily concerned with maintaining the balance and order of the universe of universes. And, more often than not, has some influence over the events that plague Tinker.
> **Dancing-All-The-Day** - Big Red's wife.
>> **Silly-All-The-Day** - their son.
>>> **Treena** - the wife of Silly.

Various - depending upon mood.
Dram - an individual often called The Evil One. He began life on Murk Wild Weald as a magician-in-training. But after long and secretive study in The Library of Arcana he slowly was transformed by his knowledge and his ambitions into one of the few pure forces in the universe of universes. Dram has a tendency to work at living up to his title.

Stumpf.
The-Mountain-That-Walks - an individual most often addressed as Mountain by his traveling companions. He is one of the original companions, selected from Stumpf, to aid John Tinker.

A Place Unnamed.
Macabre - who specializes in killing things. He is usually accompanied by his pets: The Vipers, and the Sparkling Tigers.
Gyre - his female companion, created by his vessel, Gyreship.

The Six Lands.
Sorrowful Mistidings - a professional Teller of Tales, selected from The Six Lands, as one of the original companions to aid John Tinker. He lived with his wife and sons. Now deceased.
Tears Trimblechin - his grandson, a growing Teller of Tales, trained by his grandfather.

Clear Bandler - The Land of Magicians
The $1.98 Magician - trained by Big Red and told to aid Tinker in whatever manner he could.
Plum Duff - a magician and consort to $1.98.

Bahn Duhr Tohr
Willawa, The White Warrior, Queen of all the lands.
Toucan, The King - he is the brother of Prince Goose and Princess Chicken and once was Tinker's advisor.
Hanred, Ripple's mate-for-life - he is a Master Illusionist who once traveled widely through the universe of universes and is also known by many of the folk as "Old Hanred."
Ripple, Advisor to the Royals - she is the Clan Head of the Faan witch clan.
    Shitar - her daughter, a witch.
    Sook - her daughter, a witch.

Dol Spar - Headquarters of The Monetary Control and Mirf's home.
Mirf - The Special Chief First Inspector, often sent on special assignments by The General, the overall director of The Monetary Control and her boss.
    Fred - a suk-dragon, her Assistant.
    Quan - Fred's mate - Mirf's Assistant.

Magevern - home of the Vander mage Guild.
Sa'ar - the Heart of the Vander, who made Tinker The Lord of The Vander.

Clans, Guilds, and Other Organizations.
(known individuals listed)

Anaza sorcerer Phylota located in Far Corner.
- **Netanada** -- Elixa (Clan Head), Sorceress.
- **Abadoda** -- Three Rank Sorceress.
- **Hatopa** -- Three Rank Sorcerer.
- Important Artifacts.
  - The Ancient Book of Songs.

The Divineal of Thantala located in Murklan Obscuratan. A Place Never Visited.
- **Lady Grimtouch** - The Glimmer (Clan Head) of The Divineal of Thantala.
- **Lady Fairdeath** - traveling with Sluba mage Ransapal, chosen as her consort.
- **Lady Dawnmort**
- **Lady Softtouch**
- **Lady Nightreaper**
- **Lady Final Kiss**
- **Lady Lastgift**
- Clan robe color - forest green almost black; carry a short gold staff.
- Important Artifacts
  - The Book of Death.

Potri witch Clan
    Turintor
Clan robe colors - grape and green design.

Faan witch Clan - scattered widely throughout the universe of universes.
    Ripple - Clan Head - The fifth Born.
        Hanred, the Illusionist, her Mate-For-Life.
            Shitar - their daughter, a witch.
            Sook - their daughter, a witch.
Ranna - The First Born
Riz - The Second Born.
Rekel - The Third Born.
Rbat - The Fourth Born. At one time thought by many to have gone far.
Reptar - The Sixth Born.
Rumtah - The Seventh Born. Known as The Lucky One.
Reep - The Eighth Born. Known as The Silent One.
    Married to **J. C.**
        Szaifeh - their daughter, a witch.
        Sha'gar - their daughter, a magician.
Rotak - The Ninth Born.
Raft - The Tenth Born. Known as The Fast.
R-Bar - The Eleventh Born. Called The Runt.
    Tinker - her Mate-For-Life
        Sedeem, their daughter, a magician.

Ramp - The Twelveth Born. A Magician.
> Married to **Hard**.
>> **Sa'ar**, their daughter, a magician.
>> **Shem**, their son, a magician.
> Important artifacts.
>> An immense collection of volumes dealing with the arcane collected by Hanred during his many travels through the universe of universes.

Talair witch Clan - located on Tanadra.
> **Motaiss** - a warlock
> **Mendurra** - a witch.
> Clothes colors - black with just a hint of faint grey in an ornate design that runs down the outside of each sleeve.

Sluba mage Guild, one member located in Three Trees Town.
> **Ransapal**- studied the Dark Under and ancient witch history. Traveling with Lady Fairdeath as her consort.

Vander mage Guild - located in Magevern.
> **Sa'ar** - the Heart of the Vander.
> **Tobtz** - the Soul of the Vander.
> **Cazor** - mage warrior.
> **Moonda**
> **Aada**

Bant
Arktan - adept at crafting material things.
Elend - archivist.
Imdar - the Healer.
    Rorx - Vander warlock - her son by Tinker.
    Szaifeh - his Mate-For-Life.
Clothes color - they are always dressed in garb of the faintest purple. The folk often call them "The Purple Magicians."

The Wood With located in Newlar, relocated from Blurratha. Hidden. In Plain Sight.
    Fairlan - Cluster Head
    Ringlan - Cluster Head
    Clearlar - Cluster Head
    Faerlar - Cluster Head
    Flerlan - The Observer
The Wood With are always accompanied by their beast. When the Wood With are present one might notice the smell of blooming flowers on the air.

The Garden Gnomes located in Growing Green.
    Phineas Grass
    Hiram Toadstoll
    Franny Waxflower
    Franelken Vetch
    Tiny Rosebud - the emissary
    Rose Perrywinkle

Monetary Control - located on Dol Spar.
    The General - Head of Monetary Control.
    Mirf - Head of the Special Investigations Office.
        Fred - a suk-dragon - First Assistant.
        Quan - Fred's mate - First Assistant.

Bits and Pieces of Cultural Data
(From the files of Monetary Control)

The Garden Gnomes.

The Garden Gnomes are a small folk, perhaps the smallest of all the folk. As their name implies they are fascinated by gardening and frequently visit those gardens that they recognize as being above the average in terms of arrangement and care, whether ornamental or functional.

At some point, in their past, one of them had been seen while visiting a particularly well designed ornamental garden. This kind of happening was not something that they liked to happen nor did they like to talk about it. This garden, as things seem to happen to this folk or that folk over their histories, belonged to a sculptress of some skill and very fast eyes. She made a statue of what her eyes saw as just a fleeting glance and set this statue in and among a artfully organized patch of flowers.

And as things so often happen, a visitor saw this statue and asked the owner to make one for him. And so it went. And so it went. Much to the consternation of the Garden Gnomes.

And eventually an entire industry sprang up around these statues and their production. People even wrote fanciful books about the culture of these things. They were all wrong, of course. None of the authors had ever talked with one of these small folk or had ever visited a Garden Gnome village.

The end result of all this was that the Garden Gnomes

retreated deeper and deeper into areas where they would not, or could not, be observed.

Young Garden Gnomes, every once in awhile, on a dark, a particularly dark night, would steal one of these statues and hide them away.

Of course, it had no effect on the overall population of these fake garden gnomes. The industry was to well intrenched.

The Divineal of Thantala.

In time before time almost before memory it is told that the Divineal were there, passing through the universe of universes upon business that none dared ask about and few would dare challenge. The few that did, died. This rare occurrence, challenging one of them, and the result of that challenge, was told one to the other, and thus was the tale spread, and The Divineal were left to pursue their own interests. Most of these interests appeared to have something to do with Death. Death as a being, not merely as the end of something.

All the folk of the elseplaces recognized them as none else would dare to wear a deeply hooded robe of dark forest green that was almost black. And none else would presume to carry a short gold staff.

It is said among the many cultures in the universe of universes that few have ever seen the face of the individual hidden in the blackness of the deep hoods. It is also said that to see that face is to die. But, if one had ever done so and survived, none had ever so stated.

It is known and understood by most folk that one does not approach one of The Divineal and start a conversation. One does not watch one of The Divineal closely. One tries as much as possible to ignore their existence. One hopes to stay alive. It was this understanding that brought into being the label used far and wide for them, "The Sisters of Death." But it never, ever, was used when of them could hear it.

None knew where their elseplace, their homeplace, was located. None knew which of the many elseplaces, numbers beyond counting, would be the one wherein they resided. And even if one could find out, in some mysterious way, none would dare chose to go to such an elseplace.

The Divineal were polite and very soft spoken, if and when they might chose to speak to someone. And all, but the foolish and soon to be dead, would do all that they were capable of doing, if asked to do something. That is what the folk in the universe of universes believed. And none knew of anyone that had been asked and who had refused and survived.

None knew how many Divineal there were. None knew why or what they were about and most folk felt that the best place to be when one of them was around was to be somewhere else.

The Divineal were like a pebble dropped into a still pond whose action caused ripples to flow out in all directions. And like that pebble, they were totally unconcerned about those ripples.

The Witch Clans.

The Potri witch clan came into existence, as did all the witch clans, during what all the clans call "The Great Migration." From where this migration came is a great matter of debate and argumentation, but not why.

The ancestral clan, or clans, also a matter of intense debate and argumentation, had, through arcane knowledge, come to understand that a disaster beyond the control of any user of magic was about to happen to their homeland.

So they fled out into the universe of universes and over time the witch clan, or clans, splintered and grew into the myriad of clans that are now present.

The long ago seen disaster happened in a single violent explosion that removed their homeland as their sun erupted and ate everything within reach.

Some thing, some event, during that long ago migration and scatter brought into the witch culture a sense of authority coupled with a powerful magic that each clan cultivated. Each clan developed their own clan interests and evolved their own unique concept of magic. The end result of this was a somewhat provincial sense of proper witch attire and proper witch behavior. The pairing of these beliefs with their sense of authority meant that the folk living in the many elseplaces in the universe of universes knew that any witch tended to be rather short-tempered and had a predilection toward violent behavior when the behavior of other folk, witch, magician, or non-magical user, was felt by the witches to be engaged in improper behavior, undesirable behavior, or were just plain irritating.

Most witch clans dressed in wardrobes of midnight black, the exact style of their clothing varying widely. Some of the clans, in the long before before, had, for reasons they chose not to reveal, settled on wardrobes of other colors.

The Faan witch clan is unique. Among all of the witch clans scattered across the universe of universes, they are the only one that does not maintain a clan house. And, unlike all the other clans, the members are all and only generationally linked. The magic of the Faan flows down the female line from mother to daughter.

The Faan clan, unlike the other clans, are trained almost exclusively by their female relatives, mainly by their mother and their aunts. But if a sister has learned some new and unique twist, it may be shared, sister to sister. It is due to this multi-generational sharing and training that has made the Faan noted throughout the witch clans as being the most powerful clan and to be avoided if at all possible. And some few understand that at some point in the long ago long ago, in their mating with their chosen mates-for-life, from other witch lines, that something unusual happened that twisted and transformed their genetic material.

The result of this event was that, at times, their offspring are born with new and unique abilities. This tends to explain why the Faan do not maintain a clan house. Members of their clan, most often, prefer to wander mostly by themselves and to study and collect magic and magic spells. And other things.

The Mage Guilds

The mage Guilds apparently came into existence in the long ago long ago in a manner none understand or thought to record as this event was in a time when such occurrences were not seen as being important enough to warrant special note.

Magicians are, in one sense, at the opposite end of the magical spectrum from the witches. That is why the magicians and the witches tend to avoid each other whenever possible, especially physical contact. The magics of each tend to be unstable in contact, often resulting in fatal results. However, there is the fact that, at times, in a manner none truly understand, that magicians and witches may have close association, even mates of the others, without dire affects.

The **Vander mage Guild**, as written in the *Histories of the Arcane*, was once a sub-Order of the Fanderlaine mage Guild. Little is known of the Fanderlaine and what they thought to specialize their skills upon. The Vander sub-Order eventually split away from the Fanderlaine and pushed deep into the arcane knowledge that was of particular interest to their members. The Vander became the most radical of the experimenters of the mage Guilds and explored many areas of interest to them. This was considered most strange in the mage communities as the Guilds tend to be extremely conservative in their outlook and mage knowledge. Unlike most Guilds, the Vander are almost exclusively female, each member carefully selected for skills and aptitude.

The Anaza Sorcerers.

The Sorcerers were, and are, a small clan and have forever lived in small isolated elseplaces rarely relocating. Small isolated elseplaces were more common in the universe of universes than most of the folk realized. And that suited the Sorcerer clan quite well.

Why they preferred to live this way is lost in the dim reaches of an ancient history begun in a time almost before time itself. Various of the First Sorcerers at numerous points in time in their long, long history had searched their book of lore and learning, The Book Of Songs, for clues as to why this was the way it was. But each had failed. None of them realized, or knew from the oral traditions of the clan, that the Book Of Songs had come into existence long past the time when the reason why could be remembered.

So, as these things happen, the Sorcerer clan has remained reclusive and unknown to the larger universe of universes, not really hidden so much as just being very remote and private.

There was one piece of information known to the clan, a piece of information never allowed to be transmitted to anyone not a member of the clan. And similar to the reason for their preferring small, isolated elseplaces, the acquisition of this piece of information, the how and the when and the why of it did happen, was lost in the time long before before.

Someone, way back then, had learned to recognize the presence of a folk never seen and poorly understood. This recognition was not visual but rather a matter of odor, the odor of blooming flowers. With such an olfactory clue, this small clan of magic users, the Sorcerer clan, knew when the Wood With were around. They had never seen one but the delicate and pleasant odor told them when these folk were about.

The Wood With knew of this strange thing. So they tended to keep a watch on this small group more from a matter of curiosity than of any fear of what that clan might do.

The Sorcerer clan, of course, knew when these other strange folk came and went so they, the Sorcerers, tended to keep Sorcerer business very carefully hidden from these others. And in some strange and subtle way, the clan felt that the Wood With were not to be trusted. It was a cultural tradition, never to be questioned. The reason for this was also lost in the dim historical past. And, of course, they would never attempt to affect the behavior of the Wood With. Tradition also stated that this was not to be done.

The True History of the Magic Users as Discovered by the Divineal.

Many of the witch groups, whether the Witch Clan, the Sorcerer Phylota, the Nagar sort, and the Divineal have a tale from a time long before long before, and long before written records, of fleeing their homeland before it was destroyed by an event that no magic could prevent. This tale was passed member to member as an oral tradition and eventually was written down. It appears that this event happened.

But, as the magic users scattered into the universe of universes, their knowledge and identities became unique, group to group, and most felt that they were different than all the others.

However, all the groups so far mentioned are witch, even though some felt that others were not and needed to be hunted down and destroyed.

What none of them knew, or understood, is that the magicians were also from this same single event. Witch and magician fled from the same homeland, although, in some manner not understood, the magicians lost the remembrance of that past happening.

The witch and magician groups on that homeland attempted to cast a great spell of prevention. It failed and they fled. None knew that the failure of that spell caused a great change in their magics, with witch and magician forces becoming polar opposites of each other, hence the great danger, now, of mixing, one with the other, magic or personnel, most of the time.

The Wood With.
The Wood With are a small folk. If anyone saw one of this secretive group from a distance, an event so unlikely as to be in the realm of never, it might be thought that what was seen was a very young human child of ten or twelve years of age. Of course, few human children are accompanied by a beast as tall as they are.

The Wood With, from a time before forever, have remained unobserved and unknown, which is exactly what they wish. As a group they are, for the most part, uninterested in the affairs of other sapient beings in all the universe of universes. But, every so often, there occurs a one that attracts their attention. This event is a rare, but not unusual, happening.

The Wood With prefer to live in and among the big trees, taking comfort one from the other. They and the environment blur together where ever they might be. This skill, this cultural attribute, is the main reason, but not the only reason, why they remain unseen and unnoticed.

Their beasts are as unique a species as the Wood With. From an early age one finds the other and from that instant the pair are inseparable. The beasts blend into their surroundings with the same ease as their constant companions.

It is a peculiarity of the Wood With that their presence leaves a faint odor of blooming flowers in the air. In all the time of their existence only one small group have ever realized this fact. But that group's mythology and cultural values are such that the fact that they know this is all that they know. Every thing else they believe, everything else are tales from antiquity with all the error that derives from that.

The Kingdom and Kingdoms of Bahn Duhr Tohr.

The Kingdom of Bahn Duhr Tohr had been, until its most recent merging into a whole, a series of large and small kingdoms, each with a unique name and a unique color scheme. These color schemes were relegated to their Royalty and to their armies. It was very useful to combatants to be able to recognize friend from foe in the chaos of massed combat.

Many of the kingdoms, but not all, could trace their existence back into the dimly remembered past. Some even argued that they existed long before written records came into use. The kingdoms large and small, frequently merged, or broke apart, as the normal political intrigues and royal wheeling and dealing created large kingdoms out of smaller ones, or as so often happened, smaller kingdoms out of larger.

But, in spite of the usual turmoil over boundaries and royal household alignments, all the kingdoms were dependent upon each other as no single one had all the resources necessary for true self-sufficiency.

The bonds between the rulers and the ruled are tight and mutually advantageous. Rulers who did not keep the needs of their folk foremost did not last long. Of course, the occasional battle with a neighbor was accepted as just part of life. Battles were, for the most part, short. This was due to the usual approach to warfare that assumed that most of the fighting would happen between the royalty of the houses in contention. The knights and lessor troops often suffered nothing worse than broken bones. Most of the time this occurred during the first melee and charge.

Grandeville.

Grandeville is a small, rather isolated, rural community of 8,000 population (more or less) tucked away in the mountainous corner of northeastern Oregon. It survives in a provincial unawareness of many things, being overly conscious of the ancestors who settled the place long after the westward migration brought California, Washington, Oregon, and Idaho into statehood.

The town sprawls down from "The Bench," a shallow bench along the edge of the next door mountain slope, to The Blue River, named after the color it has after the first snow melt surges from the canyon and out across the valley proper, always threatening to jump its banks and flood the surrounding farm land.

There are two newspapers published in town, a weekly and a daily (except for Sunday). The Daily, *The Grandeville News*, tends to ignore anything happening outside the edge of town. The weekly, *The Mountain View*, tends to ignore anything happening in Grandeville and prints whatever the publisher happens to feel like publishing.

There are a number of local establishments of note:
- The Two Bags Full - a grocery store.
- The Railroad Bar and Grill - also known as The Rail.
- Big Darlene's Bar - the home of the Annual Chili Cookoff and Arm Wrestling

Championship Event, All Comers Invited.
- Johnson's Everything Shop.
- Chen's Chinese Restaurant.
- Leonard's Outdoor Supply Shop.
- The Always Open Gas Pump.
- The Romp and Stomp Motel.

About the Author

George R. Mead began to study anthropology in 1962 after being discharged (honorably) from the U. S. Army, Combat Engineers. He eventually received a B.A., M. A., and Ph. D. in his chosen field. And many years later an M. S. W. in Clinical Social Work. He was worked in aerospace, taught at the college and university levels, worked in a community action agency, ran a restaurant, been unemployed, and worked for the U. S. Forest Service. He is now retired from the work-a-day world but does a certain amount of consulting, writing, and research. He lives seven miles outside of the small town of La Grande, Oregon, with his wife, one cat, and a German Shepard dog named Katy who firmly believes that staring into his face at nine-o-clock in the evening is a statement that popcorn should be made. A new dog joined the house as an eight-week old puppy found by Katy under some brush in the middle of the American Southwest desert. Rez is now four years old and weighs 93 pounds (some puppy).

www.ingramcontent.com/pod-product-compliance
Lightning Source LLC
Chambersburg PA
CBHW070712160426
43192CB00009B/1165